The Regulation of E-cigarettes

ELGAR STUDIES IN HEALTH AND THE LAW

Series Editor: Professor Amandine Garde, *University of Liverpool, UK*

This new and exciting series will tackle and explore important issues around Health and the Law as they become increasingly entwined in today's world. Public interest issues sparked by the media and new spaces of information and communication engage society on a more hands-on level, which inevitably impacts many aspects of the Law and Policies that we live by. As a field of study, Health and the Law will encompass the legal and political ramifications of various health issues within national and international law. The various and numerous aspects relating to these broad areas include healthcare law, non-communicable diseases, prevention strategies, health policies, reproductive justice, social and mental health law, bioethics, and medicinal law. Elgar Studies in Health and the Law will also be an excellent forum to discuss and debate the diverse and growing range of issues that remain unexplored. The primary mission of the series is to stimulate the development of original thinking across Health and the Law and to foster the best theoretical and empirical scholarship in the field. With valuable insights, open-minded approaches, and high quality authored and edited collections; this series will be of interest to academics and practitioners alike.

Titles in the series include:

The Law and Policy of Healthcare Financing
An International Comparison of Models and Outcomes
Edited by Wolf Sauter, Jos Boertjens, Johan van Manen and Misja Mikkers

The Regulation of E-cigarettes
International, European and National Challenges
Edited by Lukasz Gruszczynski

The Regulation of E-cigarettes

International, European and National Challenges

Edited by

Lukasz Gruszczynski

Institute of Law Studies, Polish Academy of Sciences, and Institute for Legal Studies, Centre for Social Sciences, Hungarian Academy of Sciences

ELGAR STUDIES IN HEALTH AND THE LAW

Edward Elgar PUBLISHING

Cheltenham, UK • Northampton, MA, USA

Published by
Edward Elgar Publishing Limited
The Lypiatts
15 Lansdown Road
Cheltenham
Glos GL50 2JA
UK

Edward Elgar Publishing, Inc.
William Pratt House
9 Dewey Court
Northampton
Massachusetts 01060
USA

A catalogue record for this book
is available from the British Library

Library of Congress Control Number: 2019945333

This book is available electronically in the Elgaronline
Law subject collection
DOI 10.4337/9781788970464

MIX
Paper from
responsible sources
FSC® C013604

ISBN 978 1 78897 045 7 (cased)
ISBN 978 1 78897 046 4 (eBook)

Printed and bound by CPI Group (UK) Ltd, Croydon, CR0 4YY

Contents

Contributors

EDITOR

Lukasz Gruszczynski is Associate Professor (Dr. habil.) of International Law in the Institute of Law Studies at the Polish Academy of Sciences (Warsaw, Poland) and External Research Fellow in the Institute for Legal Studies, Centre for Social Sciences, at the Hungarian Academy of Sciences (Budapest, Hungary). Professor Gruszczynski received his PhD from the European University Institute in Florence. In the past, Professor Gruszczynski has been a visiting fellow or lecturer at various foreign universities and research institutes, including, among others, the University of Michigan Law School, the Lauterpacht Centre for International Law at the University of Cambridge (as a Bohdan Winiarski Visiting Fellow), the Pázmány University (as an adjunct professor), the University of Zurich, the OSCE Academy in Bishkek, and the American University of Central Asia. In 2012 he received the Manfred Lachs Award for the best book by a Polish author in public international law.

Professor Gruszczynski is the author of more than 50 publications, many of them in respected international scientific journals or with leading publishing houses. His scientific portfolio contains four monographs, including two with Oxford University Press. His current research focuses on international trade law, international investment law, and risk regulation (in particular with respect to tobacco products and disruptive technologies). Professor Gruszczynski is a managing co-editor of the *Polish Yearbook of International Law* and correspondent editor of the *European Journal of Risk Regulation*.

AUTHORS

Allan M. Brandt is the Amalie Moses Kass Professor of the History of Medicine and Professor of the History of Science at Harvard University. Professor Brandt served as Dean of the Graduate School of Arts and Sciences at Harvard University from 2008 to 2012. He is the author of numerous publications in leading historical and scientific journals. His book on the social and cultural history of cigarette smoking in the US, *The Cigarette Century: The Rise, Fall, and Deadly Persistence of the Product that Defined America*, was published by Basic Books in 2007 (paperback in 2009). The book received the Bancroft Prize from Columbia University in 2008 and the Welch Medal from the American Association for the History of Medicine in 2011. Professor Brandt has been elected to the National Academy of Medicine and the American Academy of Arts and Sciences. His work focuses on social and ethical aspects of health, disease, medical practices, and global health in the twentieth century.

Marilyn Bromberg, PhD, is Senior Lecturer at the University of Western Australia Law School. She is also a practicing lawyer. She received her PhD from Murdoch University (Australia). In the past she studied at the London School of Economics and York University (among others) and worked as a Senior Lecturer in the law school of the University of Notre Dame Australia (Fremantle Campus). Her research interests include e-cigarettes and the law, body image law, and energy drinks and the law. She has spoken about her research at conferences and courts around the world and has authored several publications in these fields.

Giancarlo A. Ferro, PhD, is Associate Professor of Constitutional Law in the Department of Law at the University of Catania. He earned his doctorate in constitutional justice and international protection from the University of Pisa. He is a member of the Italian Association of Constitutional Scholars. He has been visiting professor at the School of Italian Law of the University of Warsaw and has authored many publications dealing with forms of government, protection of fundamental rights, and constitutional justice in Europe. He has extensive experience in normative and regulatory issues regarding vaping (such as articles in *Therapeutic Advances in Chronic Disease* and the *International Journal of Environmental Research and Public Health*). This also includes cooperation with research group CoHEAR (Centro di ricerca per la riduzione del danno da fumo), University of Catania, coordinated by Professor Riccardo Polosa, a leading international scholar in the area of e-cigarette research.

Marina Foltea, PhD, is the founder and managing director of Trade Pacts, a trade and investment consultancy based in Geneva, Switzerland. She advises governments and private companies on international trade law and policy. Dr Foltea obtained her PhD in international economic law from the University of Bern, Switzerland. She was awarded the Walther Hug prize for the best legal dissertation in Switzerland and has published extensively in leading scientific journals in the field. Her thesis "International Organisations in the WTO Dispute Settlement: How Much Institutional Sensitivity?" culminated in a book published by Cambridge University Press in 2012. Her main areas of expertise are the linkages between trade and health, WTO dispute settlement, market access, and trade negotiations. She also has extensive experience in the tobacco sector. In September 2016 she was placed on the Indicative List of WTO Panellists, making her eligible to resolve disputes between member states at the WTO.

Coral Gartner, PhD, is Associate Professor at the University of Queensland's School of Public Health (Australia) and a Theme Leader at the Queensland Alliance for Environmental Health Sciences. She is an editor for *Tobacco Control* and *PLoS Medicine*. Her research interests are tobacco control policy, nicotine and tobacco product regulation, tobacco harm reduction, health disparities, and monitoring community exposure via wastewater analysis. Associate Professor Gartner has authored numerous publications on tobacco control and tobacco harm reduction (including articles in *The Lancet*, *Tobacco Control*, *Nicotine and Tobacco Research*, and the *International Journal of Drug Policy*).

Marie Elske C. Gispen, PhD, is a postdoctoral researcher at the Department of Transboundary Legal Studies (Faculty of Law) at the University of Groningen (The Netherlands). Currently she is working together with Prof. dr. Brigit Toebes on a three-year research project, funded by the Dutch Cancer Society, on children's rights and tobacco control. She is a member of the Global Health Law Groningen Research Centre, a senior research associate of the International Centre on Human Rights and Drug Policy, and the coordinator of the recently established European Scientific Network on Law and Tobacco (ESNLT). She has broad expertise in health and human rights, with emphasis on tobacco control, drugs, medicine access, palliative care, empirical legal research, and links between bioethics and biolaw. Dr Gispen is the author or co-author of a number of publications in leading scientific journals and edited volumes. She also authored a monograph that was published in 2017 by Intersentia (*Human Rights and Drug Control*).

Aleksandra Herbeć, PhD, is a psychologist and mixed methods researcher specializing in public health, tobacco control, and behavior change. She graduated with an MSc in Health Psychology from University College London in 2012, and in 2016 trained as a Visiting Scholar at Massachusetts General Hospital in Boston, USA. In 2019 she completed her PhD under the supervision of Professor Robert West and Dr Lion Shahab at the UCL Tobacco and Alcohol Research Group. She is also Programme Lead and Consultant at the Health Promotion Foundation led by Professor Witold Zatoński in Poland. To date, Dr Herbeć has worked on several projects involving the development and evaluation of complex digital smoking cessation interventions. She has also designed capacity building resources for healthcare professionals treating patients who smoke, and conducted research on tobacco and e-cigarette use and medication adherence among general and patient populations.

Patricia I. Kovacevic, a Columbia Law School graduate, is an independent global legal and regulatory consultant. In the past she was General Counsel and Chief Compliance Officer for Nicopure Labs (USA), an independent producer of e-liquids. She has also held senior legal and compliance positions at various international tobacco companies. Her expertise includes US and global nicotine and cannabis regulation, commercial and corporate law, corporate affairs, internal investigations, antibribery, trade sanctions, privacy, and product development. Patricia serves on the board of the Global Tobacco & Nicotine Forum (a meeting point for tobacco and nicotine executives and specialists in public health, policy-making, and international relations), and has served on the board of directors of the US Vapor Technology Association. She is admitted to practice law in New York and before the Supreme Court of the United States of America.

Ching-Fu Lin, SJD, is Associate Professor of Law at National Tsing Hua University (NTHU), where he teaches international health law, food law and policy, and international law and global governance. Professor Lin received his LLM and SJD from Harvard Law School and holds a dual degree in law (LLB) and chemical engineering (BS) from National Taiwan University (NTU). His legal scholarship has appeared in numerous journals and edited collections, including the *Virginia Journal of International Law, University of Pennsylvania Journal of International Law, Columbia Science and Technology Law Review, Food and Drug Law Journal*, and the *Journal of World Trade.*

Mao-Wei Lo, LLM, is a Fellow at the Stanford Program in International Legal Studies (SPILS). He received his LLB (2012) and LLM (2015) from National Taiwan University (NTU). Before joining SPILS in 2018, Mr Lo served as the Senior Officer at the Department of Legal Affairs, Mainland Affairs Council from 2015. He also worked as a teaching assistant at NTU College of Law and Research Assistant at the Asian Center for WTO and International Health Law and Policy. In addition, he served as Chief Editor of the *Asian Journal of WTO & International Health Law and Policy* in 2014. His legal scholarship has appeared in journals and edited collections, including the *Asian Journal of WTO & International Health Law and Policy, Contemporary Asia Arbitration Journal*, and *Global Arbitration Review.*

Bryan Mercurio, PhD, is Chair Professor, Associate Dean (Research), and Vice Chancellor's Outstanding Fellow of the Faculty of Law at the Chinese University of Hong Kong (CUHK). Professor Mercurio is co-author of one of the most widely used case books on WTO law (Hart Publishing, 2018,

3rd ed), and co-editor of the leading collection on bilateral and regional trade agreements (Cambridge University Press, 2016, 2nd ed). He also maintains an active trade and investment consultancy practice, working with governments to develop, negotiate, and implement free trade agreements. Prior to relocating to Hong Kong in 2007, Professor Mercurio taught in the faculty of law at the University of New South Wales and worked in private legal practice and government.

Costanza Nicolosi is a PhD in constitutional law and comparative constitutional law. She is also affiliated with CoHEAR (Centro di ricerca per la riduzione del danno da fumo) of the University of Catania. Costanza earned a BA and MSc in economics from Bocconi University and a JD from Northwestern University in Chicago. She has practiced law in the US, Belgium (Brussels), and Costa Rica. She has authored several publications dealing with EU law and comparative constitutional law.

Anna Pudło, PhD, is a research associate in the Faculty of Law at Koźmiński University in Warsaw (Poland) and a barrister in the Warsaw Bar Association. She graduated in law from the Silesian University in Katowice and holds a PhD in EU law from the Institute of Law Studies at the Polish Academy of Sciences in Warsaw. Her professional experience includes working at the Polish Constitutional Tribunal (2009–present), the European Union Affairs Committee of the Chancellery of the Senate (as advisor, 2003–7), and the Chancellery of the President of the Republic of Poland (as an expert in EU law, 2012–13). She also completed a traineeship (*stage*) at the European Parliament and was a visiting fellow in, *inter alia*, the department of law at the European University Institute in Florence. Her research so far has led to a number of books, articles, contributions to edited volumes, and conference papers.

Lion Shahab, PhD, is Associate Professor in Health Psychology at University College London and trained in psychology, epidemiology, and neuroscience. He has a number of years' experience in addiction research, tobacco control, and health psychology, with a particular interest in novel behavioral and pharmacological smoking cessation interventions, biomarkers, tobacco product regulation and policy, digital health, and tobacco and alcohol use epidemiology. Dr Shahab's research spans a variety of techniques and methods, involving both human (randomized controlled trials, survey analysis, laboratory and experimental work) and animal studies (electrophysiology). He has collaborated with academic as well as non-academic (governmental and non-governmental) partners, and to date has authored more than 100 scientific papers, reviews, and reports.

Charlie A. Smith, MSc, is a research psychologist and a member of the Tobacco and Alcohol Research Group (UTARG) at University College London (UCL). He graduated with an MSc in Clinical Forensic Psychology from the Institute of Psychiatry, Psychology and Neuroscience (IoPPN), King's College London (KCL), in 2016. He is currently completing his PhD in Psychological and Behavioural Science in the Department of Behavioural Science and Health at UCL. In addition to his academic career, he has many years of experience working in a variety of mental healthcare settings, applying his expertise in psychology to develop and implement evidence-based treatment for patients with a range of mental health conditions.

Jacquelyn D. Veraldi, BA, LLB, is an LLM candidate at Trinity College, University of Cambridge, pursuing a specialization in European Union law. She obtained her LLB in International and European Law from the University of Groningen (the Netherlands) and her BA in Peace and Conflict Studies from the University of Waterloo (Canada). Jacquelyn has carried out research assistance and offered consultancy on a variety of health and human rights issues, having worked with the European Scientific Network on Law and Tobacco, Medicines Law & Policy, Global Health Law Groningen Research Centre, and IFHHRO—the Medical Human Rights Network, among others.

Chuan-Feng Wu, JSD, serves as Associate Research Professor at Institutum Iurisprudentiae, Academia Sinica (IIAS), and Joint Appointment Associate Professor at the Institute of Health and Welfare Policy, National Yang-Ming University (NYMU) and at the College of Public Health, National Taiwan University (NTU). He received his JSD from UC Berkeley and his LLM from Harvard Law School. In addition to degrees in law, he also holds an MA in health and welfare policy and a bachelor's degree in public health. Professor Wu has authored numerous publications in Taiwanese and foreign scientific journals. He specializes in healthcare laws and ethics, international human rights and the right to health, and healthcare distributive justice.

Mateusz Zatoński, PhD, is a Research Associate at the Department for Health, University of Bath. Mateusz holds an MSc in Public Health from the London School of Hygiene and Tropical Medicine. He is the vice-president of the Health Promotion Foundation, a major Polish non-governmental public health advocacy organization. He has taught and conducted research on public health and history at several academic institutions, including University College London and Harvard University. Mateusz is the author of peer-reviewed publications in the fields of tobacco control, alcohol policy, epidemiology, health economics, and history. He is an editor of the Journal of Health Inequalities at the President Stanisław Wojciechowski State University of Applied Sciences in Kalisz, Poland.

Acknowledgments

This book would not have been possible without the support of many people. In particular I would like to express my gratitude to Professor Władysław Czapliński, Professor Bartłomiej Krzan, Professor Cezary Mik, Professor Artur Kozłowski, and Alex Liber, as well as the anonymous reviewers of the book proposal for all their critical comments on the book as a whole as well as on its specific chapters. Of course, I take full responsibility for all mistakes and omissions.

I also would like to acknowledge the financial supported provided by the Polish National Science Centre within the research grant UMO-2016/21/B/HS5/02065 ("Regulation of electronic nicotine delivery systems (e-cigarettes): national and international legal challenges," 2017–19).

The excellent editorial work done by Dr Kaja Kowalczewska and the language correction provided by James Hartzell should be mentioned here as well.

Last but not least, special thanks go to Olga Wysocka, Franek, and Zosia. This book project would never have been successfully concluded without their encouragement and constant support.

Abbreviations

AAAQ standard of health care	standard of availability, accessibility, acceptability, and quality of health care
ACCC	Australian Competition and Consumer Commission
ACL	Australian Consumer Law
ACT	Australian Capital Territory
Altria	Altria Group, Inc.
APA	Administrative Procedure Act (US)
ARTG	Australian Register of Therapeutic Goods
ASH	Action on Smoking and Health (UK)
BAT	British American Tobacco Plc
BIC	best interests of the child
CESCR	Committee on Economic, Social and Cultural Rights (UN)
CFDA	Chinese Food and Drug Administration
CJEU	Court of Justice of the European Union
CNTC	China National Tobacco Corporation
COP	Conference of the Parties
COPD	chronic obstructive pulmonary disease
Court	Court of Justice of the European Union
CPD	cigarettes smoked per day
CPED	cross-price elasticity of demand
CRC	Convention on the Rights of the Child
CRC Committee	Committee on the Rights of the Child (UN)
CTP	Center for Tobacco Products (US)
DEA	Drug Enforcement Agency (US)
Directive	Tobacco Products Directive (EU)
e-cigarette	electronic cigarette
eCO	exhaled carbon monoxide

ECtHR	European Court of Human Rights
EHTP	electronically heated tobacco products
ENDS	Electronic Nicotine Delivery System(s)
ENNDS	Electronic Non-Nicotine Delivery System(s)
eNO	exhaled breath nitric oxide
EU	European Union
EU Charter	Charter of Fundamental Rights of the European Union
FCTC	Framework Convention on Tobacco Control
FD&C Act	Federal Food, Drug and Cosmetic Act of 1938 (US)
FDA	Food & Drug Administration (US)
FSFW	Foundation for a Smoke-Free World (US)
FTC	Federal Trade Commission (US)
GATT 1994	General Agreement on Tariffs and Trade of 1994
HNB	heat-not-burn (tobacco products)
HPA	Health Promotion Administration (Taiwan)
HRCT	high-resolution computed tomography
HS	harmonized system
ICCPR	International Covenant on Civil and Political Rights
ICESCR	International Covenant on Economic, Social and Cultural Rights
ILC	International Law Commission
JUUL	JUUL Labs, Inc.
MDD	Directive on Medical Devices (EU)
MEAs	multilateral environmental agreements
MHW	Ministry of Health and Welfare (Taiwan)
MPD	Directives on Medicinal Products (EU)
MRTP	Modified Risk Tobacco Product
NDS	National Drug Strategy (Australia)
NGPs	Next Generation (Nicotine) Products
NHIS	National Health Interview Survey (US)
NHMRC	National Health and Medical Research Council (Australia)
Nicopure	Nicopure Labs, LLC

NPHT	National Preventative Health Taskforce (Australia)
NRT	nicotine replacement therapy
NSE	non-substantial equivalence
NSW	New South Wales
NT	Northern Territory
NTS	National Tobacco Strategy (Australia)
PAA	Pharmaceutical Affairs Act (Taiwan)
Pillbox	Pillbox 38 (UK) Ltd
PG	propylene glycol
PHE	Public Health England
PMI	Philip Morris International Inc.
PMTA	premarket tobacco product authorization
QLD	Queensland
RCTs	randomized controlled trials
SA	South Australia
SE	substantial equivalence
SE Report	Substantial Equivalence Report
SKUs	stock keeping units
STMA	State Tobacco Monopoly Administration (China)
STS	Smoking Toolkit Study
TAS	Tasmania
TBT Agreement	Agreement on Technical Barriers to Trade
TCA	Family Smoking Prevention and Tobacco Control Act of 2009 (US)
TEU	Treaty on European Union
TFDA	Taiwan Food, Drug and Cosmetic Administration
TFEU	Treaty on the Functioning of the European Union
TGA	Therapeutic Goods Administration (Australia)
THPA	Tobacco Hazards Prevention Act (Taiwan)
TIRC	Tobacco Industry Research Committee (US)
TPD	Tobacco Products Directive (EU)
TTCs	transnational tobacco companies
UDHR	Universal Declaration of Human Rights

UK	United Kingdom of Great Britain and Northern Ireland
UN	United Nations
UNTS	United Nations Treaty Collection
US	United States of America
VCLT	Vienna Convention on the Law of Treaties
VIC	Victoria
WA	Western Australia
WCO	World Custom Organization
WHA	World Health Assembly
WHO	World Health Organization
WTO	World Trade Organization

Foreword

In 2014, Oxford Dictionaries chose "vape" as their "word of the year." This term is used to describe an electronic cigarette or similar device as well as the action of inhaling and exhaling the vapor produced by these. Electronic cigarettes simulate the experience of smoking a cigarette by allowing the user to inhale vapor from a solution that typically contains nicotine along with flavoring agents and other chemicals. Although the number of people vaping is growing rapidly, it remains relatively small, at 40 million vapers compared to 1 billion smokers.

The availability of e-cigarettes has proved to be intensely controversial. There is disagreement about the health risks that e-cigarettes present and about their effectiveness as a tool to encourage people to stop smoking. There are particular concerns that young people may be attracted to vaping and that this could constitute a "gateway" to smoking conventional cigarettes. There is a "flavour for every taste":[1] fresh, earthy, fruity, savory—including polar mint, passionfruit, caramel café, blueberry, and green apple!

Given the manner in which the tobacco industry harnessed junk science to manufacture "doubt" about the link between smoking and cancer,[2] it is challenging to approach the topic of e-cigarettes with an open mind. This is not made easier by the fact that some of the key protagonists are the same. British American Tobacco, Philip Morris, and Imperial are all investing heavily in e-cigarettes as well as "heat-not-burn" (HNB) technology. The Altria group which makes Marlboro cigarettes recently acquired a 35 percent share in the electronic cigarette giant JUUL Labs. A study of JUUL's marketing techniques between 2015 and 2018 suggested that its approach was "patently youth oriented" and that it "faithfully recapitulated the playbook of traditional cigarette marketers."[3]

---

1 'Discover a world of flavour' https://www.blu.com/en/GB/flavours/blu-e-liquid-flavours accessed March 1, 2019. To access this information, I was required to tick a box declaring that I am over eighteen years old.

2 E.M. Conway & N. Oreskes, *Merchants of Doubt: How a Handful of Scientists Obscured the Truth on Issues from Tobacco Smoke to Global Warming* (Bloomsbury Press 2010).

3 R.K. Jackler et al, 'JULL Advertising Over its First Three Years on the Market' (Stanford Research into the Impact of Tobacco Advertising 2019) http://tobacco.

But it would be misguided to let the wrongdoing of tobacco companies conceal the dilemmas to which electronic cigarettes give rise. This product could be a posterchild for Sunstein's critique of a strong version of the precautionary principle, because regulating or not regulating electronic cigarettes presents "risks on all sides."[4] This is apparent from a recent report produced by the National Academies of Sciences, Engineering, and Medicine in the United States.[5] On the one hand, using electronic cigarettes reduces exposure to toxic and carcinogenic substances as compared to smoking conventional cigarettes. On the other hand, young people use electronic cigarettes more than any other tobacco product and nicotine is considered to be especially harmful to children, teenagers, and young adults. There is also ongoing scientific uncertainty about the long-term health effects of electronic cigarettes.

This volume does not seek to step back from the controversy generated by electronic cigarettes or to silence the dissension that they cause. The engaging and informative chapters offer different and sometimes opposing perspectives and lay bare the challenges that both courts and regulators face in contending with this new frontier. The volume offers a sweeping overview of current approaches to the regulation of electronic cigarettes at national, regional, and international level and explores the different drivers that can help us to understand the wide variations in approach. The volume also acknowledges the central and controversial role of courts, which are called upon to appraise the lawfulness of regulations adopted in a context that is characterised by disagreement and uncertainty. The book walks a careful middle line between recognizing the specificity of the regulatory challenges presented by electronic cigarettes and acknowledging that the questions and dilemmas to which this product gives rise are to some extent familiar from previous experiments in the regulation of new technologies. This is a book about contemporary challenges in regulation as well as a book about the science, law, and governance of electronic cigarettes.

Joanne Scott
Professor of European Law at the European University Institute, Florence

---

stanford.edu/tobacco_main/publications/JUUL_Marketing_Stanford.pdf accessed March 1, 2019, at 1 and 39.

4 C.R. Sunstein, 'Beyond the Precautionary Principle' (2003) 151 U Pa L Rev 1003.

5 Committee on the Review of the Health Effects of Electronic Nicotine Delivery Systems, *Public Health Consequences of E-Cigarettes* (The National Academies Press 2018) https://www.nap.edu/catalog/24952/public-health-consequences-of-e-cigarettes accessed March 1, 2019.

1. Introduction: regulating e-cigarettes in the face of uncertainty

Lukasz Gruszczynski

1. THE CONTROVERSY OVER E-CIGARETTES

Electronic cigarettes (e-cigarettes) are as bad for your health as conventional tobacco products. Although their vapor does not contain tar, carbon monoxide, hydrogen cyanide, or many of the other dangerous substances present in tobacco smoke, it delivers equally hazardous chemicals (for example diacetyl, cinnamaldehyde, or the notorious formaldehyde) that may cause cancer and other serious diseases. So if you are a smoker, switching to e-cigarettes makes very little sense. And e-cigarettes do not help you to quit smoking. Actually, they preserve the nicotine addiction, thus making complete cessation even more difficult. E-cigarettes also attract a lot of new users, particularly among kids and adolescents. They are fashionable (as were cigarettes many years ago) and are frequently marketed (absolutely falsely!) as a safer alternative to traditional tobacco products. The availability of these products on the market thus seriously undermines the decades of efforts on the part of the health community to eradicate the tobacco epidemic. In short, they are a wolf in sheep's clothing.

But wait a minute: maybe the truth is just the opposite. E-cigarettes, although not entirely safe, are much less harmful than conventional tobacco products. They do contain nicotine, but the overall level of other hazardous substances present in the vapor is much lower than that in tobacco smoke. Nicotine as such, although addictive, poses only limited health risks as compared to other substances present in smoke. Smokers, at least those who are unable or unwilling to quit, will therefore greatly benefit from switching to these less risky products. Actually, some of them may, thanks to e-cigarettes, eventually quit the addiction. The availability of different vapor products, including a great variety of e-liquids, is more of an incentive for current smokers to switch than a hook for kids to start smoking. Overall, e-cigarettes should be seen as part of the solution, rather than a contributing factor, to the tobacco problem.

A quick review of recently published articles by more or less reputable news outlets in the general press confirms the ambiguous nature of reporting on e-cigarettes. Good evidence is offered from merely glancing at their titles. Thus, *USA Today* announces: "Depression, anxiety, nicotine withdrawal: Trying to quit vaping 'was hell',"[1] while *The Lantern* states "Safe smoking alternative e-cigarette revealed as dangerous and addictive."[2] In a similar fashion, *The Sun* warns that "Vapers [are] 'at risk of irreversible popcorn lung' if they puff on flavoured e-cigarettes,"[3] while *Eugene Weekly* has no doubt that "E-cigarettes hook a new generation of teens."[4] On the other hand, CNN explains that "E-cigarettes [are] less toxic to users than cigarettes,"[5] while *The Sun* later surprisingly claims: "Vaping isn't as bad as you think! Deluded smokers 'risk lives' by refusing to switch to e-cigarettes."[6] *The Conversation* also optimistically informs the reader that "Smokers who switch could be less likely to use cigarettes again."[7] Of course, one may downplay the significance of these differences. At the end of the day, news outlets tend to oversimplify their messages and frequently play with the titles of articles to attract the attention of potential readers. But the opposing opinions about the potential risks and benefits of e-cigarettes also deeply divide the community of scientific experts.

Some specialists, for example, confirm that e-cigarettes pose their own health risks resulting from nicotine inhalation or chronic inhalation of other toxicants present in the vapor.[8] The most important limitation of this line

---

1 J. O'Donnell, "Depression, anxiety, nicotine withdrawal: Trying to quit vaping 'was hell'" (*USA Today*, December 27, 2018) https://bit.ly/2AvuS4B accessed January 15, 2019.

2 K. Hamilton, "Safe smoking alternative e-cigarette revealed as dangerous and addictive" (*The Lantern*, January 1, 2019) https://bit.ly/2F8wR2L accessed January 15, 2019.

3 A. Downey, "Vapers 'at risk of irreversible popcorn lung' if they puff on flavoured e-cigarettes" (*The Sun*, November 20, 2018) https://bit.ly/2GT8hV2 accessed January 15, 2019.

4 C. Cruzan Morton, "E-cigarettes hook a new generation of teens" (*Eugene Weekly*, January 3, 2019) https://bit.ly/2AtRsdW accessed January 15, 2019.

5 N. Thomas, "E-cigarettes less toxic to users than cigarettes, study says" (CNN, December 14, 2018), https://cnn.it/2GjSUES accessed January 15, 2019.

6 M. Larbi, "Vaping isn't as bad as you think! Deluded smokers 'risk lives' by refusing to switch to e-cigarettes, experts say" (*The Sun*, January 4, 2019) https://bit.ly/2GW6lv1 accessed January 15, 2019.

7 M. Klonizakis, "Smokers who switch could be less likely to use cigarettes again" (*The Conversation*, January 3, 2019) https://bit.ly/2Aud4Hc accessed January 15, 2019.

8 For a detailed review of the available scientific evidence (and respective reference sources) behind the different claims presented here, see particularly Chapters 2 and 3 of this volume. Other chapters also refer extensively to various scientific data.

of reasoning—as its opponents point out—is the lack of contextualization. Although the level of some toxicants in aerosol may be as high as those in tobacco smoke, and while nicotine is not as harmless as some argue, overall the use of these products is connected with a much lower risk exposure than is the case with conventional cigarettes. A well-known report commissioned by Public Health England estimated, for example, that e-cigarettes are around 95 percent safer than smoked tobacco.[9]

There are also researchers who highlight our limited knowledge about e-cigarettes and the long-term health consequences of their use. In this context, they stress that their real impact can be verified only on the basis of comprehensive observations that will take decades to collect (owing to the lengthy lag time for the onset of many smoking-related diseases, such as cancer or emphysema). Others suggest that the use of e-cigarettes can preserve the nicotine addiction and prevent smokers from quitting completely. The efficacy of e-cigarettes as a cessation device has been questioned by many experts. It has also been argued that e-cigarettes may serve as a gateway for adolescents and kids to conventional smoking (the so-called gateway effect) or renormalize smoking by helping to make it socially acceptable behavior once again.

On the other hand, a considerable group of health experts seem to be confident that the available scientific data allow for the conclusion that e-cigarettes are much safer than traditional tobacco products. Although they admit the existence of uncertainties about their long-term health effects, they also accentuate that those uncertainties should be seen against the benchmark scenario of perpetuated use of combustible tobacco products. Some researchers also question the gateway and renormalization hypotheses, highlighting different methodological limitations in the underlying scientific studies. Finally, there are those who argue that e-cigarettes can be an effective cessation device, and others who concentrate more on their harm reduction dimension—that is, irrespective of whether e-cigarettes can help quit the nicotine addition, they present a safer and more realistic alternative to conventional smoking for those users who are unable or unwilling to quit.

2. E-CIGARETTES AS A SUBJECT OF REGULATION

Considering the disagreement in the scientific community, it is not surprising to see widely divergent regulatory approaches to e-cigarettes around the globe. In the absence of compelling science that would support a particular type of

---

9 A. McNeill et al, *E-cigarettes: An Evidence Update* (A Report Commissioned by Public Health England, Public Health England 2015) 6.

policy, regulators in various jurisdictions are taking different positions with equal justification. The result is that a broad array of policy interventions are currently in effect. In particular, countries may classify e-cigarettes as: (i) tobacco products, derivatives, or substitutes (for example Azerbaijan, Costa Rica, Georgia, Honduras, and South Korea);[10] (ii) products imitating tobacco (for example Colombia and Mexico); (iii) medicinal or pharmaceutical products, at least for those e-cigarettes that come with therapeutic claims (for example Chile, the European Union (EU), and Japan);[11] (iv) consumer products (for example Armenia, Bosnia and Herzegovina, China, and Russia);[12] (v) poisons (for example Australia, with regard to e-liquids containing nicotine);[13] or (vi) a *sui generis* category (for example Ecuador, Canada, the EU, Moldova, and New Zealand). In some places, e-cigarettes are simply banned—sometimes not only their sale but also their personal importation and possession (for example in Argentina, Brazil, Gambia, Egypt, some Indian states, Jordan, Philippines, Singapore, Thailand, Taiwan, the United Arab Emirates, Uruguay, and Vietnam).[14] Overall, there are 101 countries that do not have any specific regulations for e-cigarettes (treating them as a regular consumer good) and 39 which ban their sale, while the remaining group, which includes most of the developed nations, regulates them in a variety of other ways.[15] In terms of the legal mechanisms applied, countries have either reinterpreted or amended existing regulations to cover e-cigarettes, adopted new laws, or used some mixture of these two methods.[16]

Different rules will apply depending on the classification of e-cigarettes. Treating e-cigarettes as products imitating tobacco or poison leads in most of the jurisdictions to a ban on their sale, while qualifying them as an ordinary consumer good only subjects them to existing general product safety and liability regimes, and in in general does not affect their availability on the market. A considerable group of countries treat e-cigarettes as medicinal or pharmaceutical products. This means that before they are placed on the market, they

---

[10] All information on specific national regulatory regimes are based on data provided by the Global Tobacco Control database https://globaltobaccocontrol.org accessed January 15, 2019.

[11] For further details on the EU regime see Chapters 7 and 8 in this volume.

[12] For further details on the Chinese regulatory approach see Chapter 9 in this volume.

[13] For an in-depth discussion on the Australian legal regime for e-cigarettes see Chapter 11 in this volume.

[14] For further analysis of the Taiwanese approach see Chapter 9 in this volume.

[15] H. Shapiro, *No Fire, No Smoke: The Global State of Tobacco Harm Reduction 2018* (Knowledge-Action-Change 2018) 84.

[16] R.D. Kennedy et al, "Global approaches to regulating electronic cigarettes" (2017) 26 Tob Control 440.

need to go through a thorough and demanding authorization process, which sometimes includes a requirement of clinical trials. As yet, no e-cigarette has been registered as a medicinal/pharmaceutical device,[17] so in practice such a classification has the same effect as a complete sales ban. E-cigarettes may be also placed in two or possibly more categories in a single jurisdiction. For example, e-cigarettes featuring cessation claims can be classified as medicinal products; those without such claims may be classified either as a poison, consumer good, or *sui generis* category; and e-cigarettes imitating tobacco products may be completely prohibited.

So far, no consensus has emerged at the international level. The Conference of the Parties (COP) of the World Health Organization's (WHO) Framework Convention on Tobacco Control (FCTC), a major international point of reference for tobacco control standards, has only recently commenced work on this issue (owing to, *inter alia*, the relatively short history of e-cigarette use), and at present it remains unclear whether and to what extent the FCTC provisions are even relevant for the regulation of this category of products.[18] What is clear is that the FCTC Secretariat and the COP accept a total ban on e-cigarettes as one of the legitimate regulatory options available to states. For those countries which tolerate their presence on the market, the COP has recommended—but not required—the adoption of certain control policies that closely resemble the approach taken with respect to traditional tobacco products.

3. THE SCOPE OF THIS BOOK AND TERMINOLOGICAL CLARIFICATIONS

This book is about the regulation of e-cigarettes. The product in question, which is also referred to in the WHO nomenclature as an "electronic nicotine delivery system" (ENDS), is a battery-powered device designed to deliver nicotine by heating a solution (the so-called e-liquid) to be inhaled by a user. Technically speaking, ENDS is a broader category that includes other similar devices such as e-shisha or e-pipes (all of them have the same mode of operation). Nevertheless, e-cigarettes are by far the most common subclass, and in this book, unless stated otherwise, both terms (ENDS and e-cigarettes) are used interchangeably. Note that the WHO and FCTC COP also use the notion of "Electronic Non-Nicotine Delivery Systems," which are basically ENDS without nicotine. In principle, this category is not covered by this book (except in Chapter 9).

---

17 Shapiro (n 15) 85.

18 For a detailed discussion of this issue see Chapter 4 of this volume.

E-liquids used in e-cigarettes are composed of vegetable glycerin (VG), propylene glycol (PG), a great variety of flavorings or their mixtures (for example diacetyl, acetyl propionyl, vanillin, ethyl maltol, ethyl vanillin, or menthol),[19] and nicotine, in varying concentrations. Nicotine as such can come in two different forms: freebase and nicotine salts. The form of the nicotine affects the users' experience—for example, salts allow for a higher concentration of nicotine in e-liquids, which is more easily absorbed by the human body in this form. They also decrease the harshness of vaping that is typically experienced by users who use more potent freebase e-liquids. On the other hand, nicotine salts may also pose their own health challenges, for example because of the presence of the benzoic acid normally used to formulate nicotine salts.[20] Older e-liquids were predominantly based on the freebase form, while newer products increasingly use nicotine salts.

Modern e-cigarettes were invented in China in 2003 and quickly became popular.[21] They were introduced into Europe and the US in 2006–7 and have gradually spread around the globe.[22] The e-cigarette still remains a niche product, albeit one that is quickly gaining popularity. As of 2017 the global e-cigarette market was valued at US $13,899.9 million; it is expected to witness an annual growth rate of almost 20 percent between 2018 and 2023.[23] Various types of device are currently available on the market. Conventionally they are grouped into generational categories. The first generation, also referred to as the "cigalike," was popular about a decade ago. These e-cigarettes tended to look like combustible cigarettes and most of them came as disposable models. The second generation devices—vape pens—do not resemble traditional cigarettes. They have refillable e-liquid cartridges (allowing for a broader selection of flavors), are rechargeable, and have more powerful batteries. The third generation products ("mods") are much bigger, usually in the form of a cylinder or box, and offer a greater degree of control over a device, permitting the user to, for example, set wattage and voltage. They are refillable and rechargeable. Pod-based systems have recently become more popular. They are much smaller than mods and, in most cases, they do not look like cigarettes. They are

---

19 See for example C. Hutzler et al, "Chemical hazards present in liquids and vapors of electronic cigarettes" (2014) 88 Arch Toxicol 1295; P.A. Tierney et al, "Flavour chemicals in electronic cigarette fluids" (2016) 25 Tob Control e10.

20 See for example J.F. Pankow et al, "Benzene formation in electronic cigarettes" (2017) 12(3) PLoS One e0173055.

21 For a detailed discussion on the various prototypes of e-cigarettes and Hon Lik's invention, see Chapter 2 in this volume.

22 M.A. Rahman et al, "Electronic cigarettes: patterns of use, health effects, use in smoking cessation and regulatory issues" (2014) 12 Tob Induc Dis 21.

23 PS Market Research, *E-Cigarette Market Size, Share. Industry Analysis Report, 2023* (September 2018) https://bit.ly/2rRcUYy accessed January 15, 2019.

composed of a pod (which is basically a coil integrated with a small tank) and a battery (stronger than a cigalike but weaker than those used in the second and third generation models). Pods can be either disposable or refillable.

There are other products on the market that are used to deliver nicotine and also are not based on the combustion of tobacco. They come under different names, such as electronically heated tobacco products; novel tobacco products; vapor products (a broad category that also includes ENDS); heat-not-burn tobacco products; and electric smoking systems. With the exception of vapor products, all are based on devices that use an electric heating element to char, rather than burn, the tobacco. This requires a lower temperature, allowing for the release of nicotine in a form of aerosol (which is nevertheless regarded by some researchers as smoke[24]) without oxidization and the discharge of carbon. As a consequence, they are claimed to pose a lower risk as compared to conventional tobacco products.[25] Many health specialists indicate, however, that the scientific evidence concerning the risk profile of those products is too limited to come up with any definitive conclusions, and they also worry that most of the data come from industry-funded research projects.[26] This segment of the market has been dominated by the largest tobacco companies, and the two leading models are IQOS (owned by Philip Morris International Inc.) and Glo (owned by British American Tobacco Plc). None of these products is covered by this book.

It should be added that while the scope of the book is comprehensive, it does not pretend to exhaust all the relevant subject matter relating to the regulation of e-cigarettes. The selection of the chapters reflects both the aims of the editor and the research interests of the contributing authors (whose affiliations are disclosed in the Notes on Contributors at the beginning of this volume). When inviting the authors, the editor tried to ensure that they represented different viewpoints. As a consequence, there are contributors who advocate for rather lenient regulatory regimes for e-cigarettes, as well as those who would like to see much stricter regulatory models. This diversity of opinions clearly echoes

---

[24] R. Auer et al, "Perplexing conclusions concerning heat-not-burn tobacco cigarettes—reply" (2017) 177(11) JAMA Internal Medicine 1699.

[25] See for example PMI, "Creating less harmful alternatives to smoking" (*PMI webpage*, undated) https://bit.ly/2Hf9dSR accessed January 15, 2019.

[26] See for example FCTC COP, *Further Development of the Partial Guidelines for Implementation of Articles 9 and 10 of the WHO FCTC*, Report by WHO, FCTC/COP/7/9, July 12, 2016 (Conference of the Parties to the WHO Framework Convention on Tobacco Control, Seventh session, Delhi, India, November 7–12, 2016) 5–6; F. Moazed et al, "Assessment of industry data on pulmonary and immunosuppressive effects of IQOS" (2018) 27 (Suppl 1) Tob Control s20. For a different view, see McNeill et al (n 9).

the ongoing debate in the public health, regulatory, and business communities over the optimal way to regulate e-cigarettes.

The chapters included in this book reflect the state of scientific research and the regulatory environment as of October 31, 2018. While this book is among the most up-to-date positions on the market, readers should be aware that the field is subject to dynamic changes of a scientific, legal, and market character. Some changes have already occurred between the closing date for the book and the moment of its publication, while others might be coming in the near future. A brief summary of what has happened and what may be expected is provided in the final section of this chapter.

4. THE RESEARCH QUESTIONS, STRUCTURE, AND CONTENT OF THE BOOK

The issues and problems surrounding ENDS regulation—at the international, European and national levels—lie at the heart of this edited volume. In particular, the contributing authors have been asked to address one or more of the following questions:

1. What are the factors that influence the choice of a particular regulatory regime by regulators at the national, supranational, and international levels?
2. What is the design of the different regulatory models for e-cigarettes introduced by regulators in specific jurisdictions? What legal problems emerge in this context?
3. What is the optimal regulatory model for the regulation of e-cigarettes? Is it possible to identify one at the current stage of scientific development?
4. What roles do the precautionary and harm reduction principles play when formulating rules applicable to e-cigarettes?
5. How do certain international (for example human rights, international trade rules, FCTC obligations) and supranational (for example EU) legal standards restrict the regulatory freedom of regulators in this policy space?

This volume has been divided into three parts. The first part ("Science, regulation and e-cigarettes") provides an up-to-date review of the current scientific research on e-cigarettes in the broader historical perspective. This part constitutes the basis for the subsequent discussions on the specific regulatory challenges that are emerging in this field. The second part ("International and European law perspectives") contains several chapters that discuss various sets of international and supranational obligations that may restrict the regulatory freedom enjoyed by individual states/supranational regulators in this area. The third and final part ("National law perspectives") presents four national case studies (two of them merged into one chapter) which investigate how e-cigarettes are regulated in selected jurisdictions.

The first part is composed of two chapters. It starts with a general text by Mateusz Zatoński and Allan M. Brandt ("Divide and conquer? E-cigarettes as a disruptive technology in the history of tobacco control") which looks at e-cigarettes as an example of disruptive innovation and analyzes different societal and regulatory consequences resulting from the emergence of this new technology—for example, the polarization of the tobacco control community, the implications of technology for the viability of the endgame strategy, or the relegitimization of Big Tobacco. The second chapter in this part ("Review of the scientific evidence relating to electronic cigarettes: where do we stand now?")—authored by Charlie A. Smith, Aleksandra Herbeć, and Lion Shahab—summarizes and critically assesses the current scientific knowledge on the use of e-cigarettes, particularly with regard to their safety or efficacy as a cessation or harm reduction device, as well as the strength of the gateway effect hypothesis. It concludes that there is little evidence to suggest that e-cigarettes have renormalized smoking or act as a gateway to tobacco use among adolescents. The chapter also notes that although e-cigarettes are not completely safe and further research is still needed, the evidence available thus far indicates that these products are significantly safer than conventional cigarettes. This means that they may have a positive impact on public health in the context of tobacco harm reduction strategies.

The second part of the book consists of five chapters. In the text that opens this section ("Taming Schrödinger's cat: e-cigarettes under the Framework Convention on Tobacco Control"), Lukasz Gruszczynski investigates whether and to what extent the FCTC disciplines apply to e-cigarettes and whether the mandate enjoyed by the COP is sufficiently broad to deal with these products. He concludes that due to the formulation of the relevant FCTC provisions, the complex nature of ENDS, and the unwillingness of the COP to take a decisive position on the status of these products, the Convention regime will not reduce (at least for now) the regulatory heterogeneity among the State Parties. At the same time, the chapter proposes the development of a *sui generis* model for e-cigarettes that takes into account not only the risks posed by their use, but also their harm reduction potential. The subsequent text by Marie Elske C. Gispen and Jacquelyn D. Veraldi—"A human rights approach to the regulation of electronic cigarettes"—looks at the legal constraints imposed by international human rights law on the regulatory freedom enjoyed by states in this policy space. The authors conclude that under general international human rights law, governments are required to actively discourage the use of harmful substances, including the nicotine which is present in e-cigarettes. This baseline scenario may however be modified in light of research into the ability of ENDS to serve as a harm reduction tool and/or gateway product. In this context, the authors propose various policy recommendations on appropriate regulatory responses that take into account these two aspects and at the same time respect states' international human rights obligations. The next chapter, by Marina Foltea and Bryan Mercurio ("A ban on electronic nicotine delivery systems: step one in the WTO discrimination analysis"), carries out a similar analysis under the law of the World Trade Organization (WTO) by exploring the relevant provisions for the assessment of WTO compatibility of complete sales bans imposed on e-cigarettes in a situation where traditional combustible products are available on the market. The chapter concentrates in this context on the antidiscrimination disciplines provided by the General Agreement on Tariffs and Trade and the Agreement on Technical Barriers to Trade, looking specifically at likeness analysis (e-cigarettes versus combustible tobacco). It concludes that there is a good chance that both categories may be found to be like products. This in turn may require governments, in cases of potential trade dispute, to come up with solid scientific evidence that would explain the reasons justifying discrimination between e-cigarettes and traditional tobacco products.

The last two chapters in the section concentrate on the new EU legal regime for e-cigarettes introduced by the Tobacco Products Directive (TPD). "Regulating e-cigarettes at the EU level," authored by Anna Pudło and Lukasz Gruszczynski, analyzes the legislative process that led to the adoption of the new EU regulatory framework for e-cigarettes and attempts to identify the factors that have had an impact on its ultimate shape, at the same time presenting the main features of this framework. This chapter also assesses the legality of the new regime under the relevant EU rules, taking as a point of reference the judgment of the Court of Justice of the European Union (CJEU) in the *Pillbox 38 (UK) Ltd v Secretary of State for Health* dispute. The authors ultimately conclude that the TPD, with its *sui generis* legal regime for e-cigarettes, can be seen as a realistic (albeit not perfect) compromise between the proponents and opponents of the new technology. In the next chapter ("Vaping and the precautionary principle in EU law"), Giancarlo A. Ferro and Costanza Nicolosi come to a completely different conclusion. In their opinion the TPD primarily constitutes a missed opportunity to embrace new technology for the benefit of public health. For the most part, the EU has extended to ENDS products the restrictions already in place for traditional tobacco products, even though it seems likely that the latter are much less safe than e-cigarettes. According to the authors, the reason for such a strict approach might be that the precautionary principle (which ostensibly formed the basis of the regulatory action) has, in the EU context, been transformed from a tool aimed at balancing market and public interests to an instrument to further harmonize the EU internal market. They also note that the precautionary principle cannot be seen as compelling any specific regulatory model for e-cigarettes. It only provides a legal basis for such regulation; it does not require any regulatory actions to be taken. In the end, a relevant decision remains a political one.

The last part of the book includes three chapters that analyze the approaches taken by regulators in selected jurisdictions (Taiwan, China, the United States, and Australia). The choice of these particular countries is not accidental. They were selected not only to ensure the broad geographical diversity of the book, but also because these countries have opted for different regulatory models: a total ban on e-cigarette sales; a laissez-faire approach; and a tobacco control regime. Taking these together with the two chapters that analyze the EU *sui generis* model, the book therefore provides a good overview of the various regulatory approaches to e-cigarettes that are taken by states. Moreover, some of the analyzed countries are leaders in tobacco control policies, and they often set standards that are subsequently adopted by the rest of the world. China is a notable exception here, but it is also one of the biggest markets for e-cigarettes and the main producer of such devices.

The first chapter in this section ("E-cigarette regulation in Taiwan and China"), authored by Chuan-Feng Wu, Ching-Fu Lin, and Mao-Wei Lo, analyzes the regulatory approach to e-cigarettes in Taiwan and China (with a focus on Taiwan). The authors see the emergence of e-cigarettes primarily as a challenge rather than an opportunity for the Taiwanese regulators (for example due to the growing popularity of e-cigarettes among younger consumers). In this context, they examine the existing provisions that regulate e-cigarettes in Taiwan and China and come to the conclusion that neither of the countries provide an optimal model. In the case of Taiwan they call for a single integrated model (rather than a two track system) that incorporates elements of both the pharmaceutical regime and the comprehensive ban. As far as China is concerned, their proposal is more modest, as it only postulates a set of basic rules and standards for product safety, nicotine limits, and health controls. In her chapter, Patricia I. Kovacevic ("Regulation of e-cigarettes in US law") takes a completely different position. Although she also argues that the current legislative framework for ENDS in the US is substantially inadequate (and internally inconsistent), for her the real problem lies in the fact that the relevant framework does not differentiate ENDS from cigarettes, does not acknowledge the risk differential between tobacco products and ENDS, and places a much higher—and economically unsustainable—regulatory burden on the fledgling ENDS industry than it does on the conventional cigarette industry. As a consequence—and coupled with spotty enforcement and unfair competition on the marketplace from illicit ENDS and other types of recreational products—the US regulatory regime does not at present create a transparent and consistent tobacco harm reduction environment. In this context, Kovacevic calls for the engagement of Congress through revisiting the US Tobacco Control Act to take into account the beneficial position of ENDS on the nicotine risk continuum, while imposing safeguards regarding product design and responsible communications to various audiences.

The final chapter looks at the Australian regulatory approach to e-cigarettes ("One does not simply sell e-cigarettes in Australia: an overview of Australian e-cigarette regulations"). The authors, Coral Gartner and Marilyn Bromberg, note that the Australian laws concerning e-cigarettes are complex and have been inconsistently interpreted by different jurisdictions and government ministers, while the type of enforcement action related to e-cigarettes has varied by jurisdiction. Although there have been some attempts to liberalize the very strict regulatory model currently in place, these have been met with strong opposition from various organizations, the government, and prominent public figures. According to the authors, the hostility to tobacco harm reduction is likely to have been influenced by the previous Australian experience with low tar cigarettes and an enduring distrust of and animosity toward the tobacco industry. At the same time, the authors note that there are practical and ethical issues associated with the current policy, which penalizes smokers for switching to a lower risk nicotine product, and argue that a more coherent and ethical policy approach would be to allow the legal sale of nontherapeutic nicotine-containing e-cigarette products to adults, with regulations imposed to minimize potential risks.

5. SOME REMARKS ON THE SELECTED FINDINGS OF THE CONTRIBUTING AUTHORS

Overall, the contributing authors have addressed all the questions put forward by the editor. Having said this, one also needs to acknowledge that while some research problems have received considerable attention, others have been tackled only at the margins of the main discussion. A careful review of the individual chapters shows both common points and areas of disagreement among the authors. For example, all of the authors who deal with the relevant question agree that the optimal regulatory strategy for e-cigarettes should take into account not only the risks (actual and potential) posed by e-cigarette use, but also the harm reduction potential of those products. At the same time, the authors disagree as to how this general approach should be translated into specific regulatory mechanisms. Some of them see a traditional tobacco regulatory model as appropriate, as it allows for keeping ENDS out of the reach of children and discouraging non-smokers without preventing the realization of e-cigarettes' potential as smoking cessation aids (Chapter 2). Others disagree and argue that the regulatory response should be tailored to the risks posed by these products (particularly for minors and non-smokers), without however undermining their potential to serve as a less harmful replacement for current tobacco users. This means that ENDS should be treated as a special category, one that is different from traditional tobacco products (Chapter 4). In this context, Pudło and Gruszczynski see the TPD, with its *sui generis* legal regime for e-cigarettes, as a realistic, albeit not perfect, compromise between the proponents and opponents of the new technology—one that recognizes the harm reduction potential of the products but also acknowledges the existing uncertainties resulting from the gaps in knowledge and contradictory scientific views (Chapter 7). Ferro and Nicolosi do not share this opinion. On the one hand, they see the TPD as a welcome example of European law-makers' attention to a new sector, where it is necessary to establish a balance between market rules and other objectives. On the other, they believe that the TPD borrows excessively from the tobacco control regulatory repertoire, thus bypassing the opportunity to set up a truly innovative regulatory regime (Chapter 8). This sentiment is also shared by Kovacevic in Chapter 10. The position taken by Wu, Lin, and Lo is just the opposite: they prefer a total ban combined with the pharmaceutical model for e-cigarettes with therapeutic claims (Chapter 9). Gartner and Bromberg are probably somewhere in the middle (Chapter 11).

Obviously it is not possible to summarize here all the details of the analyses presented in the individual chapters. For the purposes of this introduction, the editor selected two specific issues that appear to be particularly interesting, to wit: (i) the factors behind the choice of a specific regulatory model for e-cigarettes; and (ii) the extent of regulatory freedom enjoyed by regulators under the applicable international and supranational rules.

Since science remains inconclusive as to the risks and benefits of e-cigarette use, other factors have to play a role in determining the shape of the regulatory regime applicable to these products.[27] It seems that the normative stance held by key decision-makers within a country (or other important public figures able to influence the regulatory process in this specific area) on how to optimally deal with the tobacco epidemic is particularly important. If these people see it mainly as a problem of nicotine (rather than tobacco addiction), and believe in the effectiveness of current tobacco control methods (which will ultimately lead to the eradication of the tobacco problem rather than its replacement with nicotine addiction), or are deeply suspicious (rightly, by the

---

[27] See an interesting observation by Professor Stanton A. Glantz on the recent study concerning the gateway effect: "This result shows that the gateway of e-cigarettes in Great Britain is about four times as powerful in Great Britain, where health authorities have embraced e-cigarettes, more than in the US (where most health authorities have been skeptical of e-cigarettes), where the odds of youth who initiate with e-cigarettes progressing to smoking are 'only' tripled." S.A. Glantz, "Strong evidence for a huge gateway effect for e-cigs in Britain, even stronger than in USA" (Centre for Tobacco Control Research and Education, March 7, 2018) https://bit.ly/2SPBrGr accessed January 15, 2019.

way) of any initiatives that come from the tobacco (or, more broadly, nicotine) industry, it makes little sense for them to support this new technology. On the other hand, if key players are predominantly interested in the harm reduction approach and/or are skeptical about the efficiency of existing tobacco control measures, they may be more willing to embrace an e-cigarette friendly regulatory approach. Chapter 11 indicates that this factor was relevant in shaping the Australian approach to e-cigarettes.

History also matters. Past positive experiences with harm reduction policies may constitute an incentive for regulatory experimentation with e-cigarettes. Conversely, past failures in the implementation of harm reduction strategies (or limited experience with such policies) will push countries in the opposite direction. Again, Australia—as discussed in Chapter 11—seems to confirm this, while the UK is probably on the other side of the spectrum.

The political strength of various actors whose interests are directly and indirectly affected by e-cigarette regulations can also play a significant role. Such actors include users and their associations (both formal and informal). If the consumer base is large enough, as the EU case study attests (see Chapter 7), they can more easily translate their expectations into political claims and put pressure on relevant decision-makers (which also means that it might be more difficult to introduce a strict regulatory regime in those countries that have established strong markets for e-cigarettes).[28] Other groups that can also influence the regulatory process include not only the e-cigarette companies, but also the tobacco and pharmaceutical industry. The first of these was initially rather hostile to e-cigarettes, considering them a disruptive technology (as explained in Chapter 2), but since then has gradually embraced this new market niche by creating its own products and/or taking over its competitors. This means that the tobacco industry could take different strategic positions depending on the point in time. For example, it was in favor of extending the US Food & Drug Administration's (FDA) authority to e-cigarettes,[29] but against the recent sales ban that was introduced by Hong Kong (see also the discussion in Chapter 9 on the tobacco industry's influence on the regulatory process in China).[30] Pharmaceutical companies also have interests in restricting the sales of e-cigarettes, as those products potentially constitute competition to

---

[28] Of course, this assumes a certain quality of the regulatory process, which is a characteristic feature of democratic regimes. In authoritarian and quasi-authoritarian states, this factor (at least as far as users are concerned) is less relevant.

[29] J.H. Adler et al, "Baptists, bootleggers & electronic cigarettes" (2016) 33(2) Yale J Regul 313, at 348.

[30] L. Du, D. Wei, "Hong Kong bans e-cigarettes in latest blow for Big Tobacco" (*Bloomberg*, October 10, 2018) https://bloom.bg/2AKkplN accessed January 15, 2019.

the nicotine replacement therapies (NRT) they market.[31] This consideration was highlighted by the European Commission in the context of its initial TPD proposal. According to the Commission, e-cigarettes enjoyed an unjustified advantage, undermining the level playing field as compared to NRT products. There is also evidence that some pharmaceutical companies lobbied against the "light touch" approach to e-cigarettes during the TPD legislative process (again, see Chapter 7 for more details).

There also seems to be some cross-learning between countries (an issue not addressed in this volume). The introduction of a specific regulatory regime in one state may sometimes lead to its spread to neighbors or even more distant countries, without any real internal discussion as to the rationality of specific regulatory solutions or their fitness to the local conditions.[32] Certain countries—as well as their domestic institutions—occupy a privileged position in this context, acting as norm makers rather than norm takers. This may be a consequence of, among other things, their political and cultural strength, their epistemic and technical superiority, or the importance of their market for other countries. The FDA seems to be such an institution. In the context of e-cigarettes its influence is highlighted by several countries' decisions to ban e-cigarettes following the FDA 2009 import alert (66-41) concerning e-cigarettes (directing US Customs and Border Protection to reject their entry into the country on the basis that they were unapproved drug delivery devices), as well as the subsequent FDA report that found diethylene glycol and certain carcinogens in examined e-liquids. Shortly after, bans were introduced in Argentina, Brazil, Colombia, Panama, Saudi Arabia, and the United Arab Emirates. Some of those countries explicitly referred to the 2009 FDA position as a justification for their strict approach to e-cigarettes.[33]

---

31 N. Fides, "Glaxo boss bemoans rise of vaping" (*The Times*, January 17, 2015) https://bit.ly/2H8shmW accessed January 15, 2019. The statistical figures appear to confirm that fear (at least in the UK), as there seems to be a correlation between the rise of e-cigarettes and a sharp decline in NRT sales (see for example R. West, E. Beard, J. Brown, "Trends in electronic cigarette use in England" (*Smoking Toolkit Study*, 2018) http://smokinginengland.info/latest-statistics/ accessed January 15, 2019.

32 For more on the process of the diffusion of law, see W. Twining, "Diffusion of law: a global perspective" (2014) 36 JLP 1.

33 See for example Panama: Y.G. Mojica, "Advierten sobre cigarillos con veneno" [Warning about cigarettes with poison] (*La Prensa*, October 22, 2009) https://bit.ly/2VO6ap9; Argentina: Administracion Nacional de Medicamentos, Alimentos y Tecnologia Medica, Disposicion 3226/2011: Prohibese la commercialiacion y usi en todo el territorio nacional de un determinado product [Prohibits the sale and use throughout the national territory of a certain product] https://bit.ly/2SRdGxJ; and Brazil: N.V. Eich, "Anvisa proíbe comercialização do cigarro eletrônico" [Anvisa prohibits the commercialization of electronic cigarettes] (*Estadao*, August 31, 2009) https://bit.ly/2D74gJ0, all accessed January 15, 2019.

The activities of the FCTC COP also appear to affect the choice of a specific regulatory model for e-cigarettes. As noted above, both the FCTC COP and the Secretariat have endorsed a total ban as one of the legitimate regulatory options available to states (alongside a regulatory regime that would aim at addressing specific risks posed by these products). It seems that Taiwan, despite not being a party to the Convention, was inspired by the strict approach promoted by both bodies (see Chapter 9). The adoption of the FCTC was also indicated as one of the reasons behind the need to reform the EU regulatory framework for tobacco and tobacco-related products. Moreover, in the *Pillbox 38 (UK) Ltd* judgment the CJEU referred not only to the Convention but also to one of the COP decisions, noting that it recommended the consideration of specific restrictions for e-cigarettes (for example with regard to advertising and sponsorship) and the monitoring of their use (for more details see Chapter 7). Other countries which have decided to regulate e-cigarettes, or even banned these products, sometimes also refer to the FCTC documents. What seems to be interesting is that these documents can serve as a basis for completely different regulatory actions (which, as discussed in Chapter 4, is the result of the uncertain status of ENDS under the Convention and the lack of clear guidance from the COP).

Sometimes domestic legal norms (including constitutional ones) and internal political constraints may also have an impact (at least temporarily) on the shape of the regulatory model applicable to e-cigarettes in a specific country. Two case studies analyzed in this volume may serve as an example. The FDA's unsuccessful attempt to assert its jurisdiction over e-cigarettes in 2009 (as drug devices), and the court proceedings that ensued, delayed the FDA regulation by a few years and enabled the creation of an e-cigarette market in the US (see Chapter 10). A similar situation occurred in the EU. The prolonged process surrounding the adoption of the TPD stalled regulatory activities with respect to e-cigarettes at the national level in some Member States, effectively freezing the existing regulatory environment (ranging from complete prohibition to a laissez-faire model) (Chapter 8). More recently, Switzerland's Federal Administrative Court has overturned a ban on the sale of electronic cigarettes with nicotine, finding it incompatible with the existing applicable laws.[34]

The contributing authors have also confirmed that the extent of regulatory freedom enjoyed by regulators in this policy space is determined not only by national laws (for example constitutional norms), but also by international

---

[34] "Court overturns Swiss ban on e-cigarettes" (*Swissinfo*, April 28, 2018) https://bit.ly/2FqWtrA accessed January 15, 2019. Various e-cigarette restrictions were also challenged in other jurisdictions, such as Mexico, the Netherlands, Germany, and Estonia.

obligations and, in the case of the EU, by the relevant treaty rules and general principles of European law. This means that it is not possible to investigate and fully understand the regulatory activities of states with respect to e-cigarettes without analyzing the relevant applicable international and supranational rules.

Intuitively, one would think of the FCTC as an international treaty which constrains states' autonomy in regulating e-cigarettes by imposing certain common standards. However, as explained in detail in Chapter 4, a careful analysis of its text reveals that this is not the case. It seems that it is entirely up to the Parties of the Convention how they classify e-cigarettes for the purposes of the FCTC. They may interpret the conventional notion of "tobacco products" broadly, thus bringing e-cigarettes within the purview of the FCTC, or opt for a narrow interpretation and remove those products from the scope of most of FCTC obligations. Another option for the Parties is to rely on Art. 5.2(b) of the FCTC, which requires implementation of effective measures for preventing and reducing tobacco consumption, nicotine addiction, and exposure to tobacco smoke. As explained in Chapter 4, the formulation of this provision is sufficiently broad to cover e-cigarettes. However, this provision leaves the Parties with an almost unlimited discretion as to their choice of a preferred policy. Within this discretion a particular Party may decide to classify e-cigarettes, at the national level, as tobacco products, medicinal products, or simply ordinary consumer goods. It may also decide to entirely prohibit their sales and use. Of course, it is also always possible for the Parties to classify e-cigarettes at the national level as they wish, even without any reference to the Convention. Consequently, a particular Party may decide on its own regulatory framework for e-cigarettes, as well as on the classification of those products, by simply using its inherent sovereign powers. Thus, from the legal point of view the Convention does little to constrain its State Parties.

In Chapter 5, Gispen and Veraldi look at international human rights law as a relevant international framework which does not merely guide states when designing their e-cigarette regulatory regimes, but may actually restrict their regulatory autonomy in this field. In particular, State Parties to human rights treaties must protect and promote the health of individuals, especially children. This means that there is a positive obligation for states, under the right to health, to discourage (but not necessarily ban) the use of harmful substances (such as nicotine); to regulate industries that produce these products; and to actively inform individuals about the harmful effects of their use in proportion to the risks they pose. When marketed with therapeutic claims (as harm reduction tools), e-cigarettes should be required to conform to the relevant medical laws. An additional layer of complexity emerges if e-cigarettes are identified as gateway products. In such a case, a set of supplementary requirements will be activated, ranging from the obligation to regulate the use of e-cigarettes at places where children congregate, to additional advertising restrictions.

In Chapter 6, Foltea and Mercurio identify the WTO system as potentially relevant when determining the scope of the regulatory freedom enjoyed by states. As they correctly note, international trade rules that are concerned with discrimination may have the potential to be pertinent to an assessment of complete bans on e-cigarettes in a situation wherein traditional combustible products remain legally available on the market. In this context, they argue that there are sound grounds to conclude that both categories of product are either similar or likely to be considered as such in the future (depending on the development of science and the market situation), and therefore they should receive identical regulatory treatment under WTO rules. If such treatment is not provided, countries need to ensure that their e-cigarette bans are supported by sufficient scientific justification and that they constitute the least trade restrictive alternative available. The authors also indicate that similar problems may emerge with respect to other regulatory measures applied at the national level to e-cigarettes in situations where there are no equivalent restrictions for traditional combustible products. This group particularly includes bans on the registration and use of intellectual property linked to e-cigarettes, display bans, or indoor vaping bans.

As shown in Chapters 7 and 8, the supranational rules applicable in the context of the EU can restrict the freedom of individual Member States as well as European law-makers. In principle, until the adoption of the TPD, Members were free to regulate e-cigarettes as they considered appropriate. This resulted in a great variety of regulatory approaches, potentially undermining the establishment of the internal market for this category of products. Since this situation was qualified as an internal market problem rather than a public health protection issue, it fell within the scope of shared (and not supporting) competences. This means that since the adoption of the TPD, Member States can exercise their competences only with respect to those issues that are left unregulated by the Directive or other pieces of EU law (for example, excise taxes on e-cigarettes or the regulation of flavors). This has obviously circumscribed their regulatory freedom and completely changed the regulatory landscape in Europe. The EU rules, however, are also relevant for decision-makers at the European level. The EU legal system is of a constitutional character and establishes a clear hierarchy of norms. Secondary EU law (for example, directives and regulations) needs to be compatible with the provisions of the founding Treaties as well as the Charter of Fundamental Rights of the European Union. In the context of the TPD, this particularly meant that EU law-makers had to comply with: (i) the principle of subsidiarity, which provides that the Union can take action only if and to the extent that the objectives of the intended action cannot be sufficiently achieved by its Member States and if, due to the scale or effects of the proposed action, the objective can be better achieved at the EU level; (ii) the principle of proportionality, which stipulates that an adopted measure cannot exceed the limits of what is appropriate and necessary in order to achieve a particular objective set out in the Treaties; (iii) the principle of equal treatment, which means that comparable situations cannot be treated differently, and different situations should not be treated in the same way unless such treatment is objectively justified; and (iv) the EU's fundamental freedoms (here the right to property and the freedom to conduct a business). Although the TPD has been ruled to have passed all the applicable legal thresholds, these principles also mark out the future parameters of the regulatory freedom enjoyed by the EU regulators.

6. WHAT TO EXPECT IN THE FUTURE?

As was mentioned above, the field is subject to dynamic changes of a scientific, regulatory, and market character. As far as the first category is concerned, it should be stressed that in recent years e-cigarettes have attracted growing interest from the scientific community (with a corresponding increase in available funding). Consequently, many of the leading universities currently host research teams that work on various aspects of their use, and a number of major research reports (including those which are based on clinical studies) are expected in the upcoming years.[35] They may shed new light on our current assumptions, determining more clearly the risks that are connected with e-cigarette use (as well as their extent), the efficiency of e-cigarettes as a cessation method, or broader societal consequences of their presence on the market. If sufficiently conclusive, they may affect the direction of regulatory policies taken by states, either by making them more restrictive or more liberal.

When it comes to regulatory developments, probably the most important was the FDA's decision to restrict sales of flavored e-cigarette products in order to limit their availability and use among minors. The agency announced in November 2018 that such products will be sold only in age-restricted in-person locations, with online sales subject to tightened age verification procedures. The FDA also promised to strengthen its enforcement efforts against those retailers that violate age restrictions on the sale of e-cigarettes.[36] This may not be its final word: initially it planned to completely ban sales of flavored e-liquids (except for mint and menthol) in all convenience stores

---

[35] See for example the list of ongoing research projects at Clinical Trials (US National Library of Medicine) https://bit.ly/2C8g77N accessed January 15, 2018 (indicating almost 100 active projects relating to e-cigarettes).

[36] FDA, "Statement from FDA Commissioner Scott Gottlieb, M.D., on proposed new steps to protect youth by preventing access to flavored tobacco products and banning menthol in cigarettes" (November 15, 2018) https://bit.ly/2CatNyX accessed January 15, 2019.

and gas stations in the US.[37] Some individual American states are also active in this area. For example, California is currently working on a total ban on all retail sales of flavored e-liquids.[38] Some other states, or countries, may follow suit and introduce various restrictions on flavored e-cigarette products in the future. This issue may become relevant during the next meeting of the Conference of the Parties, which is scheduled for 2020.

While on one side of the Atlantic the regulatory regime is becoming more restrictive, on the other side it may soon be relaxed. The UK government is planning to review the current rules applicable to e-cigarettes (to a great extent determined by the TPD[39]) after the country leaves the EU, as is currently planned for 2019.[40] This is in reaction to the House of Commons Science and Technology Committee's report on e-cigarettes, published in August 2018, which pictured e-cigarettes not as a risk but rather as "an opportunity to significantly accelerate already declining smoking rates" and proposed "a shift to a more risk-proportionate regulatory environment; where regulations, advertising rules and tax duties reflect the evidence of the relative harms of the various e-cigarette and tobacco products available."[41]

Regulators are also busy in other parts of the world. For example, China has recently banned the sale of e-cigarettes to minors,[42] and is contemplating the introduction of certain additional restrictions (note that the market here is currently largely unregulated).[43] It is not clear, however, what this reform will ultimately look like, or whether it will actually materialize. New Zealand, after liberalizing its e-cigarette market, is also planning to tighten the applicable laws by introducing a ban on the use of e-cigarettes in public places and

---

[37] L. McGinley, "FDA plans curbs on e-cigarette sales over concerns about surge in teen vaping" (*The Washington Post*, November 8, 2018) https://wapo.st/2GXiXC3 accessed January 15, 2019.

[38] J. McDonald, "California lawmakers will introduce a statewide flavor ban" (*Vaping360*, November 30, 2018) https://bit.ly/2sgXOJ7 accessed January 15, 2019.

[39] For a detailed discussion of EU rules see Chapter 7 in this volume.

[40] Department of Health & Social Care, *The Government Response to the Science and Technology Committee's Seventh Report of the Session 2017–19 on E-cigarettes* (December 2018) Cm 9738.

[41] House of Commons Science and Technology Committee, *E-cigarettes* (Seventh Report of Session 2017–19, August 17, 2018) HC 505.

[42] L. Zhang, "China: central government bans sale of e-cigarettes to minors" (*Global Legal Monitor*, September 19, 2018) https://bit.ly/2ARo1CT accessed January 15, 2019.

[43] Z. Yu, "Cities mull ban on e-cigarettes in public even though China is the biggest producer" (*Global Times*, November 7, 2018) http://globaltimes.cn/content/1126288.shtml accessed January 15, 2019. For a more detailed discussion of the Chinese approach to e-cigarettes see Chapter 9 in this volume.

restricting their display at points of sale.[44] In another example of a country that has recently taken a more restrictive approach, Israel is planning requirements of plain packaging for all e-cigarette products and restrictions on their advertising.[45]

The most significant event in terms of market development was probably the purchase of a 35 percent stake in JUUL Labs, Inc. (JUUL), for US $12.8 billion, by Altria Group, Inc. (Altria)—one of the biggest producers of combustible tobacco products in the US. This is apparently part of Altria's business solution to the emergence of the post-tobacco world (particularly understandable if one considers the difficulties it faces in getting FDA approval for its IQOS system).[46] For JUUL this was probably a way to expand its customer base (for example, the company will gain access to Altria's marketing and distribution channels, and Altria will allow JUUL to advertise its product to smokers in the form of package inserts in cigarettes), as well as a way to face the regulatory challenges that have emerged recently as a consequence of the various FDA actions.[47] Not surprisingly, the transaction was met with heavy criticism from those in public health circles. For example, Matthew L. Myers, President of the Campaign for Tobacco-Free Kids, said that this was "a truly alarming development for public health and brings together the two companies that have been the most successful in marketing their highly addictive products to kids."[48] Another observer also alarmingly noted "[t]his move signals that vaping has now crossed a Rubicon. No longer the nemesis of big tobacco, it has become big tobacco."[49]

Another important market development is the expansion of JUUL outside of the US. Initially, the company marketed its products (based on a pod system) only to American consumers, but in 2018 it started to offer its products in

---

44 D. Caruana, "New Zealand moves to tighten vaping laws" (*VapingPost*, November 26, 2018) https://bit.ly/2RFGXhi accessed January 15, 2019.

45 L. Bauer, "Israel to paint cigarette, e-cigarette packages with world's ugliest color" (*CTech*, January 1, 2019) https://bit.ly/2H4YGL1 accessed January 15, 2019.

46 See the discussion in Chapter 2 on the strategy of transforming big tobacco companies into quasi-pharmaceutical corporations and regaining the influence over regulatory processes as a legitimate socially engaged actor.

47 S. Kaplan, M. Richtel, "Juul closes deal with tobacco giant Altria" (*The New York Times*, December 20, 2018) https://nyti.ms/2A5Xvoz accessed January 15, 2019.

48 Campaign for Tobacco-Free Kids, "Altria–Juul deal is alarming development for public health and shows need for strong FDA regulation" (Statement of Matthew L. Myers, December 20, 2018) https://bit.ly/2PQlsWc accessed January 15, 2019.

49 D. Marcus, "Why the Marlboro Man just bought a big chunk of Juul" (*The Federalist*, December 21, 2018) https://bit.ly/2CUSuRD accessed January 15, 2019.

several other countries, notably in the UK, Ireland, and Canada.[50] In the near future JUUL is planning to expand its operations further to the rest of the EU, Russia (where it has already an operative webpage), Indonesia, and other Asian countries.[51] Considering the popularity of JUUL products in the US (as well as the dynamics of the company's growth), one may expect its entrance into new countries' markets to have a significant effect, potentially attracting a lot of new customers (current smokers, but arguably also fresh users).

The twentieth century was, in the phrase famously coined by Professor Allan M. Brandt, a cigarette century. Will the current one be an e-cigarette century? If a world without nicotine is not possible, this indeed may be the case. For better or for worse.

---

[50] Note that in some countries JUUL has encountered some serious regulatory obstacles. For example, in Israel, almost immediately after entering the market, import and sale of its products was prohibited. The government cited the high level of nicotine concentration as reason behind the ban. "Israel bans Juul e-cigarette, 'a grave danger to public health'" (*The Times of Israel*, August 22, 2018) https://bit.ly/2RjNvTy accessed January 15, 2019.

[51] F. Potkin, C. Kirkham, "Juul sounds out Indonesia for expansion, other Asian countries in its sights" (*Reuters*, November 13, 2018) https://reut.rs/2qFAeoC accessed January 15, 2019.

PART I

Science, regulation and e-cigarettes

2. Divide and conquer? E-cigarettes as a disruptive technology in the history of tobacco control

Mateusz Zatoński and Allan M. Brandt

1. PREPARING FOR A WORLD "AFTER TOBACCO"

In their 2011 book *After Tobacco*, Peter Bearman and colleagues presented their readers with a series of hypothetical developments in tobacco control. They described a scenario in which the tightening of tobacco regulation in the United States of America (US) leads to no new smoking initiation under the age of 18, a doubling of the quit rate among adults under the age of 40, and a reduction by half in smoking prevalence in just five years. The authors then explored the ramifications this would have for the US economy, health, and society.[1] Bearman et al admitted that such tobacco control policy measures "seem unlikely," but they were not the only tobacco control experts to start planning for a future without smoking. Between 2011 and 2013 several countries around the globe, including New Zealand, Singapore, Scotland, and Finland, announced that they were setting hard target dates within the 25 years to come by which they planned to reach a tobacco "endgame"—a situation in which less than 5 percent of their populations would continue to use tobacco products.[2] The continuous decline of smoking rates to the point of negligibility seemed to be the broad agreement among many, if not most, tobacco control scholars.

The previous decades of development in smoking seemed to warrant such optimism. Since the 1980s the estimated global daily smoking prevalence

---

[1] P. Bearman et al (eds), *After Tobacco: What Would Happen if Americans Stopped Smoking?* (Columbia University Press 2011).

[2] R.E. Malone, "The race to a tobacco endgame" (2016) 25 Tob Control 607; Y. van der Eijk, "Development of an integrated tobacco endgame strategy" (2013) 24 Tob Control 336.

underwent large reductions for both sexes.[3] In the US, one of the first countries to experience mass popularity of smoking, adult smoking prevalence decreased from 42.4 percent in 1965 to 24.7 percent in 1997.[4] Countries that experienced later peaks of the tobacco epidemic also began to see smoking declines—in Poland, the country with the highest smoking rates in the world in the 1980s, cigarette sales decreased by 10 percent in the 1990s.[5]

The social acceptability of smoking was undergoing a similar change. Smoking first disappeared from the workplace and from airplanes, then from public transport, and finally from public venues and even from some outdoor settings.[6] When Ireland and Italy became the first European Union (EU) Member States to announce smoking bans in pubs and restaurants in 2004 and 2005, many commentators ridiculed the measures as zealotry and predicted mass disobedience.[7] Instead, the resounding success of these smoke-free provisions, which surprised even some tobacco control advocates, led to the introduction of similar regulations in most EU countries.[8] A shift in public attitudes toward smoking was also recorded in the US. Gallup polls indicated that between 2001 and 2011 the percentage of Americans favoring a ban on smoking in all public places increased from 39 percent to 59 percent.[9]

Finally, when the tobacco industry's attempts over decades to conceal data and mislead regulators about the health effects and addictive nature of smoking were exposed to the public, transnational tobacco companies (TTCs) became culturally and politically marginalized. A survey conducted in 2004 in

---

3 M. Ng et al, "Smoking prevalence and cigarette consumption in 187 countries, 1980–2012" (2014) 311 Jama 183.

4 CDC Office on Smoking and Health, "Achievements in public health, 1900–1999: tobacco use—United States, 1900–1999" (1999) 48 MMWR Morb Mortal Wkly Rep 986.

5 W.A. Zatoński et al, "Hundred years of cigarette smoking in Poland: three phases of the tobacco epidemic" (2017) 3 J Health Inequal 118.

6 A.M. Brandt, "Difference and diffusion: cross-cultural perspectives on the rise of anti-tobacco policies" in E.A. Feldman, R. Bayer (eds), *Unfiltered: Conflicts over Tobacco Policy and Public Health* (Harvard University Press 2004).

7 "Italians fume over cigarette curb" (*BBC News*, January 10, 2005) http://news.bbc.co.uk/1/hi/world/europe/4159587.stm; "Rebel Irish pubs flout smoking ban on the quiet" (*The Telegraph*, October 9, 2004) http://telegraph.co.uk/news/worldnews/europe/ireland/1473755/Rebel-Irish-pubs-flout-smoking-ban-on-the-quiet.html; A. Guidera, "No smoking! Ireland makes history with cigarette ban" (*Irish Independent*, January 20, 2014) http://independent.ie/lifestyle/no-smoking-ireland-makes-history-with-cigarette-ban-29926186.html, all accessed October 31, 2018.

8 L. Joosens, M. Raw, *Progress in Tobacco Control in 30 European Countries, 2005 to 2007* (Report financed by Swiss Cancer League 2007).

9 K.M. Cummings, R.N. Proctor, "The changing public image of smoking in the United States: 1964–2014" (2014) 23 Cancer Epidemiol Biomarkers Prev 32.

Australia reported that 79 percent of adults thought tobacco companies either never or mostly do not tell the truth in relation to issues about smoking.[10] For politicians, an association with TTCs became a "kind of reputational 'mark of Cain'."[11] In this cultural and political environment new opportunities for successful tort litigation arose, leading to further exposure of malfeasance and deception used by the tobacco industry in order to avoid regulation.

1.1 Advent of the Framework Convention on Tobacco Control

The adoption of the Framework Convention on Tobacco Control (FCTC) by the World Health Assembly in May 2003 constituted the institutional manifestation of this period of great optimism about tobacco control.[12] This pioneering global public health agreement was to become one of the most rapidly embraced treaties in United Nations history. It carried the promise of a new, global, evidence-based approach to tobacco control that would ensure the development of internationally coordinated strategies for reducing the demand and supply of cigarettes. The FCTC also institutionalized the tobacco industry's status as a corporate pariah in Art. 5.3, which set the rules of interaction with tobacco industry representatives, suggesting that the TTCs had lost their place at the regulatory table for good.[13]

Of course, a multitude of challenges for tobacco control advocates persisted. Tobacco continued to be aggressively marketed in lower and middle income countries. After a decade of rapid decrease in global smoking prevalence, the rate of decline decelerated after 2006 due to an increase in smoking in large countries such as Bangladesh, China, and Indonesia.[14] Due to population growth, the number of smokers globally actually grew after 1980, from more than 700 million to almost 1 billion in the first decade of the twenty-first century, as did the number of cigarettes smoked, from under 5 trillion to 6.25 trillion.[15] The increasingly global commercial reach of the TTCs meant that, while they were losing ground in regions such as Western Europe (where smoking prevalence declined by approximately 26 percent between 1990 and

---

10 S. Durkin, D. Germain, M. Wakefield, "Adults' perceptions about whether tobacco companies tell the truth in relation to issues about smoking" (2005) 14 Tob Control 429.

11 S. Chapman, B. Freeman, "Markers of the denormalisation of smoking and the tobacco industry" (2008) 17 Tob Control 25.

12 For detailed discussion of the FCTC regime and its applicability to e-cigarettes, see Chapter 4 in this volume.

13 R.E. Malone, S.A. Bialous, "WHO FCTC Article 5.3: promise but little progress" (2014) 23 Tob Control 279.

14 Ng et al (n 3).

15 Ibid.

2009), they were simultaneously addicting scores of people in the developing world, notably Sub-Saharan Africa and the Middle East (which registered a smoking prevalence increase of 57 percent in 1990–2009).[16] These appeared to be significant but nonetheless temporary setbacks in efforts to curtail the global tobacco epidemic. Matthew Myers, president of the Campaign for Tobacco-Free Kids, declared that the FCTC "is the closest thing we have to a vaccine against tobacco-caused death in the developing world."[17] The tobacco control community worldwide was united around a common goal and the FCTC was to provide the global governance tools necessary to pave the way to a smoke-free future. The tobacco industry, arguably one of the most successful businesses of the past hundred years, seemed to be in serious trouble in this new phase of global regulation and exposure.

1.2 Arrival of the E-cigarette

In 2003, as tobacco control leaders were celebrating the World Health Organization's (WHO) newly acquired mandate for promoting public health through treatymaking power, in China the pharmacist Hon Lik patented a technology which vaporized a nicotine solution in a device resembling a cigarette.[18] Today, he is credited as the inventor of "vaping"—obtaining nicotine from an electronic device rather than from a combustible, tobacco-based cigarette. Thus was born the modern e-cigarette (or Electronic Nicotine Delivery System—ENDS).[19]

The new product initially saw only modest interest in China and the TTCs seemed to have little faith in its commercial success. Instead, small independent manufacturers dominated the market.[20] However, ENDS technology quickly developed to make the e-cigarette a more attractive consumer product. Battery-powered heating replaced Hon Lik's bulky ultrasound elements and

---

16 R. Brathwaite et al, "A systematic review of tobacco smoking prevalence and description of tobacco control strategies in Sub-Saharan African countries: 2007 to 2014" (2015) 10 PloS One e0132401.

17 A.M. Brandt, *The Cigarette Century* (Basic Books 2007) 482.

18 S. Boseley, "Hon Lik invented the e-cigarette to quit smoking—but now he's a dual user" (*The Guardian*, June 9, 2015) http://theguardian.com/society/2015/jun/09/hon-lik-e-cigarette-inventor-quit-smoking-dual-user accessed October 31, 2018.

19 In this chapter the terms "e-cigarettes" and "ENDS" will be used interchangeably. Note, however, that sometimes "ENDS" is used as a broader category that also refers to other Next Generation Nicotine Products, such as heat-not-burn tobacco systems.

20 C. Abate, "Tobacco companies taking over the e-cigarette industry" (Healthline, February 16, 2017) http://healthline.com/health-news/tobacco-companies-taking-over-e-cigarette accessed October 31, 2018.

helped achieve miniaturization. E-cigarettes began to be exported abroad in 2005 and entered the US market in 2007, increasingly gaining popularity in the West.[21] Imperial Tobacco estimated that by 2014 total sales of vaping devices stood at just under US $5 billion and expected this to rise to more than US $15 billion by 2019, with sales highest in China, US, Japan, Russia, and Germany.[22] As the market potential of e-cigarettes became apparent, TTCs decided not so much to enter the fray as to take over. In 2013, Imperial Tobacco, through its Dutch subsidiary Fontem Ventures, bought Hon Lik's patents for US $75 million.[23] Other TTCs and their subsidiaries began to launch their own brands or acquire smaller private companies producing e-cigarettes.[24] Today, according to Jeff Drope, "Big Tobacco is now dominating [the e-cigarette market] in dollars in sales."[25]

In recent years e-cigarettes, and more recently other Next Generation (Nicotine) Products (NGPs), such as heat-not-burn (HNB) tobacco, seem to have dominated not only media headlines but also the programs of tobacco control summits, political regulatory debates, and public health research agendas. Some financial analysts have predicted that e-cigarette sales will overtake combustibles within a decade.[26] Scholars began to speculate as to whether e-cigarettes will become a "disruptive technology" that could precipitate a dramatic transformation in the consumption of nicotine products, potentially leading conventional cigarettes to obsolescence.[27] With this explosion of global interest and public health hopes around e-cigarettes one can perhaps see why Hon Lik, in a 2015 interview with the British weekly *The Spectator*, declared that some people "in China have called it the fifth invention—after navigation, gunpowder, printing and paper."[28]

---

21 Unknown, "Hon Lik: the man who invented vaping" (Blu, 7 July 2016) http://blu.com/en/US/blog/industry-news/hon-lik-man-invented-vaping.html accessed October 31, 2018.

22 Ibid.

23 Boseley (n 18).

24 Trefis Team, "E-cigarette market in the U.K. part 2: Big Tobacco enters the fray" (*Forbes*, 2 February 2016) https://bit.ly/2QJFWQH accessed October 31, 2018.

25 Abate (n 20).

26 B. Herzog, "US tobacco trends: disruptive innovation should drive outsized growth" (PowerPoint slides, Wells Fargo Securities 2014).

27 D.B. Abrams, "Promise and peril of e-cigarettes: can disruptive technology make cigarettes obsolete?" (2014) 311 Jama 135; G.V. Stimson, B. Thom, P. Costall, "Disruptive innovations: the rise of the electronic cigarette" (2014) 25 Int J Drug Policy 653; K. Fagerstrom, J.-F. Etter, J.B. Unger, "E-cigarettes: a disruptive technology that revolutionizes our field?" (2015) 17 Nicotine Tob Res 125.

28 M. Ridley, "'Quitting is suffering': Hon Lik, inventor of the e-cigarette, on why he did it" (*The Spectator*, June 20, 2015) http://spectator.co.uk/2015/06/quitting-is-

2. THE TOBACCO INDUSTRY'S HISTORY OF DISRUPTIVE INNOVATION

The concept of "disruptive innovation" was first introduced by Clayton Christensen and Joseph Bower in the *Harvard Business Review* in 1995. It sought to explain why some well-established companies failed to make technological investments that would help them to stay at the top of their industries and succumbed to newer challengers. The authors suggested that in order to survive, companies must be able to spot and develop innovative technologies that, while not necessarily appealing to current customers, would cater to the demands of the customers of the future.[29] Christensen's theory has become hugely influential in the past two decades, in both the academic and the business communities, despite more recent criticism of its theoretical overreach and the careful handpicking of case studies on which it was based.[30]

Tobacco companies have been engaging in industrial strategies reminiscent of disruptive innovation since long before the concept was coined. Whether faced with challenges from competitors, new findings about the harmfulness of its products threatening its public image, or increasingly restrictive regulation of its products, time and time again the tobacco industry has turned to technological innovation in its attempts to endure and expand. The very birth of mass cigarette production would be impossible without successful disruptive innovation.[31] The invention of the Bonsack machine in the early 1880s, combined with the ensuing reduction in the labor costs of cigarette manufacture, allowed cigarettes to become a mass produced good.[32] Later, technological advancements such as safe, toxic-free matches made cigarettes more "user-friendly," paving the way to their ubiquity.[33] The tobacco industry was also one of the first commercial entities to effectively harness the power of mass

---

suffering-hon-lik-inventor-of-the-e-cigarette-on-why-he-did-it/ accessed October 31, 2018.

[29] J.L. Bower, C.M. Christensen, "Disruptive technologies: catching the wave" (1995) 73 Harv Bus Rev 43.

[30] J. Lepore, "The disruption machine" (The New Yorker, June 16, 2014).

[31] V. Berridge, "Electronic cigarettes and history" (2014) 383 The Lancet 2204; A.M. Brandt, "From nicotine to nicotrol: addiction, cigarettes, and American culture" in S.W. Tracy, C.J. Acker (eds), *Altering American Consciousness: The History of Alcohol and Drug Use in the United States, 1800–2000* (University of Massachusetts Press 2004).

[32] M.C. Jensen, "The modern industrial revolution, exit, and the failure of internal control systems" (1993) 48 J Finance 831.

[33] R. Sobel, *They Satisfy: The Cigarette in American Life* (Anchor Books 1978) 64.

communication technology through the aggressive advertising of its products, attracting scores of new customers.[34]

Throughout the twentieth century the industry tweaked the design and composition of cigarettes, introducing flavorings that would mask the harshness of smoke and increasing nicotine levels to optimize their addictiveness.[35] The tobacco industry's success in periodically "disrupting" the market and renewing its customer base did not just happen by chance. It was a conscious effort on the part of the TTCs, investing significant means into research and development efforts and constantly monitoring the market in search of approaching trends and threats.[36]

2.1 In Search of a "Safer" Cigarette

The seminal studies of Doll & Hill and Wynder & Graham,[37] both published in 1950, were followed by a flurry of research proving beyond reasonable doubt that cigarettes are a uniquely harmful consumer product and giving rise to the threat of regulatory attempts aiming at decreasing their consumption. From that point on, the bulk of Big Tobacco's attempts at technological innovation have focused on developing a product that could be marketed as allowing its users to engage in "safer smoking."[38] In the 1950s and 1960s governments and public health organizations were often a willing partner in those efforts. In this they were driven by the belief in the desirability of *harm reduction*—defined by the British National Institute for Health and Care Excellence as "reducing the illness and deaths caused by smoking tobacco—among people who smoke and those around them."[39]

The idea was to offer smokers a less dangerous version of the cigarette, one that would be attractive enough for them to transition away from traditional cigarettes while at the same time reducing undesirable health effects. In the United Kingdom (UK), the tobacco industry contributed money to the Medical Research Council in the 1950s for a research program aiming to remove the

---

34 Brandt, *The Cigarette Century* (n 17).

35 Campaign for Tobacco-Free Kids, *Designed for Addiction* (2014).

36 R.N. Proctor, *Golden Holocaust: Origins of the Cigarette Catastrophe and the Case for Abolition* (University of California Press 2011); Brandt, *The Cigarette Century* (n 17).

37 R. Doll, A. Bradford Hill, "Smoking and carcinoma of the lung" (1950) 2 BMJ 739; E.L. Wynder, E.A. Graham, "Tobacco smoking as a possible etiologic factor in bronchiogenic carcinoma; a study of 684 proved cases" (1950) 143 J Am Med Assoc 329.

38 Berridge, "Electronic cigarettes and history" (n 31).

39 NICE, *Public Health Guidance Scope: Tobacco: Harm-Reduction Approaches to Smoking* (2011).

harmful components of cigarettes.[40] In 1968 in the US, Ernst Wynder himself convinced Kenneth Endicott, the head of the National Cancer Institute, to set up a study group to conduct research that would help remove the biologically active components in smoke, such as tar.[41]

In the communist Eastern Bloc too, many health advocates believed that the best route to containing the epidemic of tobacco-related diseases was through the development of a "safer cigarette." In 1971 the Polish Tobacco Monopoly, spurred on by the public health community, began to experiment with the production of a type of crop that, through the application of a special chemical process, yielded a low nicotine and low tar nicotine leaf.[42] This aroused the interest of the international press. In an article published in the *New York Post* on April 26, 1971, the author described his experience of smoking what he calls "probably the safest cigarette in the world. If I smoked 50 a day for the rest of my life I'd be in no greater danger than if I was gulping sea air, according to its manufacturers."[43]

However, the development of low tar and low nicotine cigarettes failed to make smoking "safer." The former simply led smokers to take in more tar (compensatory smoking).[44] The latter, perhaps unsurprisingly, never took off as a mass consumer product as smokers did not receive their nicotine fix. Probably the most commercially successful of this long line of industry-sponsored harm reduction products, if equally ineffective when it came to health benefits, were cigarette filters. In 1963 Addison Yeaman, the General Counsel and Vice President of Brown & Williamson, wrote that, faced with the Surgeon General's Committee's likely conclusion that there is a causal relation between smoking and cancer, the company must of course "challenge these charges," but must also say to the public: "here is our triple, or quadruple, or quintuple filter, capable of removing whatever constituent of smoke is currently suspect while delivering full flavor—and incidentally a nice

---

40 Berridge, "Electronic cigarettes and history" (n 31).

41 Brandt, *The Cigarette Century* (n 17) 275.

42 Unknown, "Monopoly tests nicotine-free brand" (May 12–14, 1971) http://industrydocumentslibrary.ucsf.edu/tobacco/docs/#id=xpnk0027 accessed October 31, 2018, 52.

43 D. Blewett, "Poles taking smokers off hook" (April 26, 1971) http://industrydocumentslibrary.ucsf.edu/tobacco/docs/#id=xpnk0027 accessed October 31, 2018, 53.

44 N.L. Benowitz, "Compensatory smoking of low-yield cigarettes" in National Cancer Institute (ed), *Risks Associated with Smoking Cigarettes with Low Machine-Measured Yields of Tar and Nicotine* (US Department of Health and Human Services, National Institutes of Health, National Cancer Institute 2001).

jolt of nicotine."[45] The encouraging claims for filtered cigarettes helped distort the public's understanding of smoking harm at a time when it seemed that the verdict of science was clear. They were accompanied by aggressive marketing and slogans such as Viceroys' "Double-Barreled Health Protection." The prevalence of filtered cigarettes leaped from 10 percent of the US cigarette market in 1954 to 90 percent by the mid-1970s—disruptive innovation was complete.[46] Filter cigarettes, just as low tar and low nicotine cigarettes before them, were ineffective in reducing harm, but they allowed the tobacco industry to reassure customers and reinforce smoking behavior.

2.2 Developing the Proto-ENDS

Frustrated by the industry's false claims and aggressive marketing, public health advocates' and regulators' desire to collaborate with the tobacco industry in developing a "safer cigarette" had waned by the 1970s.[47] From this point on, the strategy of the tobacco industry moved from making smoking safer by creating a healthier cigarette to developing completely new replacement products, such as oral tobacco.[48] Despite its claim to be committed to harm reduction, internal documents indicate that the tobacco industry saw medical nicotine replacement therapy (NRT) predominantly as a threat to its business. "Products of this type," a Philip Morris report argued, "pose a dual threat to PM USA . . . they make it easier for smokers to quit, and smokers who quit are the major cause of loss of sales of our products. We lose far more customers to quitting than we do to competitive brands."[49]

A solution considered by the industry was the development of its own nicotine aerosol devices as a way to address smokers' health concerns, satisfy their desire for nicotine, and preempt regulation, all the while creating a product which could have the potential for long-term use rather than serving purely as an aid to quitting smoking. Therefore, while the conventional narrative of the history of ENDS begins with Hon Lik's patent of 2003,[50] tobacco companies' attempts to develop nicotine delivery products that were not

---

[45] A. Yeaman, *Implications of Battelle Hippo I & II and the Griffith Filter* (Philip Morris Records 1963).

[46] Brandt, *The Cigarette Century* (n 17) 244.

[47] V. Berridge, "History and the future: looking back to look forward?" (2016) 37 Int J Drug Policy 119.

[48] Berridge, "Electronic cigarettes and history" (n 31).

[49] Philip Morris USA, "Operations 1992–1996" (undated) http://industrydocumentslibrary.ucsf.edu/tobacco/docs/#id=llch0116 accessed October 31, 2018, 13.

[50] Boseley (n 18).

dissimilar to modern e-cigarettes date back to a much earlier period, with the first patent for a smokeless non-tobacco cigarette dating back to 1963 in the US.[51] Since then, the tobacco industry has released a long line of products that heat tobacco instead of burning it or that vaporize nicotine, including British American Tobacco's (BAT) Ariel cigarettes in the 1960s, R.J. Reynolds Tobacco Company's Premier in the 1980s, and Philip Morris' Accord in the 1990s. Even Philip Morris' MarkTen e-cigarettes, launched in 2013, entered development in 1990.[52]

3. E-CIGARETTES—A DISRUPTIVE MOMENT IN TOBACCO CONTROL?

The modern e-cigarette might be seen as effectively another in a continuum of reduced harm products picked up by the tobacco industry as part of its drive to find socially acceptable alternatives to cigarettes. Most of these earlier products, including reduced harm cigarettes and early nicotine aerosol devices, proved unconvincing to customers and never gained a mass following. Others, such as cigarette filters or "light" cigarettes, were examples of new technologies which successfully "disrupted" the tobacco market and are until this day erroneously perceived by many consumers as healthier alternatives to what came before them.[53] Which group of products will the e-cigarettes join?

Some of the developments accompanying e-cigarettes' entry to the market seem to indicate that they might indeed constitute the tobacco industry's new disruptive technology coup. In many countries, legislators have allowed ENDS companies to launch aggressive marketing efforts. An example is the UK, where spending on e-cigarette promotion grew between 2010 and 2012 from £1.7 million to £13.1 million.[54] In a country in which cigarette promotion was banned 15 years previously, e-cigarette adverts suddenly began to crop up on television, in the press, in electronic media. A powerful symbol of this was the appearance of images promoting e-cigarettes on the iconic London double decker buses. Decades after being pushed out of public places, cigarette adverts seemed to have made a comeback in the streets of British cities. In addition, in the UK, as in many other countries, confusion still reigns as to

---

[51] US Department of Health and Human Services, *E-Cigarette Use among Youth and Young Adults: A Report of the Surgeon General—Executive Summary* (2016) 10.

[52] L.M. Dutra, R. Grana, S.A. Glantz, "Philip Morris research on precursors to the modern e-cigarette since 1990" (2017) 26 Tob Control e97.

[53] M.A. Song et al, "Cigarette filter ventilation and its relationship to increasing rates of lung adenocarcinoma" (2017) 109 JNCI djx075.

[54] L. Conway, *Advertising of E-Cigarette Products* (Briefing Paper 2017).

the status of vaping in public places, with many British pubs allowing their customers to use e-cigarettes indoors.[55]

In the years after e-cigarettes' first appearance in western markets, the increase in their popularity was spectacular. Revenues from the sale of ENDS doubled each year between 2008 and 2013.[56] In the US, by 2013, 11.4 percent of current smokers reported ever having used e-cigarettes.[57] In the UK there are almost three million e-cigarette users.[58] In European countries the use of e-cigarettes seems particularly high in Germany and Greece, where almost 13 percent of smokers declare they are current e-cigarette users.[59]

However, there are signs that, at least among adult smokers, this growth is slowing. After reaching a 5 percent prevalence of use in the UK population in 2013, the use of e-cigarettes has plateaued.[60] Analyses from the US show a slight decrease in current use of e-cigarettes, from 3.7 percent in 2014 to 3.5 percent in 2016.[61] While these data must be taken cautiously, especially given that it is difficult to track the accuracy of self-reported use, there is some evidence that among adult conditioned smokers conversion rates to e-cigarettes are low, as their delivery of nicotine remains inferior to that of combustible cigarettes.[62] Despite its unquestionable growth, the e-cigarette market remains

---

55 G. Townshend, "Up in smoke: the rules of vaping inside pubs" (*The Morning Advertiser*, June 29, 2018) http://morningadvertiser.co.uk/Article/2017/06/30/Up-in-smoke-the-rules-of-vaping-inside-pubs accessed October 31, 2018.

56 D. Robinson, "Japan Tobacco joins rivals in e-cigarette market with E-Lites buy" (*The Financial Times*, June 11, 2014) http://ft.com/content/28e13462-f179-11e3-9161-00144feabdc0 accessed October 31, 2018; Abrams (n 27).

57 J.L. Pearson et al, "E-cigarette awareness, use, and harm perceptions in US adults" (2012) 102 Am J Public Health 1758.

58 Action on Smoking and Health, "Large national survey finds 2.9 million people now vape in Britain: for the first time over half don't smoke" (Action on Smoking and Health, May 8, 2017) http://ash.org.uk/media-and-news/press-releases-media-and-news/large-national-survey-finds-2-9-million-people-now-vape-in-britain-for-the-first-time-over-half-no-longer-smoke/ accessed October 31, 2018.

59 C.N. Kyriakos et al, "Characteristics and correlates of electronic cigarette product attributes and undesirable events during e-cigarette use in six countries of the EUREST-PLUS ITC Europe Surveys" (2018) 16 Tob Induc Dis A1.

60 R. West, E. Beard, J. Brown, "Trends in electronic cigarette use in England" (Smoking Toolkit Study, 2018) http://smokinginengland.info/latest-statistics/ accessed October 31, 2018.

61 W. Bao et al, "Changes in electronic cigarette use among adults in the United States, 2014–2016" (2018) 319 Jama 2039.

62 D. O'Connell, "Philip Morris could stop making conventional cigarettes" (BBC, November 30, 2016) http://bbc.com/news/business-38152297 accessed October 31, 2018; M. Zatoński, M. Stokłosa, "Report from the seminar on the past, present, and future of tobacco control, Harvard University Department of the History of Science, Cambridge, Massachusetts, October 2016" (2016) 3 J Health Inequal 16.

a fraction of the conventional tobacco market—BAT approximated global conventional cigarette sales in 2016 at US $680 billion, compared with less than US $15 billion for e-cigarettes.[63]

Perhaps more concerning is the appeal e-cigarettes seem to have for teenagers. A study conducted in Poland found that use of e-cigarettes among adolescents rose from 5.5 percent in 2010–11 to 29.9 percent in 2013–14 (although current use was defined broadly in the study, as having had even a single puff in the preceding 30 days).[64] In the US, 50 percent more high- and middle-schoolers vaped than smoked in 2017.[65] Recently, more refined products such as JUUL have been attracting affluent and middle class teenagers in America's big cities; according to Nielsen data, by mid-2018 this brand controlled 72 percent of the US e-cigarette market.[66] JUUL's producers claim that the product is intended for adults, just as the tobacco industry has done for decades with combustible cigarettes.[67] However, their marketing efforts (using young models and celebrities) and flavor offers (such as crème brûlée and cotton candy) found themselves at the center of a federal investigation into whether they were intentionally directed at youth.[68] Almost one fifth of middle and high school students in the US have declared that they have seen JUUL used in school and two thirds of the brand's youngest users state they are not aware that the product always contains nicotine.[69]

From a long-term business perspective, ENDS offer the tobacco industry an opportunity to tailor its corporate strategies to markets with different characteristics. As the denormalization of combustible cigarettes progresses in North America, Europe, and Australia, reduced harm nicotine and tobacco products could offer an opportunity to restore growth to TTCs in those markets. Due to their elevated price and technological requirements they might not be suited for

---

63 BAT, "The global market: trends affecting our industry" (British American Tobacco, 2016) http://bat.com/group/sites/UK__9D9KCY.nsf/vwPagesWebLive/DO9DCKFM# accessed October 31, 2018; Unknown (n 21).

64 M.L. Goniewicz et al, "Rise in electronic cigarette use among adolescents in Poland" (2014) 55 J Adolesc Health 713.

65 J. Tolentino, "The Promise of Vaping and the Rise of Juul" (The New Yorker, May 7, 2018).

66 M. Richtel, S. Kaplan, "Did Juul lure teenagers and get 'customers for life'?" (*The New York Times*, August 27, 2018 https://nytimes.com/2018/08/27/science/juul-vaping-teen-marketing.html accessed October 31, 2018.

67 G. Bellafante, "Cool-looking and sweet, Juul is a vice teens can't resist" (*The New York Times*, February 16, 2018) https://nytimes.com/2018/02/16/nyregion/juul-teenagers-vaping-ecigarettes-dangers.html accessed October 31, 2018.

68 Richtel, Kaplan (n 66).

69 *Truth Initiative*, "Nearly 1 in 5 youth say they have seen Juul used in school" (Truth Initiative, May 23, 2018) https://truthinitiative.org/news/nearly-1-5-youth-say-they-have-seen-juul-used-school accessed October 31, 2018.

markets in some lower income countries. However, in many of those countries the sale of traditional cigarettes continues to grow and smoking prevalence is on the rise.[70] In this context, the success of a very expensive electronic unit in Japan might make it possible for the TTCs to continue promoting inexpensive tobacco products with higher profit margins in poorer settings. A similar mechanism can be replicated within countries by targeting communities with different socio-economic statuses with different products.

3.1 Polarization of the Tobacco Control Community

While it still remains to be seen whether e-cigarettes will constitute a long-term commercial success, there is one way in which they have most certainly constituted a disruptive force—namely in the deep polarization of the tobacco control community caused by their appearance on the market. The success of e-cigarettes took most tobacco control experts by surprise, just as it did regulators. Neither the FCTC,[71] nor national smoke-free laws—as mentioned above—contained provisions that would help manage the new challenge. The public health community had not worked out a position on how the issue should be tackled. As a result, deep fissures quickly appeared among different groups. The main bone of contention regards whether e-cigarettes could be a useful tool in helping smokers quit, in which case they should be regulated less strictly than combustible tobacco, or whether they are just another addictive and potentially dangerous device, often used in conjunction with combustible products, in which case they should be measured with the same regulatory yardstick as traditional cigarettes.

A significant section of the health community sees e-cigarettes as a huge opportunity for public health progress. In 2014 Karl-Olov Fagerström, one of the world's leading authorities on nicotine addiction, recalled Michael Russell's dictum that "people smoke for nicotine but they die from the tar" and cautiously suggested that e-cigarettes might be another offer in the line of harm reduction products, such as NRT, which can help wean people off combustible cigarettes.[72] Public Health England (PHE), in its 2018 evidence review, argued that e-cigarettes help 20,000 people in the UK quit smoking

---

[70] J. Drope, N.W. Schluger, *The Tobacco Atlas* (6th ed, American Cancer Society 2018).

[71] For further details see Chapter 4 in this volume.

[72] K.O. Fagerström, K. Bridgman, "Tobacco harm reduction: the need for new products that can compete with cigarettes" (2014) 39 Addict Behav 507. It is worth noting that the article's second author was an employee of Nicoventures Limited, a standalone company within the British American Tobacco Group.

every year and called for hospitals and employers to provide vaping areas.[73] A good overview of the current state of knowledge on the health harm posed by ENDS, their utility as cessation aids, and the risk they pose as a gateway to the use of combustible tobacco for youth or non-smokers is included in Chapter 3 of this volume.

Other scholars challenged this view, suggesting that, while helpful for individual smokers otherwise unable to quit, e-cigarettes would ultimately be detrimental to public health. In 2014 a group of leading tobacco control scholars cautioned about the potential of e-cigarettes to renormalize smoking.[74] Others pointed out that many of the e-cigarette models that appeared in advertising, sponsorship, and popular culture replicated the look of traditional cigarettes very closely, leading to concerns about effectively promoting smoking.[75] A 2018 review led by Stanton Glantz directly contradicted PHE's findings, suggesting that e-cigarettes actually depress quitting rates and expand the nicotine market by attracting youth while the adult users of e-cigarettes continue to also smoke combustibles (dual users).[76]

The split within the public health tobacco control community is perhaps best illustrated by the two open letters sent to WHO Director General Margaret Chan in 2014. The first, from May 26, which was signed by 53 prominent tobacco addiction specialists and epidemiologists, urged the WHO not to "control and suppress" e-cigarettes, which the signatories considered low risk nicotine products which can be "part of the solution, not part of the problem," in its upcoming global guidelines.[77] Less than a month later, on June 16, 129 public health and medical experts delivered another open letter to Margaret Chan, this time warning the WHO about the danger of leaving ENDS unregulated and of buying "into the tobacco industry's well-documented strategy of presenting itself as a partner."[78]

---

[73] A. McNeill et al, *Evidence Review of E-Cigarettes and Heated Tobacco Products 2018* (A report commissioned by Public Health England, Public Health England 2018).

[74] M. McKee et al, "The debate on electronic cigarettes" (2014) 384 The Lancet 2107.

[75] M. de Andrade, G. Hastings, K. Angus, "Promotion of electronic cigarettes: tobacco marketing reinvented?" (2013) 347 BMJ f7473.

[76] S.A. Glantz, D.W. Bareham, "E-cigarettes: use, effects on smoking, risks, and policy implications" (2018) 39 Annu Rev Public Health 215.

[77] Press Association, "WHO urged not to 'suppress and control' e-cigarettes" (*The Guardian*, May 29, 2014) https://theguardian.com/world/2014/may/29/who-suppress-control-e-cigarettes-uk-health-tobacco accessed October 31, 2018.

[78] S.A. Glantz, "129 public health and medical authorities from 31 countries write WHO DG Chan urging evidence-based approach to ecigs" (UCSF Center for Tobacco Control Research and Education, June 15, 2014) https://tobacco.ucsf.edu/129-public-health-

Some have sought to characterize the main fault line of the debate on e-cigarettes as lying between the US, with its prohibitionist leanings, and the UK, where less antipathy to harm reduction has existed historically.[79] However, this can give a false impression of a broader consensus within either of these countries. In fact, e-cigarettes have been a highly polarizing question for the public health community within both the UK and the US. As recently as February 2018, the British Medical Association cautioned that while "there is growing consensus that using an e-cigarette is substantially safer than smoking tobacco . . . Given the limited time for which these products have been widely available, there is limited information about the long-term health impact of their use."[80]

A less explored rift in the tobacco control community over the issue of e-cigarettes is the one dividing clinicians and smoking cessation practitioners from public health generalists. Members of the first group have argued that the "provision of clean nicotine . . . in the form of NRTs has been in use for nearly 30 years and has proven to be a safe way to facilitate smoking cessation."[81] In their view, e-cigarettes can constitute another useful element in the clinician's cessation support toolbox, one that can be useful with patients who have tried and failed using different methods of quitting. In 2014 David Abrams voiced his opinion that "e-cigarettes, with prudent tobacco control regulations, do have the potential to make the combusting of tobacco obsolete."[82] According to this approach, burdensome regulation could stifle e-cigarettes and decrease their viability as popular cessation aids.

The second group, and in particular researchers who have conducted work on tobacco industry tactics, are concerned about the disruptive impact e-cigarettes could have on tobacco control. They point out that enormous progress has been made in the struggle against cigarettes in high income countries in the past decades, with a sustainable decline observed in smoking rates and effective new anti-tobacco legislation, most recently in the form of Australia's plain

---

and-medical-authorities-31-countries-write-who-dg-chan-urging-evidence-based-approach-ecigs#_edn1 accessed October 31, 2018.

[79] J. Glenza, "E-cigarette bans highlight public health divide between US and UK researchers" (*The Guardian*, October 24, 2017) https://theguardian.com/society/2017/oct/24/e-cigarette-bans-highlight-public-health-divide-between-us-and-uk-researchers accessed October 31, 2018; Berridge, "History and the future" (n 47).

[80] BMA, "E-cigarettes" (British Medical Association, February 27, 2018) http://bma.org.uk/collective-voice/policy-and-research/public-and-population-health/tobacco/e-cigarettes accessed October 31, 2018.

[81] N.L. Benowitz, M.L. Goniewicz, "The regulatory challenge of electronic cigarettes" (2013) 310 Jama 685.

[82] Abrams (n 27).

packaging law.[83] All this has been achieved without the help of e-cigarettes and many health advocates are worried that the new product will unnecessarily thwart a positive trend. In other words, in many countries the advent of e-cigarettes came at a time when the existing tobacco control measures, as well as more recent measures such as plain packaging, seemed already to be effective in driving significant progress in the reduction of smoking rates. In the US, the decline in consumption since 2000 pointed to a smoking prevalence of under 5 percent by the 2030s.[84] Similarly, projections for Poland indicate that by the 2030s cigarette sales will decrease to under ten billion sticks per year, down from a peak of more than 100 billion in the 1990s.[85] In Norway, the prevalence of daily smoking among 15-year-old adolescents had fallen to under 2 percent by 2014, making headway for a new generation that could be effectively tobacco free.[86] Introducing a new, technologically advanced product, attractive to teenagers and with enormous addictive potential, could, according to many public health scholars, disrupt these positive trends.

The TTCs further fanned the flames of interest and controversy around the issue of e-cigarettes. In January 2018 Philip Morris ran full-page adverts in several UK newspapers claiming that the firm's "New Year's Resolution" for 2018 is to "stop selling cigarettes in the UK." The ad contained one caveat: "But many will continue to smoke. That's why we want to replace cigarettes with products, such as e-cigarettes and heated tobacco, which are a better choice for the millions of men and women in the UK who would otherwise not stop smoking."[87]

3.2 The Relegitimization of Big Tobacco

Throughout the twentieth century, Big Tobacco sought to affect the policy debate in a way that would limit the impact of regulation on its business—preferably by scrapping the undesirable policies altogether. It has used a range of tactics to this end, including commissioning economic analyses exaggerating the costs of anti-tobacco legislation, conducting studies questioning their effectiveness, and directly lobbying politicians. With the growing unwilling-

---

83 Office of Parliamentary Counsel, Tobacco Plain Packaging Act 2011 (2016).

84 Zatoński, Stokłosa (n 62).

85 Zatoński et al, "Hundred years of cigarette smoking in Poland" (n 5).

86 W.A. Zatoński et al, "Smoking- or nicotine-free generation, or both? What should be the public health priority?" (2016) 2 J Health Inequal 105.

87 D. Carrig, "Philip Morris says its New Year's resolution is to give up cigarettes" (*USA Today*, 3 January 2018) https://usatoday.com/story/money/business/2018/01/03/philip-morris-marlboro-wants-give-up-cigarettes-go-smoke-free/1001442001/ accessed October 31, 2018.

ness of politicians to be seen directly dealing with the industry and in particular with the advent of FCTC Art. 5.3, the TTCs needed to focus on tactics which would allow them to stay out of the spotlight, while retaining their influence over tobacco policy-making. In order to achieve this, the industry increasingly acted through third parties, political allies, and front groups—including tobacco growers and distributors, other businesses (notably retail and hospitality industry), and libertarian pressure groups, but also trade unions, women's groups, or organizations representing ethnic minorities. Constant and careful monitoring by the tobacco control community was required to expose and stigmatize those links.[88]

The support given to e-cigarettes by some public health advocates has raised concern regarding a potentially disruptive development to the fragile balance in this war of attrition between the tobacco industry and its opponents. The e-cigarette producers can now link their promotional efforts with the rhetoric of the harm reduction advocates, suggesting that they stand on the side of public health. E-cigarette marketing focuses on employing claims of health benefits compared with smoking cigarettes, including in terms of secondhand smoking, as well as advertising the products as cessation aids.[89]

As a result, the tobacco industry has already been partly successful in shedding its social and political pariah status. Prominent tobacco researchers have begun to openly advocate for a normalization of relations with the tobacco industry, arguing that public health regulators should treat cigarette companies as they would any other business. The economists Branston and Sweanor argued that public health regulation should provide TTCs with incentives that would encourage them to "develop in such a way that they no longer achieve the greatest shareholder value by focusing on cigarettes." In their view, less regulated and increasingly popular e-cigarettes could provide an "escape route" for tobacco companies, making them "less inclined to fight so hard for the continuation of tobacco markets as we know them."[90]

This softening approach to the industry gave the TTCs a new avenue to put themselves back into a position where they could influence regulation. With the assumption that e-cigarette producers could be allies of public health, the tobacco industry can now conduct policy lobbying via vaping associations and ENDS-producing subsidiaries. The TTCs are engaging in a strategy of renormalization, asserting that they have become powerful advocates for

---

88 S. Ulucanlar, G.J. Fooks, A.B. Gilmore, "The policy dystopia model: an interpretive analysis of tobacco industry political activity" (2016) 13(9) PLoS Med e1002125.

89 J.K. Noel, V.W. Rees, G.N. Connolly, "Electronic cigarettes: a new 'tobacco' industry?" (2011) 20 Tob Control 81.

90 J.R. Branston, D. Sweanor, "Big tobacco, e-cigarettes, and a road to the smoking endgame" (2016) 29 Int J Drug Policy 14.

global "corporate responsibility." Philip Morris took this approach one step further in September 2017 by launching the Foundation for a Smoke-Free World (FSFW), to which it will contribute approximately US $80 million per year over 12 years. The stated aim of the organization, headed by the former Cabinet Director for Noncommunicable Diseases at the WHO, Derek Yach, is to "accelerate an end to smoking . . . by producing better science and research to underpin cessation and harm reduction."[91] The WHO, along with the bulk of the public health community, identified the hypocrisy of Philip Morris' actions, pointing out that if the company were truly committed to a smoke-free world it would support tobacco control policies such as tobacco taxes, graphic warning labels, and advertising bans, instead of vehemently challenging them.[92] Nonetheless, FSFW continues a forceful recruitment campaign targeting public health researchers, especially from lower income settings, with grant offers.[93]

Initiatives such as FSFW are not new in the history of tobacco control. This consistent strategic approach of the industry dates back at least to 1953 and the establishment of the Tobacco Industry Research Committee (TIRC). In the "Frank Statement" accompanying the launch of the TIRC, the cigarette companies pledged to provide "aid and assistance to the research effort into all phases of tobacco use and health," a statement closely resonating with the FSFW's mission statement.[94] The declaration, claiming that the health of its consumers was the industry's primary concern, was followed by decades of industry-supported research criticizing studies that found evidence of smoking harm and denial of smoking's addictive nature.[95] To head the TIRC, the tobacco industry chose a prominent researcher, of a status similar to Derek Yach—the biologist Clarence Cook Little. Finally, to recruit collaborators, the TIRC would often approach young researchers struggling to secure funding, enticing them with the opportunity for financial support to continue their work. While the TIRC's efforts focused on manufacturing doubt about the

---

91 D. Yach, "Building a foundation to accelerate an end to smoking" (*British Medical Journal*, 23 January 2018) https://blogs.bmj.com/bmj/2018/01/23/derek-yach-building-a-foundation-to-accelerate-an-end-to-smoking/ accessed October 31, 2018.

92 WHO, "WHO statement on Philip Morris funded Foundation for a Smoke-Free World" (World Health Organization, September 28, 2017) https://who.int/mediacentre/news/statements/2017/philip-morris-foundation/en/ accessed October 31, 2018.

93 A. Bhuya, "Philip Morris funded anti-smoking foundation targeting public health leaders with grants" (*The Wire*, December 13, 2017) https://thewire.in/health/leaked-email-reveals-philip-morris-funded-anti-smoking-foundation-targeting-public-health-leaders-grants accessed October 31, 2018.

94 Brandt, *The Cigarette Century* (n 17) 170–1.

95 K.D. Brownell, K.E. Warner, "The perils of ignoring history: Big Tobacco played dirty and millions died. How similar is Big Food?" (2009) 87 Milbank Q 259.

harm of smoking, the FSFW's principal concern seems to be the promotion of e-cigarettes and NGPs.[96] This was confirmed by the Philip Morris CEO André Calantzopoulos, who declared that his company welcomes the FSFW's "recommendations to accelerate smoker adoption of less harmful alternatives."[97]

3.3 Big Tobacco as a Pharmaceutical Company

Big Tobacco is increasingly modeling its strategy on other commercial actors which, while often criticized for engaging in controversial corporate practices, do not share the tobacco industry's political pariah status, and have their voices openly heard in policy discussions—Big Sugar and Big Pharma.

The first approach is modeled after the producers of high calorie foods. Precedents exist, for instance, in the corporate strategy of the soda industry, which uses the sale of low sugar drinks as a sign of its commitment to harm reduction while it continues the production of high sugar sodas and their sale to less affluent and health conscious customers.[98] Such companies argue that most of the products they sell are not unhealthy. Yes, they might be releasing high calorie sweets and candy to the market, but they often also offer healthier alternatives and healthy foodstuffs. In effect, they claim, they are offering adult consumers a choice. Often this is accompanied by declarations of willingness to work with the public health community and to self-regulate, for example by decreasing marketing of unhealthy products to kids. This approach has thus far been largely successful in helping Big Sugar companies avoid governmental regulation.[99] By using ENDS in the same way the food industry uses low calorie products and by offering assurances of consumer choice and self-regulation, tobacco companies attempt to portray themselves as exemplary "corporate citizens" and allies of public health.

The second approach is based on the example of the pharmaceutical industry. By declaring a willingness to stop selling traditional cigarettes at an ill-defined future point in time, companies such as Philip Morris try to build their image as a business operator which, while selling chemical products with secondary

---

[96] N. Hirschhorn, "Another perspective on the Foundation for a Smoke-Free World" (2018) 391 The Lancet 25.

[97] Philip Morris International, "Philip Morris International announces support for the establishment of the Foundation for a Smoke-Free World" (Philip Morris International, September 12, 2017) https://pmi.com/media-center/press-releases/press-release-details/?newsId=2300228 accessed October 31, 2018.

[98] M. Nestle, *Soda Politics: Taking on Big Soda (and Winning)* (Oxford University Press 2015).

[99] K.D. Brownell, K.B. Horgen, *Food Fight: The Inside Story of the Food Industry, America's Obesity Crisis, and What We Can Do About It* (Contemporary Books 2004).

risks, can package them as "medicine"—in the case of e-cigarettes, as a tool to quit smoking. Effectively such a company positions itself as a pharmaceutical company—but one trying to solve a health problem which it created itself. Even more hypocritically, while Big Tobacco firms would like to acquire the social acceptability of pharmaceutical companies, they continue to resist the regulatory apparatus that would go with it—after all, the pharmaceutical market is one of the most heavily regulated in the world. Meanwhile, tobacco companies not only continue to oppose the regulation of e-cigarettes, but also persist in aggressive attacks against legislation of combustible products, such as the strict packaging laws in Uruguay[100] or in Australia.

This paradigm of an e-cigarette industry that can be a legitimate partner for tobacco control efforts could mean that some health researchers will have fewer misgivings about collaborating with Big Tobacco, for example by conducting trials sponsored by heat-not-burn producers or attending e-cigarette conferences coorganized by the industry. The first signs of this relegitimization of the industry are evident, and not only in English-speaking western countries. In June 2016 the renowned Nencki Institute of Experimental Biology in Poland announced its collaboration with Philip Morris, in which the scientists of the Institute were to conduct research on the impact of tobacco heat-not-burn NGP (that is, IQOS) use on the cellular level.[101] Conferences such as the Global Forum on Nicotine, attended by many bona fide smoking cessation researchers, have become events showcasing e-cigarettes, with the participation of tobacco industry representatives and offers of industry-funded scholarships to academics.[102] At the 2015 meeting of the American Association for the Advancement of Science, Deborah Arnott, chief executive of the UK Action on Smoking and Health, shared a symposium with Kevin Bridgman, chief medical officer of BAT's e-cigarette company, Nicoventures. Will Hill, public relations manager for BAT, remarked: "Imagine that happening 10 years ago. We're now starting to share podiums with people like ASH at e-cigarette conferences."[103]

---

[100] E. Crosbie, P. Sosa, S.A. Glantz, "Defending strong tobacco packaging and labelling regulations in Uruguay: transnational tobacco control network versus Philip Morris International" (2017) Tob Control doi: 10.1136/tobaccocontrol-2017-053690.

[101] Ł. Kaniewski, "Uczeni, papierosy i mniejsze zło" [Scientists, cigarettes, and the lesser evil] (*Rzeczpospolita*, June 8, 2016) http://rp.pl/Nowe-technologie/306079887-Uczeni-papierosy-i-mniejsze-zlo.html accessed October 31, 2018.

[102] Tobacco Tactics, "Global Forum on Nicotine" (Tobacco Tactics, June 20, 2018) https://tobaccotactics.org/index.php?title=Global_Forum_on_Nicotine accessed October 31, 2018.

[103] J. Gornall, "Why e-cigarettes are dividing the public health community" (2015) 350 BMJ h3317.

All these developments also have an impact on how public opinion perceives Big Tobacco. As Philip Morris announced the creation of FSFW in September 2017, the Polish Press Agency declared that "even transnational tobacco companies are joining the fight against cigarettes."[104] Tobacco companies' entry into the ENDS market has given them a strong hand to play, with a good public relations message and claims of commitment to harm reduction. E-cigarettes have sorely split the tobacco control community and redirected a significant proportion of public health resources into research focusing on vaping. For tobacco control advocates who have struggled for decades to expose the manipulations and overt lies of the tobacco industry, engagement with e-cigarettes is a step back for public health. In this view, any harm reduction approaches involving the collaboration of disgraced industrial actors should include boundaries preventing the renormalization of their most successful product—the combustible cigarette. A situation in which Big Tobacco is allowed to move toward vaping products in wealthy countries while continuing to aggressively and successfully market traditional cigarettes in low and middle income countries upends both public health interests and global health.

4. TOBACCO CONTROL IN TIMES OF SCIENTIFIC UNCERTAINTY

A strong conviction persists, both in certain sections of the tobacco control community and in public opinion, that the question of ENDS regulation, while highly divisive at the moment, will be put to rest as soon as conclusive evidence of the products' harmfulness or lack thereof emerges from the data.[105] Scientific investigation into the health consequences of tobacco smoking marked one of the high points of public health research in the twentieth century. Doll & Hill's study of British doctors, published in 1954, not only conclusively solved the mystery of the rapid rise in lung cancer among adult men in western countries, but also largely pioneered the use of prospective epidemiology and medical statistics in public health—methods that have become fundamental for the

---

[104] W. Szczepaniak, "Papierosy są w odwrocie, prawie cały świat walczy z epidemią palenia" [Cigarettes are on the retreat; almost the entire world is fighting the smoking epidemic] (*Polska Agencja Prasowa*, September 19, 2017) https://zdrowie.pap.pl/uzaleznienia/papierosy-sa-w-odwrocie-prawie-caly-swiat-walczy-z-epidemia-palenia accessed October 31, 2018.

[105] L. Bauld, "The evidence keeps piling up: e-cigarettes are definitely safer than smoking" (*The Guardian*, December 29, 2017) https://theguardian.com/science/sifting-the-evidence/2017/dec/29/e-cigarettes-vaping-safer-than-smoking, accessed October 31, 2018; D. Saitta, G.A. Ferro, R. Polosa, "Achieving appropriate regulations for electronic cigarettes" (2014) 5 Ther Adv Chronic Dis 50.

development of the field in the decades to come.[106] Throughout the half century that followed, meticulous research was successful in exposing a broad range of negative health effects of tobacco both for smokers and, by the 1990s, also for people inhaling secondhand smoke. The fact that smoking is so uniformly harmful also helped—the magnitude of differences in disease incidence and mortality between smokers and controls made the research results relatively easy to interpret persuasively and decisively.

With e-cigarettes, tobacco control research became the victim of its own success. The advent of ENDS' popularity was followed by an expectation on the part of media and consumers that the public health community would promptly provide them with conclusive evidence of the health effects of e-cigarettes. However, unlike in the case of traditional cigarettes, ENDS researchers do not have at their disposal large quantities of good quality data collected from subjects with a history of use often spanning multiple decades. In addition, the research environment has become much more complex than was the case in the era when standardized cigarettes ruled supreme. It remains uncertain whether e-cigarettes predominantly help smokers quit, or whether they promote dual use alongside traditional cigarettes, flavored brands of tobacco, NGPs, heat-not-burn products, marijuana, water pipes, and so on. Concerns remain as to whether they might serve as a gateway to smoking combustible cigarettes for children. Other sequelae of nicotine addiction of children must also be taken into account, such as alcohol or marijuana consumption. The public health community is not even entirely sure whether it is sufficient to research the same type of harm that has been associated with traditional cigarettes, as evidenced, for example, by media reports on exploding e-cigarettes.[107]

The history of science shows that trials often fail when they are conducted around issues that are hotly contested by the scientific community. This is because those on both sides of the argument tend to be very good at pointing out the weaknesses and critiquing the limitations of the methods used by their opponents. An example of such an issue comes from the history of cardiovascular diseases, where the practice of angioplasty and the use of stents have been at the center of a fraught methodological debate between cardiologists and cardiac surgeons since the 1980s, even as thousands of angioplasty procedures are carried out in the US every year.[108] Similarly loaded debates are

---

[106] R. Doll, A. Bradford Hill, "The mortality of doctors in relation to their smoking habits" (1954) 1 BMJ 1451.

[107] E.G. Brownson et al, "Explosion injuries from e-cigarettes" (2016) 375 N Engl J Med 1400.

[108] D.S. Jones, *Broken Hearts: The Tangled History of Cardiac Care* (Johns Hopkins University Press 2013).

taking place among e-cigarette researchers, with scientists seemingly drawing contradictory conclusions from the same data. Particularly strong disagreement exists over the question of utility of e-cigarettes as smoking cessation tools. For instance, a study by Kulik et al published in February 2018 indicated that the use of e-cigarettes in Great Britain depressed quitting, while the Public Health England report released a month later claimed the opposite, suggesting that "e-cigarettes have contributed tens of thousands of additional quitters in England."[109]

The complexities surrounding e-cigarette research pose a methodological challenge for scientists that can be hard to solve using the available methods. This is exacerbated by the fact that new and enhanced next generation nicotine and tobacco delivery devices are being released on the market at a pace that far outstrips the speed of research conducted into them.[110] As a result, when a new piece of research on e-cigarettes is released, frequently it describes a product that has already become obsolete and replaced by a new model. The truth is that the debate on e-cigarettes will be impossible to resolve with a few, even well-conducted, rigorous studies. A review article published in the *New England Journal of Medicine* in October 2016 concluded that "it is impossible to reach a consensus on the safety of e-cigarettes except perhaps to say that they may be safer than conventional cigarettes."[111] Two years later, this is still the case. The fact that e-cigarettes are possibly less harmful than cigarettes does not seem like a solid enough base for public health recommendations—it would effectively amount to letting the regulatory standards be set by a product that kills half of its consumers. The jury is still out on vaping and the ambiguity of evidence will not diminish in the short term.

4.1 Implications for Policy

In an ideal world, the issue of e-cigarette regulation would be resolved consensually, through evidence-based findings. The problem would be studied and the results of the investigation would serve to inform policy. It seems increasingly clear that suspending the regulatory debate in order to let science resolve the issue might not work in the context of ENDS and other nicotine and tobacco NGPs. Even as further studies are published, evidence will remain

---

[109] M.C. Kulik, N.E. Lisha, S.A. Glantz, "E-cigarettes associated with depressed smoking cessation: a cross-sectional study of 28 European Union countries" (2018) 54 Am J Prev Med 603; McNeill et al (n 73).

[110] S.-Z. Zhu et al, "Four hundred and sixty brands of e-cigarettes and counting: implications for product regulation" (2014) 23 Tob Control iii3.

[111] C. Dinakar, G.T. O'Connor, "The health effects of electronic cigarettes" (2016) 375 N Engl J Med 1372.

ambiguous, highly politicized, and unable to isolate each of the wide range of variables in the usage and impact of e-cigarettes. Even more complexity is added by the rapid developments in technology, which mean that every year, subsequent models of e-cigarettes released are often radically different from their predecessors, whole range of new products are available on the open market, dual use patterns change, and so on.

As the delivery of accepted cessation treatment in the form of behavioral support and cessation medicine demands specialized expertise and consumes a lot of health providers' time, e-cigarettes can be a tempting tool, providing a technological aid for clinical responsibility. The example of the UK, where the market for cessation medicine has effectively collapsed since the introduction of e-cigarettes, can be seen as a forecast for what would happen in other countries should they begin to regulate e-cigarettes as smoking cessation aids.[112] The challenge is complicated further by the fact that many cessation drugs with proven effectiveness are subject to strict regulation (for example varenicline) or even face severe regulatory obstacles in even seeking to enter western markets (for example generic drugs such as cytisine). Meanwhile, e-cigarettes in many countries remain largely unregulated and easily accessible—which results in a situation in which tobacco cessation is tackled via nicotine addiction.

Public health regulators in this situation must weigh the claims of harm reduction with the precautionary principle and the need to prevent tobacco industry interests guiding their hand. Policy will need to be made in the imperfect conditions of scientific and market uncertainty. This is perhaps the most "disruptive" feature of ENDS—they have disturbed the public health status quo on tobacco and nicotine, as rapid technological innovation and dissemination outstripped the knowledge context. The notion that Big Tobacco corporations have finally matured to become responsible civil actors is one that a significant section of the public health community finds very appealing. For most health advocates, the ultimate value to which they are striving is saving lives—this means that compromise solutions promising to bring about this outcome will always be tempting, even if they mean collaborating with an industry with a proven track record of deception.

Evidence suggests that the tobacco industry has been looking for a product that would help polarize and disrupt tobacco control efforts for decades. An example of this is Philip Morris's Project Sunrise, initiated in 1995 and planning to use "carefully orchestrated efforts" to exploit existing differences of opinion within tobacco control, as well as repositioning the company as

---

[112] West, Beard, Brown (n 60).

"responsible."[113] Therefore, for historians of public health monitoring current affairs, e-cigarettes constitute a potentially alarming development. History shows that industrial actors, in both the case of tobacco harm and that of climate change, have been extremely adept at exploiting "soft edges" of scientific debate in order to serve their corporate interests and delay regulatory solutions.[114] The tobacco industry, in particular, has thrived whenever the public health community is divided, scientific consensus is not evident, and the promise of a "reduced risk" product can be fostered, while simultaneously continuing to aggressively push its most profitable product—the traditional cigarette.[115]

4.2 Implications for the Public Health Community

E-cigarettes have proved to be a disruptive technology, not just as a potentially marketable solution for the tobacco industry to overcome commercial stagnation, but also as a disruptive factor for the global public health regime that has emerged in the past decades. On one hand, they threaten to disrupt our traditional concepts of tobacco regulation and the cohesiveness of the anti-tobacco advocacy movement. On the other, some academics' hardening attitudes toward ENDS could undo the progress in understanding the need for harm reduction in other contexts, such as drug policy. This could be especially damaging in the US, where the opioid crisis has been exacerbated by the historical hostility to harm reduction substances such as methadone.[116]

The thinking about the regulatory framework of e-cigarettes must adapt to the possibility that public health is facing an instance in which empirical investigation will not be able to unambiguously guide us toward the ideal policy in the immediate or even medium term. The wait and see approach is not viable, as it will delay regulation indefinitely or promote solutions based on idiosyncratic clinical practice and, more worryingly, commercial and political interests. The regulatory question will need to be settled, for the time being at least, based on a political and cultural consensus. What should be the values guiding our approach to e-cigarettes? What new pieces of information would allow the tobacco control community to form a more united front? Is

---

113 P.A. McDaniel, E.A. Smith, R.E. Malone, "Philip Morris's Project Sunrise: weakening tobacco control by working with it" (2006) 15 Tob Control 215.

114 N. Oreskes, *Merchants of Doubt: How a Handful of Scientists Obscured the Truth on Issues from Tobacco Smoke to Global Warming* (Bloomsbury Press 2010).

115 Ibid; Brandt, *The Cigarette Century* (n 17).

116 J. Woo et al, "'Don't judge a book by its cover': a qualitative study of methadone patients' experiences of stigma" (2017) 11 Substance Abuse: Research and Treatment 1178221816685087.

there an appropriate regulatory framework for dealing with products which are inherently dangerous, but the moderate use of which might be preferable to the alternative?

The precautionary principle is one possibility offering an easy answer[117]—regulating ENDS in the same way as traditional combustible cigarettes. This would help put ENDS out of the reach of children and discourage non-smokers—but it would also stop the realization of their potential as smoking cessation aids. The option of lighter regulation of e-cigarettes proposed by tobacco harm reduction supporters and smoking cessation practitioners also warrants a serious discussion. However, the tobacco industry would first need to show its commitment to harm reduction. As Simon Capewell has rightly suggested, if Big Tobacco is truly concerned about the health toll of smoking, it should cease the production of combustible cigarettes and "go into e-cigarette production 100 percent."[118]

First, the tobacco industry should make explicit efforts toward restricting e-cigarette marketing and sales to adult current smokers and former smokers who have switched.[119] More importantly, it would need to accept anti-smoking policies that it currently opposes as too restrictive—including further smoking bans and the minimization of nicotine levels in cigarettes. This would need to apply not just to developed countries but also to low income settings, which are often made more vulnerable to tobacco by a lack of strong tobacco control legislation. Without such far reaching compromises from the tobacco companies, any collaboration between health advocates and industrial actors would merely contribute to deepening the disruption of public health progress in tobacco control—something that the industry has historically, and effectively, sought.

---

[117] For details on the precautionary principle in the context of EU law see Chapter 8 in this volume.

[118] Gornall (n 103).

[119] E.N. Lindblom, "Effectively regulating e-cigarettes and their advertising—and the First Amendment" (2015) 70 Food Drug Law J 55.

3. Review of the scientific evidence relating to electronic cigarettes: where do we stand now?

Charlie A. Smith, Aleksandra Herbeć and Lion Shahab

1. AN OVERVIEW OF ELECTRONIC CIGARETTES AND TOBACCO CONTROL

The debate over the benefits and the role of electronic nicotine delivery systems (e-cigarettes, or—referred to both in singular and in plural—ENDS) for public health and tobacco control concerns three main dimensions:[1] whether ENDS pose health harms to their users;[2] whether they can aid cessation efforts among current smokers;[3] and whether they constitute a gateway to using combustible tobacco for youth or non-smokers. All three aspects are discussed in detail in this chapter. At the same time, it should be stressed that the chapter does not address general societal issues that appear in the context of ENDS emergence. In particular, it does not discuss the broader implications of this technology for the viability of the endgame strategy or the legitimacy of the tobacco industry. Those issues are analyzed in Chapter 2.

Although combustible tobacco smoking prevalence has been decreasing in many countries, the absolute number of smokers continues to increase due to population growth.[4] Current estimates suggest there are more than a billion daily smokers worldwide, with more than six million dying from smoking-attributed causes every year.[5] Many efforts within tobacco control are

---

[1] M. Ng et al, "Smoking prevalence and cigarette consumption in 187 countries, 1980–2012" (2014) 311 Jama 183.

[2] J. Britton, "Death, disease, and tobacco" (2017) 389 The Lancet 1861.

[3] WHO, *WHO Report on the Global Tobacco Epidemic 2008: The MPOWER Package* (World Health Organization 2008) 342.

[4] Ng et al (n 1).

[5] Britton (n 2).

focused on preventing the uptake of cigarettes by lowering demand, such as by increasing prices of tobacco or limiting advertisements, as well as establishing smoking bans and smoke-free places.[6] However, given the scale of the tobacco epidemic, the measure that could bring the greatest gains in health and quality of life in the immediate future is increasing the number of current smokers who completely cease tobacco use.[7]

Several types of intervention are considered gold standard and the first line of recommended treatment for tobacco dependence.[8] These include either a combination of pharmacotherapy and behavioral support, or offering at least one of these. However, access to evidence-based smoking cessation treatments differs considerably between and within countries.[9] Additionally, only a very small minority of smokers access such support when trying to quit, even when it is free at the point of access.[10] Furthermore, even with the most intensive support, the success rate in clinical trials, after biochemical verification, is below 20 percent after 12 months.[11]

Most smokers attempting to quit traditional cigarettes do so without any assistance, going "cold turkey," using willpower alone.[12] Such attempts tend to be unsuccessful, with less than 5 percent of smokers still abstinent after 12 months.[13] Additionally, smokers have been shown to adhere poorly to licensed pharmacotherapy for smoking cessation, often using it too little or for too short a time.[14] Among the reasons for poor use are side effects (although these are

---

6 WHO, *WHO Report on the Global Tobacco Epidemic 2008: The MPOWER Package* (n 3).

7 WHO, *Framework Convention on Tobacco Control Adopted Guidelines* (2017).

8 M.C. Fiore et al, *Treating Tobacco Use and Dependence: 2008 Update* (Clinical Practice Guideline, US Department of Health and Human Services, Public Health Service 2008).

9 Action on Smoking and Health, "New government data shows valuable stop smoking services continue to decline" (August 18, 2017) http://ash.org.uk/media-and-news/press-releases-media-and-news/new-government-data-shows-valuable-stop-smoking-services-continue-to-decline/ accessed October 31, 2018; S. Regan, N.A. Rigotti, A. McNeill, "A survey of tobacco dependence treatment services in 36 countries" (2009) 104 Addiction 279.

10 D. Kotz, J. Brown, R. West, "Prospective cohort study of the effectiveness of smoking cessation treatments used in the 'real world'" (2014) 89 Mayo Clin Proc 1360.

11 J. Ferguson et al, "The English smoking treatment services: one-year outcomes" (2005) 100 Addiction 59.

12 T. Raupach, R. West, J. Brown, "The most 'successful' method for failing to quit smoking is unassisted cessation" (2013) 15 Nicotine Tob Res 748.

13 Ibid.

14 L.R. Pacek, F.J. McClernon, H.B. Bosworth, "Adherence to pharmacological smoking cessation interventions: a literature review and synthesis of correlates and barriers" (2017) 20 Nicotine Tob Res 1163; J.T. Hays et al, "Adherence to treatment for

often overestimated or misattributed), concerns over safety and effectiveness, negative views, and poor evaluations of the medications' attractiveness and practicality.[15] Finally, there are also important sociodemographic determinants of cessation,[16] as well as of use of treatment.[17] Taken together, it can be seen that attaining complete cessation from tobacco products is a public health imperative, but without appropriate support most smokers fail to quit. The available support is relatively effective, but no treatment guarantees success, and both access and uptake of traditional treatments are suboptimal.

In this context, ENDS emerge as a class of products that deliver nicotine, the substance that confers addictive properties to tobacco, and which offer behavioral and sensory experiences that resemble smoking, making them potentially a more acceptable cessation aid than traditional pharmacotherapy. Additionally, ENDS are widely promoted by a range of interest groups and across many channels, and hundreds of different types, forms, and models have been developed that could appeal to diverse customer groups.

2. PREVALENCE

2.1 ENDS Use in Adults

Use of ENDS has increased rapidly in recent years, although globally it remains low. Heterogeneity across countries in terms of legislation, availability, research priorities, and study methodology make it impossible to provide a global prevalence estimate of ENDS use, as well as making it extremely difficult to systematically compare data between countries.

A large national survey conducted by Action on Smoking and Health (ASH) estimated there were 2.9 million adult e-cigarette users in Great Britain in 2017, accounting for 6 percent of the adult population.[18] This figure is similar

---

tobacco dependence: association with smoking abstinence and predictors of adherence" (2010) 12 Nicotine Tob Res 574.

15 Ibid; A. Herbeć et al, "'If I'd known . . .'—a theory-informed systematic analysis of missed opportunities in optimising use of nicotine replacement therapy and accessing relevant support: a qualitative study" (2018) 25 Int J Behav Med 579.

16 N. Herd, R. Borland, A. Hyland, "Predictors of smoking relapse by duration of abstinence: findings from the International Tobacco Control (ITC) Four Country Survey" (2009) 104 Addiction 2088.

17 D. Kotz, J. Fidler, R. West, "Factors associated with the use of aids to cessation in English smokers" (2009) 104 Addiction 1403.

18 ASH, *Use of E-Cigarettes (Vapourisers) among Adults in Great Britain* (September 2017).

to that of a large national survey in England which estimated 5.5 percent.[19] Data from the United States of America (US) estimated e-cigarette prevalence at 3.2 percent of the adult population in 2016.[20] E-cigarette prevalence in Europe is intermediate, with around 2 percent of adults currently using them.[21] In all cases, ENDS use is dominated by past or current smokers.

3. ENDS CONSTITUENTS

3.1 Nicotine

Nicotine is the main psychoactive compound that perpetuates the use of tobacco.[22] As the majority of ENDS use involves nicotine, studying this compound is fundamental to improving our understanding regarding the safety of ENDS use. In 1976, the late Professor Michael Russell, who was a pioneer in nicotine research, wrote: "People smoke for nicotine but they die from the tar"[23]—nicotine in itself is not a highly hazardous drug, and although it increases heart rate and blood pressure, it is not a carcinogen.[24] A 2016 report by the Royal College of Physicians concluded that nicotine does not result in clinically significant harm, and that cessation medications which provide nicotine (nicotine replacement therapy—NRT) do not appear to be associated with an increased risk of heart attack, stroke, or death.[25] Furthermore, although many concerns have arisen from animal research which has identified a relationship between nicotine and health adversity, it should be noted that such findings cannot be easily applied to humans. The best evidence to date which has explored the effect of nicotine on user health comes from a randomized controlled trial

---

19 J. Brown, R. West, "Latest trends on smoking in England from the Smoking Toolkit Study" (*Smoking in England*, 2018) http://smokinginengland.info/latest-statistics/ accesssed October 31, 2018.

20 W. Bao et al, "Changes in electronic cigarette use among adults in the United States, 2014–2016" (2018) 319 Jama 2039.

21 K.E. Farsalinos et al, "Electronic cigarette use in the European Union: analysis of a representative sample of 27,460 Europeans from 28 countries" (2016) 111 Addiction 2032.

22 N.L. Benowitz, "Nicotine addiction" (2010) 362 N Engl J Med 2295.

23 M.A.H. Russell, "Low-tar medium-nicotine cigarettes: a new approach to safer smoking" (1976) 1 Br Med J 1430.

24 IARC, *Agents Classified by the IARC Monographs, Volumes 1–104* (IARC Monographs 2012) https://monographs.iarc.fr/ENG/Classification/ClassificationsAlphaOrder.pdf accessed October 31, 2018.

25 Royal College of Physicians, *Supporting Doctors to Improve Care: Annual Report 2016* (2016).

(RCT) which measured NRT use over a five year period.[26] This study found NRT was safe to use for this duration, while continued smoking was predictive of cancer development.

3.2 Propylene Glycol and Glycerin

Propylene glycol (PG) and glycerin are organic compounds which are commonly used ingredients in e-liquid. There has been much speculation regarding the potential impact that these compounds have on health. There have been documented incidences whereby PG was identified as an airway irritant in humans, and some research suggests there is an association between asthma and rhinitis onset in children and PG exposure in the home.[27] It is important to note that such cases are rare and research has generally found both compounds to be harmless in their natural form.[28]

However, vaping requires heating a solution which contains these compounds, and researchers have found that heating PG or glycerin at high temperatures can release aldehydes into the atmosphere. These include formaldehyde, acrolein, and acetaldehyde, all of which are toxic components that have been identified in tobacco smoke. In most cases, the levels identified in vapor are lower than levels identified in tobacco smoke,[29] though this has not always been the case for formaldehyde. For instance, one study found that a variable voltage ENDS set on maximum power emitted up to 15 times more formaldehyde than tobacco cigarettes.[30] However, as is the case for nearly all studies of this nature, findings have generally been interpreted out of context. For example, studies which have detected aldehydes such as formaldehyde resulting from heating PG and/or glycerin have done so only in laboratory

---

[26] R.P. Murray, J.E. Connett, L.M. Zapawa, "Does nicotine replacement therapy cause cancer? Evidence from the Lung Health Study" (2009) 11 Nicotine Tob Res 1076.

[27] H. Choi et al, "Common household chemicals and the allergy risks in pre-school age children" (2010) 5 PLoS One e13423.

[28] A.M. Glasser et al, "Overview of Electronic Nicotine Delivery Systems: a systematic review" (2017) 52 Am J Prev Med e33.

[29] N. Beauval et al, "Chemical evaluation of electronic cigarettes: multicomponent analysis of liquid refills and their corresponding aerosols" (2017) 41 J Anal Toxicol 670; S.S. Hecht et al, "Evaluation of toxicant and carcinogen metabolites in the urine of e-cigarette users versus cigarette smokers" (2015) 6 Nicotine Tob Res 704; H. McRobbie et al, "Effects of switching to electronic cigarettes with and without concurrent smoking on exposure to nicotine, carbon monoxide, and acrolein" (2015) 8 Cancer Prev Res 873.

[30] R.P. Jensen et al, "Formaldehyde in e-cigarette aerosols" (2015) 372 N Engl J Med 392.

settings where heating temperatures have been set above those typically used by vapers. The main account for this is a phenomenon known as "dry puff," an unpleasant phenomenon caused by overheating the e-liquid which causes adverse taste and so is avoided by ENDS users. There is evidence from one study which has found ENDS users experienced dry puff even when temperatures were well below that which generated detectable aldehyde levels.[31] One study which adopted a realistic temperature setting and puffing regime reported formaldehyde levels of 0.4 to 1.5 ng/mL in e-liquid aerosol emissions, compared with 82 ng/mL in tobacco smoke.[32] Therefore, it may be concluded that, although vaping can release aldehydes when overheating e-liquid solution, the levels inhaled at normal vaping temperatures are only a small fraction of those inhaled by smokers.

3.3 Flavors

Flavorings used in e-liquid are generally considered safe when ingested orally from food and drink; however, the safety of most flavors after heating and inhalation remains unknown.[33] Findings thus far suggest that vapor which is produced from e-liquids containing flavoring, especially cinnamon, is more cytotoxic than that without, though still significantly less than tobacco smoke.[34] Flavors that received most attention are those which contain diacetyl, an organic compound which is typically added to food to create a sweet taste, for example in popcorn production. Diacetyl, when ingested orally, has not been associated with health adversity, though there is some evidence which has found a link between inhaled diacetyl and bronchiolitis.[35] Some e-liquid brands have been found to use diacetyl in their flavorings, although, as with other potentially harmful components, this has been at substantially lower levels in comparison with cigarette smoke.[36] One recent study which analyzed 49 commercially available e-liquid flavors found that almost half modulated

---

[31] K.E. Farsalinos et al, "E-cigarettes emit very high formaldehyde levels only in conditions that are aversive to users: a replication study under verified realistic use conditions" (2017) 109 Food Chem Toxicol 90.

[32] Beauval et al (n 29).

[33] P.A. Tierney et al, "Flavour chemicals in electronic cigarette fluids" (2016) 25 Tob Control e10.

[34] F. Cervellati et al, "Comparative effects between electronic and cigarette smoke in human keratinocytes and epithelial lung cells" (2014) 28 Toxicol Vitr 999; Glasser et al (n 28).

[35] K. Kreiss et al, "Clinical bronchiolitis obliterans in workers at a microwave-popcorn plant" (2002) 347 N Engl J Med 330.

[36] K. Fujioka, T. Shibamoto, "Determination of toxic carbonyl compounds in cigarette smoke" (2006) 21 Environ Toxicol 47.

free radical formation. This was linked with the capacity to oxidize biologically relevant lipids which has been associated with adverse health effects such as coronary heart disease.[37] Further research is required to explore whether or not the inclusion of certain flavoring compounds is a potential source of preventable risk.

3.4 Other

In addition to the ingredients present in e-liquids, other materials which are used for ENDS compartments (for example metals, ceramics, rubber, plastics, and so on) may become aerosolized in the process of vapor generation. Although research in this area is still developing, to date several metals have been identified in both e-liquid solutions and the aerosol produced, albeit at considerably lower levels than those found in cigarette smoke.[38] One recent study sampled 56 e-cigarette devices and investigated metal concentrations in both the e-liquids and aerosol.[39] The authors of this study concluded that similar levels of metal were present in both ENDS and tobacco smoke; the purpose of this study was not to compare ENDS and conventional cigarettes, though, and so the methods leading to this conclusion were based on non-definitive assumptions. What is more, even studies which have reported higher concentrations of certain metals in e-liquid and aerosol compared with tobacco smoke have reported total level of exposure to be far less in the former.[40] Indeed, research in this area has highlighted the issue of heterogeneity among e-cigarette products which subsequently results in differential metal emissions.[41] Therefore, although metals present in e-liquid and aerosol are unlikely to pose significant health risks to users, manufacturers can and should strive to keep metal emissions to a minimum. Additional research is needed to explore these issues further.

---

[37] Z.T. Bitzer et al, "Effect of flavoring chemicals on free radical formation in electronic cigarette aerosols" (2018) 120 Free Radic Biol Med 72.

[38] K.E. Farsalinos, V. Voudris, K. Poulas, "Are metals emitted from electronic cigarettes a reason for health concern? A risk-assessment analysis of currently available literature" (2015) 12 Int J Environ Res Public Health 5215.

[39] P. Olmedo et al, "Metal concentrations in e-cigarette liquid and aerosol samples: the contribution of metallic coils" (2018) 126 Environ Health Perspect 027010.

[40] A. Saffari et al, "Particulate metals and organic compounds from electronic and tobacco-containing cigarettes: comparison of emission rates and secondhand exposure" (2014) 16 Environ Sci Process Impacts 2259.

[41] C.A. Hess et al, "E-cigarettes as a source of toxic and potentially carcinogenic metals" (2017) 152 Environ Res 221.

4. HEALTH EFFECTS OF ENDS

4.1 General Population

Relatively little research exists on the safety of ENDS for humans, although available data suggest that e-cigarettes are considerably less risky than combustible tobacco. To date, the majority of research exploring potential adversity of vapor has used animal and cell studies, which poses challenges for interpreting their findings in the context of real-life human vapers. Moreover, we lack data on the long-term impact of ENDS use, both among short-term and long-term ENDS users. Additionally, very little research has been conducted exploring toxicant and carcinogenic metabolites in humans using validated laboratory measures.

One study analyzed urine samples of ENDS users who abstained from tobacco smoking for two months and compared the presence of numerous toxicant and carcinogen metabolites with samples of smokers from three previous studies.[42] The authors concluded that ENDS have a more favorable toxicity profile than cigarettes. Reductions in measured metabolites were also found in the urine of dual ENDS and cigarette users following a four week period.[43] Shahab and colleagues conducted a pioneering study which measured the presence of biomarkers of nicotine and a range of carcinogens and toxins following a six-month period among smokers, ENDS users who quit smoking, NRT users who quit smoking, and dual users of NRT/ENDS and cigarettes.[44] This study found no difference in nicotine intake between groups, although ENDS and NRT only users had significantly lowered levels of all biomarkers compared with those who continued to smoke. Similar findings were also found by another study which reported a reduction in exposure to a range of carcinogens and toxins among smokers who converted to vaping for two weeks. These smokers were also able to maintain their usual intake of nicotine.[45] These studies suggest that converting from smoking to vaping can lead to maintenance of nicotine levels while reducing exposure to harmful elements. However, it remains unclear whether dual use has any significant health benefits, and so further research is needed to explore the health implications of this behavior.

---

[42] Hecht et al (n 29).

[43] McRobbie et al (n 29).

[44] L. Shahab et al, "Nicotine, carcinogen, and toxin exposure in long-term e-cigarette and nicotine replacement therapy users" (2017) 166 Ann Intern Med 390.

[45] L.M. Goniewicz et al, "Exposure to nicotine and selected toxicants in cigarette smokers who switched to electronic cigarettes: A longitudinal within-subjects observational study" (2017) 19 Nicotine Tob Res 160.

With regard to health outcomes following ENDS use, the small number of studies available have failed to indicate any substantial health threats among those who have vaped for up to two years.[46] One recent three-and-a-half-year observational cohort study was the first to measure health outcomes among ENDS users who had never smoked (n=9), compared with a reference group of never smokers (n=12).[47] The authors did not find any significant changes in blood pressure, heart rate, body weight, lung function, respiratory symptoms, exhaled breath nitric oxide (eNO), exhaled carbon monoxide (eCO), and high-resolution computed tomography (HRCT).

Moreover, one RCT failed to find a significant difference in adverse reactions between users of nicotine-containing ENDS, placebo ENDS, and NRT patch.[48] Similarly, another RCT reported no significant difference in adverse events at 3 and 12-month follow-ups between the three study conditions: 7.2 mg nicotine for 12 weeks; 7.2 mg nicotine for six weeks followed by 5.2 mg for six weeks; and 0 mg nicotine (placebo) for 12 weeks.[49] This study reported the most common adverse effects were a cough (26 percent), dry mouth (22 percent), shortness of breath (20 percent), throat irritation (17 percent), and headaches (17 percent); all of which diminished over time, except for throat irritation. Similarly, adverse events that have been reported by cohort studies are relatively shortlived and mostly consist of mouth and throat irritation, which reflects the findings of both RCTs.[50] Moreover, adverse effects caused by e-cigarette use do not appear to be moderated by the presence of nicotine in the e-liquid solution; pooled results of three RCTs (n=421) found no difference in adverse events between nicotine ENDS users and non-nicotine ENDS (RR 1.1 (95 percent CI 0.87 to 1.56)).[51] These findings are reassuring, although further long-term studies are needed to explore the safety of ENDS.

---

[46] J. Hartmann-Boyce et al, "Electronic cigarettes for smoking cessation" (2016) Cochrane Database Syst Rev doi.wiley.com/10.1002/14651858.CD010216.pub3.

[47] R. Polosa et al, "Health impact of e-cigarettes: a prospective 3.5-year study of regular daily users who have never smoked" (2017) 7 Sci Rep 13825.

[48] C. Bullen et al, "Electronic cigarettes for smoking cessation: a randomised controlled trial" (2013) 382 Lancet 1629.

[49] P. Caponnetto et al, "EffiCiency and Safety of an eLectronic cigAreTte (ECLAT) as tobacco cigarettes substitute: a prospective 12-month randomized control design study" (2013) 8 PLoS One :e66317.

[50] Hartmann-Boyce et al (n 46).

[51] J. Hartmann-Boyce, R. Begh, P. Aveyard, "Electronic cigarettes for smoking cessation" (2018) 360 BMJ j5543.

4.2 Pre-existing Physical Health Conditions

As is the case for the general population, only a few studies have specifically aimed at measuring health outcomes among smokers with pre-existing medical conditions who switched to ENDS. One study used data from the 2014/15 National Health Interview Survey (NHIS) in the US and found high prevalence of ENDS use among current and ex-smokers with chronic obstructive pulmonary disease (COPD).[52] A large survey of 1,190 COPD ENDS users found improvements in respiratory symptoms among 75.7 percent of respondents, and worsening of symptoms among 0.8 percent.[53] Moreover, a fifth of all the participants terminated use of their routine respiratory medication following the switch to ENDS, which could be explained by less frequent inhalation of tobacco smoke. Another study examined medical records of COPD patients and found that those who switched from cigarettes to ENDS had significant reductions in COPD exacerbation, improved general health status, and improved physical activity levels when assessed over a two-year period, while no changes in health were found among matched controls who continued to smoke.[54]

Studies have also reported benefits of converting to ENDS among patients with hypertension. One study found that in comparison to those who still smoked, patients with hypertension who switched to ENDS had lower systolic and diastolic blood pressure at 12 months.[55] Similarly, in the ECLAT trial,[56] smokers who had elevated blood pressure and had switched to vaping experienced an initial decrease in their systolic blood pressure. One uncontrolled longitudinal study with a small sample size (n=16) of asthmatic smokers who converted to ENDS found an improvement in lung function and respiratory symptoms which was maintained for 24 months after switching. This study also found this effect for dual cigarette and e-cigarette users.

---

52 G.R. Kruse, S. Kalkhoran, N.A. Rigotti, "Use of electronic cigarettes among U.S. adults with medical comorbidities" (2017) 52 Am J Prev Med 798.

53 K.E. Farsalinos et al, "Characteristics, perceived side effects and benefits of electronic cigarette use: a worldwide survey of more than 19,000 consumers" (2014) 11 Int J Environ Res Public Health 4356.

54 R. Polosa et al, "Evidence for harm reduction in COPD smokers who switch to electronic cigarettes" (2016) 17 Respir Res 166.

55 R. Polosa et al, "Blood pressure control in smokers with arterial hypertension who switched to electronic cigarettes" (2016) 13 Int J Environ Res Public Health pii: E1123.

56 Caponnetto et al, "EffiCiency and Safety of an eLectronic cigAreTte (ECLAT) as Tobacco Cigarettes Substitute: A Prospective 12-Month Randomized Control Design Study" (n 49).

Therefore, although ENDS are not risk free, the evidence suggests that the switch from cigarettes to ENDS may improve some of the symptoms of pre-existing health conditions which are exacerbated by tobacco smoking.

4.3 Passive Exposure

ENDS do not produce sidestream vapor. However, users exhale the vapor produced through heating the solution, and therefore it is feasible that this may be inhaled by bystanders, resulting in passive exposure.[57] One recent study which modeled passive exposure did suggest that bystanders could be exposed to aldehydes;[58] however, the study lacked ecological validity due to generating dry puffs in a laboratory setting.[59] Conversely, most of the evidence available thus far does not indicate that passive vaping causes any significant harm. A recent review examined studies of secondhand vaping and concluded the level of nicotine and other compound exposure to bystanders was much lower when compared with secondhand smoke.[60] Another study which measured the exhaled breath of ENDS users found that only 6 percent nicotine, 8 percent of PG, and 16 percent of glycerine was exhaled, suggesting that the majority of vapor is retained by the user.[61]

Furthermore, some studies have investigated the air quality of environments in which vaping takes place, such as vape shops and households which are occupied by ENDS users. Unpublished reports of studies on aerosol exposure in vape shops conducted by governmental bodies in the US have found that flavoring compounds and formaldehyde were all below the lowest occupational exposure limit and nicotine was almost undetectable.[62] Additionally, one study assessed the impact of occupant activities and home characteristics on

---

[57] J. Czogala et al, "Secondhand exposure to vapors from electronic cigarettes" (2014) 16 Nicotine Tob Res 655.

[58] J.M. Logue et al, "Emissions from electronic cigarettes: assessing vapers' intake of toxic compounds, secondhand exposures, and the associated health impacts" (2017) 51 Environ Sci Technol 9271.

[59] M. Sleiman et al, "Emissions from electronic cigarettes: key parameters affecting the release of harmful chemicals" (2016) 50 Environ Sci Technol 9644.

[60] Glasser et al (n 28).

[61] G. St. Helen et al, "Nicotine delivery, retention and pharmacokinetics from various electronic cigarettes" (2016) 111 Addiction 535.

[62] L.M. Zwack, A.B. Stefaniak, R.F. LeBouf, *Evaluation of Chemical Exposures at a Vape Shop* (US Department of Health and Human Services, Centers for Disease Control and Prevention, National Institute for Occupational Safety and Health, Health Hazard Evaluation Report 2017) https://cdc.gov/niosh/hhe/reports/pdfs/2015-0107-3279.pdf accessed October 31, 2018.

the air quality of 193 households (including 43 where vaping was present).[63] This study concluded that vaping had no discernible effect on mean weekly particle counts, in contrast to activities such as smoking and candle burning. These findings are comparable to another recent study which failed to find a difference in home surface nicotine levels between homes of e-cigarette users and non-tobacco users.[64] Therefore, although research is limited, it is believed that passive vaping is extremely unlikely to pose any significant health risks to bystanders.

4.4 Safety Profile of ENDS

Although there is substantial scientific evidence to suggest that ENDS are much safer than traditional combustible cigarettes, uncertainty remains regarding the likely level of risk reduction obtained when switching over completely to ENDS. Therefore, it is important to be aware of the residual risks and unanswered questions which remain when evaluating the safety profile of ENDS. First, although nicotine poses a low risk to health, it is not risk-free. One meta-analysis reported that NRT use was associated with lower level cardiovascular disease events, such as arrhythmia.[65] The authors reported that this was mostly the case in studies with longer periods of follow-up. Further research indicates a low cardiovascular risk in healthy users of nicotine, although nicotine medications and smokeless tobacco may still be of concern in people with cardiovascular disease.[66] Moreover, nicotine has been found to have teratogenic effects in animals.[67] Second, possible ENDS-specific risks may not be captured by tobacco-related outcomes. For instance, some research has identified the presence of glycidol, a probable carcinogen, in some vapor produced by ENDS.[68] The degree of exposure to toxins has also been found to be dependent on flavoring, with liquids containing, for example, cinnamal-

---

[63] N.E. Klepeis et al, "Fine particles in homes of predominantly lowincome families with children and smokers: key physical and behavioral determinants to inform indoor-air-quality interventions" (2017) 12 PloS One e0177718.

[64] D. Bush, M.L. Goniewicz, "A pilot study on nicotine residues in houses of electronic cigarette users, tobacco smokers, and non-users of nicotine-containing products" (2015) 26 Int J Drug Policy 609.

[65] E.J. Mills et al, "Cardiovascular events associated with smoking cessation pharmacotherapies: a network meta-analysis" (2014) 129 Circulation 28.

[66] N.L. Benowitz, A.D. Burbank, "Cardiovascular toxicity of nicotine: implications for electronic cigarette use" (2016) 26 Trends Cardiovasc Med 515.

[67] D.A. Dempsey, N.L. Benowitz, "Risks and benefits of nicotine to aid smoking cessation in pregnancy" (2011) 24 Drug Saf 277.

[68] Sleiman et al (n 59).

dehyde being more toxic.[69] Third, product and user characteristics may affect the safety of ENDS use. For instance, advanced modifiable products allow aerosolization at higher temperatures, which has been associated with toxic carbonyl production.[70] In addition, users of more advanced models may engage in a behavior known as "cloud chasing," whereby they intake larger amounts of e-liquid to create large masses of vapor. Finally, the majority of research investigating the safety of ENDS constituents has been based on oral and not pulmonary administration, and so further research into pulmonary administration is required.

5. ENDS IMPACT ON TOBACCO USE

5.1 Initiation[71]

A major concern is that ENDS may act as a gateway for non-smokers to take up smoking. This phenomenon is commonly known as the "gateway hypothesis."[72] First generation ENDS were designed to visually resemble cigarettes, and so it is feasible that the tobacco industry could cross-promote smoking imagery and hence tobacco products through e-cigarette advertising. However, first generation ENDS are visually distinguishable from cigarettes, and exhaled vapor differs from tobacco smoke in appearance, smell, and irritancy.[73] What is more, later generation ENDS have very little resemblance to conventional cigarettes. Indeed, one qualitative study which interviewed 50 vapers aged between 16 and 26 years old (including 28 current smokers, 19 former smokers, and 3 never smokers) did not find evidence to suggest that ENDS renormalize smoking. Specifically, the authors reported that the interviews indicated that increased availability of vaping products may be contributing to worse perceptions of tobacco.[74]

However, the possibility of a gateway effect, particularly among youth, remains a major concern. One systematic review of multiple US-based longitudinal studies concluded that ENDS use predicts subsequent tobacco use among

---

[69] R.Z. Behar et al, "Distribution, quantification and toxicity of cinnamaldehyde in electronic cigarette refill fluids and aerosols" (2016) 25 Tob Control ii94.

[70] P. Wang et al, "A device-independent evaluation of carbonyl emissions from heated electronic cigarette solvents" (2017) 12 PLoS One e0169811.

[71] See Chapter 2 of this book for an alternative discussion.

[72] J.F. Etter, "Gateway effects and electronic cigarettes" (2017) 13 Addiction 1776.

[73] Royal College of Physicians, *Nicotine without Smoke: Tobacco Harm Reduction* (2016).

[74] N. McKeganey, M. Barnard, C. Russell, "Vapers and vaping: e-cigarettes users views of vaping and smoking" (2018) 25 Drugs Educ Prev Policy 13.

youths;[75] similar findings apply to Canada,[76] and to the United Kingdom (UK).[77] However, although all of these studies suggest that ENDS use is associated with subsequent smoking in young people, they all share similar limitations which make it difficult to infer a causal relationship. First, the UK studies defined ENDS and cigarette use as "ever use," meaning many young people who were included could have used the product just once. Likewise, the "ever use" measure of tobacco at follow-up includes experimentation. In comparison, the US studies defined use as "past 30 days," rather than regular use of ENDS and cigarettes. Such differences highlight methodological differences which should be considered when interpreting results. Second, all of these studies adopted statistical modeling; however, it is impossible to control for all potential confounders. For instance, studies only partially controlled for factors which are known to be related with cigarette experimentation (for example genetic vulnerabilities, sensation seeking, risk taking, personality, and so on).

Given these limitations, population data can shine more light on the gateway hypothesis. These appear to contradict a strong causal effect. Recent survey data from the UK indicate that smoking prevalence continues to decline among youth. For instance, between 2000 and 2015 in Scotland, regular smoking among 15 year olds declined from 30 percent to 7 percent, and that among 13 year olds from 10 percent to 2 percent.[78] Similarly in England, between 2002 and 2014, weekly smoking declined from 10 percent to 3 percent among 11–15 year olds.[79] This survey also found that 18 percent of youth in England reported having ever tried smoking—the lowest ever percentage since the survey began in 1982. In the US, a 2016 Surgeon General report concluded that e-cigarette use among young people was becoming a major public concern, yet a reanalysis of this data actually found the sharpest declines in US youth smoking rates

---

[75] S. Soneji et al, "Association between initial use of e-cigarettes and subsequent cigarette smoking among adolescents and young adults: a systematic review and meta-analysis" (2017) 171 Jama Pediatrics 788.

[76] D. Hammond et al, "Electronic cigarette use and smoking initiation among youth: a longitudinal cohort study" (2017) 189 Can Med Assoc J E1328.

[77] C. Best et al, "Relationship between trying an electronic cigarette and subsequent cigarette experimentation in Scottish adolescents: a cohort study" (2018) 27 Tob Control 373.

[78] C. Black, L. Murray, L.S.A. Setterfield, *Scottish Schools Lifestyle and Substance Use Survey 2015—Mode Effect Study* (Edinburgh 2015).

[79] E. Fuller, *Smoking, Drinking and Drug Use among Young People in England in 2014* (Health and Social Care Information Centre, UK Statistics Authority, National Centre for Social Research, National Foundation for Educational Research in England and Wales 2015).

to occur as ENDS became increasingly available.[80] Therefore, if ENDS were acting as a gateway to smoking, the impact would have to be minimal, given continuing declines in youth smoking prevalence and experimentation.

5.2 Smoking Cessation

5.2.1 Observational studies

Rather than preventing quit attempts, as has been documented in some literature,[81] research generally shows the opposite, that is, ENDS successfully encouraging smoking cessation and reduction among smokers. A large Eurobarometer study explored e-cigarette use across 28 Member States of the European Union (EU).[82] Of 3,612 respondents who were either current or ex-smokers and had tried ENDS, 14 percent indicated that an e-cigarette enabled them to stop smoking tobacco entirely; individuals who found e-cigarettes most useful were those who were long-term smokers, former daily smokers, males, and those aged 55 or over.

The Tobacco Use Supplement of the Current Population survey included data from five US population surveys to assess the relationship between ENDS use and smoking cessation in a representative sample of the US population.[83] The five surveys included collected data in 2001–2, 2003, 2006–7, 2010–11, and 2014–15 and found that in comparison to non-ENDS users, ENDS users were more likely to make a quit attempt (65.1 percent versus 40.1 percent) and were more likely to succeed in quitting (8.2 percent versus 4.8 percent). Additionally, quitting rates increased from 2010–11 (4.5 percent) to 2014–15 (5.6 percent), the latter representing approximately 350,000 additional US ex-smokers.

A time series analysis examined data from English Stop Smoking Services and the Smoking Toolkit Study (STS) from 2006 to 2015 in order to determine how population level ENDS use had been associated with changes in quit attempts and quitting success.[84] This study did not show clear evidence of an

---

[80] R. Polosa et al, "A critique of the US Surgeon General's conclusions regarding e-cigarette use among youth and young adults in the United States of America" (2017) 14 Harm Reduct J 61.

[81] S. Kalkhoran, S.A. Glantz, "E-cigarettes and smoking cessation in real-world and clinical settings: a systematic review and meta-analysis" (2016) 4 Lancet Respir Med 116.

[82] Special Eurobarometer, *458—Attitudes of Europeans towards tobacco and electronic cigarettes* (2017).

[83] S.-H. Zhu et al, "E-cigarette use and associated changes in population smoking cessation: evidence from US current population surveys" (2017) 358 BMJ j3262.

[84] E. Beard et al, "Association between electronic cigarette use and changes in quit attempts, success of quit attempts, use of smoking cessation pharmacotherapy, and use

association between e-cigarette use and attempts to quit smoking. However, the authors reported that a rise in ENDS use prevalence was positively associated with the success rates of quit attempts, and that this association remained following adjustment for a range of confounding variables. Specifically, the authors estimated that ENDS use may have contributed to around 16,000 additional long-term ex-smokers in 2015, the same as the estimate of West and colleagues for 2014.[85]

In one small early observational study, 40 regular smokers who were unwilling to quit were provided with ENDS and followed up for up to 24 months. At 24-week follow-up, 22.5 percent reported abstinence.[86] The findings attenuated at 24 months, with 12.5 percent reporting abstinence. One large and ongoing prospective cohort study examined follow-up data from 236 e-cigarette users (ex-smokers), 491 current tobacco smokers, and 232 dual users.[87] Results at 12-month follow-up showed continued abstinence from tobacco among 61.9 percent of solely e-cigarette users, as well as abstinence among 20.6 percent of tobacco smokers and abstinence among 22 percent of dual users. After adjusting for potential confounders, abstinence remained significantly higher among e-cigarette users; this was not observed among dual users. These results suggest that replacing all cigarettes with ENDS can aid in sustained smoking cessation, whereas this may not be the case if e-cigarette users continue to smoke tobacco.

5.2.2 Randomized controlled trials

Randomized controlled trials are the gold standard for measuring the effectiveness of any given intervention and involve randomly allocating participants willing to enroll on the study to two or more conditions, thus limiting the impact of participant characteristics or other circumstances on the outcomes. Unfortunately, few RCTs have been conducted to measure the impact of ENDS on smoking cessation, although many are currently ongoing and are expected to be published in the foreseeable future.[88] However, data from the available RCTs thus far provide some promising, albeit inconclusive, results.

---

of stop smoking services in England: time series analysis of population trends" (2016) 354 BMJ i4645.

[85] R. West, L. Shahab, J. Brown, "Estimating the population impact of e-cigarettes on smoking cessation and smoking prevalence in England" (2015) 111 Addiction 1.

[86] R. Polosa et al, "Effect of an electronic nicotine delivery device (e-cigarette) on smoking reduction and cessation: a prospective 6-month pilot study" (2011) 11 BMC Public Health 786.

[87] L. Manzoli et al, "Electronic cigarettes efficacy and safety at 12 months: cohort study" (2015) 10 PLoS One e0129443.

[88] Hartmann-Boyce et al (n 46).

To date, only two RCTs have been conducted which have measured the effectiveness of ENDS in relation to smoking cessation over a six-month period. The first, known as the ASCEND trial,[89] randomized 657 highly dependent smokers who were motivated to quit to one of three conditions: ENDS containing 16 mg nicotine, or 21 mg/24 hour nicotine patches (an effective, but not the most effective, type of all NRT products), or ENDS with non-nicotine cartridges (placebo condition). At six-month follow-up, the biochemically verified continuous abstinence rates were low in all groups and there was no statistically significant difference in outcomes between the treatment arms, although abstinence rates were numerically higher in the treatment conditions that offered some nicotine to the users. Very similar findings were found in a three arm ECLAT trial that randomized 300 highly dependent smokers who were not intending to quit smoking in the next 30 days to one of three conditions: cigalike with disposable cartridges containing 7.2 mg nicotine for 12 weeks; 7.2 mg nicotine for six weeks which was then replaced with 5.2 mg nicotine for six weeks; or 0 mg nicotine for 12 weeks (placebo).[90] Abstinence at 12 months was defined as self-reported abstinence since the six-month follow-up, confirmed with carbon monoxide readings at 6 and 12 months. At 12-month follow-up, abstinence rates were higher in both nicotine conditions (13 percent and 9 percent) compared with placebo (4 percent), but these results were not statistically significant.

5.2.3 Meta-analyses

Over the years, several systematic reviews and meta-analyses have been published which have attempted to synthesize the findings from individual studies to answer the question of whether or not ENDS aid smoking cessation and reduction. Of seven meta-analyses, two reported a positive effect,[91] one reported a negative effect,[92] and four reported inconclusive findings.[93]

---

[89] Bullen et al (n 48).

[90] Caponnetto et al, "EffiCiency and Safety of an eLectronic cigAreTte (ECLAT) as Tobacco Cigarettes Substitute: A Prospective 12-Month Randomized Control Design Study" (n 49).

[91] Hartmann-Boyce et al (n 46); M.A. Rahman et al, "E-cigarettes and smoking cessation: evidence from a systematic review and meta-analysis" (2015) 10 PLoS One e0122544.

[92] Kalkhoran, Glantz (n 81).

[93] M. Malas et al, "Electronic cigarettes for smoking cessation: a systematic review" (2016) 18 Nicotine Tob Res 1926; R. El Dib et al, "Electronic nicotine delivery systems and/or electronic non-nicotine delivery systems for tobacco smoking cessation or reduction: a systematic review and meta-analysis" (2017) 7 BMJ e012680; S. Khoudigian et al, "The efficacy and short-term effects of electronic cigarettes as a method for smoking cessation: a systematic review and a meta-analysis" (2016) 61

There are likely many explanations as to why this is the case, as discussed in a recent Public Health England report.[94] First, four of the meta-analyses only included the RCTs which intentionally measured the impact of ENDS use on smoking cessation or reduction, whereas the remainder included observational studies which did not have a primary aim to measure smoking cessation as a result of ENDS use and which cannot exclude the possibility of confounding. Second, some reviews incorporated studies which enrolled only current smokers, whereas others included studies that also enrolled current or ex-smokers and dual users. Therefore, studies which analyzed results of smokers based on ENDS use at baseline had already excluded individuals who have successfully quit smoking through use of an ENDS, thus retaining participants who are classed as treatment failures or who are in the process of cutting down as a first step toward quitting. This methodological fault is likely to underestimate the impact of ENDS for smoking cessation. Finally, discrepancies between meta-analyses are likely to be accounted for by the differences relating to how missing data was handled and the length of follow-up time. Only the two meta-analyses which reported a positive effect of ENDS on cessation incorporated studies which had the longest follow-ups from the start of the interventions (that is, 6 and 12 months), whereas two analyses which reported inconclusive results only incorporated data at six months from both the RCTs.

More generally, at the time most studies were conducted, cigalikes (that is, first generation products) were the most commonly used ENDS among consumers. More recent data now suggest that less than 5 percent of experienced vapers use these first generation products,[95] with second and third generation devices now being the most popular. As these products have been found to be more efficient in delivering nicotine compared with first generation products (see section 2.5.3), it is likely that they may be more effective.

5.3 Factors which Affect ENDS Effectiveness

ENDS allow the user to inhale a vaporous solution of water, nicotine, propylene glycol, vegetable glycerin, and flavoring, which is suspended in a humectant. Nicotine is absorbed through the airways and is then metabolized by the liver

---

Int J Public Health 257; P. Vanderkam et al, "Efficacité et sécurité de la cigarette électronique pour la réduction du tabagisme: revue systématique et méta-analyse" (2016) 45 Press Medicale 971.

94 A. McNeill et al, *Evidence Review of E-Cigarettes and Heated Tobacco Products 2018* (A report commissioned by Public Health England, Public Health England 2018).

95 Farsalinos et al, "Characteristics, perceived side effects and benefits of electronic cigarette use: A worldwide survey of more than 19,000 consumers" (n 53).

into cotinine as one of the metabolites. The dose and speed of nicotine delivery from ENDS use has been shown to be dependent on many variables. As may be expected, e-liquids with higher nicotine concentrations deliver more nicotine than those with lower concentrations,[96] and nicotine delivery has improved with successive generations of ENDS.[97] Moreover, studies have found that nicotine delivery is also dependent on how much experience users have with these products. One study found naïve users of a first generation e-cigarette containing 24 mg/mL of nicotine achieved a peak plasma concentration of 5.7 ng/mL after four weeks of use, compared with 4.6 ng/ML achieved at baseline (that is, following the first five minutes of use).[98] Similarly, with third generation devices, research has found that experienced users achieve a greater rise in blood nicotine levels than naïve users under the same prescribed five-minute puffing regime (5.8 ng/mL versus 2.7 ng/mL).[99] Another study found that experienced users of third generation devices achieved peak nicotine levels within the first two to five minutes after puffing, suggesting comparable, if still somewhat slower, pulmonary delivery.[100] Although this route of delivery makes it likely for users to become addicted, this study did note that not all nicotine retained was absorbed through the lungs, meaning addictiveness is less likely compared with cigarettes. Therefore, as similar levels of the nicotine metabolite cotinine are achieved by experienced ENDS users and smokers, it can be concluded that ENDS are capable of delivering similar nicotine doses as cigarettes, albeit at a slower speed than cigarettes.[101]

6. HARM REDUCTION

Smoking cessation is the ideal outcome for all smoking cessation interventions. However, it does not appeal to smokers who do not hold abstinence as their primary goal. For these smokers, harm reduction may be more suitable.

---

[96] C. P. Ramôa et al, "Electronic cigarette nicotine delivery can exceed that of combustible cigarettes: a preliminary report" (2016) 25 Tob Control e6.

[97] S. Talih et al, "Effects of user puff topography, device voltage, and liquid nicotine concentration on electronic cigarette nicotine yield: measurements and model predictions" (2015) 17 Nicotine Tob Res 150.

[98] P. Hajek et al, "Nicotine intake from electronic cigarettes on initial use and after 4 weeks of regular use" (2015) 17 Nicotine Tob Res 175.

[99] K.E. Farsalinos et al, "Nicotine absorption from electronic cigarette use: comparison between experienced consumers (vapers) and naïve users (smokers)" (2017) 5 Sci Rep 11269.

[100] Helen et al (n 61).

[101] J.F. Etter, C. Bullen, "Saliva cotinine levels in users of electronic cigarettes" (2011) 38 Eur Respir J 1219; J.F. Etter, "Levels of saliva cotinine in electronic cigarette users" (2014) 109 Addiction 825.

Tobacco harm reduction is defined as complete or partial substitution of cigarettes with less dangerous products, such as smokeless tobacco, NRT, and ENDS. Research from Sweden (where snus is popular) indicates that snus has contributed to the low rates of smoking among Swedish men, as well as a significant decrease in rates of lung cancer and myocardial infarction in this population.[102] Additionally, research has supported the use of NRT in achieving long-term abstinence (minimum six-month follow-up) among smokers who had no intention to, or were unable to, quit abruptly.[103] Although this relationship is not as well established for ENDS, the most recent Cochrane review supports their ability to aid smoking cessation.[104] In some countries, such as Sweden and the UK, tobacco harm reduction has been more popular as an approach to tobacco control, and it has also recently become a national strategy in the UK.[105]

Data from the STS in England show that 18 percent of current smokers and 29 percent of ex-smokers currently use ENDS.[106] Only a few studies have specifically investigated the impact of e-cigarettes on reduction of cigarettes smoked per day (CPD) and some found that it can aid such efforts. One study showed that among 40 regular smokers unwilling to quit, almost half had managed to cut down at 24-week follow-up,[107] and 40 percent at 24 months.[108] One small RCT found that smokers randomized to receive nicotine-containing ENDS or placebo ENDS for three weeks achieved significant reductions in CPD, though those in the nicotine condition were more likely to reduce CPD by at least 50 percent at the end of treatment following adjustment for ENDS use and readiness to quit at baseline.[109] However, this study also suggests that ENDS without nicotine may help smokers cut down by providing sensory and behavioral sensations that accompany smoking.

---

[102] J. Foulds et al, "Effect of smokeless tobacco (snus) on smoking and public health in Sweden" (2003) 12 Tob Control 349.

[103] D. Moore et al, "Effectiveness and safety of nicotine replacement therapy assisted reduction to stop smoking: systematic review and meta-analysis" (2009) 338 BMJ Br Med J 867.

[104] Hartmann-Boyce et al (n 46).

[105] Royal College of Physicians, *Nicotine without Smoke: Tobacco Harm Reduction* (n 73).

[106] Brown, West (n 19).

[107] Polosa et al, "Effect of an electronic nicotine delivery device (e-cigarette) on smoking reduction and cessation: a prospective 6-month pilot study" (n 86).

[108] R. Polosa et al, "Effectiveness and tolerability of electronic cigarette in real-life: a 24-month prospective observational study" (2014) 9 Intern Emerg Med 537.

[109] T.Y. Tseng et al, "A randomized trial comparing the effect of nicotine versus placebo electronic cigarettes on smoking reduction among young adult smokers" (2016) 18 Nicotine Tob Res 1937.

The large Eurobarometer study mentioned above,[110] which included the responses of 3,612 participants, found that ENDS had helped 17 percent of participants to reduce the amount of tobacco smoked. In one small early observational study, 40 regular smokers unwilling to quit were provided with ENDS and followed up for up to 24 months. At 24-week follow-up, 32.5 percent of participants reported a sustained 50 percent reduction in cigarettes smoked per day and 12.5 percent of participants reported an 80 percent sustained reduction.[111] The findings attenuated at 24 months, with 12.5 percent reporting abstinence, and a combined 40 percent of respondents reporting either a >50 percent reduction in cigarettes smoked per day or abstinence.[112]

6.1 Vulnerable and Disadvantaged Populations

An important and long neglected issue is that smoking prevalence tends to be significantly higher in disadvantaged and vulnerable groups compared with the general population. Groups which are impacted include, but are not limited to, people living with mental illness, personality disorders, and/or substance misuse disorders, as well as prisoners and homeless people.[113] Smokers with mental health conditions are still not receiving adequate cessation support, although more recently this seems to be changing in countries such as the UK.[114] It remains the case that although smoking cessation interventions can work for these individuals, they do find it more difficult to remain abstinent, which is likely due to greater addiction to nicotine, in addition to social and cultural norms.[115] As a result of this heavy addiction and tobacco use, premature death as a result of smoking within this population is at between 10 and 20

---

110 Special Eurobarometer (n 82).

111 Polosa et al, "Effect of an electronic nicotine delivery device (e-cigarette) on smoking reduction and cessation: a prospective 6-month pilot study" (n 86).

112 Polosa et al, "Effectiveness and tolerability of electronic cigarette in real-life: a 24-month prospective observational study" (n 108).

113 L. Szatkowski, A. McNeill, "Diverging trends in smoking behaviors according to mental health status" (2015) 17 Nicotine Tob Res 356; C. Cookson et al, "Smoking and its treatment in addiction services: clients' and staff behaviour and attitudes" (2014) 14 BMC 304; C.Y. Wu et al, "Evaluation of smoking status identification using electronic health records and open-text information in a large mental health case register" (2013) 8 PLoS One e74262; Public Health England, *Reducing Smoking in Prisons: Management of Tobacco Use and Nicotine Withdrawal* (2015).

114 E. Ratschen, J. Britton, A. McNeill, "Implementation of smoke-free policies in mental health in-patient settings in England" (2009) 194 Br J Psychiatry 547.

115 E. Ratschen, J. Britton, A. McNeill, "The smoking culture in psychiatry: time for change" (2011) 198 Br J Psychiatry 6.

years in comparison with smokers of the general population.[116] In light of these wider challenges, it has been proposed that ENDS are one potential solution to address this ongoing disparity.[117]

Only a few studies to date have investigated the effectiveness of ENDS among smokers with mental health conditions. Secondary data analysis from community mental health patients in the ASCEND clinical trial showed that ENDS are just as effective as nicotine patches in achieving abstinence at six-month follow-up,[118] and that ENDS lead to higher levels of smoking reduction when compared with nicotine patches, as well as higher levels of treatment compliance and acceptability. Similar results have been reported for patients with schizophrenia,[119] as well as for patients with bipolar disorder.[120] These studies did not report any adverse implications for mental health, underlining the utility of ENDS as a tobacco harm reduction product for smokers with a severe mental health condition.

7. MISINTERPRETATION OF ENDS RESEARCH IN THE MEDIA

ENDS have received much media attention over recent years and the potential risks of vaping have been highly publicized. Although most studies covered in this chapter concluded that ENDS are safer than tobacco smoking, they have been covered less frequently in the media, distorting the presentation of scientific evidence. Authors of the PHE report suggest the following reasons for this:[121]

- studies which show ENDS to be harmful are considered much more "newsworthy" than studies which demonstrate ENDS to be safer than smoking;

---

[116] E. Chesney, G.M. Goodwin, S. Fazel, "Risks of all-cause and suicide mortality in mental disorders: a meta-review" (2014) 12 World Psychiatry 153.

[117] E. Ratschen, "Electronic cigarettes in mental health settings—solving a conundrum?" (2014) 38 Psychiatr Bull 226.

[118] B. O'Brien et al, "E-cigarettes versus NRT for smoking reduction or cessation in people with mental illness: secondary analysis of data from the ASCEND trial" (2015) 13 Tob Induc Dis 5.

[119] P. Caponnetto et al, "Impact of an electronic cigarette on smoking reduction and cessation in schizophrenic smokers: a prospective 12-month pilot study" (2013) 10 Int J Environ Res Public Health 446.

[120] S.I. Pratt et al, "Appeal of electronic cigarettes in smokers with serious mental illness" (2016) 59 Addict Behav 3.

[121] McNeill et al (n 94).

- stakeholders of research, including journals, authors, and research organizations, strive for publicity to achieve high impact, which can lead to certain findings being inaccurately represented;
- media outlets, such as newspapers, can exaggerate scientific findings.

Even now, stories which exaggerate the risks of ENDS continue to be published in UK and international media outlets. For example, multiple stories regarding ENDS use and increased risk of developing certain cancers were covered in one English newspaper with headlines that were not supported by the research studies to which they refer.[122] As a result, smokers may be deterred from trying an ENDS and may continue to smoke instead. Misperceptions about the safety of ENDS are common among the general public.[123] What is more, healthcare professionals also hold misconceptions, which may discourage them from supporting service users who are interested in converting to vaping in order to quit smoking.[124]

Much (though not all) of the research that raises concerns regarding ENDS use has particular methodological flaws. The first problem is that studies have often used animal models and so generalizability to human health is unclear.[125] Furthermore, studies which have explored the effect of ENDS solution and aerosol on human cells do not reflect appropriate levels of exposure to which humans would be exposed, as these studies often soak the cells in the e-liquid, thus significantly amplifying the risks.[126] Therefore, findings from such studies should be interpreted with caution, as their applicability to real-life human vapers is unknown.

Second, some studies that analyzed the constituents of aerosol following the heating of e-liquids adopted unrealistic use conditions under artificial lab-

---

[122] C. Tanner, "E-cigarette smokers have a high bladder cancer risk" (*Daily Mail Online*, May 17, 2017) https://dailymail.co.uk/health/article-4514542/E-cigarette-smokers-high-bladder-cancer-risk.html; M. de Graaf, "Vaping causes DNA mutations leading to cancer" (*Daily Mail Online*, January 29, 2018) https://dailymail.co.uk/health/article-5325945/Vaping-causes-cancer-new-study-warns.html, both accessed October 31, 2018.

[123] B.A. Majeed et al, "Changing perceptions of harm of e-cigarettes among U.S. adults, 2012–2015" (2017) 52 Am J Prev Med 331.

[124] R. Hiscock et al, "E-cigarettes: online survey of UK smoking cessation practitioners" (2014) 12 Tob Induc Dis 13; D. Van Gucht, F. Baeyens, "Health professionals in Flanders perceive the potential health risks of vaping as lower than those of smoking but do not recommend using e-cigarettes to their smoking patients" (2016) 13 Harm Reduct J 22.

[125] K.E. Farsalinos, R. Polosa, "Safety evaluation and risk assessment of electronic cigarettes as tobacco cigarette substitutes: a systematic review" (2014) 5 Ther Adv Drug Saf 67.

[126] Ibid.

oratory conditions. As a result, these studies overestimate risks due to heating e-liquid at particularly high temperatures. As discussed in section 2.3.2, overheating e-liquid at such temperatures generates an acrid and aversive taste which ENDS users would avoid. Third, studies often use inappropriate control conditions, comparing exposure in never smokers with that in e-cigarette users. Because most current e-cigarette users are former or current smokers, this introduces bias, as many of the health effects of smoking are irreversible and longlasting. Thus, effects observed between never smokers and e-cigarette users may simply be due to confounding from tobacco use and not e-cigarette use: past or current smokers are more appropriate controls in this context.

8. FUTURE DIRECTIONS FOR ENDS RESEARCH

Although the growing consensus is that ENDS are significantly safer than cigarettes, future research still needs to evaluate long-term health effects by assessing a wider array of outcomes. What is more, further studies are required to adopt sophisticated analytical methods (for example, propensity score matching, agent-based modeling, time series analyses) to determine the impact of ENDS on smoking initiation at a population level.

With regard to the impact of ENDS on smoking cessation, the overall quality of research remains low due to the lack of available data from RCTs.[127] Further RCTs are therefore required to determine the impact of ENDS on smoking cessation and reduction, as this methodology is considered the gold standard study design for evaluating an intervention.

9. CONCLUSIONS

There is little evidence to suggest that ENDS have "renormalized" smoking or act as a gateway to tobacco use among adolescents. Rather, the evidence suggests that ENDS are more likely to be a gateway away from tobacco use. Indeed, increasing evidence has supported e-cigarette use as an aid to smoking cessation, suggesting ENDS are just as effective as NRT. Furthermore, though ENDS are not completely safe and further research is still needed, the evidence available thus far indicates that these products are significantly safer than conventional cigarettes, and as a result, sophisticated modeling analyses predict

---

127 Hartmann-Boyce et al (n 46); A.C. Villanti et al, "How do we determine the impact of e-cigarettes on cigarette smoking cessation or reduction? Review and recommendations for answering the research question with scientific rigor" (2018) 113 Addiction 391.

ENDS have a positive impact on population health in the context of tobacco harm reduction.

PART II

International and European law perspectives

4. Taming Schrödinger's cat: e-cigarettes under the Framework Convention on Tobacco Control

Lukasz Gruszczynski

1. INTRODUCTION

The Framework Convention on Tobacco Control (FCTC or the Convention)[1] is a treaty that establishes certain global standards for tobacco control policies. It is widely seen as one of the major achievements of the international community in the field of public health protection. However, the emergence of various alternative technologies for nicotine delivery, and in particular e-cigarettes (which are, in the context of the FCTC, conventionally referred to as "Electronic Nicotine Delivery Systems" or simply "ENDS"), appears to pose certain tactical and legal challenges for the FCTC Parties. Some countries see those products as yet another incarnation of traditional tobacco and thus an obstacle to effective implementation of the endgame strategy.[2] It is therefore not surprising that those states favor strict regulatory solutions, such as outright sales bans or treating ENDS as traditional tobacco products. Others, however, disagree and see them as a part of the solution to the global tobacco epidemic rather than a factor that prevents its complete eradication. This means that regulators, rather than constraining ENDS use, should aim at increasing their popularity by treating e-cigarettes more favorably than traditional tobacco products.

The existing regulatory diversity among the FCTC Parties corresponds with the uncertain status of ENDS under the Convention. Does the FCTC apply to

[1] WHO Framework Convention on Tobacco Control, opened for signature June 16, 2003 (entered into force February 27, 2005) 2302 UNTS 166.

[2] For a discussion of the concept of an "endgame" and a review of the relevant literature, see P.A. McDaniel, E.A. Smith, R.E. Malone, "The tobacco endgame: a qualitative review and synthesis" (2016) 25 Tob Control 594. See also Chapter 2 of this volume.

them because they need to be classified as tobacco products? Or maybe they constitute a *sui generis* category that falls outside the scope of the FCTC? If the answer to the second question is positive, can the Conference of the Parties (COP)—the highest "governing body" of the Convention—address them as a part of its mandate?

These are precisely the problems tackled in this chapter. In particular, the chapter investigates whether and to what extent the FCTC disciplines apply to ENDS and whether the mandate enjoyed by the COP is sufficiently broad to deal with those products. Considering the scope of this book, the analysis presented here is limited to e-cigarettes and does not extend to other so-called novel tobacco products, such as heat-not-burn tobacco.[3] This narrow approach is, however, also justified by two additional reasons. First, due to their physical properties (the lack of actual tobacco in the final product), e-cigarettes seem to be a separate category that is different from tobacco products, irrespective of whether they are novel or traditional. This fact may have an impact on the applicability of the FCTC and the choice of an optimal regulatory strategy (or, at a minimum, it calls for a separate legal assessment). Second, the body of scientific evidence on e-cigarettes—despite all the existing loopholes—seems to be more robust as compared to that on novel tobacco products.[4] This body of evidence is also more diverse, consisting of mostly independent research studies. This is not the case for novel tobacco products, which are under-investigated and for which most of the health-related research comes from industry-funded projects.[5] The existing disparity in the knowledge may also influence how ENDS are (or should be) addressed under the Convention.

This chapter proceeds as follows. Section 2 briefly introduces the basic disciplines of the FCTC. Section 3 looks at the legal status of ENDS under the Convention. In this context, it discusses the position taken so far by the COP and the approach promoted by the FCTC Secretariat. Section 4 critically explores the available legal options and attempts to explain the existing heterogeneity in the classification of ENDS under the FCTC. The last section offers

---

[3] The World Health Organization makes a distinction between these two categories (e-cigarettes and novel tobacco products), as do many countries. For the set of detailed criteria used by the WHO to define "novel tobacco products" see WHO, *Work in Progress in Relation to Articles 9 and 10 of the WHO FCTC. Report by WHO*, FCTC/COP/6/14, July 24, 2014 (Conference of the Parties to the WHO Framework Convention on Tobacco Control, Sixth session, Moscow, Russian Federation, October 13–18, 2014) paras 3–4.

[4] For an up to date summary of scientific evidence relating to e-cigarettes, see Chapter 3 of this volume.

[5] See for example A. McNeill et al, *Evidence Review of E-Cigarettes and Heated Tobacco Products 2018* (A Report Commissioned by Public Health England, Public Health England 2018) 22.

conclusions together with recommendations as to the most desirable approach to e-cigarettes at the international level.

2. THE FCTC: A VERY BRIEF INTRODUCTION

The FCTC is the first convention, and until now the only one, negotiated under the auspices of the World Health Organization (WHO).[6] The idea of an international treaty that would set standards for national tobacco control policies was conceived in a small circle of likeminded public health specialists in the 1990s. It reflected the growing awareness of the global character of the tobacco epidemic, connected with the progressive internationalization of tobacco industry operations (for example in the form of foreign direct investments, liberalization of international trade, or implementation of global marketing campaigns). Gradually the idea gained broader support and was included by the WHO in its official agenda (1996).[7] Three years later, the World Health Assembly (WHA)—the WHO's highest governing body—established a working group and an intergovernmental negotiating body responsible for the preparation of the first draft of the Convention and subsequent technical negotiations.[8] The provisional text of the FCTC was finalized by 2000, while the complex technical negotiations that followed lasted for an additional 2.5 years. Eventually, the WHA unanimously adopted the Convention on May 21, 2003. The FCTC entered into force on February 27, 2005—90 days after the date of deposit of the fortieth instrument of ratification (or acceptance, approval, formal confirmation, or accession, as the case may be) with the UN Secretary General.[9] Currently, there are 181 Parties to the Convention, making it one of the most widely accepted international treaties in history.[10]

The Convention identifies as its objective the protection of

> present and future generations from the devastating health, social, environmental and economic consequences of tobacco consumption and exposure to tobacco smoke by providing a framework for tobacco control measures to be implemented by the Parties at the national, regional and international levels in order to reduce

---

[6] For a more detailed discussion, see WHO, *History of the WHO Framework Convention on Tobacco Control* (World Health Organization 2009).

[7] WHA, *Resolution WHA49.17: International framework convention for tobacco control* (Sixth plenary meeting, May 25, 1996—Committee B, third report).

[8] WHA, *Resolution WHA52.18: Towards a WHO framework convention on tobacco control* (Ninth plenary meeting, May 24, 1999—Committee A, second report).

[9] Compare with Art. 36 of the FCTC.

[10] The full list of Parties is available at http://bit.ly/2nxt0k1 accessed October 31, 2018. Except for the European Union, all the other Parties are states.

> continually and substantially the prevalence of tobacco use and exposure to tobacco smoke.[11]

To this end the FCTC sets certain tobacco control standards for its Parties, covering both demand side and supply side reduction measures. The first group encompasses various regulatory instruments that aim at diminishing the demand for tobacco products, and particularly includes: (i) price and tax measures (Art. 6); (ii) measures protecting from exposure to tobacco smoke (Art. 8); (iii) regulation of the contents of tobacco products (Art. 9); (iv) regulation of tobacco products' disclosures (Art. 10); (v) packaging and labeling of tobacco products (Art. 11); (vi) education, communication, training, and public awareness (Art. 12); (vii) tobacco advertising, promotion, and sponsorship (Art. 13); and (viii) measures to reduce tobacco dependency and to assist cessation (Art. 14). The supply side is addressed through the following: (i) measures that aim at eliminating illicit trade in tobacco products (Art. 15); (ii) restrictions on sales to and by minors (Art. 16); and (iii) promotion of economically viable alternatives to tobacco workers, growers, and individual sellers (Art. 17).

The FCTC also includes a number of other obligations. Probably the most important is Art. 5.3, which requires all the Parties to protect their public health policies relating to tobacco control from commercial and other vested interests of the tobacco industry. There are also special provisions on research, surveillance, and exchange of information as well as reporting (Arts 20 and 21). At the same time, the Convention clearly confirms that it only sets minimum standards and does not prevent the Parties from introducing stricter tobacco control measures if they are consistent with its other provisions (Art. 2.1).

Most of the FCTC obligations are formulated in rather general language which provides the Parties with only limited guidance as to their proper implementation—a standard problem with any framework treaty. In practice, various provisions are further developed and elucidated through the more technical guidelines which are adopted from time to time by the COP (as of October 31, 2018 there are altogether eight such guidelines).[12] For example, Art. 8 of the FCTC merely requires "adoption and implementation of effective . . . measures, providing for protection from exposure to tobacco smoke in indoor workplaces, public transport, indoor public places and, as appropriate, other public places." The relevant guidelines not only define a number of specific expressions (such as "smoking," "public places," or "workplace") but also clarify the scope of effective regulatory measures, enforcement aspects

---

[11] Art. 3 of the FCTC.

[12] For the full list of the adopted guidelines, see https://who.int/fctc/treaty_instruments/adopted/en/ accessed October 31, 2018.

(penalties, enforcement strategies, and infrastructure), and standards for monitoring and evaluation of the actions undertaken.[13] Although the guidelines are not legally binding, in practice they are followed by the Parties. As a general rule they are adopted in the form of COP decisions taken by consensus, but if this is not possible, a qualified majority of three fourths of the Parties present and voting is sufficient.[14]

The COP may also adopt protocols, annexes, and amendments to the Convention, which however become legally binding only after the conclusion of national ratification, acceptance, or an approval process. The Protocol to Eliminate Illicit Trade in Tobacco Products, which builds on Art. 15 of the FCTC, has been adopted, and recently entered into force.[15] Unlike other international treaties, the FCTC does not provide the COP with an explicit mandate to make binding interpretations of its provisions. It envisages, however, a dispute settlement system (regarding interpretation and application of its provisions), which is composed of a diplomatic mechanism and an *ad hoc* arbitration procedure, but only for those Parties that explicitly accept that option.[16]

3. E-CIGARETTES UNDER THE FCTC REGIME

In principle most of the provisions of the Convention only apply to tobacco and tobacco products. The latter are defined by the FCTC as "products entirely or partly made of the leaf tobacco as raw material which are manufactured to be used for smoking, sucking, chewing or snuffing."[17] At the same time, the Convention is silent about e-cigarettes. This should not come as a surprise, as the FCTC was drafted before these products entered the market.[18] Of course, this does not necessarily mean that ENDS are not covered by the Convention, as they may fall within the scope of some of its generally formulated provisions. However, before proceeding further with the analysis, it is worth looking at the approach taken so far by the COP and FCTC Secretariat.

---

13 FCTC COP, *Guidelines for implementation of Article 8: Protection from exposure to tobacco smoke*, FCTC/COP2(7), April 26, 2007.

14 FCTC COP, *Rules of Procedure of the Conference of the Parties to the WHO Framework Convention on Tobacco Control*, 2017 edition https://who.int/fctc/cop/who-fctc-rop-2017-en.pdf accessed October 31, 2018.

15 For more details, see https://who.int/fctc/protocol/en/ accessed October 31, 2018.

16 For more details, see section 4 of this chapter.

17 Art. 1(f) of the FCTC.

18 For a detailed discussion on the history of ENDS, see Chapter 2 in this volume.

3.1 Dealing with ENDS at the COPs' Meetings

E-cigarettes were discussed by the COP for the first time during its fourth session (in 2010).[19] This discussion was based on a report prepared by the FCTC Secretariat which provided a brief overview of scientific evidence relating to ENDS. It also included some general recommendations for the Parties, drawing on the outcomes of the Regulatory Consultation on the Safety of Electronic Nicotine Delivery Systems (so-called TobReg), for example encouraging them to ensure collaboration between regulators of medical and tobacco products in order to design appropriate regulatory frameworks.[20] Separately, the working group on draft guidelines for the implementation of Arts 9 and 10 of the FCTC requested advice from the COP as to whether e-cigarettes were to be considered as "tobacco products" (given the fact that they do not contain any tobacco *per se*) and whether they should be a part of its future work.[21] The issue did not attract any significant attention from the delegates, however, and eventually the COP4 only adopted a quite enigmatic decision in which it simply requested the Secretariat to prepare, jointly with WHO's Tobacco Free Initiative, a report on the relevant experiences of the Parties.[22] The question posed by the working group remained unanswered.

The FCTC Secretariat submitted such a report in 2012 during the COP5 meeting. The report, based on information received from the Parties, highlighted gaps in the existing knowledge (particularly with regard to the safety of e-cigarettes and their efficiency as a smoking cessation aid) and described a variety of regulatory responses employed by the Parties, including a total ban, regulation of ENDS with health claims, regulation of ENDS as pharmaceutical products, and a laissez-faire approach.[23] It also attempted to clarify the

---

[19] Note, however, that this was not the first time when e-cigarettes were addressed by the WHO. The WHO Study Group on Tobacco Product Regulations discussed the issue and prepared a report a couple of months before, WHO Study Group on Tobacco Product Regulation, *Report on the Scientific Basis of Tobacco Product Regulation: Third Report of a WHO Study Group* (World Health Organization, WHO Technical Report Series No 955, 2010).

[20] FCTC Secretariat, *Control and Prevention of Smokeless Tobacco Products and Electronic Cigarettes. Report by the Convention Secretariat*, FCTC/COP/4/12, September 15, 2010.

[21] FCTC COP, *Draft guidelines for the implementation of Articles 9 and 10 of the WHO Framework Convention on Tobacco Control*, FCTC/COP/4/6 Rev.1, November 18, 2010, para 14.

[22] FCTC COP, *Decision: Control and prevention of smokeless tobacco products and electronic cigarettes*, FCTC/COP4(14), November 20, 2010.

[23] FCTC Secretariat, *Electronic Nicotine Delivery Systems, including Electronic Cigarettes. Report by the Convention Secretariat*, FCTC/COP/5/13, June 18, 2012.

status of e-cigarettes under the Convention and identified several provisions that could potentially apply to such products.[24] These issues were subsequently discussed during the meeting of Committee A (one of the subsidiary bodies to the COP which is responsible, among other things, for preparation of the COP's draft decisions). Many delegates sought clarifications from the FCTC Secretariat as to the applicability of the Convention to e-cigarettes and on the regulatory standards that should be used for such products. The position of the Secretariat is discussed in the subsequent subsection.[25] Although the COP5 noted the report of the FCTC Secretariat in its decision, it only instructed the Secretariat to invite the WHO to review the available scientific evidence on ENDS and identify options for the prevention and control of such products.[26]

The WHO report was presented in 2014.[27] It addressed three distinct issues: (i) health risks connected with ENDS use; (ii) the effectiveness of ENDS as a cessation device; and (iii) their impact on existing tobacco control efforts (including implementation of the FCTC provisions). With respect to the first two issues, the report concluded that the available scientific evidence was limited, but also noted the existence of certain risks (for example related to nicotine exposure). It nevertheless confirmed that "average ENDS use produces lower exposures to toxicants than combustible products."[28] In the context of the third issue, the report identified the so-called gateway and renormalization problems,[29] but found that due to the lack of empirical data their accurate assessment was not possible.[30] At the same time, the report recognized banning ENDS as a legitimate regulatory approach, but also proposed a set of other regulatory options.[31] These included measures such as prohibiting health claims

---

24 Ibid 7–8. For more extensive discussion see subsequent section.

25 FCTC COP, *Summary records of Committees*, FCTC/COP/5/REC/2 (Conference of the Parties to the WHO Framework Convention on Tobacco Control, Fifth session, Seoul, Republic of Korea, November 12–17, 2012) 68–72.

26 FCTC COP, *Decision: Control and prevention of smokeless tobacco products and electronic nicotine delivery systems, including electronic cigarettes*, FCTC/COP5(10), November 17, 2012 (Conference of the Parties to the WHO Framework Convention on Tobacco Control, Fifth session, Seoul, Republic of Korea, November 12–17 2012).

27 FCTC COP, *Electronic Nicotine Delivery Systems. Report by WHO*, FCTC/COP/6/10 Rev.1, September 1, 2014 (Conference of the Parties to the WHO Framework Convention on Tobacco Control, Sixth session, Moscow, Russian Federation, October 13–18, 2014).

28 Ibid para 15.

29 See generally Chapter 3 of this volume; see also the discussion in subsection 3.2 of this chapter.

30 FCTC COP, *Electronic Nicotine Delivery Systems. Report by WHO* (n 27) paras 23–29.

31 Ibid para 39.

for ENDS (unless approved by a state on the basis of convincing scientific evidence); a ban on the use of ENDS in public places; restrictions on ENDS advertising, promotion, and sponsorship; protecting regulatory processes from the vested commercial interests of ENDS and tobacco companies; product design and information (for example banning ENDS solutions with certain flavors until empirical evidence shows that they are not attractive to minors); use of appropriate health warnings; and a prohibition on selling ENDS products to minors.[32] Overall, the regulatory measures proposed by the report were similar to those which are envisaged by the Convention for traditional tobacco products. They differed, however, in their stringency. For example, the WHO seemed to accept some forms of promotion if empirical evidence could show that ENDS could play a role in helping some smokers to quit. In a similar vein, it noted that ENDS health warnings should be commensurate with the identified health risks. Considering the limited health risk potential of ENDS, these warnings could be formulated differently than in the case of traditional tobacco products (for example "potential respiratory, eyes, nose and throat irritant effect" or "potential adverse effect on pregnancy,"[33] rather than "vaping kills"). The report also did not recommend the introduction of any graphic health warnings.

The 2014 WHO report constituted a point of reference for the subsequent COP6 decision, which invited the Parties to "consider prohibiting or regulating ENDS/ENNDS, including as tobacco products, medicinal products, consumer products, or other categories, as appropriate, taking into account a high level of protection for human health."[34] The decision also indicated a number of objectives that should be reflected in any national regulatory regime on ENDS (other than a total prohibition on their sale and use). This specifically included: (i) prevention of the initiation of ENDS by non-smokers and youth; (ii) minimization of potential health risks to ENDS users and protection of non-users from exposure to their emissions; (iii) preventing unproven health claims from being made about ENDS; and (iv) protection of tobacco control activities from all commercial and other vested interests related to ENDS. The decision once again asked the FCTC Secretariat to invite the WHO to prepare an updated expert report for the next COP meeting. It also requested the Secretariat to invite the Parties to monitor and report on scientific, regulatory, and market

---

32 Ibid paras 40–51.

33 Ibid para 49.

34 FCTC COP, *Decision: Electronic nicotine delivery systems and electronic non-nicotine delivery systems*, FCTC/COP6(9), October 18, 2014 (Conference of the Parties to the WHO Framework Convention on Tobacco Control, Sixth session, Moscow, Russian Federation, October 13–18, 2014). Note that "ENNDS" refers to Electronic Non-Nicotine Delivery System.

developments such as initiation, cessation, advertising, and promotion of ENDS.

That WHO report was delivered in 2016—just before the COP7 meeting—and in principle it repeated the previous findings.[35] In particular, the WHO noted still persisting gaps in the scientific knowledge and offered a more detailed set of regulatory recommendations. As previously, those guidelines were formulated less stringently than the FCTC obligations.[36] Interestingly, the WHO 2016 report did not mention a total ban on the sale and use of ENDS as a suggested regulatory option. The COP7, in its decision, only recommended that the Parties consider the application of measures identified by the report and asked the FCTC Secretariat to invite the WHO to prepare yet another report—this time on the standard setting activities of international and regional bodies vis-à-vis testing and measuring of the contents and emissions of ENDS.[37]

However, the FCTC Secretariat only delivered, at the request of the COP7 Bureau, a progress report on the regulatory and market developments on ENDS,[38] while preparation of the report on standard setting activities was postponed to the COP9 meeting.[39] The progress report updated the previous information on national experiences and noted that a large number of the Parties did not have any regulatory scheme for ENDS. In this context, it recommended that the Parties develop a relevant policy based on the recommendations in the previous reports.[40] During the meeting of Committee A, the Parties apparently could not agree on the proper treatment of ENDS. Some of them concentrated on potential risks (health and systemic), while others highlighted the harm reduction potential of those products.[41] In response to this discussion, the

---

35 WHO, *Electronic Nicotine Delivery Systems and Electronic Non-Nicotine Delivery Systems (ENDS/ENNDS)*, FCTC/COP/7/11 August 2016 (Conference of the Parties to the WHO Framework Convention on Tobacco Control, Seventh session, Delhi, India, November 7–12, 2016).

36 Ibid paras 28–32.

37 FCTC COP, *Decision: Electronic nicotine delivery systems and electronic non-nicotine delivery systems*, FCTC/COP7(9), November 12, 2016 (Conference of the Parties to the WHO Framework Convention on Tobacco Control, Seventh session, Delhi, India, November 7–12, 2016).

38 WHO, *Progress Report on Regulatory and Market Developments on Electronic Nicotine Delivery Systems (ENDS) and Electronic Non-Nicotine Delivery Systems (ENNDS)*, FCTC/COP/8/10, June 27, 2018 (Conference of the Parties to the WHO Framework Convention on Tobacco Control, Eighth session Geneva, Switzerland, October 1–6, 2018).

39 Ibid para 10.

40 Ibid para 28.

41 FCTC COP, *Report of the Eighth Session of the Conference of the Parties to the WHO Framework Convention on Tobacco Control* (Conference of the Parties

Secretariat indicated that the COP might eventually produce recommendations for a regulatory framework for ENDS.[42] However, the COP8 ultimately did not take any action in this regard.

3.2 The Position of the FCTC Secretariat

As mentioned above, the Parties have frequently sought clarifications from the FCTC Secretariat on the Convention's applicability to e-cigarettes. This issue was addressed extensively during COP5 (2012), but the position of the Secretariat was far from clear. At the meeting of Committee A, the Secretariat maintained that the applicability of the Convention entirely depended on the subjective decision of an individual Party. If a particular state classifies ENDS at the national level as tobacco products, then all the FCTC provisions would apply to them,[43] albeit of course only with respect to that Party. On the other hand, the Secretariat also claimed that the applicability of the Convention was determined by a certain objective criterion. In particular, if an e-cigarette *included tobacco* it would qualify (irrespective of the decision of a particular Party) as a "tobacco product," triggering the application of all the Convention's disciplines.[44] At the same time, the Secretariat did not explain what it meant by "ENDS that include tobacco" (see below for additional discussion of this issue). To make the entire classification even more obscure, the FCTC Secretariat advised that e-cigarettes may be also regarded as "objects in the form of tobacco products which appeal to minors" (irrespective of whether they contain tobacco extracts or nicotine) and therefore fall within the scope of the sales ban envisaged by Art. 16.1(c) of the FCTC.[45]

A more structured and elaborated evaluation of the FCTC applicability to e-cigarettes can be found in the Secretariat report prepared for the very same COP meeting.[46] The document repeated that the Convention applies to ENDS if they are categorized at the national level as tobacco products (para 38). The document also indicated several other provisions that may be relevant for the regulation of ENDS. In addition to Art. 16.1 of the Convention that regulates

---

to the WHO Framework Convention on Tobacco Control, Eighth session, Geneva, Switzerland, October 1–6, 2018) 17.

42 Ibid 18.

43 FCTC COP, *Summary records of Committees* (n 25) 67.

44 Ibid 84.

45 Ibid (arguing that there is "a strong argument to be made that electronic nicotine delivery systems, even those not containing tobacco, could be subject to prohibition under Article 16.1(c)").

46 FCTC Secretariat, *Electronic Nicotine Delivery Systems, including Electronic Cigarettes. Report by the Convention Secretariat* (n 23).

"objects in the form of tobacco products which appeal to minors," the report pointed to Art. 5.2(b), which requires Parties to "implement effective legislative, executive, administrative and/or other measures and cooperate, as appropriate, with other Parties in developing appropriate policies for preventing and reducing tobacco consumption, *nicotine addiction* and exposure to tobacco smoke" (para 34) [emphasis added]. Since all ENDS contain nicotine (otherwise they would be qualified as ENNDS), their regulation could be regarded as a way of preventing and reducing nicotine addiction. The Secretariat also argued that because e-cigarettes are used to mimic smoking, the sale and use of ENDS could be seen as an indirect form of advertising and promotion of tobacco use,[47] and that as a consequence it fell within the scope of Art. 13.2 of the FCTC, which also calls for a comprehensive ban (para 35). In addition, the Secretariat indicated that the use of e-cigarettes might undermine an effective implementation of Art. 8 ("Protection from exposure to tobacco smoke") as their users in public places could claim that their ENDS neither contain tobacco nor produce secondhand tobacco smoke (para 36). According to the FCTC Secretariat, this may lead to confusion and enforcement problems. Finally Art. 14, which requires the Parties to take effective measures to promote the cessation of tobacco use and adequate treatment for tobacco dependence, could be relevant. In this context, the Secretariat pointed to the implementing guidelines,[48] which require the Parties to apply an evidence-based approach to dependence and tobacco cessation actions and to make available only those medications that have been clearly shown to increase the chances of tobacco cessation. This condition could be hardly met by e-cigarettes, as relevant evidence is limited and inconclusive.

To complicate the issue even further, one should also recall the various COP decisions discussed in the previous subsection, which suggest that ENDS are apparently regarded by the Parties as a *sui generis* category (despite the fact they are not treated as such in the various regulatory models at home), distinct from regular tobacco products. Why otherwise include recommendations that provide less stringent standards than those which are provided by the Convention for tobacco products? Overall, it seems that the FCTC Secretariat has a preference for a total ban on the sale and use of ENDS rather than some

---

[47] Art. 1(c) of the FCTC defines tobacco advertising and promotion as "any form of commercial communication, recommendation or action with the aim, effect or likely effect of promoting a tobacco product or tobacco use either directly or indirectly."

[48] *Guidelines for implementation of Article 14 of the WHO Framework Convention on Tobacco Control (Demand reduction measures concerning tobacco dependence and cessation)* FCTC/COP4(8) para 9.

regulatory model that would mimic the regime introduced by the Convention,[49] while the COP as a whole has taken a more moderate approach that seeks to regulate rather than prohibit the use of e-cigarettes (probably reflecting the regulatory diversity existing among the FCTC Parties).

4. TAMING SCHRÖDINGER'S CAT: WHAT ARE THE AVAILABLE OPTIONS?

The previous subsection highlighted the elusive nature of e-cigarettes under the FCTC. It appears that they may be simultaneously regarded, depending on the decision of a specific Party, as tobacco products, objects in the form of tobacco products which appeal to minors, indirect forms of advertising and promotion of tobacco use, or cessation devices, or may fit none of these categories (for example, they may be regarded as a simple consumer product or fall into some type of *sui generis* category). This situation constitutes a real Schrödinger's cat problem in the chamber of international public health protection, and one may rightly ask: Is such a situation permissible under the rules of public international law? If so, is it desirable?

Before addressing these issues, it should be stressed that, depending on the classification of ENDS under the FCTC, different regulatory responses will be required from the Parties. If e-cigarettes are classified under the Convention as tobacco products, all the FCTC obligations would apply to them. If they are regarded as objects in the form of tobacco products which appeal to minors or indirect forms of advertising, they *have to be* banned. If none of those categories apply to them, but they are seen as products contributing to nicotine addiction, the Parties need to take, as required by Art. 5.2(b), effective legislative, executive, administrative, and/or other measures that would prevent and reduce nicotine addiction. Obviously, the language of the latter provision leaves the Parties with the broadest discretion (essentially unlimited) as to how to deal with ENDS. For example, one may argue that this provision provides an equal basis for a whole spectrum of responses, ranging from a total ban (because this is a logical way of preventing and reducing the nicotine addiction resulting from ENDS use) to a laissez-faire approach, or even some form of proactive strategy (if e-cigarettes are seen by a particular state as a useful harm reduction tool, that would lead to reductions in tobacco consumption, exposure

---

[49] Compare with FCTC Secretariat, *Electronic Nicotine Delivery Systems, including Electronic Cigarettes. Report by the Convention Secretariat* (n 23) para 37 (noting "if ENDS are not banned, a two-pronged strategy—regulating ENDS as both a tobacco and a medical product—could close potential loopholes in their regulation. *However, Parties may again wish to consider the desirability of allowing the sale of new products that may have the capacity to maintain a nicotine addiction*" [emphasis added]).

to tobacco smoke, and to a lesser extent nicotine addiction).[50] Such a vague formulation of the provision suggests, however, that it may only have an aspiratory character and in practice is deprived of any normative value.

One way of clarifying the existing heterogeneity would be for at least some Parties to formulate interpretative declarations in which they explain their understanding of the status of e-cigarettes under the Convention. Since these declarations could differ from each other, the classification of ENDS would vary from one Party to another, but still remain (as shown below) within the limits established by the Convention. In such a case, the resulting heterogeneity would be perfectly fine from the point of view of international law.

Although interpretative declarations are not codified in the Vienna Convention on the Law of Treaties (VCLT),[51] they are conventionally used by states in their treaty practice as an instrument of international customary law.[52] The International Law Commission (ILC) defines an "interpretative declaration" as "a unilateral statement, however phrased or named, made by a State . . . whereby that State . . . purports to specify or clarify [rather than modify] the meaning or scope attributed by the declarant to a treaty or to certain of its provisions."[53] Although the ILC expressed its preference for written interpretative declarations,[54] such a statement can be actually made in any form, including a verbal announcement. Unlike a reservation, an interpretative declaration can be formulated at any time,[55] and can be modified afterward (unless a specific treaty provides otherwise).[56] What is also important is that such a declaration "must be formulated by a person who is considered as representing a State . . . for the purpose of adopting or authenticating the text of a treaty or expressing

---

[50] Arts 8 and 14 of the FCTC, which are recalled by the Secretariat as well, cannot be regarded as potentially determining the general regulatory regime for e-cigarettes. The first provision could only require banning the use of e-cigarettes in public places, while the second could only justify the prevention of sales of e-cigarettes as cessation devices (or a ban on making any claims in this regard).

[51] Vienna Convention on the Law of Treaties (adopted May 23, 1969, entered into force January 27, 1980) 1155 UNTS 331.

[52] For an extensive analysis of interpretative declarations, see F. Horn, *Reservations and Interpretative Declarations to Multilateral Treaties* (TMC Asser Instituut 1988).

[53] UN General Assembly, *Report of the International Law Commission on the Work of Its 63rd Session (Guide to Practice on Reservations to Treaties)*, Official Records, 66th Session, Supplement No 1 Addendum 1, Doc. A/66/10/Add. 1, para 1.2.

[54] Ibid para 2.4.1.

[55] Ibid para 2.4.4. Note that a reservation can be formulated only when signing, ratifying, accepting, approving, or acceding to a treaty (compare with Arts 2(1)(d) and 19 of the VCLT). A subsequent reservation is only possible if a specific treaty envisages such an option or if none of the other contracting parties opposes the late formulation.

[56] Ibid para 2.4.8.

the consent of the State . . . to be bound by a treaty."[57] According to Art. 7 of the VCLT, this group includes heads of states, heads of governments, and ministers for foreign affairs. Other officials (including those at the ministerial level) can also represent a state, but only on the basis of full powers delegated by one of the above authorities. Once a declaration is formulated by a Party, it serves as an element which is taken into account, vis-à-vis a declarant, when interpreting a particular treaty provision.[58]

The United Nations Treaty Collection database does not mention any interpretative declarations made under the FCTC and relating to the classification of ENDS.[59] It is also hard to argue that any of the statements made by various delegates during one of the COP meetings may amount to a verbal interpretative declaration (provided that those persons were authorized to formulate such a declaration in the first place[60]). Delegates have, on different occasions, simply informed the COP about the classification of ENDS under their national law, rather than specified or clarified the meaning or scope of specific provisions of the FCTC (such as Art. 1(f) or Art. 16.1). For example, a delegate from Turkey simply declared during the COP6 meeting that "all these products [ENDS]—with or without tobacco—are subject to all legal regulations as tobacco products are."[61] Similarly, a South Korean delegate stated that "with respect to the emerging tobacco products, including electronic cigarettes and other types of nicotine delivery devices, my government decided to categorize these as tobacco products."[62] None of those statements can be qualified, however, as an interpretative declaration.[63]

---

57 Ibid para 2.4.2.

58 Ibid para 4.7.1.

59 Note that FCTC Parties made a number of such declarations relating to other provisions of the Convention. This was done, depending in the specific Party, upon signature, ratification, or formal confirmation of the Convention (for details see the United Nations Treaty Collection webpage https://bit.ly/2s8X6x2 accessed October 31, 2018).

60 The Rules of Procedure of the COP provide that a Party can be represented at the meeting of the COP only by delegates with proper credentials issued by the Head of State or Government, the Minister for Foreign Affairs, or the Minister of Health—thus authorities with power to bind the State (FCTC COP, *Rules of Procedure of the Conference of the Parties to the WHO Framework Convention on Tobacco Control* (n 14) rule 18. Credentials are, however, not publicly available, so it is not possible to analyze their content.

61 FCTC COP, *Verbatim Records of Plenary Meetings*, FCTC/COP/6/VR (Conference of the Parties to the WHO Framework Convention on Tobacco Control, Sixth session, Moscow, Russian Federation, October 13–18, 2014) 52.

62 Ibid 43.

63 Note that such a statement could be also made during the meeting of the Committee. Unfortunately, it is not possible to verify this as after COP5 the FCTC Secretariat ceased to publish, the verbatim records of the meetings.

If the existing heterogeneity cannot be explained by interpretative declarations, then what are the other possible options? In my opinion, there are at least three.

First, the FCTC Parties, when implementing the Convention into their domestic legal orders, have to interpret its specific provisions. In doing so, they are bound by the general rules of treaty interpretation as provided by Arts 31–33 of the VCLT. In particular, "a treaty shall be interpreted in good faith in accordance with the ordinary meaning to be given to the terms of the treaty in their context and in the light of its object and purpose." The instructions included in those provisions are general and leave a considerable margin of discretion to an interpreter, for example as to the balancing between textual ("ordinary meaning") and teleological aspects of interpretation ("object and purpose").[64] Consequently, different interpreters may reach, on the basis of the same treaty text, completely different outcomes.

As already noted above, the FCTC defines tobacco products as "[i] products entirely or partly made of the leaf tobacco as raw material [ii] which are manufactured to be used for smoking, sucking, chewing or snuffing." On one hand, a purely textual interpretation would suggest that generally ENDS cannot, under the Convention, be classified as tobacco products. Note that most of the e-liquids available on the market do not contain tobacco extracts,[65] but instead, in the case of tobacco flavors, use synthetic flavors that attempt to replicate tobacco taste. The same is true for non-tobacco flavored e-liquids, which in practice have the biggest share of the market. Such e-liquids do contain nicotine, which is currently derived from tobacco,[66] but not tobacco itself. This obviously does not fit into the phrase "made of [rather than "made

---

64 As noted by Jan Klabbers, "not too much should be expected from any rules on interpretation. Interpretation is, so to speak, not entirely a rule-governed activity, in much the same way as playing the violin or the piano is not entirely rule-governed." In this context he also added that "rules on interpretation can do little more than set the outward parameters" (J. Klabbers, "Interpretation as the Continuation of Politics by Other Means" (*Opinio Juris*, March 2, 2009) http://opiniojuris.org/2009/03/02/continuation/ accessed October 31, 2018.

65 Notable exceptions are so-called naturally extracted tobacco (NET) e-liquids and whole tobacco alkaloids (WTA) e-liquids, which do contain extract from tobacco leaves. Those products can be easily classified as "products entirely or partly made of the leaf tobacco as raw material."

66 Theoretically it is even possible to use nicotine that is synthetized in laboratories or derived from plants other than tobacco. This option is currently not used in the production of e-liquids, mainly because the costs are considerably higher compared to normal extraction (compare with L.K. Lempert, R. Grana, S.A. Glantz, "The importance of product definitions in US e-cigarette law and regulations" (2016) 25 Tob Control e50).

from"] the leaf tobacco as raw material."[67] ENDS are not used for smoking (understood as a practice whereby a substance is burned and the resulting smoke is breathed in), sucking, chewing, or snuffing, but rather for puffing or vaping, which could be defined as an act of inhaling vapor produced by a vaporizer. Finally, it is not clear what exactly *does* classify as a "tobacco product." While this problem does not emerge for dispensable e-cigarettes, for other types (second and third generation ENDS) one will need to decide how wide the scope of the definition will be. Would it cover only e-liquids, or also devices (or parts of them, such as vaporizers)?

On the other hand, under the approach that puts more emphasis on the object and purpose of the treaty (without, however, disregarding the text), it may be easier to come to the conclusion that ENDS are indeed covered by the definition of tobacco products. As discussed below, the presence of e-cigarettes on the market may, if left unregulated, undermine the effective implementation of the Convention and national tobacco policies. As a consequence, ENDS may prevent Parties from "protect[ing] present and future generations from the devastating health, social, environmental and economic consequences of tobacco consumption."[68] The objective of the FCTC may therefore require a broad reading of both terms, that is, "products . . . made of leaf tobacco" and "smoking." In particular, it may be argued that the verb "made of" simply describes a specific form of making something (note that nicotine used in the production of e-liquids was physically part of the raw tobacco leaf). Similarly, since vaping intends to mimic smoking, and ENDS vapor resembles smoke (even if its chemical composition is very different), this activity may be regarded as a specific form of smoking.[69] At the same time, such an interpretative approach does not necessarily inflate the definition. Note that in order for a specific object to qualify as a tobacco product, both conditions of the FCTC definition need to be met. The second condition will thus control its scope and will ensure that various cessation products that also contain nicotine derived from tobacco (that is, nicotine replacement therapies) do not qualify as tobacco products, because no smoking, even as broadly understood, is involved.

Such differences in interpretation could be addressed and eventually eliminated in the dispute settlement process.[70] As mentioned in section 2 of this

---

[67] For a similar argument made in the context of Taiwanese law, see Chapter 9 of this volume.

[68] Art. 3 of the FCTC.

[69] Compare also with one of the definitions of "smoking" at dictionary.com ("to draw into the mouth and puff out the smoke of . . .").

[70] It should be acknowledged that formally the decisions of international dispute settlement bodies are relevant only to particular disputes. In practice, however, they frequently enjoy a quasi-precedential character and elucidate the normative meaning

chapter, the Convention envisages such a system in its Art. 27, making it available for any "dispute between two or more Parties concerning the *interpretation* or application of this Convention" [emphasis added]. In practice, however, this provision establishes a very weak mechanism that to date has been never used by the Parties. In particular, an *ad hoc* arbitration, which could lead to a "quasi-authoritative" interpretation of FCTC provisions, may be used only by those Parties that have formally accepted it. So far this has been done only by three countries (out of 181 Parties),[71] and there are no indications that the situation will change any time soon. Consequently, there is only a very limited chance that the scope of any FCTC provisions that are potentially relevant for ENDS will be clarified through this channel. Moreover, due to the low level of acceptance of *ad hoc* arbitration among the Parties, it may be difficult to argue that decisions produced in this process will indeed have some kind of quasi-precedential value.

Arguably this task could also be undertaken by the COP itself. It is clear that the meeting of the Parties has a mandate to deal with ENDS. It also seems to have sufficient instruments at its disposal to effectively clarify, through quasi-authoritative interpretations rather than formal interpretations or amendments of the Convention,[72] the status of ENDS under the FCTC.

Note that the FCTC describes the functions of its COP broadly, providing that it shall take all necessary decisions to promote the effective implementation of the Convention. To this end, the COP can "consider . . . action, as appropriate, for the achievement of the objective of the Convention in the light of experience gained in its implementation."[73] As a general rule, the COP decisions are taken by consensus, but as has been noted, if this is not possible,

---

of treaty provisions in a more general way. For more details, see A. Bogdandy, I. Venzke, "The spell of precedents: lawmaking by international courts and tribunals" in C.P.R. Romano, K.J. Alter, Y. Shany (eds), *The Oxford Handbook of International Adjudication* (Oxford University Press 2014) 503–22; G. Guillaume, "The use of precedent by international judges and arbitrators" (2011) 2(1) JIDS 5.

[71] According to information in the United Nations Treaty Series database, only two countries (Azerbaijan and Belgium) have unconditionally declared their acceptance of the compulsory *ad hoc* arbitration provided in Art. 27.2 of the FCTC. In addition, Vietnam made a conditional declaration, subject to a separate agreement between parties to a dispute on a case by case basis: see https://bit.ly/242f68b accessed October 31, 2018.

[72] Amendments to the Convention are also adopted by the COP (by consensus, or if this is not achievable, by a three-quarters majority vote of the Parties present and voting at the session). Of course, an amendment enters into force only for those Parties that have accepted it.

[73] Art. 23.5 of the FCTC.

a three fourths majority vote of the Parties present and voting is sufficient.[74] At the same time, however, COP decisions as such should be seen as mere recommendations, as the body formally lacks any law-making authority.[75]

While ENDS may have a certain potential to reduce the prevalence of tobacco use (and thus contribute to the achievement of the FCTC objective), they can also pose specific challenges to the existing tobacco control measures taken by the Parties and the implementation of the FCTC obligations. In particular, as already mentioned in subsection 3.1, e-cigarettes may potentially produce a gateway effect, meaning that non-smokers (and in particular minors) may start nicotine use with such products (at a rate greater than if ENDS did not exist) and switch, after developing an addiction to nicotine, to regular tobacco.[76] The availability of ENDS on the market may also undermine the effectiveness of denormalization efforts (various strategies that aim at redefining smoking as an undesirable and abnormal social behavior) undertaken with respect to traditional tobacco products. As noted by the WHO in its 2014 report, "everything that makes ENDS attractive to smokers may enhance the attractiveness of smoking itself and perpetuate the smoking epidemic."[77] There are also concerns among some public health experts that the marketing of ENDS could provide a back door for the tobacco industry to reenter and influence the public debate about the future of tobacco control strategies, as well as legitimize its status as a legitimate stakeholder genuinely interested in addressing the smoking epidemic.[78] Finally, it may be argued that the availability of ENDS could undermine smoke-free policies, as it could reduce quitting

---

[74] FCTC COP, *Rules of Procedure of the Conference of the Parties to the WHO Framework Convention on Tobacco Control* (n 14).

[75] For a more detailed analysis of this aspect, see L. Gruszczynski, "Tobacco and international trade: recent activities of the FCTC Conference of the Parties" (2015) 49(4) J World Trade 665, 670–5.

[76] See for example S. Soneji et al, "Association between initial use of e-cigarettes and subsequent cigarette smoking among adolescents and young adults. A systematic review and meta-analysis" (2017) 171(8) JAMA Pediatrics 788.

[77] FCTC COP, *Electronic Nicotine Delivery Systems. Report by WHO* (n 27) para 24.

[78] While the ENDS market was initially dominated by small independent producers that had no interest in perpetuating tobacco use, this has changed dramatically over the last couple of years. Through acquisitions, transnational tobacco companies have become increasingly dominant on the market (see for example L. Bauld et al, *Electronic Cigarette Marketing: Current Research and Policy* (Report commissioned by Cancer Research UK, October 2016); C. Abate, "Tobacco companies taking over the e-cigarette industry" (*Huffington Post*, February 27, 2017) https://bit.ly/2I3TxCk accessed October 31, 2018. See also the discussion in Chapter 2 in this volume.

incentives and may conflict with the smoking denormalization effect.[79] If one considers all these elements (which are of systemic rather than individual character), it seems reasonable to argue that actions taken by the COP with respect to ENDS fall within the mandate given to the body by the Convention. This is also confirmed, as subsection 3.1 described in detail, by the actual practice of the FCTC Parties.

Although the Convention does not grant its COP power to make binding interpretations of FCTC provisions, a very similar effect could be achieved through a mere COP decision. Although such decisions are not binding, there is broad consensus in the literature that, in practice, the decisions of the Conference of the Parties do produce certain consequences. For example, Churchill and Ulfstein argue, in the context of COPs operating under multilateral environmental agreements (MEAs), that "decisions [which] have not been challenged [should be regarded] as agreements in simplified form between parties to the MEA."[80] Such an agreement becomes relevant in the process of interpretation as it needs to be taken into account together with the context of the interpreted provision (compare with Art. 31.3(a) of the VCLT). This conclusion has also recently been confirmed by the ILC.[81] Others claim that the decisions of COPs may have some kind of *de facto* binding force, with parties simply following their prescriptions (for the sake of effective functioning of the agreement and/or because of reputational costs), without really determining or contesting their legal status.[82]

So far, however, the FCTC COP has avoided taking any specific position on the issue of ENDS. It should be recalled that in its 2012 decision it limited itself to noting the report of the Convention Secretariat, which set out possible options for the classification of ENDS.[83] Although it took a more proactive stance two years later, the language used in the decision was nevertheless both weak and indecisive. The COP recognized that the Parties had adopted

---

[79] FCTC COP, *Electronic Nicotine Delivery Systems. Report by WHO* (n 27) para 28.

[80] R. Churchill, G. Ulfstein, "Autonomous institutional arrangements in multilateral environmental agreements: a little-noticed phenomenon in international law" (2000) 94 AJIL 640. See also FCTC COP, *Rules of Procedure of the Conference of the Parties to the WHO Framework Convention on Tobacco Control* (n 14).

[81] ILC, *Report of the International Law Commission, Sixty-sixth session* (May 5–June 6 and July 7–August 8, 2014, A/69/10) 209.

[82] See for example T. Gehring, "Treaty-making and treaty evolution" in D. Bodansky, J. Brunnée, E. Hey (eds), *The Oxford Handbook of International Environmental Law* (Oxford University Press 2007) 467–97.

[83] FCTC COP, *Decision: Control and prevention of smokeless tobacco products and electronic nicotine delivery systems, including electronic cigarettes* (n 26) preamble.

different regulatory strategies with respect to ENDS and invited them "to consider prohibiting or regulating ENDS/ENNDS, including as tobacco products, medicinal products, consumer products, or other categories, as appropriate, taking into account a high level of protection for human health."[84] A similar approach was taken in 2016, when the COP again invited the Parties "*to consider* applying regulatory measures *such as* those referred to in document FCTC/COP/7/11 [the 2016 WHO report] to prohibit or restrict the manufacture, importation, distribution, presentation, sale and use of ENDS/ENNDS, as appropriate to their national laws and public health objectives"[85] [emphasis added].

Consequently, it seems that until such time as a decision is taken either by an *ad hoc* arbitration panel or the COP, the existing heterogeneity in the classification of ENDS must simply be tolerated.

Second, when regulating ENDS the Parties may rely on Art. 5.2(b) of the FCTC, which requires implementation of effective measures for preventing and reducing tobacco consumption, nicotine addiction, and exposure to tobacco smoke. As explained above, the formulation of this provision is sufficiently broad to cover ENDS. At the same time, it leaves the Parties with almost unlimited discretion as to the choice of their preferred policy. Within this discretion a particular Party may decide to classify ENDS, at the national level, as tobacco products, medicinal products, or simply ordinary consumer goods. It may also decide to entirely prohibit their sale and use. However, in this context it should be noted that if ENDS are qualified as tobacco products at the national level (as a part of policy pursued under Art. 5.2(b) of the FCTC, rather than through the interpretation described above) this will not make the entire Convention automatically applicable to them (in the way it is applicable to traditional tobacco products). The FCTC has its own definition of tobacco products, the scope of which is determined through the process of interpretation of relevant treaty provisions. This process cannot be affected by classification at the national level. The two legal systems (the international and domestic ones), although related, operate autonomously at two different levels. Consequently, the application to ENDS of specific legal standards envisaged by the Convention can be done as a matter of national law and as a result of the sovereign decision of a particular Party, rather than because it is required by the Convention that ENDS be classified at the national level as tobacco products.

---

84 FCTC COP, *Decision: Electronic nicotine delivery systems and electronic non-nicotine delivery systems* (n 34) preamble and para 3.

85 FCTC COP, *Decision: Electronic nicotine delivery systems and electronic non-nicotine delivery systems* (n 37) para 2.

Third, it is also always possible for the Parties to classify ENDS as they wish at the national level, even without any reference to the Convention. The FCTC, as shown above, does not restrict the sovereign prerogatives enjoyed by countries in this regard, while Art. 5.2(b) is formulated so generally that it provides very little guidance as to the required conduct. Consequently, a particular Party may decide on its own regulatory framework for ENDS, as well as on the classification of those products, simply by using its inherent sovereign powers.

5. CONCLUSIONS: A RECOMMENDED STRATEGY

The analysis presented in the previous sections shows that due to the formulation of the relevant FCTC provisions, the complex nature of ENDS, and the COP's unwillingness to take a decisive stance on the status of those products, regulatory heterogeneity between various Parties may persist for some time.[86] This situation, although not necessarily desirable, is perfectly legal from the point of view of international law (or, at least, it is tolerable). It is also not surprising. The lack of definitive scientific evidence as to the real risks and benefits of ENDS—both from the public and individual health perspectives—makes any international-level decision on a preferred regulatory strategy very problematic. Note that it would be difficult to design a regulatory model that would be able to take into account all the particularities (for example different market structures, smoking prevalence, available enforcement mechanisms) and risk preferences of the specific Parties.

Does the above mean that the COP should refrain from taking any actions on ENDS? Quite the contrary. The caution that needs to be expressed in this policy space does not mean that the COP has to remain inactive, and, as explained above, the Convention provides a sufficient legal basis for the COP to deal with these products. A lack of action at the international level (with the FCTC COP being a natural point of reference in this regard) may be interpreted by some Parties as a green light to leave the market for ENDS unregulated. Considering the potential negative consequences and the overall aim of the FCTC, this cannot be viewed as the preferable option.[87] Note also that the activities of the COP have an "educational" aspect. They raise governments' awareness with respect to emerging problems in the implementation of the Convention and provide the required epistemic credibility (and thus legitimacy) for various actions that are subsequently undertaken, in response to COP decisions, by states themselves at the national level. They also provide

[86] Compare with the discussion in Chapter 2; the authors do not expect any scientific consensus to emerge on ENDS in any foreseeable future.

[87] For a similar conclusion see also Chapter 2.

guidance—even though they are not binding—on how to approach specific problems. This guidance is particularly important for developing countries with limited financial and technical resources. At the same time, it would be wrong to seek to maintain the current status quo by preserving the existing confusion as to the status of ENDS under the FCTC. Such a situation has the potential to be exploited by the tobacco industry and ultimately may weaken the position of the national governments vis-à-vis special interest groups.

Having said the above, it also seems that classifying ENDS as tobacco products is not the best available strategy. As already noted, e-cigarettes clearly pose certain challenges in light of the tobacco control policies currently applied. At the same time, a considerable body of evidence strongly suggests that they are less risky than traditional tobacco products.[88] Putting them in the same category as tobacco (because of gateway and renormalization concerns) would be throwing the baby out with the bathwater. The regulatory response should be tailored to the risks posed by these products (particularly for minors and non-smokers), without however undermining their potential to serve as a less harmful replacement for current tobacco users. This means that ENDS should be treated as a *sui generis* category, one that is different from both traditional as well as novel tobacco products (insofar as the latter group is concerned, at least until sufficient data from independent sources are collected and analyzed). For the same reasons, it would be a mistake to generally classify ENDS as an indirect form of advertising and promotion of tobacco use, or of objects in the form of tobacco products which appeal to minors (irrespective of whether this makes any sense from the textual point of view).

Arguably the best legal basis in the Convention to deal with ENDS is Art. 5.2(b). There seems to be no doubt, from the textual point of view, that it could cover diverse regulatory measures relating to e-cigarettes. At the same time, it is sufficiently broad to provide the necessary flexibility to create a well tailored regulatory model that could be used by the Parties. However, as noted above, the general character of the provisions of Art 5.2(b) is also its drawback. To remedy this, the COP could consider developing recommendations for ENDS in the form of guidelines rather than in the form of "ordinary" decisions (as has been the case so far).[89] In this context, for the reasons indicated above, the COP should clearly recommend treating ENDS as a *sui generis* category rather than passively abdicating responsibility to the decisions of the individual Parties (as once again has been the case so far). Note that this would not prevent the Parties from taking a very strict approach if this is required by some particu-

---

88 For a detailed review of the available evidence, see Chapter 3 in this volume.

89 This would elevate their importance, without however changing their legal status (that is, they would still be regarded as non-binding recommendations).

larities of the local situation. As noted above, countries can always do this by exercising their inherent sovereign powers. The Convention itself also confirms that it only sets minimum standards, and does not prevent the Parties from introducing stricter measures.

There are already visible signs of such an approach in the documents prepared by the WHO and the decisions taken by the COP. Although both entities still accept the classification of e-cigarettes as regular tobacco products and/or a total prohibition of their sale and use as possible regulatory options, they have also developed a set of guidelines (for those Parties that decided to regulate ENDS rather than ban them) on the recommended approach to e-cigarettes. This is definitely a move in the right direction and gives some hope for a rational approach to ENDS products in the future.

5. A human rights approach to the regulation of electronic cigarettes

Marie Elske C. Gispen and Jacquelyn D. Veraldi[1]

1. INTRODUCTION

As discussed in Chapter 2 of this book, the scientific community remains largely divided as to the public health effects and related safety of electronic cigarettes (also referred to as Electronic Nicotine Delivery Systems or ENDS). There are divided opinions as to the potential utility of ENDS as a smoking cessation tool, and thus harm reduction device, on the one hand, and whether ENDS may act as a gateway product for youth to start smoking combustible cigarettes, on the other.[2] Not surprisingly, these differing views have led to dramatically different ENDS policy recommendations and regulatory approaches among countries. Moreover, the question of whether ENDS—a new form of device that transcends the design of combustible cigarettes yet still facilitates nicotine dependence[3]—

---

[1] The research underlying this chapter is part of a three-year research project into children's rights and tobacco control funded by the Dutch Cancer Society. The funding body did not play any role in drafting the study design, in the data collection and analysis, nor in the writing or reviewing of this manuscript. The authors declare no conflict of interest. The authors thank Prof. dr. Brigit Toebes for valuable feedback on earlier drafts. Any errors are directly and only attributable to the authors.

[2] Note that various reports have concluded that ENDS may serve as a cessation device and that there is no persuasive evidence that the use of e-cigarettes may produce gateway effects: A. McNeill et al, *Evidence Review of E-Cigarettes and Heated Tobacco Products 2018* (A report commissioned by Public Health England, Public Health England 2018). For less optimistic conclusions, see: K. Stratton, L.Y. Kwan, D.L. Eaton (eds), *Public Health Consequences of E-Cigarettes* (National Academies Press 2018) 30, 426; WHO, *Electronic Nicotine Delivery Systems and Electronic Non-Nicotine Delivery Systems (ENDS/ENNDS)* (FCTC/COP/7/11 2016) 4, 6.

[3] In drug control policies, the terms "addiction" and "drug addict" are generally considered stigmatizing. Consequently, this chapter refers to "nicotine dependence" and not "addiction."

can or must fall under traditional tobacco control laws and policies influences the different perspectives on ENDS regulation. There is a need for overarching principles that can guide this debate, and human rights law can fulfill this role.[4] In line with one of the objectives of this book, this chapter looks at the legal constraints imposed by international human rights law on the regulatory freedom enjoyed by states in this policy space.

Human rights law is increasingly important in international and domestic tobacco control debates.[5] More generally, human rights have proven essential in shaping health and socio-economic policies and in ensuring accountability.[6] As argued in this chapter, human rights are also directly relevant to the regulation of ENDS products.

State Parties to human rights treaties must protect and promote the health of individuals, and children in particular. Although most scientific debates on ENDS are not yet settled, it is clear that these products are, at least, not beneficial to health. Research demonstrates that ENDS remain harmful to health in various ways (albeit much less so than combustible tobacco products).[7] They contain substances that may not only cause health-related harm but also raise human rights concerns in light of product safety and quality issues.[8]

---

[4] Yvette van der Eijk and colleagues similarly propose that human rights reflects a "common set of principles" necessary to guide the regulation of e-cigarettes in pregnancy. See Y. van der Eijk et al, "E-cigarette Use in Pregnancy" (2017) 93 Acta Obstet Gynecol Scand 1283.

[5] See e.g. WHO, *Electronic Nicotine Delivery Systems and Electronic Non-Nicotine Delivery Systems (ENDS/ENNDS)* (n 2) 7–12.

[6] For instance, there is a wealth of case law on access to medicines in which human rights play an important role. See K. Perehudoff, B. Toebes, H. Hogerzeil, "Essential Medicines in National Constitutions" (2016) 18 Health Hum Rights 141. Even though the rulings of the European Committee of Social Rights are not legally binding in domestic law, they may influence domestic policy. See for example *Conference of European Churches v. Netherlands* (2013) Decision No 90/2013 of the European Committee of Social Rights. This case led to the adoption of the "bed, bath, and bread" policy in the Netherlands offering refugees basic needs: "Factsheet Bed-bad-brood regeling" (*Vereniging van Nederlandse Gemeenten*, March 2015) https://vng.nl/files/vng/publicaties/2016/20150326-factsheet-bed-bad-brood.pdf accessed October 31, 2018. On accountability, see Y. Zhang, *Advancing the Right to Health Care in China* (Intersentia 2018).

[7] See, among the other literature mentioned in section 3: G. Maina, "Skin Contamination as Pathway for Nicotine Intoxication in Vapers" (2017) 41 Toxicol in Vitro 102; R.C. McMillen et al, "Trends in Electronic Cigarette Use among U.S. Adults" (2015) 17 Nicotine Tob Res 1995; J.M. Cameron, "Variable and Potentially Fatal Amounts of Nicotine in E-Cigarette Nicotine Solutions" (2014) 23 Tob Control 77.

[8] The potential health hazards of nicotine use and dependence as such are not further addressed in this chapter.

The regulatory approach to ENDS may also be influenced by harm reduction considerations, as well as their gateway potential, leading to conflicting views on how these two aspects can be balanced. Consequently, this may require modification of an initial regulatory approach whereby ENDS are considered solely in the light of their harmful nature.

Notably, while this chapter is based on the assumption that ENDS may be harmful to health (in light of the reasons explained above), it does not take a position in the current scientific debate on the costs and benefits of ENDS as either a harm reduction tool or a gateway product (section 2). It does not do so because its objective is to demonstrate which human rights frameworks apply to certain aspects of ENDS regulation, and to inform law and policy discussions in the regulation of ENDS from a broad human rights perspective.

The chapter focuses both on general and child-specific human rights, and therefore in particular analyses provisions in the International Covenant on Economic, Social, and Cultural Rights (ICESCR) and the Convention on the Rights of the Child (CRC), as well as the General Comments developed under both treaty systems.[9] Because of the specific focus of this edited collection, the present chapter focuses primarily on positive human rights norms in international law—that is, those norms that are included in (quasi-)legal instruments and documents—and generally does not address related normative frameworks such as the precautionary principle.[10]

Including the introduction, this chapter is organized into six sections. Section 2 provides an overview of the links between human rights and tobacco control in general, and places ENDS as new products in this context. Section 3 analyzes ENDS as devices containing harmful substances. This section mainly focuses on the use of and exposure to vapor. For reasons of scope and space limitations, issues of product safety are only marginally addressed in this analysis. This section is based on the ICESCR and only partially on the CRC. Section 4 analyzes ENDS as a potential harm reduction tool, in which the primary focus is on the ICESCR. Section 5 analyses the gateway hypothesis from a child rights perspective, addressing both general norms and

---

[9] International Covenant on Economic, Social and Cultural Rights (adopted December 16, 1966, entered into force January 3, 1976) 993 UNTS 3; Convention on the Rights of the Child (adopted November 20, 1989, entered into force September 2, 1990) 1577 UNTS 39. This chapter does not deal with regional human rights systems or documents of international health law, such as the WHO Framework Convention on Tobacco Control (FCTC). The latter is the subject of analysis in Chapter 4 of this book. The Concluding Observations of the CRC Committee and CESCR were also searched through, but no results regarding ENDS regulation were found and therefore they are not included in the analysis.

[10] For an in-depth analysis of the precautionary principle and ENDS regulation under EU law, see Chapter 8 of this book.

specific rights included in the CRC as relevant to the regulation of ENDS. Some overlap between sections 3 and 5 is unavoidable because ENDS, by their nature, may be considered as devices containing substances harmful to both adults and children. The chapter concludes with a set of recommendations to inform the current debates on ENDS regulation.

2. HUMAN RIGHTS AND TOBACCO CONTROL

Human rights are fundamental entitlements that every person has simply because he or she is a human.[11] The modern notion of human rights originated in the Charter of the United Nations (UN) and the Universal Declaration of Human Rights (UDHR) in 1948.[12] The UDHR reflects the importance of protecting individuals against illegitimate government interference and of vesting individuals with rights claims against governments to demand, *inter alia*, access to facilities, goods, and services essential to address at least basic needs.[13] While the UDHR is one of the most pivotal documents within international human rights law, the civil and political rights as well as the social, economic, and cultural rights and obligations set forth therein have remained largely unenforceable because it is a declaration and not a legally binding treaty.[14] In order to give the UDHR legal teeth, the international community adopted the International Covenant on Civil and Political Rights (ICCPR) and the ICESCR in 1969.[15] Since the adoption of these two documents the UN human rights treaty system has vastly expanded, and now includes agreements that provide specific rights protection in the areas of racial discrimination, torture, and enforced disappearances, as well as agreements protecting specific groups, including migrant workers, women, children, and persons with disabilities. These treaties jointly reflect a comprehensive body of law that includes

---

[11] A. Henriksen, *International Law* (Oxford University Press 2017) 178.

[12] Ibid; Charter of the United Nations (adopted June 26, 1945, entered into force October 24, 1945) 1 UNTS XVI, preamble and Art. 1.3; Universal Declaration of Human Rights (adopted December 10, 1948 UNGA Res 217 A(III)) Art. 1.

[13] The UDHR includes both civil and political rights as well as economic, social, and cultural rights. Art. 3 UDHR includes the right to life, which is a classic civil right. Art. 25 UDHR includes the right to health, which is a typical social right.

[14] For more on the origins of the UDHR and the differing political views at the time of its adoption, see A. Samnoy, "The Origins of the Universal Declaration of Human Rights" in G. Alfredsson, A. Eide (eds), *The Universal Declaration of Human Rights* (Martinus Nijhoff Publishers 1999) 3–22; J. Donnelly, *International Human Rights* (4th ed, Westview Press 2013) 7–8; M.E.C. Gispen, *Human Rights and Drug Control* (Intersentia 2017) 81.

[15] International Covenant on Economic, Social and Cultural Rights (adopted December 16, 1966, entered into force January 3, 1976) 993 UNTS 3.

relevant standards and obligations for governments in relation to tobacco control. Indeed, human rights law is integrally relevant to tobacco control and, as mentioned in the introduction to this chapter, is considered increasingly important in international and domestic tobacco control debates.[16]

Under human rights law, states have obligations to respect, protect, and fulfill human rights.[17] Depending on the context and the applicable right, states have obligations to abstain from illegitimate interference with a right (respect), to protect individuals from illegitimate interference with their rights by others (protect), and to take deliberate and active steps toward the full realization of human rights (fulfill). All three types of obligation are generally applicable to all rights.[18] However, as regards tobacco control policies, governments have, in particular, obligations to protect and fulfill the right to health and related rights.

Finally, as mentioned above, human rights law traditionally places duties upon states and vests individuals with rights claims invokable against governments.[19] This means that private actors such as tobacco companies are, strictly speaking, not legally bound dutybearers within human rights law, despite their significant contribution to tobacco-related harm to health. They are not official parties to UN human rights treaties and the obligations flowing therefrom are not directly transferable to the tobacco industry.[20] Even though they are formally not bound to human rights treaties, it is increasingly accepted that private actors have a responsibility to respect human rights.[21]

---

16 See for example WHO, *Electronic Nicotine Delivery Systems and Electronic Non-Nicotine Delivery Systems (ENDS/ENNDS)* (n 2) 7–12, but also C. Dresler, S. Marks, "The Emerging Human Right to Tobacco Control" (2006) 28 HRQ 599; C. Dresler et al, "Human Rights-Based Approach to Tobacco Control" (2012) 21 Tob Control 208; Y. van der Eijk, "The Convention on the Rights of Persons with Disabilities as a Tobacco Control Tool in the Mental Health Setting" (2017) Tob Control 1; B. Toebes et al, "A Missing Voice: The Human Rights of Children to a Tobacco-Free Environment" (2018) 27 Tob Control 3.

17 Maastricht Guidelines on Violations of Economic, Social, and Cultural Rights (1997) para 6, reissued by the CESCR in UN Doc E/C.12/2000/13; CESCR, "General Comment No 14 on The Right to the Highest Attainable Standard of Health (Art. 12)" (August 11, 2000) UN Doc E/C.12/2000/4 (CESCR GC 14) para 4.

18 I.E. Koch, "Dichotomies, Trichotomies or Waves of Duties?" (2005) 5 HRL Rev 81.

19 Henriksen (n 11) 177.

20 For more on human rights and the tobacco industry, see for example B. Toebes, "Human Rights and the Tobacco Industry" (2018) 7 IJHPM 677.

21 See for example J. Ruggie, *Guiding Principles on Business and Human Rights* (United Nations 2011), endorsed by the UN Human Rights Council in its resolution "Human Rights and Transnational Corporations and Other Business Enterprises" (July 6, 2011) A/HRC/RES/17/4.

Research into international and regional human rights law and tobacco control demonstrates that governments have obligations to regulate the entire supply chain of tobacco products.[22] Moreover, governments have specific obligations in this regard, based on the CRC, to protect the health, life, development, and well-being of children along their life course.[23] Overall, the question is whether and to what extent these obligations may inform the regulation of ENDS.

3. E-CIGARETTES AS A HARMFUL DEVICE/ DEVICE CONTAINING HARMFUL SUBSTANCES

The ongoing debate on the risks posed by ENDS is largely polarized.[24] Within this polarized debate, however, it is generally accepted that ENDS contain harmful substances. McNeill and colleagues observe that the use of ENDS is "less harmful than smoking";[25] however, this still implies that ENDS are harmful to a certain degree. Additionally, Cameron and others found some e-liquid solutions contained potentially fatal doses of nicotine.[26] These devices pose numerous other health risks, regardless of the extent of their severity. In other words, no matter how much less harmful than combustible cigarettes they may be, they are harmful. Such risks relate to dermal exposure to e-liquid chemicals,[27] toxicity from consumption,[28] and poisoning by metals contained in e-liquids and aerosol.[29]

---

[22] See for example Dresler and Marks (n 16); R. de Silva de Alwis, R. Daynard, "Reconceptualizing Human Rights to Challenge Tobacco" (2008–9) 17 Mich St J Int l L 304; C. Dresler et al (n 16); O.A. Cabrera, A. Madrazo, "Human Rights as a Tool for Tobacco Control in Latin America" (2010) 52 Salud pública México S288; van der Eijk, "The Convention on the Rights of Persons with Disabilities as a Tobacco Control Tool in the Mental Health Setting" (n 16).

[23] CRC (n 9); M.E.C. Gispen, B. Toebes, "The Human Rights of Children in Tobacco Control" (2019) 41 HRQ 340; Toebes et al (n 16); A.K. Ramos, "Child Labor in Global Tobacco Production" (2018) 20(2) HHRJ 235.

[24] For more details of this debate, see Chapter 2 of this book.

[25] McNeill et al, *Evidence Review of E-Cigarettes and Heated Tobacco Products 2018* (n 2) 20.

[26] Cameron (n 7).

[27] Maina (n 7).

[28] US Department of Health and Human Services, *E-Cigarette Use Among Youth and Young Adults* (US Department of Health and Human Services 2016) 7.

[29] McNeill et al, *Evidence Review of E-Cigarettes and Heated Tobacco Products 2018* (n 2) 151; M. Williams et al, "Metal and Silicate Particles Including Nanoparticles Are Present in Electronic Cigarette Cartomizer Fluid and Aerosol" (2013) 8 PLOS e57987.

While e-liquids may contain substances that are harmful in themselves, additional risks may be produced by the devices as such. For instance, the heavy metals, such as tin and nickel, contained in heating elements have been also found in e-liquids and aerosol. Grana and colleagues assert that it is likely that engineering features influence the "nature, number and size" of the relevant particles, which may cause local respiratory toxicity.[30] Kumetz and colleagues show that power sources in ENDS devices have been reported to have caused severe thermal and blast injuries.[31] Moreover, the fact that ENDS exposure frequency in children is said to be "increasing rapidly and severe outcomes are being reported" amplifies these concerns.[32] A 2016 US study found that, in comparison to child exposure to cigarettes, "children exposed to e-cigarettes had 5.2 times higher odds of health care facility admission and 2.6 times higher odds of severe medical outcomes."[33]

The following subsection seeks to assess in detail the issue of ENDS-related risks by investigating the regulatory implications that can be deduced from the human rights law framework.

3.1 Regulating ENDS-related Harm under the Right to Health

Art. 12 ICESCR includes the right to the highest attainable standard of physical and mental health, commonly referred to as the right to health. The right to health is an inclusive right, which means that it encompasses aspects of both access to (health) care and the underlying social determinants of health.[34] Art. 12 ICESCR is the most authoritative health law provision in international law and includes relevant obligations in relation to not only the regulation of tobacco, but also "other harmful substances."[35]

---

30 R. Grana et al, "E-Cigarettes" (2014) 129 Circulation 1972.

31 E.A. Kumetz et al, "Electronic Cigarette Explosion Injuries" (2016) 34 Am J Emerg Med 252e1. As regards the relationship between human rights and consumer protection, which encompasses product safety issues, see I. Benöhr, "The Evolution of Consumer Protection and Human Rights" in I. Benöhr, *EU Consumer Law and Human Rights* (Oxford University Press 2013) 49–50, 72–5. Support can be found for this relationship in CESCR GC 14 (n 17) para 51, which states that breaches of obligations to protect include "the failure to regulate the activities of individuals, groups or corporations so as to prevent them from violating the right to health of others; the failure to protect consumers and workers from practices detrimental to health."

32 A. Kamboj et al, "Pediatric Exposure to E-Cigarettes, Nicotine, and Tobacco Products in the United States" (2016) 137 Pediatrics 1. Over the time of this study, child exposure reports increased 1492.9 percent.

33 Ibid.

34 CESCR GC 14 (n 17) para 4.

35 Ibid paras 15, 36, and 51.

In their references to government obligations with respect to tobacco products, the Committee on Economic, Social and Cultural Rights (CESCR)—the monitoring body of the ICESCR—consistently adds that these obligations also apply to "other harmful substances."[36] Devices such as ENDS that contain harmful substances would fit squarely into this category. The Committee has stated that the failure to discourage the production, marketing, and consumption of other harmful substances (in addition to tobacco and narcotics) amounts to a violation of the duty to protect the rights enshrined in Art. 12 ICESCR.[37] The CESCR has also established that the obligation to fulfill the right to health requires governments to adopt information campaigns on the use of "cigarettes, drugs, and other harmful substances."[38] Hence, human rights law requires governments to regulate ENDS based on the products' harmful nature regardless of whether ENDS would be considered a tobacco product in the traditional sense, which is a common theme discussed in the context of the FCTC.[39]

With respect to the risks posed by defective ENDS devices, human rights law may also be relevant for the development of appropriate consumer protection and product safety standards. The obligation to protect the rights set out in Art. 12 ICESCR requires states to regulate the activities of corporations in order to protect individuals from practices that may harm their health.[40] Based on this line of reasoning, insufficient manufacturing practices liable to give rise to ENDS malfunctions would arguably be encompassed within the scope of those industry activities that governments should regulate.[41] The CESCR specifically mentions that the failure to protect consumers from practices detrimental to health amounts to a failure to protect the right to health.[42] Governments should thus make efforts to increase product safety standards to protect individuals' right to health,[43] and in particular children's rights to protection of their interest, life, development, and health.[44]

---

36 Ibid para 15 and 51.
37 Ibid para 51.
38 Ibid para 36.
39 For more on the FCTC, see Chapter 4 of this book.
40 CESCR GC 14 (n 17).
41 For more on product safety and human rights, see Benöhr (n 31).
42 CESCR GC 14 (n 17) para 51.
43 Benöhr (n 31) and CESCR GC 14 (n 17) para 51.
44 Arts 3, 6, 24 CRC (n 9).

3.2 Environmental Health and Protection against Vapor as Part of the Right to Health

Another dimension of regulating ENDS as devices containing harmful substances is the issue of vapor exposure. Art. 12.2(b) ICESCR imposes on State Parties the obligation to improve "all aspects of environmental and industrial hygiene," and has been interpreted by the CESCR to include "the prevention and reduction of the population's exposure to . . . detrimental environmental conditions that directly or indirectly impact upon human health."[45] Environmental health protection obligations therefore specifically require governments to discourage the use of tobacco and other harmful substances.[46]

Within tobacco control, governments have to regulate exposure to tobacco smoke via smoking bans in public spaces, and increasingly even do so by adopting smoking bans in private spaces (for example cars).[47] Although research suggests that exposure to ENDS vapor generally does not lead to harm, some studies also highlight that ENDS use reduces (indoor) air quality.[48] Specifically with regard to children, Art. 24 CRC enshrining the right to health for children requires governments to develop, among their other obligations, preventive health care measures and to address environmental health issues, including tobacco control.[49] In identifying the relationship between environmental pollution and the right to health, the Committee on the Rights of the Child (CRC Committee) considers "adequate housing" to include smoke-free environments.[50] So if exposure to mainstream vapor exhaled by ENDS users poses health risks then, as similarly argued above, tobacco smoking bans should likewise apply to ENDS—both for adults and for children. This is

---

45 CESCR GC 14 (n 17) para 15.

46 Ibid.

47 Art. 8 of the FCTC requires governments to adopt smoking bans in "indoor workplaces, public transport, indoor public places and, as appropriate, other public places." Some countries, like the United Kingdom, have decided to go beyond those minimum requirements and regulated tobacco use in cars where minors are present, "Smoking in Vehicles" (Gov.uk, July 17, 2015) https://gov.uk/government/news/smoking-in-vehicles accessed October 31, 2018.

48 R. Chen et al, "Assessment of Indoor Air Quality at an Electronic Cigarette (Vaping) Convention" (2017) J Expo Sci Environ Epidemiol doi:10.1038/s41370-017-0005-x; W. Schober, "Use of Electronic Cigarettes (e-Cigarettes) Impairs Indoor Air Quality and Increases FeNO Levels of E-cigarette Consumers" (2014) 217 Int J Hyg Environ Health 628. See also Chapter 3 in this volume.

49 Art. 24(c)(f) CRC (n 9).

50 CRC Committee, "General Comment No 15" (17 April 2013) UN Doc CRC/C/GC/15 (CRC Committee GC 15) para 49. As mentioned in the Introduction, the child rights framework applicable to tobacco and possibly to ENDS is further elaborated upon in section 5 of this chapter.

particularly so because the CESCR requires governments to "take measures that prevent third parties from interfering with the right to health."[51] The demonstrated effectiveness of tobacco control policies, including smoking bans, shows that such policies could be useful to fulfill the obligations imposed by the CESCR.[52]

3.3 Access to Information and the Right to Health

Within the regulatory measures that states should take, access to impartial health-related information is of key importance. Information accessibility is a central component of the adequate realization of the right to health, as complemented by the right to information enshrined in Art. 19 ICCPR.[53] According to the CESCR, information accessibility in light of Art. 12 ICESCR broadly includes "the right to seek, receive and impart information and ideas concerning health issues."[54]

Whether in reference to the alleged benefits or harms of ENDS, promoting misinformation or not taking steps to prevent interested third parties from promoting misinformation could also lead to a breach of a government's health-related information obligations. For instance, it is well known that cigarette manufacturers misled consumers by marketing their products as "light," giving rise to the belief that these products contained fewer toxicants.[55] As the traditional tobacco market seems no longer to exist but instead has transformed into a market of nicotine-containing products, including both combustible cigarettes and ENDS, it is important to distinguish between the degrees of harm caused by these products. Scholars have argued that individuals are equally misled when all nicotine-containing products are gathered under the same umbrella as equally harmful.[56] Therefore, as Rodu puts it, "greater efforts should be undertaken to promote more accurate perceptions of relative health

---

51 CESCR GC 14 (n 17) para 33.

52 J.V. Been et al, "Effect of Smoke-free Legislation on Perinatal and Child Health" (2014) 383 Lancet 1549; T. Faber et al, "Effect of Tobacco Control Policies on Perinatal and Child Health" (2017) 2 Lancet Public Health PE420.

53 CESCR GC 14 (n 17) para 11; WHO, "Fact Sheet—The Right to Health" (August 2007) WHO/OHCHR/323 https://ohchr.org/Documents/Publications/Factsheet31.pdf accessed October 31, 2018. On the link between the right to information and tobacco control more generally, see, *inter alia*, Dresler, Marks (n 16) 647; de Silva de Alwis, Daynard (n 22) 341.

54 CESCR GC 14 (n 17) para 12.b.

55 Z. Cahn, M. Siegel, "Electronic Cigarettes as a Harm Reduction Strategy for Tobacco Control" (2011) 32 J Public Health Policy 16.

56 B. Rodu, W.T. Godshall, "Tobacco Harm Reduction" (2006) 3 Harm Reduct J 15. For an analysis of both sides of the misinformation issue, see: L.T. Kozlowski,

risks between tobacco product[s]."[57] This is also important in light of the harm reduction hypothesis elaborated on in section 4.2.

In sum, there are thus different grounds upon which governments must regulate ENDS according to human rights law. However, as was also mentioned in the introduction to the chapter, there are two scenarios that may affect the degree of regulation that countries need to exercise: (1) ENDS as a potential harm reduction tool; and/or (2) ENDS as potential gateway products. Sections 4 and 5 will further elaborate upon these frameworks.

4. E-CIGARETTES AS A HARM REDUCTION TOOL

One side of the ENDS regulation debate emphasizes the potential of ENDS in harm reduction strategies.[58] There is no fixed definition of harm reduction. Harm Reduction International, one of the core NGOs in this area, defines harm reduction as "policies, programmes, and practices that aim to reduce the harms associated with the use of psychoactive drugs in people unable or unwilling to stop."[59] The Harm Reduction Coalition, another key NGO in this policy space, stresses more specifically that harm reduction "incorporates a spectrum of strategies from safer use, to managed use, to abstinence in order to meet drug users 'where they're at', addressing the conditions of use along with the use itself."[60] In other words, harm reduction strategies may generally include both substitutes and cessation tools and programs, tailored to meet the needs of the user.

In tobacco control, products such as nicotine replacement therapies (NRT) that contain tobacco-related toxicants but which lower tobacco-related deaths are covered by such an approach.[61] Application of the harm reduction approach in the ENDS context could prevent what some currently perceive as the mistaken "lumping of all tobacco/nicotine products into the same bin of being

---

D.B. Abrams, "Obsolete Tobacco Control Themes Can be Hazardous to Public Health" (2016) 16 BMC Public Health 4.

[57] B. Rodu, "The Scientific Foundation for Tobacco Harm Reduction, 2006–2011" (2011) 8 Harm Reduct J 7.

[58] D.B. Abrams, "Promise and Peril of E-Cigarettes" (2014) 311 Jama 135.

[59] "What is Harm Reduction?" (Harm Reduction International) https://hri.global/what-is-harm-reduction accessed October 31, 2018.

[60] "Principles of Harm Reduction" (Harm Reduction Coalition) http://harmreduction.org/about-us/principles-of-harm-reduction/ accessed October 31, 2018.

[61] "Editorial: Applying the Risk/Use Equilibrium" (2001) 10 Tob Control 201. See the special communication by the Institute of Medicine, Committee to Assess the Science Base for Tobacco Harm Reduction, and the Board on Health Promotion and Disease Prevention: K. Stratton et al, "Clearing the Smoke: The Science Base for Tobacco Harm Reduction" (2001) 10 Tob Control 189.

highly lethal."[62] However, the US Commissioner of Food and Drugs has rightly pointed out that the "debate over the past decade on harm reduction and e-cigarettes has essentially reached a stalemate."[63]

The extent to which the use of ENDS as a harm reduction approach is promoted varies. In the literature, for instance, Goniewicz and colleagues found ENDS to contain 9–450 times fewer potentially toxic compounds than combustible cigarettes, and indicated that the "use of e-cigarettes as a harm reduction strategy among cigarette smokers who are unable to quit warrants further study."[64] One of the US studies went further, stating that ENDS "show tremendous promise in the fight against tobacco-related morbidity and mortality" and finding the marketing ban promoted by numerous organizations and the Food and Drug Administration "unfortunate" in light of the review of the evidence.[65]

The United Kingdom (in particular England) appears to be the only country where, in recent years, public bodies have largely embraced ENDS as a tool to promote smoking cessation, as seen in the recommendations made by several national institutions.[66] While it is generally acknowledged that ENDS products do not work for everyone, Public Health England (PHE) cautiously concluded in 2018 that "evidence suggests that e-cigarettes have contributed tens of thousands of additional quitters in England."[67] In this context, ENDS are a tool for both cessation and conversion to a less dangerous substitute product. They substitute nicotine consumption via combustible cigarettes with nicotine consumption via ENDS, which are generally considered less dangerous to health than combustible cigarettes. Yet at the same time, they are a cessation tool because, if successfully substituted, they keep people from using combustible cigarettes. Notably, there appear to be no studies that analyze the use of ENDS

---

[62] Kozlowski, Abrams (n 56) 5.

[63] S. Gottlieb, "Remarks by Dr. Gottlieb on the Regulation of Nicotine" (Public Discussion on The Regulation of Nicotine, Baltimore, October 19, 2017) https://fda.gov/newsevents/speeches/ucm581314.htm accessed October 31, 2018.

[64] Goniewicz et al, "Levels of Selected Carcinogens and Toxicants in Vapour from Electronic Cigarettes" (2014) 23 Tob Control 113.

[65] Cahn, Siegel (n 55).

[66] Tobacco Advisory Group of the Royal College of Physicians, *Nicotine Without Smoke* (Working Party Report 2016) 130–1 http://rcplondon.ac.uk/projects/outputs/nicotine-without-smoke-tobacco-harm-reduction-0; "Promote E-Cigarettes Widely as Substitute for Smoking Says New RCP Report" (*RCP*, April 28, 2016) http://rcplondon.ac.uk/news/promote-e-cigarettes-widely-substitute-smoking-says-new-rcp-report; A. McNeill et al, *E-Cigarettes* (Public Health England Report 2015) 45 https://bit.ly/2lnx6en all accessed 31 October 2018.

[67] McNeill et al, *Evidence Review of E-Cigarettes and Heated Tobacco Products 2018* (n 2).

and total nicotine cessation. In this context, ENDS products are hence not a classical abstinence tool in the same way that NRTs can be.

By contrast, the World Health Organization (WHO) finds that the evidence on ENDS as a smoking cessation aid is "scant and of low certainty, making it difficult to draw credible inferences,"[68] and has therefore paid little attention to the potential role of ENDS in harm reduction. The US Surgeon General's report likewise found the current evidence to be insufficient in terms of the ability to determine whether ENDS may play a role in harm reduction.[69]

Taking a harm reduction approach necessarily requires one to consider dependence as a disease and to view substance users as patients, or individuals in need of medical (including mental) care. Nicotine can clearly be understood as a psychoactive substance. Hence, if one assumes that ENDS are less harmful than combustible cigarettes and that the use of ENDS may consequently reduce the harm associated with combustible cigarette use, then ENDS should be understood as a harm reduction tool. In that case, the human rights framework applicable to harm reduction (as initially developed to deal with illicit drugs) also applies to ENDS.

4.1 Access to Harm Reduction Programs under the Right to Health

Art. 12 ICESCR provides various grounds upon which governments have to ensure access to harm reduction programs. Primarily, Art. 12.2(d) ICESCR requires governments to ensure access to health facilities, goods, and services. While the CESCR requires governments to ensure health facilities, goods, and services generally, rehabilitative health is referred to specifically in this context. Indeed, the CESCR has interpreted Art. 12.2(d) ICESCR as including rehabilitative health services and education.[70] In addition, the CRC emphasizes the importance of harm reduction strategies.[71] The former UN Special Rapporteur on the Right to the Highest Attainable Standard of Health, Paul Hunt, stated in 2008 that states are "obliged to have an effective, national, comprehensive harm reduction policy and plan, [which] delivers essential harm reduction services."[72]

---

68 WHO, *Electronic Nicotine Delivery Systems and Electronic Non-Nicotine Delivery Systems (ENDS/ENNDS)* (n 2).

69 US Department of Health and Human Services (n 28) 11.

70 CESCR GC 14 (n 17) para 17.

71 CRC Committee GC 15 (n 50) para 66.

72 P. Hunt, "Human Rights, Health, and Harm Reduction" (IHRA's 19th International Conference, Barcelona, May 11, 2008) https://bit.ly/2nv8RMf accessed October 31, 2018.

In the case of tobacco control, NRT products such as nicotine patches, gum, or mouth spray are generally considered products with a harm reduction and rehabilitative purpose.[73] Should the use of ENDS be found to have a similar replacement or cessation effect (even in the event that it does not lead to absolute nicotine abstinence because of the broad definition of harm reduction), their availability would also fall within the scope of this obligation.

In addition, governments have to ensure access to essential medicines in light of the right to health. The CESCR Committee refers to the WHO List of Essential Medicines in defining which medicines are considered essential within the scope of the right to health. Some forms of NRT are included in this list.[74] The latter inclusion in particular provides an important benchmark in defining a regulatory approach to ENDS, because access to medicines is considered a priority (or "core") obligation under the right to health.[75] In general, the right to health and its related obligations are subject to progressive realization.[76] As it is impossible for governments to realize all conditions of the right to health overnight, they should allocate and maximize all available financial and human resources toward fulfillment of the right to health, which they have an independent obligation to do "as expeditiously and effectively as possible."[77] The CESCR holds that the steps governments must take should be "deliberate, concrete and targeted as clearly as possible towards meeting the obligations recognized in the [ICESCR]."[78] At the same time, in order to make sure that the rights included in the ICESCR are not void, some parts of the right are considered so important that their realization should be a priority.[79]

---

[73] Nicotine has been on the pharmaceutical market since 1978 for tobacco dependence: N. Gomez-Coronado et al, "Current and Emerging Pharmacotherapies for Cessation of Tobacco Smoking" (2017) 38 Pharmacotherapy 235.

[74] WHO, "WHO Model List of Essential Medicines" (WHO, 2017) https://who.int/medicines/publications/essentialmedicines/en/ accessed October 31, 2018.

[75] CESCR GC 14 (n 17) para 43.

[76] Art. 2.1 ICESCR.

[77] CESCR GC 14 (n 17) para 31.

[78] Art. 2(1) ICESCR; CESCR GC 3, para 2.

[79] CESCR GC 14 (n 17) para 10.

In this respect, the CESCR has also established that adequate realization of the right to health implies that all health facilities, goods, and services—hence including rehabilitative services – should be:

(a) available in sufficient quantity in a country;
(b) physically and economically accessible on a non-discriminatory basis and with access to due information;
(c) culturally acceptable; and
(d) of sound scientific quality.[80]

Viewing ENDS as a harm reduction tool and thus as a rehabilitative service requires governments to ensure that their use conforms to the necessary standards of availability, accessibility, acceptability, and quality of health care (the AAAQ standard of health care).[81] According to this line of reasoning, states would be in violation of the obligation to respect the right to health if they were to impose a complete prohibition on the sale, possession, or use of ENDS and not make an exception for harm reduction purposes. The question therefore arises as to how strictly ENDS should be regulated in a country. However, the aforementioned grounds do not yet set any standard as to how international human rights law would limit the regulatory freedom of governments with respect to ENDS.

4.2 Different Regulatory Approaches under the Right to Health

As human rights law often includes open norms, it does not lay down a specific or explicit standard on the nature, scope, and level of regulation of ENDS. Analogous interpretations also fail to set out a clear standard; hence, different regulatory approaches seem possible under the right to health.

For example, methadone is an illicit drug under the Single Convention on Narcotic Drugs.[82] As an opioid substitute medicine for heroin dependence, methadone is also a prescription medicine in some domestic legal orders and therewith subject to advanced international and domestic regulatory control to ensure its medical availability.[83] Notably, within the framework of the right to health, access to methadone treatment is considered a core obligation subject to priority realization, as it appears on the essential medicines list of the WHO and thus should be available in health systems on the basis of the

---

80 Ibid at para 12.b.

81 Ibid para 12.a–d. See also WHO, "Fact Sheet–The Right to Health" (n 53) 2.

82 Schedule I of the Single Convention on Narcotic Drugs, 1961, as amended (adopted August 9, 1961, entered into force August 7, 1975) 976 UNTS 105.

83 On the implications of those regulations on access to care, see Gispen (n 14).

right to health.[84] Nevertheless, whereas methadone is subject to rigorous regulation, NRT products are available both over the counter and on prescription: Champix, for example, is available only on prescription,[85] while NRT products such as nicotine patches, gum, and inhalers are available over the counter as well as on prescription.[86]

It should be noted that harm reduction tools presented with health claims fall under the general legal measures concerning medicinal goods. These include, for instance, the European Union (EU) Directives on Medicinal Products (MPD) and on Medical Devices (MDD).[87] Hence substances and devices falling within their scope require marketing authorization by the designated national medicine regulatory agencies or the European Medicines Agency in order to be allowed onto the pharmaceutical market.[88] As a result, NRT access is also subject to different regulatory models.[89] In the Tobacco Products Directive, the EU lays down standards for ENDS, but it excludes from that Directive's scope those ENDS products encompassed by the MPD and MDD—that is those making health claims—as transposed in Member State legislation.[90] In the Netherlands, for example, general ENDS regulations are not applicable to those products that are registered as medicinal products and have received marketing approval by the Medicines Evaluation Board of the Netherlands.[91] Similarly, in New Zealand nicotine is a restricted substance and selling it while making a therapeutic claim requires prior marketing approval.[92]

---

84 Art. 12.2(d) ICESCR; CESCR GC 14 (n 17) para 43.

85 "Highlights of Prescribing Information" (Pfizer, June 2018) https://bit.ly/2fg0odU; "Stop Smoking Treatments" (*NHS*, July 19, 2016) https://bit.ly/2JkyUzC both accessed October 31, 2018.

86 See for example "Nicorette Invisi Pleister" (*College ter Beoordeling van Geneesmiddelen*, March 7, 2013) https://bit.ly/2MiyRsk accessed October 31, 2018.

87 Art. 1.2(a)–(b) Directive 2001/83/EC on the Community Code Relating to Medicinal Products for Human Use [2001] OJ L311/67; Art. 1.2(a) Directive 93/42/EEC Concerning Medical Devices [1993] OJ L169/1.

88 See Title III Directive 2001/83/EC for the marketing authorization requirements in respect to medicinal products in the EU (ibid).

89 Whether harm reduction tools falling under the EU Medicinal Directives, such as NRT, require prescription is determined by Arts 70–72 Directive 2001/83/EC (ibid).

90 Art. 20.1 Directive 2014/40/EU on the Approximation of the Laws, Regulations and Administrative Provisions of the Member States concerning the Manufacture, Presentation and Sale of Tobacco [2014] OJ L127/1. It is noteworthy that the requirements laid down in the Tobacco Product Directive, for example in relation to marketing and nicotine concentration, do not apply to those falling under the MPD or MDD: Art 20.1. For additional details, see Chapters 7 and 8 in this volume.

91 "Regels voor de e-sigaret" [Regulations for the E-cigarette] (*Rijksoverheid*) https://bit.ly/2MBPHPH accessed October 31, 2018.

92 "Vaping, Smokeless, including Heated Tobacco" (Ministry of Health, June 6, 2018) https://bit.ly/2ryvLov accessed October 31, 2018.

Although regulatory approaches differ, it seems it is generally the intention of the producer that determines the type of regulation applicable to ENDS: is the product accompanied by a therapeutic claim or not? If the purpose is therapeutic, which is the case for those products making harm reduction claims, general medicine marketing authorization rules apply.

One could also frame regulatory issues from the perspective of the right to health and the AAAQ standard of health care. Classifying ENDS within the scope of the right to health as a rehabilitative service requires the product to conform to the AAAQ standard of health care. This means that such ENDS products must be "scientifically and medically appropriate and of good quality";[93] medicine marketing approval regulations undoubtedly contribute to this.

Finally, if one understands ENDS as a harm reduction tool then, based on human rights law, governments should both provide access to impartial information on ENDS, actively discourage (combustible) tobacco use and encourage replacement therapies.[94] This obligation is in line with the general health-related information obligations elaborated in section 3.3 of this chapter. As has been pointed out by Carl Phillips, discouraging a smoker from using a less harmful alternative "is more likely to kill him than it is to save him," and is thereby in opposition to promoting the individual's right to health.[95]

4.3 Protection against Secondhand (Tobacco) Smoke and the Right to Health

In contrast to the earlier reflections in section 3.2 concerning environmental health protection and harm caused by ENDS via the exhalation of vapor, it is now important to consider the potential for ENDS to assist in reducing the negative health impacts of secondhand smoke caused by combustible cigarettes. Protection against secondhand smoke is one of the main drivers behind international and domestic tobacco control efforts, as the negative health impact is significant. The WHO estimates that about 890,000 people die each year because of diseases caused by exposure to tobacco smoke.[96] If ENDS replace combustible cigarettes, they could thereby reduce secondhand smoke exposure and protect the health of non-users. Nevertheless, it should be reiterated that, as indicated in section 3.2, research demonstrates that (indoor)

---

[93] CESCR GC 14 (n 17) para 12.d.

[94] Ibid paras 15 and 17.

[95] C.V. Phillips, "Debunking the Claim that Abstinence is Usually Healthier for Smokers than Switching to Low-Risk Alternative, and Other Observations About Anti-Tobacco-Harm-Reduction Arguments" (2009) 6 Harm Reduct J 9.

[96] WHO, "Tobacco" (WHO, March 9, 2018) https://bit.ly/2xr7hCP accessed October 31, 2018.

air quality may be reduced because of ENDS use. As argued in that section, if ENDS themselves pose any risk of effects from secondhand vapor, more invasive policies limiting exposure to ENDS vapor, similar to those found in traditional tobacco control policies, would be required to ensure compliance with a state's obligation to protect the right to health. This is so even if the risk, or harm, is found to be lower than that associated with combustible cigarettes.

5. E-CIGARETTES AS A GATEWAY PRODUCT

Another important issue to contemplate when considering the human rights implications of ENDS regulation is how these nicotine products may be harmful to children. The present section will assess the scenario of ENDS' potential to act as a gateway to the use of combustible cigarettes, and the implications that can be derived therefrom.

The gateway hypothesis is a theory founded by Eric Kandel and Denise Kandel and is used to describe "a developmental process of involvement in drugs in the general population in which certain drugs serve as a gateway for the use of other substances in a specific temporal sequence."[97] For the purposes of ENDS, this chapter applies the gateway theory as a possible link between ENDS use and the likelihood of combustible cigarette use, particularly in children.

In the US, a 2018 report by the National Academies of Sciences, Engineering, and Medicine indicated that there "is substantial evidence that e-cigarette use increases risk of ever using combustible tobacco cigarettes among youth and young adults."[98] This is in line with the findings of a 2017 systematic review and meta-analysis which found that ENDS use increased the risk of both initiation and current use of combustible cigarettes in children and young adults.[99] Chapman, Bareham, and Maziak hold that ENDS are more attractive to youth in light of their "perceived lower health risks, attractive flavors, lower price, inconspicuous use, higher acceptance among peers and others."[100] They allege that this attractiveness familiarizes youth with nicotine and increases the

---

[97] E. Kandel, D. Kandel, "The Gateway Hypothesis of Substance Abuse" (2015) 104 Acta Pædiatrica 130.

[98] Stratton, Kwan, Eaton (n 2) 416.

[99] S. Soneji et al, "Association between Initial Use of E-Cigarettes and Subsequent Cigarette Smoking Among Adolescents and Young Adults" (2017) 171 Jama Pediatrics 788. On the correlation between the use of ENDS and combustible cigarette uptake by adolescents, see also L.D. Makadia et al, "Tobacco Use and Smoke Exposure in Children" (2017) 17 Curr Allergy Asthma Rep 2.

[100] S. Chapman, D. Bareham, W. Maziak, "The Gateway Effect of E-Cigarettes" (2018) Nicotine Tob Res 1.

likelihood of combustible cigarette use.[101] An additional possible reaction by children, which Faletau and colleagues put forward as one that could "undermine [tobacco] de-normalization strategies," is to perceive ENDS as the same as combustible cigarettes.[102]

Other scholars are skeptical about the gateway effect. Cahn and Berg, for instance, note that studies "that allow for a direct determination of a causal gateway effect of vaping on smoking are notoriously difficult to undertake."[103] A 2018 study found "no evidence that e-cigarettes increase nicotine dependence," which Seyla and colleagues interpreted as raising "doubts about concerns that e-cigarettes introduce a risk for later cigarette use via nicotine dependence."[104] In the UK, PHE does not endorse the gateway hypothesis,[105] and found that in fact "e-cigarettes are attracting very few young people who have never smoked into regular use."[106]

In light of the specific concerns regarding children's health that have arisen with the introduction of ENDS, the remainder of this section seeks to analyze the applicable human rights framework with respect to the potential gateway effect. While acknowledging that the gateway question is still under debate, this analysis will start from the assumption that ENDS may indeed pose risks to child health and development. By doing so, it may serve to inform policy considerations in the event that a gateway effect is indeed found to exist.

5.1 Child Health and Development in the CRC as Relevant to Tobacco Control

Even though children fall within the general remit of human rights law, the CRC provides for a child-specific interpretation and application of human rights. Based on the CRC, State Parties have a range of obligations to protect children from tobacco and other harmful substances.

---

[101] Ibid.

[102] J. Faletau et al, "Looks Like Smoking, Is It Smoking? Children's Perceptions of Cigarette-Like Nicotine Delivery Systems, Smoking and Cessation" (2013) 10 Harm Reduct J 4.

[103] Z. Cahn, C.J. Berg, "Commentary on Seyla et al. (2018)" (2018) 113 Addiction 334. See also discussion in Chapter 3 in this volume.

[104] A. Seyla et al, "Evaluating the Mutual Pathways among Electronic Cigarette Use, Conventional Smoking and Nicotine Dependence" (2018) 113 Addiction 325.

[105] Royal Society for Public Health, "New PHE Review Strengthens Consensus on Harm Reduction Role of E-Cigarettes" (Royal Society for Public Health, February 6, 2018) https://bit.ly/2nvgEtt accessed October 31, 2018.

[106] McNeill et al, *Evidence Review of E-Cigarettes and Heated Tobacco Products 2018* (n 2) 75.

In analyzing the relevant child rights framework, it is important to note that research shows that children's (ill-)health and (under)development is cumulative and transgenerational, also in relation to tobacco-related harm.[107] The CRC Committee has also acknowledged that (ill-)health is cumulative.[108] Previous analyses have demonstrated that in order to ensure the healthy development of children, State Parties to the CRC should take preventive measures to ensure prenatal care as well as healthy and smoke-free environments, and to provide adequate access to information for adolescents—in particular to empower them to make healthy life choices.[109] In addition, across all stages of (child) development and in all sectors of the tobacco supply chain, the CRC requires states to regulate the tobacco industry such that its business operations do not violate the rights of children.[110] The CRC thus necessarily invokes a baseline of obligations to regulate ENDS, similar to those obligations addressed in section 3. Moreover, it may provide for an additional level of protection if ENDS are indeed considered gateway products. The issue whether ENDS are a gateway to combustible cigarettes or a device containing harmful substances as such is not immediately important here. This is because, as also seen in the case of harmful substances addressed under the general human rights framework in section 3, harmful substances and tobacco are often referred to in the same way by human rights monitoring bodies.

Although a range of rights may be relevant across the tobacco supply chain to address different aspects of child health and development, several rights are particularly important in regulating ENDS as possible gateway products. These rights include the best interests of the child (Art. 3 CRC); the right to life, survival, and development (Art. 6 CRC); the right to health (Art. 24 CRC); and the right to information (Art. 17 CRC).[111] The right to be heard and the notion of evolving capacities (Art. 12 CRC) are important as well.

Finally, as a general observation it should be noted that the above-mentioned rights are in principle relevant for those up to the age of 18, despite the fact that adolescence, for instance, is generally considered to include a wider group of

---

[107] See for example W. Hofhuis, J.C. de Jongste, P.J.F.M. Merkus, "Adverse Health Effects of Prenatal and Postnatal Tobacco Smoke Exposure on Children" (2003) 88 Arch Dis Child 1086; Been et al (n 52); E.M. Hollams, "Persistent Effects of Maternal Smoking During Pregnancy on Lung Function and Asthma in Adolescents" (2014) 189 Am J Respir Crit Care Med 401; Gispen, Toebes (n 23).

[108] CRC Committee GC 15 (n 50) para 20.

[109] See Gispen, Toebes (n 23).

[110] Ibid.

[111] Gispen and Toebes (n 23) identify a range of rights included in the CRC that are relevant to tobacco control and child health. They provide for additional analysis into the nature and scope of these rights as relevant to the different aspects of tobacco harm along various stages of child development.

youth.[112] One would assume that if the risks are similar for 17 and 19 year olds, then the rights framework would be similar; however, in light of the maximum age limit set in Art. 1 CRC (that is, 18 years of age) this is not the case. Hence, the analysis below is only applicable to children up to the age of 18 despite the seemingly broader potential of the normative reasoning portrayed.[113]

5.2 Best Interests of the Child and the Right to Life, Survival and Development

As included in Art. 3 CRC, states should use the best interests of the child (BIC) as a primary consideration in "all actions concerning children."[114] According to the CRC Committee, which monitors implementation of the CRC, Art. 3 is one of the four general provisions of the Convention.[115] The CRC Committee holds that the BIC norm should be applied on a case by case basis and is applicable both to individual circumstances and to groups of children.[116] State Parties should thus also take the BIC norm into account in their social, health and economic policies.[117] Hence, in the same way that the BIC norm is relevant to tobacco control policies, it is also a determinative factor in regulating ENDS.[118] In adopting new laws and policies, State Parties should carry out an impact assessment to determine how proposed norms may impact the interests of children.[119]

The BIC norm does not set out clear or defined standards in relation to specific factors harmful to health and development. Nevertheless, it does require

---

[112] See for example the WHO's reference to adolescence as occurring between the ages of 10 and 19: WHO, "Adolescents: Health Risks and Solutions" (WHO, February 5, 2018) https://bit.ly/2kDRyHw accessed October 31, 2018. There is no fixed definition of adolescence; it is merely important here that the age limit of 18 is somewhat artificial when considering health and developmental factors.

[113] Gispen, Toebes (n 23).

[114] Art. 3 CRC (n 9).

[115] The other general provisions include Art. 2 CRC (non-discrimination), Art. 6 (right to life, survival, and development) and Art. 12 CRC (the right to be heard/expression of views). CRC Committee, "General Comment No 5" (November 27, 2003) UN Doc CRC/GC/2003/5 (CRC Committee GC 5) para 12.

[116] CRC "General Comment No 14" (May 29, 2013) UN Doc CRC/C/GC/14 paras 19. 32.

[117] Ibid para 6.c. See also M.E.C. Gispen, M. Hesselman, B. Toebes "De rol en potentie van het internationaal recht in het reguleren van ongezond gedrag" [The role and potential of international law in regulating unhealthy behaviour] in A. Keirse et al, *Ongezond en (on)geoorloofd* (Boom Juridisch 2018); Gispen, Toebes (n 23).

[118] On the BIC norm and tobacco control, see, *inter alia*, Gispen, Hesselman, Toebes (n 117) and Gispen, Toebes (n 23).

[119] CRC Committee GC 14 (n 116) para 35.

governments to create "an environment that respects human dignity and ensures the holistic development of every child."[120] Addressing cumulative and transgenerational (ill-)health across a child's life course by taking preventive health measures and regulating behavioral risk factors such as tobacco use fits squarely into the BIC obligation and is linked to Art. 6 CRC.[121]

Art. 6 CRC includes the right to life, survival, and development. The CRC Committee notes in this regard that preventable diseases remain an obstacle to realizing rights in early childhood.[122] Although the gateway hypothesis seems most relevant for youth, there might also be a link to early childhood and even prenatal care in light of the cumulative and transgenerational nature of health. Research shows, for instance, that children of smoking parents/caretakers are more likely to take up smoking themselves.[123] Similarly, as addressed by van der Eijk and colleagues, there is research showing that nicotine exposure during pregnancy may hamper a child's development in general, and a cautious approach is necessary in this context.[124]

Finally, if ENDS are indeed a gateway product in one way or another (that is, not necessarily for youth exclusively, but where young children also have a higher chance of taking up vaping and smoking), then governments should certainly regulate ENDS in order to ensure the holistic development of children in light of Arts 3 and 6 CRC. It is very likely that such regulation would model general tobacco control efforts because of the gateway hypothesis and because the CRC Committee reinforces the links between the CRC framework and the FCTC.[125]

5.3 Right to Health, Information, and Participation in Decision-making

Art. 24 CRC is the child-specific interpretation of the right to health included in Art. 12 ICESCR. Giving specific meaning to Art. 24 CRC, the CRC Committee has articulated that states should protect children from tobacco and other harmful substances.[126] In particular, State Parties should regulate the

---

120 Ibid para 42.

121 See Gispen, Toebes (n 23). See also Toebes et al (n 16).

122 CRC Committee, "General Comment No 7" (September 20, 2006) UN Doc CRC/C/GC/7/Rev.1 para 10. See also Gispen, Toebes (n 23).

123 See for example K.G. Hill et al, "Family Influences on the Risk of Daily Smoking Initiation" (205) 37 J Adolesc Health 202; Gispen, Toebes (n 23).

124 Van der Eijk et al, "E-Cigarette Use in Pregnancy" (n 4) 1285–7.

125 CRC Committee GC 15 (n 50) para 44 and 66.

126 Ibid. See also, on adolescent health and access to health-related information and tobacco control, Gispen, Toebes (n 23).

advertising and sale of substances harmful to children's health, as well as the promotion of these substances "in places where children congregate" and in media accessed by children.[127] The CRC Committee has also highlighted the due diligence responsibilities of private actors with respect to children, and requires governments to regulate industries so that their operations no longer harm the rights of children, including in the area of health.[128] In doing so, the CRC Committee has also specifically referred to private actors themselves and recommended that companies refrain from advertising, marketing, and selling "tobacco and other toxic substances" to children.[129]

The rights to health and to information of Art. 17 CRC are also intertwined with respect to children. Indeed, as emphasized in Art. 17 CRC, Art. 24.2(e) CRC also reiterates the child's right to access to information. The CRC Committee has interpreted this to encompass health-related information and education,[130] including "the dangers of alcohol, tobacco and psychoactive substance use."[131]

Access to information to make well informed lifestyle choices also fits directly within the notion of evolving capacities and the right to be heard found in Art. 12 CRC. The concepts of evolving capacities and the right to be heard embody the importance of children participating in decision-making that affects them. The level of their involvement and the status of their views depends on their incremental development.[132] If youth are particularly vulnerable to the gateway effect, it is essential that their views are taken into consideration when regulating ENDS in light of Art. 12 CRC. Research shows that adolescents generally welcome tobacco control measures, but that they could be more effective if the factors behind such support are taken into account.[133]

The long embedded strategies of the tobacco industry in which children are specifically targeted as the next generation of smokers are well documented.[134] Based on this extensive experience and the negative consequences thereof, states are increasingly well prepared in their capacity to make efforts to prevent these practices from materializing in the first place. If it is found that ENDS may serve as a gateway to tobacco use, and if states are under

---

[127] CRC Committee GC 15 (n 50) para 65.

[128] Ibid para 80.

[129] Ibid para 81.

[130] Ibid para 58.

[131] Ibid para 59.

[132] G. Lansdown, *Evolving Capacities of the Child* (UNICEF 2005) 3–5.

[133] M. Schreuders et al, "To What Extent and Why Adolescents Do or Do Not Support Future Tobacco Control Measures" (2017) Tob Control doi:10.1136/tobaccocontrol-2017-053770. This is also briefly addressed in Gispen, Toebes (n 23).

[134] L. Bach, "Tobacco Company Marketing to Kids" (Tobacco Free Kids, 2018) https://bit.ly/2OyjU31 accessed October 31, 2018.

the obligation to protect children from tobacco, it can be deduced that states should equally protect children from ENDS. This would also give rise to the recommendation that states take similar measures in terms of the marketing of ENDS as they should in respect to tobacco products. As the Committee also addressed private actors, its recommendations on corporate responsibilities are particularly relevant to the ENDS industry. If ENDS may cause harm to children—and particularly if they may act as a gateway to tobacco use—ENDS manufacturers and suppliers should refrain from directing their marketing activities at children and should make these products less attractive to children, for example with respect to e-liquid flavoring. States should likewise enact legislation to enforce these responsibilities.

6. CONCLUSIONS AND RECOMMENDATIONS

ENDS regulatory approaches differ widely from country to country, and both international and regional laws have so far failed to set clear and consistent legal standards as to their regulation. This chapter has aimed to demonstrate the importance of taking into account human rights law as an overarching set of rights and obligations when demarcating governments' regulatory freedom to regulate ENDS. Human rights are indeed of great importance and of immediate relevance to this debate. They have proven essential and of great use both in tobacco control specifically and in broader policy areas more generally. Human rights law often includes open norms and is less specific than the minimum requirements included in the FCTC. However, this chapter demonstrates that this body of law provides an important framework to guide states in their domestic approaches to ENDS regulation. In light of the current scientific and policy discussions on the effects of ENDS, this chapter has elaborated three interrelated human rights frameworks: from the perspective of ENDS as devices containing harmful substances; that of ENDS as harm reduction tools; and that of ENDS as gateway products.

First, regardless of whether ENDS may indeed serve as successful harm reduction tools or gateway products, research demonstrates that they are nevertheless devices containing harmful substances, use of and exposure to which may pose certain health risks. Based on the right to health and the right to information, governments are bound to discourage the use of harmful substances (and thus necessarily also those devices that contain harmful substances) and regulate industries that produce these products. More specifically, states should:

- implement information campaigns about the use of ENDS (also in comparison to other products);
- discourage the production, marketing, and consumption of ENDS;

- improve product safety standards to ensure consumer protection; and
- limit vapor exposure in public spaces.

Precisely because there is no situation in which the use of ENDS is entirely safe, regulations concerning the products' harmful nature can be considered the baseline.[135] As was mentioned in the introduction to the chapter, it may however be necessary to depart from this baseline of regulation in light of research on ENDS' ability to serve as harm reduction tools and/or gateway products.

In relation to harm reduction, this chapter has shown that, if marketed with a therapeutic aim, ENDS as harm reduction tools should be regulated to conform to medicine regulation laws. Considering ENDS as part of a harm reduction strategy (which can include both cessation and replacement) is a general matter of providing access to health facilities, goods and services; ensuring rehabilitative care within this context; and even providing access to essential medicines, as has been done with NRT. Within the context of the right to health, ENDS must then be available, accessible, acceptable, and compliant with the corresponding rules on (product) quality if used for medical purposes. At the same time, as in the case of harmful substances, governments should actively inform individuals about the harmful effects of both combustible cigarettes and ENDS in proportion to their respective health impacts.

As a result, on the one hand governments must regulate ENDS on the grounds that they are devices containing harmful substances. Yet at the same time, if the products may serve a harm reduction purpose, governments should ensure their availability for medical purposes (if the producer aims to place its product on the market with an explicit therapeutic aim). This may seem contradictory at the policy level—notably since ENDS may assist with harm reduction precisely because they are subject to milder regulation than combustible cigarettes (for example, flavors are often allowed) and are widely available.

---

[135] It is not suggested here that this baseline reflects the minimum core of the rights analyzed. Rather, it reflects the idea that in regulating ENDS governments must adopt a level of control relative to its harmfulness in light of human rights principles. Acknowledging that there is no safe use of ENDS hence necessarily makes this level of protection the minimum threshold or baseline below which governments cannot fall. This is different from minimum core human rights, which requires governments to respect, protect, and fulfill certain core or basic elements of a human right. The minimum core is thus related to how the different aspects of a right are prioritized in rights realization while the idea of the baseline introduced in this piece specifically focuses on the regulatory aspects of the substance at hand. On minimum core rights protection see CESCR, "General Comment No 3" (December 14, 1990) UN Doc E/1991/23; I. Leijten, *Core Socio-Economic Rights and the European Court of Human Rights* (Cambridge University Press 2018).

There is no one size fits all approach to regulating harm reduction strategies. As also shown in this chapter, methadone for opioid substitute treatment is subject to stringent regulations making it much more complex to prescribe and use than NRT products, which are available both on prescription and over the counter. A staged, incremental process may also be applicable to ENDS, striking a balance between general regulation (because it is a harmful product) and the need to ensure access for medical (rehabilitative) purposes in a safe manner.[136] The notion of balancing and the principle of proportionality may be guiding mechanisms in this context, although they have not been scrutinized within the scope of this chapter.

A possible human rights-based regulatory approach becomes even more complex if ENDS are indeed gateway products. Children's rights as included in the CRC provide for a comprehensive approach to tobacco control, which may well be extended to cover ENDS if ENDS use increases the likelihood of combustible tobacco use. Based on the CRC, governments should protect and promote the interests, health, and development of children by:

- applying the BIC norm in domestic law and policy discussions and conducting impact assessments on how ENDS regulations may affect the interests of children and on whether the proposed measures sufficiently take into account the best interests of children;
- implementing preventive health care, including in relation to tobacco and other substances harmful to the health, well-being, and development of children;
- regulating tobacco and other harmful substances in places where children congregate and in media channels;
- protecting children from indoor/outdoor air pollution, similarly as with tobacco;
- discouraging the use of tobacco and other harmful substances and providing cessation support to those who need it;
- regulating the tobacco and ENDS industries such that their business activities do not harm the rights of children, notably by regulating the marketing and advertisement of these products;
- taking a precautious approach in the absence of clear evidence on the best interests of the child, and acknowledging that (ill-)health and (ill-)development are cumulative and transgenerational.[137]

---

[136] For instance, in some countries certain medicines are only available over the counter in specified locations (for example pharmacies), as seen in the Netherlands: Art. 56 Medicines Act [2007].

[137] The chapter refers to a precautious approach instead of the "precautionary principle" as such because the latter has not been extensively addressed in this chapter.

Some of these approaches seeking to avoid the gateway effect may also lead to tensions at a policy level. In this context, it should be taken into consideration that the BIC norm is considered a cornerstone of the CRC. Although it is acknowledged that it is not the single overriding factor, the importance of the BIC norm carries substantial normative weight, and therefore concerns regarding children should be a leading concern in regulating ENDS.

6. A ban on electronic nicotine delivery systems: step one in the WTO discrimination analysis

Marina Foltea and Bryan Mercurio

1. INTRODUCTION

This chapter discusses the law of the World Trade Organization (WTO) as it applies to bans on electronic nicotine delivery systems (ENDS), that is, products which deliver nicotine through inhalation of vapor. As discussed in detail below, the most common examples of ENDS are various types of electronic cigarettes (e-cigarettes).[1] Given the novelty of ENDS, consumer perceptions have been based on a constant flow of flawed and/or erroneous information regarding the products. Governments have responded to the new products, but they have done so in a stilted and incoherent manner. While some countries regulate ENDS in the same way as traditional tobacco products, others classify them as medicinal products or create a *sui generis* category subject to unique rules. There are also countries that simply prohibit their sale and possession—directly or indirectly—on a precautionary basis.[2] The World Health Organization (WHO) has not yet developed and maintained a clear position on ENDS, but does endorse an outright ban as one of the regulatory options available to State Parties of the Framework Convention on Tobacco Control (FCTC).[3]

1 Note that the authors of this chapter use the terms "ENDS" and "e-cigarettes" interchangeably.

2 For a more detailed analysis of various approaches taken by states, see Chapters 7 to 11 in this volume.

3 FCTC COP, *Decision: Electronic nicotine delivery systems and electronic non-nicotine delivery systems*, FCTC/COP6(9) October 18, 2014 (Conference of the Parties to the WHO Framework Convention on Tobacco Control Sixth Session, Moscow, Russian Federation, October 13–18, 2014). A more detailed discussion of the WHO approach can be found in Chapter 4 of this volume.

The sale of all types of e-cigarettes is banned in at least 27 countries,[4] and a further eight countries prohibit the sale of e-cigarettes containing nicotine (Australia, Canada, Costa Rica, Jamaica, Japan, Malaysia, Mexico, and Switzerland).[5] Other countries, including heavily populated nations such as India, are also deliberating over the introduction of a sales ban on ENDS.[6] Of these countries, in addition to e-cigarettes, electronically heated tobacco products (EHTPs) are banned in Brazil, Panama, New Zealand, Taiwan, Thailand, and Norway. A few of these countries, however, are considering changes to their regulations on e-cigarettes—for example, Australia and Switzerland—while New Zealand has recently lifted its ban and now promotes ENDS as a matter of public health.[7]

From an international trade perspective, a complete sales ban on ENDS is far more restrictive than the regime currently applied to conventional cigarettes, which are highly regulated but freely commercialized, and simply treated as all other goods under the rules of international trade law. As the treatment of ENDS and conventional cigarettes widely differs between countries, the question which arises is whether a complete ban is discriminatory under WTO law. This question is quite topical, as more governments are considering legislation in the field and the answer has important implications for the future regulation of these products. Governments contemplating a general ban must therefore carefully assess their regulatory plans against their international obligations—including those contained in the WTO agreements. In this context, this chapter examines the first essential (but not sole) step in determining discrimination under WTO law: the "likeness" between ENDS and conventional cigarettes. At the same time, this chapter leaves for future determination the discussion over whether a sales ban on ENDS would result in less favorable treatment, as well as other factors that are relevant when assessing the legality of national measures under WTO rules (for example, the availability of a justification under the general exception clause).

The chapter proceeds as follows. In order to provide the necessary context to the above question, section 2 defines ENDS in more detail and briefly

---

4 Argentina, Bahrain, Brazil, Brunei Darussalam, Cambodia, Colombia, Gambia, Greece, Jordan, Kuwait, Lebanon, Mauritius, Nepal, Nicaragua, Oman, Panama, Qatar, Saudi Arabia, Seychelles, Singapore, Suriname, Thailand, Turkey, Turkmenistan, Uganda, United Arab Emirates, and Uruguay.

5 All data sourced from Global Tobacco Control http://globaltobaccocontrol.org/e-cigarette/policy-domains accessed October 31, 2018.

6 M. Foltea, "Tough Times Ahead for Taiwan's E-cig Market" (*Trade Pacts*, 21 March 2017) https://tradepacts.com/news/tough-times-ahead-for-taiwans-e-cig-market/; S. Dey, "Govt Likely to Stub Out 'Toxic' E-Cigarettes" (*The Times of India*, August 1, 2017) https://bit.ly/2D0H93E both accessed October 31, 2018.

7 For additional details of the Australian case, see Chapter 11 in this volume.

describes the ENDS market. Section 3 introduces the concept of discrimination under WTO law. In particular, this section examines the antidiscrimination provisions enshrined in the two agreements relevant to this issue: the General Agreement on Tariffs and Trade (GATT 1994)[8] and the Agreement on Technical Barriers to Trade (TBT Agreement).[9] Section 4 introduces other relevant provisions which need to be assessed in order for a WTO panel to ultimately make findings on the legality of banning ENDS sales. Section 5 concludes and indicates further research questions.

2. DEFINING ENDS AND THE SCOPE OF THE CHAPTER; ASSESSING THE ENDS MARKET

E-cigarettes are the most common type of ENDS. This category has witnessed constant evolution: first generation "cigalikes," second generation "tank systems," and now the more successful third generation "personal vaporizers." These devices can also be classified into closed and open systems, depending mainly on the degree of control that users have over the e-liquid used in the e-cigarettes, the voltage and resistance applied to heating the e-liquid, and ventilation features.[10] One of the main features of e-cigarettes is that their use does not entail combustion of tobacco, as in the case of traditional cigarettes. The main constituents of the solution, in addition to nicotine (when nicotine is present), are propylene glycol, with or without glycerol, and flavoring agents. E-cigarette solutions and emissions can also contain other chemicals, some of them considered to be toxicants.[11] The choice of e-liquid, the user's puffing style, and the device's capacity to aerosolize the e-liquid at increasing temperatures by modulating its wattage and resistance will all determine whether the use of e-cigarettes produces a satisfactory experience to the user in terms of the speedy delivery of sufficient nicotine to mimic the sensory feel of smoking.

---

[8] General Agreement on Tariffs and Trade 1994, Marrakesh Agreement Establishing the World Trade Organization, Annex 1A (adopted April 15, 1994, entered into force January 1, 1995) 1867 UNTS 187.

[9] Agreement on Technical Barriers to Trade, Marrakesh Agreement Establishing the World Trade Organization, Annex 1A (adopted April 15, 1994, entered into force January 1, 1995) 1868 UNTS 120.

[10] WHO, *Electronic Nicotine Delivery Systems and Electronic Non-Nicotine Delivery Systems (ENDS/ENNDS)*, FCTC/COP/7/11 August 2016 (Conference of the Parties to the WHO Framework Convention on Tobacco Control, Seventh session, Delhi, India, November 7–12, 2016).

[11] WHO, "E-Cigarettes or Electronic Nicotine Delivery Systems" (Tobacco Free Initiative, March 30, 2015) www.who.int/tobacco/communications/statements/electronic_cigarettes/en/ accessed October 31, 2018.

ENDS are not to be conflated with two other categories of next generation tobacco products, neither of which is covered by this chapter. The first of these is EHTPs, a category that also delivers nicotine, in this case not from a liquid but by heating compressed tobacco leaves. The second is a cigarette that actually heats tobacco without the use of any electronic device (for example, heat may be provided by a pressed carbon tip heat source). Nor does this chapter examine the applicability of the relevant arguments and WTO obligations to another category of product—non-nicotine e-cigarettes, which are also called electronic non-nicotine delivery systems.

In 2013, the investment bank Goldman Sachs identified e-cigarettes as one of the eight emergent themes in the global economy capable of what is now commonly termed "creative destruction," representing a whole new and totally disruptive technology, offering consumers a far safer product and forcing companies to either adapt or die.[12] The ENDS market is characterized by its fast moving and dynamic environment. In such circumstances it is quite challenging to account for the size of this sector in terms of financial value, units sold, market share, or number of consumers. Some measures, such as number of units sold, are difficult to acquire owing to the absence of reporting systems, especially from independent shops and online sales. Another limitation on ENDS data is posed by the fact that some important independent sources of this information do not make a distinction in their statistics between ENDS and EHTPs, which form the vaping (or "vape") market together with ENDS.

The global size of the ENDS and vape market was estimated to amount to US $8.6 billion in 2018. North America is by far the largest ENDS market, followed by Western Europe, then Eastern Europe, Asia Pacific, and the rest of the world.[13] In the USA, the world's most mature and valuable market for e-cigarettes, it is estimated that the value of the market reached US $5.1 billion in 2018. US tobacco companies have no more than an 18–25 percent share of the ENDS market.[14]

The global e-cigarette market is segmented based on product type, flavor, distribution channel, and region. Based on product type, the market is divided into disposable, rechargeable, and modular products. As regards distribution channels, the market is categorized into specialist e-cigarette shops, online, supermarkets, tobacco shops, and others.

---

[12] R.D. Boroujerdi, "The Search for Creative Destruction" (Goldman Sachs, March 24, 2014) http://goldmansachs.com/investor-relations/financials/archived/annual-reports/2013-annual-report-files/search.pdf accessed October 31, 2018. See also Chapter 2 for an additional discussion on the disruptive technologies.

[13] H. Shapiro, *Global Tobacco: Key Findings. Part II. Vapour Products* (Euromonitor International, October 2017).

[14] Wells Fargo, *Nielsen: Tobacco "All Channel" Data 5/19*, May 29, 2018.

The e-cigarette companies, which may belong to the tobacco industry or be fully independent, either produce their own products or source them from elsewhere. The key components in both cases mostly originate (about 90 percent) from Shenzhen, China.

3. NON-DISCRIMINATION UNDER WTO LAW

General sales bans of ENDS differentiate the product from other tobacco products on the market, and therefore may be discriminatory and *prima facie* inconsistent with the relevant rules of the WTO. With its virtually universal membership (currently 164 Members), one of the key features of the WTO is that it provides a level playing field for all Members to trade across borders, irrespective of the origin of the traded goods or services. Its goal is to avoid the competitive disadvantages that producers may face as a result of protectionist or discriminatory regulations in the global market. Such measures are, at times, used to insulate domestic industries against like (meaning similar) imported products, or are applied to grant an advantage to a specific importer over others.

The determination of likeness relies on a holistic interpretation of four criteria, each of which is set out below. In the main, the analysis is primarily concerned with a determination of the existence of a competitive relationship between the two products at issue. This interpretation has been confirmed in a number of cases, including by the Appellate Body in *EC—Asbestos*, which found that "a determination of 'likeness' under Article III:4 of the GATT 1994 is, fundamentally, a determination about the nature and extent of a competitive relationship between and among products."[15] The Appellate Body emphasized that in each case all pertinent evidence, whether or not related to one of the traditional criteria of "likeness," must be examined and considered to determine whether the products are, and more importantly *could be*, in a competitive relationship in a particular marketplace.[16] Without a competitive relationship between domestic and imported product(s), the internal regulation at issue cannot be regarded as affording protection to domestic products and thus cannot be qualified as discriminatory. Therefore, the existence of a competitive relationship is a fundamental pillar of "likeness" and an essential element of the non-discrimination obligation of WTO Members.

---

[15] Appellate Body Report, *European Communities—Measures Affecting Asbestos and Products Containing Asbestos* (WT/DS135/AB/R, adopted March 12, 2011) para 99.

[16] Ibid para 103.

The case law suggests that although ENDS may present a lower risk profile than cigarettes, the two categories may nevertheless be found to be "like" under WTO law simply because they may be in commercial competition with each other. Such differing treatment may be deemed inconsistent with the WTO non-discrimination rules unless a valid GATT Art. XX justification can be invoked by a state. The remainder of this section explores the extent to which ENDS and cigarettes may be deemed to be "like" products under WTO law.

3.1 Non-discrimination under the GATT 1994

Non-discrimination is one of the central market access principles of the GATT/WTO system. This principle is underpinned by two fundamental WTO obligations: national treatment and the most favored nation principle. With respect to goods, the national treatment obligation (Art. III of the GATT 1994) requires that once the "like" imported products (in this case, ENDS) have cleared customs and the applicable tariff or duty has been collected, it must be treated not less favorably than the "like" domestic products (as argued in this chapter, that means cigarettes which are freely sold on the market).

Thus, the objective of the national treatment principle is "to protect expectations of the contracting parties as to the competitive relationship between their products and those of the other contracting parties . . . to protect current trade [and] to create the predictability needed to plan future trade."[17] This serves both to preserve fair competition on the international market and to foster the predictability necessary to plan future trade.

The relevant national treatment provision is set out in Art. III:4 of GATT 1994:

> The products of the territory of any contracting party imported into the territory of any other contracting party shall be accorded treatment no less favorable than that accorded to like products of national origin in respect of all laws, regulations and requirements affecting their internal sale, offering for sale, purchase, transportation, distribution or use.

The national treatment argument advanced here would therefore apply to the situation where there is domestic production of cigarettes in a specific market, while ENDS (of both domestic and imported origin) are generally banned from sale in that market.

---

[17] GATT Panel Report, *United States—Taxes on Petroleum and Certain Imported Substances* (June 17, 1987, GATT BISD 1988 (34th Supp.)) para 5.2.2.

The most favored nation obligation (Art. I of GATT 1994) is similar, but is concerned instead with equal treatment between "like" imports: this is where discrimination exists not between an imported and domestic product, but rather between imported products depending on their origin. This principle may apply where, for example, one market does not produce cigarettes, but sources them from another country through importation. If cigarettes are freely imported into that country, the argument is that the treatment accorded to imported cigarettes should be applied to the "like" products (a category which, as argued in this chapter, covers ENDS).

If two products are found to be "like" while they are not treated equally, and in the absence of a valid applicable general exception existing in WTO law (for example, Art. XX(b) of GATT 1994), a ban on ENDS may be regarded as being inconsistent with the relevant trade rules. Establishing "likeness" is therefore crucial in determining whether a ban or other trade restrictive measure is discriminatory. This exercise is routinely conducted in the WTO dispute settlement system and there is a solid body of case law which may be used as a reference to make this determination.

In the WTO context, "likeness" is assessed based upon four criteria derived from the case law: (i) physical properties, (ii) end use, (iii) consumers' tastes and habits, and (iv) tariff classification.[18] These criteria are briefly examined below.

3.1.1 Physical properties

It can be argued that although ENDS and conventional cigarettes are certainly not identical, depending on the category and generation discussed they share some important physical characteristics. ENDS may mimic many features of cigarettes, but they do not emit all cigarette-related chemical substances (like carbon monoxide, for example). However, depending on the category of ENDS, they may offer a similar taste and sensory experience. Some categories also physically resemble conventional cigarettes (for example, the first generation "cigalikes," although today these represent only a small share of the market).

However, while ENDS are designed to mimic conventional cigarettes in order to create a similar experience, it may be argued that there are several physical differences which distinguish the two products. Most notably, ENDS are noncombustible while conventional cigarettes are combustible. Another

---

[18] Appellate Body Report, *Japan—Taxes on Alcoholic Beverages* (WT/DS8/AB/R, WT/DS10/AB/R, WT/DS11/AB/R, adopted November 1, 1996); Appellate Body Report, *Chile—Taxes on Alcoholic Beverages* (WT/DS87/AB/R, WT/DS110/AB/R, adopted January 12, 2000); Appellate Body Reports, *Philippines—Taxes on Distilled Spirits* (WT/DS396/AB/R, WT/DS403/AB/R, adopted January 20, 2012).

important difference is the prevalence of flavorings—while numerous countries have banned the use of flavorings in conventional tobacco products, they are quite common in ENDS, with more than 7,700 e-cigarette flavors.[19] Likewise, the actual physical properties of ENDS and cigarettes differ, with the former comprising metal and liquid and the latter made of tobacco leaf and paper.

Another important issue relating to the physical properties of ENDS and conventional cigarettes is health risk. The lead case on physical properties, *EC—Asbestos*, held that health risks are part of the "like" product analysis, meaning that they can play a major role in determining the likeness of physical properties. In that case, the Appellate Body found that as a result of different structures and a different health risk profile, "physically, chrysotile asbestos and PCG fibers are very different."[20] The Appellate Body even called the carcinogenicity or toxicity of a product—that is, the health risk associated with asbestos—the "defining aspect" of physical properties.[21] Moreover, the Appellate Body stated that physical properties are a "useful indicator" of likeness that can also influence end uses, consumer attitudes, and tariff classification.[22] In this regard, the Appellate Body stated that where physical characteristics are different, there is a "high burden" on the complainant to establish that, despite the physical differences, there is a competitive relationship between the products. Thus, while health risks can be taken into account in determining physical characteristics (and their impact on the other factors), this does not detract from the preeminence of the test itself—that is, whether the products are in a competitive relationship. It should be noted, however, that in order to meet this "high burden" the competitive relationship between cigarettes and ENDS would need to be proven to be strong. This may depend on the point in time at which a WTO case challenging an ENDS ban may be launched, as this will determine the abundance or scarcity of relevant data proving a competitive relationship. The picture in this regard may look very different ten years from now.

While the WHO has publicly adopted a cautious approach to the health-related claims of e-cigarettes, current research supports the conclusion that ENDS are less harmful than conventional cigarettes.[23] However, this point could be

---

19 M. Eriksen et al, *The Tobacco Atlas* (5th ed. American Cancer Society 2015) chapter 12.

20 Appellate Body Report, *European Communities—Measures Affecting Asbestos and Products Containing Asbestos* (n 15) para 136.

21 Ibid para 151.

22 Ibid para 111.

23 S.S. Hecht et al, "Evaluation of Toxicant and Carcinogen Metabolites in the Urine of E-Cigarette Users Versus Cigarette Smokers" (2015) 17 Nicotine Tob Res

argued in a WTO dispute, as there are limited scientific studies evaluating the risks of using e-cigarettes, especially where the user also smokes conventional cigarettes at the same time.[24] Moreover, the role that e-cigarettes play in reducing smoking rates is also unclear.[25] However, according to a recent report prepared for the WHO, "in a simple product-to-product comparison most e-cigarettes are probably less, and some products may even be much less, harmful than conventional cigarettes."[26] The New Zealand Ministry of Health, in promoting e-cigarettes as a replacement for conventional tobacco products, is more to the point: "e-cigarettes are significantly less harmful than smoking tobacco."[27]

Given the similarities between the products, but also the differences outlined above, it is difficult to predict what a WTO panel/Appellate Body might find under this "likeness" criterion. What is clear is that the jurisprudence points out the importance of clearly demonstrating a competitive relationship between products that do not share many physical characteristics, which may be the case with cigarettes and ENDS.

3.1.2 End use

The end use criterion refers to "the extent to which the products are capable of serving the same or similar end-uses."[28] E-cigarettes and conventional tobacco products are all capable of performing the same function and in essence serve to deliver nicotine and contribute to the "ritual" of smoking (or, in the case of e-cigarettes, vaping). The evidence suggests that a large proportion of e-cigarette consumers formerly smoked conventional tobacco products, with some consuming the various products interchangeably.[29] This may suggest that ENDS serve a similar, if not identical, end use as conventional cigarettes

---

704; H. McRobbie et al, "Effects of Switching to Electronic Cigarettes with and without Concurrent Smoking on Exposure to Nicotine, Carbon Monoxide, and Acrolein" (2015) 8(9) Cancer Prev Rese 873. For a more detailed and up to date summary of the literature on this topic, see Chapters 2 and 3 in this volume.

[24] See C. Pisinger, "A Systematic Review of Health Effects of Electronic Cigarettes" (Document prepared for the World Health Organization, December 2015) https://bit.ly/2yVmycN accessed October 31, 2018.

[25] M. McKee, S. Capewell, "Evidence about Electronic Cigarettes: A Foundation Built on Rock or Sand?" (2015) 351 BMJ h4863.

[26] Pisinger (n 24).

[27] Ministry of Health of New Zealand, *Vaping and Smokeless Tobacco* (August 2, 2016) www.health.govt.nz/our-work/preventative-health-wellness/tobacco-control/e-cigarettes accessed October 31, 2018.

[28] Appellate Body Report, *European Communities—Measures Affecting Asbestos and Products Containing Asbestos* (n 15) para 101.

[29] The Tobacco Atlas, "E-Cigarettes Should Be Regulated in Such a Way as to Reduce Smoking of Combusted Tobacco to the Greatest Extent Possible" (Call to

and thus should be considered as "like" products for the purposes of a WTO discrimination assessment.

On the other hand, while it is true that all these products can deliver nicotine, for some users ENDS serve the function of assisting the user in ceasing the consumption of conventional cigarettes. Insofar as it can be established that ENDS may serve as a method of cessation of smoking conventional cigarettes,[30] it could be argued that their end use is not "like" conventional tobacco products. This may help to explain why in some jurisdictions, e-cigarettes are classified as medical devices (in cases where the manufacturer makes claims associated with health).[31]

While in many respects e-cigarettes have a similar, if not identical, end use to conventional tobacco products, there can be important differences between and among users and their uses. For this reason, while it is likely that a panel/Appellate Body would find the products are "like" conventional tobacco products under the criterion of end use, this cannot be stated with absolute certainty.

3.1.3 Consumers' tastes and preferences

The criterion of consumer tastes and habits refers to "the extent to which consumers perceive and treat the products as alternative means of performing particular functions in order to satisfy a particular want or demand."[32] Factors relevant to this criterion include price (for example, price elasticity and substitutability), and whether information, distribution, brand recognition, and/or habits and tastes limit consumers' ability or willingness to switch products or brands. Thus, this criterion focuses on consumer attitudes and opinions vis-à-vis the interchangeability of ENDS and conventional cigarettes.

The available evidence on tastes and preferences is mixed. On one hand, some evidence points to consumers increasingly viewing ENDS as a safer alternative for those who want to continue to use nicotine products. For example, in 2014 the *British Medical Journal* reported that the use of ENDS was especially high among smokers. In the same year, data from UK Action on Smoking and Health (ASH) in the UK showed that 2.8 million adults in the

action, undated) http://3pk43x313ggr4cy0lh3tctjh.wpengine.netdna-cdn.com/topic/e-cigarettes/ accessed October 31, 2018.

30 S.-H. Zhu et al, "E-Cigarette Use and Associated Changes in Population Smoking Cessation: Evidence from US Current Population Surveys" (2017) 358 BMJ :j3262.

31 R.D. Kennedy et al, "Global Approaches to Regulating Electronic Cigarettes" (2017) 26 Tob Control 441 (citing Australia, Japan, Belgium, Chile, and Denmark as examples).

32 Appellate Body Report, *European Communities—Measures Affecting Asbestos and Products Containing Asbestos* (n 15) para 101.

United Kingdom used ENDS (6 percent of the adult population), and of these approximately 1.3 million (47 percent of users) were former smokers. In total, ASH reported that 1.4 million Britons (51 percent of users) continued to use both combustible cigarettes and e-cigarettes. In 2018, YouGov surveyed more than 12,000 adults for ASH, with a further analysis by King's College London, and estimated that the number of vapers in Great Britain was 3.2 million.[33]

A number of consumer surveys also show that there is significant switching to ENDS by cigarette users.[34] Notably, some consumers use ENDS simultaneously (dual use), as a permanent alternative to tobacco, in situations where smoking conventional cigarettes is not allowed, or simply as a lifestyle choice.[35] Thus, consumers' behavior when faced with a choice between cigarettes and vaping products (both ENDS and EHTPs) shows that there is a certain perception that the new products can be used interchangeably with the old ones. To a certain degree, however, this may depend on the category of the vaping product (for example, this perception may be stronger with respect to EHTPs than ENDS).

What is clear is that both awareness and use of ENDS have increased exponentially in recent years. Data obtained from the HealthStyles survey showed that awareness of ENDS in the US rose from 40.9 percent in 2010 to 57.9 percent in 2011. The statistics also showed that some regular smokers switched to ENDS in a relatively short period of time: 2.9 percent in one year in the US and 4 percent in two years in the United Kingdom—and this tendency persists. As mentioned, some surveys estimate that by 2025 ENDS could displace 30 percent of cigarette sales in high income markets.[36] Therefore, awareness of ENDS as a substitute for cigarettes is growing, with an increasing number of consumers switching from cigarettes to ENDS.

On the other hand, a recent report by the WHO concluded that the two main reasons for the use of e-cigarettes are to reduce or stop smoking, and for use in smoke-free environments.[37] When used as a mechanism to reduce or quit smoking conventional tobacco products, it may be hard to argue that these

---

[33] ASH, "New Data Shows Smokers Are Getting the Message on E-Cigarettes" (*ASH*, September 14, 2018) http://ash.org.uk/media-and-news/press-releases-media-and-news/ash-news-release-new-data-shows-smokers-are-getting-the-message-on-e-cigarettes/ accessed October 31, 2018.

[34] McKee, Capewell (n 25).

[35] J. Pepper et al, "Effects of Advertisements on Smokers' Interest in Trying E-Cigarettes: The Roles of Product Comparison and Visual Cues" (2014) 23 Tob Control iii31.

[36] Unknown, "Smoke Signals. Philip Morris Health Company?" (*The Economist*, April 23, 2016) https://econ.st/2T1cpDT accessed October 31, 2018.

[37] FCTC COP, *Electronic Nicotine Delivery Systems. Report by WHO*, FCTC/COP/6/10 Rev.1, September 1, 2014 (Conference of the Parties to the WHO Framework

products are viewed as interchangeable—in this regard, while some consumers may use cigarettes and ENDS interchangeably, other consumers may view them as separate and distinct product lines.

With ENDS still relatively new and seeking to establish their place in the market, the scientific evidence to date may be insufficient to reach discernible and broad conclusions. A user who has "tried" an e-cigarette does not necessarily become a consumer of the product. Moreover, the market share and user profile of ENDS users both differ widely between markets, which indicates that a "like" product analysis on consumer tastes and preferences may not yield consistent results across markets and may need to be performed on a case by case basis.

Even more, a case can be made that a growing share of e-cigarette users are non-smokers, who may be attracted by ease of access/use, diverse and tasty flavors, and/or more limited health risks.[38] For this group of users, it is hard to argue interchangeability with conventional tobacco products. Of course, some argue that once non-smokers begin to use e-cigarettes the next step will be transition to conventional cigarettes, which would increase the chances of these products being qualified as interchangeable.

3.1.4 Tariff classification

There is no doubt that ENDS and conventional cigarettes have different ingredients and are manufactured differently. Depending on the country, e-cigarettes are currently classified in chapters other than tobacco, such as Chapter 30—Pharmaceutical Products or Chapter 85—Electrical Machinery, Equipment and Parts.

However, there is a strong push to include ENDS in Harmonized System (HS) Chapter 24, which is designed to cover tobacco products despite the fact that ENDS are not a tobacco product. The issue was discussed at the World Custom Organization (WCO) Harmonized System Committee (HSC) in May 2018, although without reaching a final decision on the matter.[39] The HSC has however agreed in its March 2019 meeting to include ENDS in Chapter 24 by creating (a new) heading 24.04. This will cover all nicotine containing products including both ENDS and EHTPs. If no opposition on this decision will raised by any HS Contracting Party to the Customs Co-operation Council, the new classification will be effective as of 2022 as HS2022.

Convention on Tobacco Control, Sixth session, Moscow, Russian Federation, October 13–18, 2014).

[38] Kennedy et al (n 31) 440; McKee, Capewell (n 25); Pepper et al (n 35).

[39] C. Snowdon, "E-Cigarettes to Be Re-Classified as Tobacco?" (*Velvet Glove, Iron Fist*, May 24, 2018) https://velvetgloveironfist.blogspot.com/2018/05/e-cigarettes-to-be-re-classified-as.html accessed October 31, 2018.

While the classification of a non-tobacco product in the tobacco chapter perhaps seems counterintuitive, it is not without more subtle implications. Such a reclassification would actually only raise the probability that ENDS and conventional cigarettes would be found "like" in the context of the WTO discrimination analysis. This would, in turn, raise the probability that a ban of e-cigarettes would be found discriminatory under WTO law.

3.1.5 Additional "likeness" criteria

Additional criteria may inform the panel regarding its "likeness" analysis. In fact, the Appellate Body has stressed that the four "likeness" criteria discussed above are "neither a treaty-mandated nor a closed list of criteria that will determine the legal characterization of products."[40] There is no established hierarchy of the "likeness" criteria,[41] and therefore none of them is determinative as such; each should be assessed in the context of all other criteria.

In light of the above, at least two more criteria (discussed below) can help WTO panels to determine the "likeness" of the two products: (i) the cross-price elasticity of demand; and (ii) their regulatory regimes or relevant legislation. The cross-price elasticity of demand (CPED) measures the rate of response of the quantity demanded of one product due to a price change of another product. In other words, it measures how the demand on one product changes if the price for its substitute product increases or decreases. Thus, a CPED showing that the two products are substitutes, while not being a decisive criterion, could be taken into account as an additional criterion which speaks in favor of a likeness between the two products. There are economic studies that tackle this issue directly. One study, conducted in New Zealand, concluded that e-cigarettes are potentially substitutable for regular cigarettes and that their availability will reduce tobacco consumption.[42] Another study, conducted in the European Union (EU), stated that e-cigarettes and regular cigarettes are substitutes, with higher cigarette prices being associated with increased e-cigarette sales.[43] As the Appellate Body noted, the CPED alone may not suffice to assess the WTO "likeness" of two products, but it can provide impor-

---

[40] Appellate Body Report, *European Communities—Measures Affecting Asbestos and Products Containing Asbestos* (n 15) para 101.

[41] A. Mitchell, T. Voon, "Regulating Tobacco Flavors: Implications of WTO Law" (2011) 29 Boston Uni Intl L J 398 (referring to the Appellate Body Report, *European Communities—Measures Affecting Asbestos and Products Containing Asbestos* (n 15) para 102).

[42] R. Grace, B. Kivell, M. Laugessen, "Estimating Cross-Price Elasticity of E-Cigarettes Using a Simulated Demand Procedure" (2015) 17(5) Nicotine Tob Res 592.

[43] M. Stoklosa, J. Drope, F.J. Chaloupka, "Prices and E-Cigarette Demand: Evidence from the European Union" (2016) 18(10) Nicotine Tob Res 1973.

tant guidance to panels in sorting and examining the relevant evidence.[44] These and future studies showing substitution in different markets between the two products examined in this chapter may have a bearing on a positive finding of "likeness" by a WTO panel.

An additional criterion is the classification of ENDS under a specific regulatory regime (or legal framework). A party to a WTO case challenging a ban on ENDS may argue that the "likeness" should also be assessed based on the regulatory or legal regime which regulates the two different products. In other words, do the same laws which regulate conventional cigarettes apply also to ENDS, and if so, to what extent? A positive finding along these lines may strengthen a WTO panel's assumption of a positive likeness. Two big economies, the USA and EU, currently regulate ENDS under legislation dealing with cigarettes and other tobacco products. Additionally, in about 62 countries in the world, ENDS are controlled as a "tobacco product."[45]

3.1.6 Preliminary conclusions

Under the WTO case law, "likeness" is determined not on the basis of a single factor but as a broad assessment of all of the relevant criteria taken together. There is no hierarchy between the factors, nor a single "likeness" criterion which will trump the others; in fact, the list of considerations for determining "likeness" may also extend beyond the criteria described above. By taking a holistic view of the above analyses of the four criteria and considering the additional "likeness" criteria discussed in this chapter, in spite of many unknowns, a positive "likeness" finding by a panel is possible. Moreover, the further scientific, legal, and market developments might over time increase the chances of such a finding.

3.2 Non-discrimination under the TBT Agreement

The first and perhaps most important part of any analysis under the TBT Agreement is to determine whether a measure falls within the scope of the Agreement itself—in other words, whether the measure at issue is a "technical regulation" within the meaning of Annex 1.1 of the TBT Agreement. If so, it must be determined whether the imported and domestic products at issue are "like products." If further so, then it must be determined whether the imported products are accorded "treatment no less favorable" than "like"

---

44 Appellate Body Report, *European Communities—Measures Affecting Asbestos and Products Containing Asbestos* (n 15) para 102.

45 H. Shapiro, *No Fire, No Smoke: The Global State of Tobacco Harm Reduction* (GSTHR Report 2018) 85 https://gsthr.org/downloads/GSTHR%20Report/Global-State-of-Tobacco-Harm-Reduction-2018.pdf accessed October 31, 2018.

domestic products and "like products" originating in any other country. While it remains debatable whether a general ENDS ban will be covered by the TBT Agreement—which will have to be determined on a case by case basis[46]—for the sake of a more comprehensive discussion in this chapter, we assume such a measure to be a "technical regulation" under the TBT Agreement.[47]

Assuming that a ban on ENDS constitutes a technical regulation, the TBT Agreement employs a similar logic and argumentation as the GATT with respect to a complete ban on ENDS.[48] The national treatment and most favored nation obligations are contained in Art. 2.1 of the TBT Agreement, according to which: "Members shall ensure that in respect of technical regulations, products imported from the territory of any Member shall be accorded treatment no less favorable than that accorded to 'like' products of national origin and to 'like' products originating in any other country."

As under the GATT 1994, the TBT Agreement's non-discrimination obligations apply only to "like products"; therefore the concept is an essential element in the analysis of whether a measure is discriminatory.[49] Art. 2.1 of the TBT does not explicitly specify which criteria should be used in order to determine if two products are "like products" for the purposes of establishing discrimination. The important analytical issue for our purposes is that a technical regulation is a measure which usually has a particular regulatory purpose (for example, ensuring the quality of its exports; protecting human, animal, or plant life or health). This begs the question whether the concept of "likeness" under the TBT Agreement should be evaluated using the traditional GATT "likeness" criteria—which assign prominence to the competitive relationship of the two products—or should be premised on the regulatory purpose of the measure in issue.

---

[46] Appellate Body Report, *European Communities—Measures Affecting Asbestos and Products Containing Asbestos* (n 15) para 24.

[47] Panel Report, *European Communities—Measures Affecting Asbestos and Asbestos Containing Products* (WT/DS/135/R, adopted September 18, 2000) para 8.35. For a detailed analysis on whether a measure qualifies as a technical regulation under the TBT Agreement, see L. Gruszczynski, "The TBT Agreement and Tobacco Control Regulations" (2013) 8 AJWH 115.

[48] For a more detailed analysis of the argument under the TBT Agreement, see M. Foltea, A. Markitanova, "The 'Likeness' of E-Cigarettes and Cigarettes at WTO" (2017) 8 EJRR 342.

[49] Appellate Body Report, *United States—Measures Affecting the Production and Sale of Clove Cigarettes* (WT/DS406/AB/R, adopted April 4, 2012) para 87. Other elements of the analysis include the findings on (i) whether the measure at issue is a "technical regulation" and (ii) whether the imported products are accorded "treatment no less favourable" than like domestic products. These elements do not fall within the purview of this chapter.

A number of WTO cases are relevant for addressing this question, including *EC—Asbestos*, *Japan—Alcoholic Beverages*, *US—Clove Cigarettes*, and *US—Tuna II (Mexico)*. All these cases generally conclude that the traditional likeness criteria approach will prevail. For instance, the Appellate Body in *US—Clove Cigarettes* explicitly transferred the "competitive relationship" logic of Art. III:4 of GATT 1994 to determining "likeness" under Art. 2.1 of the TBT Agreement, stating that "[w]e consider that the determination of 'likeness' under Article 2.1 of the TBT Agreement, as well as under Article III:4 of the GATT 1994, is a determination about the nature and extent of a competitive relationship between and among the products at issue."[50]

This makes a lot of sense given that products which are in a competitive relationship are precisely the ones which can be discriminated against through technical regulations. This view, however, departed from and overturned the panel's reasoning in the lower instance. The panel believed that the weighing of the traditional evidence relating to "likeness" should have been influenced by the fact that the measure at issue was a technical regulation, having the immediate purpose of regulating flavored cigarettes for public health reasons.[51] It found that menthol cigarettes are "like" clove cigarettes not so much because they compete but because they both raise the same "regulatory concern" invoked by the United States, namely, they are both flavored cigarettes that are particularly attractive to youth.[52]

The Appellate Body rejected this attempt to return to the "aims and effects" test of the GATT and specifically and decisively stated that "the concept of 'like products' in Article 2.1 of the TBT Agreement [does not] lend itself to distinctions between products based on the regulatory objectives of a measure."[53] Otherwise, in the view of the Appellate Body, the outcome of any case could allow for the "likeness" analysis to include the products covered by a regulatory purpose, but exclude those which are not. In such a case, the finding on "likeness" would be questionable, as it would inevitably distort the less favorable treatment comparison. Accordingly, the Appellate Body relied on the jurisprudence concerning Art. III:4 of GATT 1994 to determine that the

---

[50] Ibid para 120. See also Panel Report, *United States—Measures Concerning the Importation, Marketing and Sale of Tuna and Tuna Products* (WT/DS381/R, adopted July 15, 2011) paras 7.223–7.225; Appellate Body Report, *United States—Measures Concerning the Importation, Marketing and Sale of Tuna and Tuna Products* (WT/DS381/AB/R, adopted May 16, 2012) para 235.

[51] Panel Report, *United States—Measures Affecting the Production and Sale of Clove Cigarettes* (WT/DS406/R, adopted September 2, 2011) para 7.119.

[52] Ibid paras 7.231, 7.247.

[53] Appellate Body Report, *United States—Measures Affecting the Production and Sale of Clove Cigarettes* (n 49) para 116.

very concept of "treatment no less favorable" influences the determination of "likeness" "to the extent they have an impact on the competitive relationship between and among the products concerned."[54] This means that regulatory concerns underlying technical regulations (for example, health risks) may play a role in the determination of "likeness" to the extent that they are relevant to the examination of other "likeness" criteria (for example, product characteristics and consumer preferences) and are reflected in the products' competitive relationship. Such concerns, and more directly the regulatory intent behind a measure, are not however directly relevant to the determination of likeness.

Having rejected the "regulatory purpose of the measure" approach for determining "likeness," the Appellate Body clearly stated the determination of "likeness" under both GATT 1994 and the TBT Agreement is about the "nature and extent of a competitive relationship between and among products."[55] The Appellate Body instructed panels to "discount any distortive effects that the measure at issue and its regulatory purpose may have on the competitive relationship, and reserve the consideration of such effects for the analysis of less favourable treatment," which is perhaps easier said than done but nevertheless a useful instruction. Therefore, while the regulatory purpose of the measure at issue may influence the finding on whether the treatment accorded is less favorable, the determination of "likeness" remains a finding about the nature and extent of a competitive relationship between the products concerned.

Some academic commentary exists which asserts that the case law has applied the concept of "likeness" in the TBT context (that is, *US—Clove Cigarettes*, *US—Tuna*, and *US—COOL*) in the wrong manner.[56] For instance, Professor Mavroidis believes it should not have been for the consumers to decide (as was done in the three cases) whether two goods are "like" under the TBT (described as "market-likeness"), but rather that the panels should have understood the term "likeness" as denoting policy likeness, meaning that the concept should have been assessed through the eyes of the regulator, who intervenes and corrects a specific market outcome.[57] While there may be some

---

[54] Ibid para 156. See also A.E. Appleton, "National Treatment under the TBT Agreement" in A. Kamperman Sanders (eds), *The Principle of National Treatment in International Economic Law* (Edward Elgar Publishing 2014).

[55] Appellate Body Report, *United States—Measures Affecting the Production and Sale of Clove Cigarettes* (n 49) para 111.

[56] P. Mavroidis, "Driftin' Too Far from Shore—Why the Test for Compliance with the TBT Agreement Developed by the WTO Appellate Body is Wrong, and What Should the AB Have Done Instead" (2013) 3(2) World Trade Rev 509; R. Howse, P.I. Levy, "The TBT Panels: *US—Clove Cigarettes*, *US—Tuna*, and *US—COOL*" in C.P. Bown, P. Mavroidis (eds), *The WTO Case Law of 2011* (The American Law Institute 2012).

[57] Mavroidis (n 56) 529.

merit to this argument, it is not the purpose of this chapter to enter into the debate: our task is limited to assessing the law as it stands and not the direction in which the interpretation of "likeness" under TBT Agreement should take. The case law is clear: the interpretation of "likeness" in Art. 2.1 should be guided by establishing whether there is a competitive relationship between the two products at issue, and use of the four criteria used under Art. III:4 of GATT 1994 to do so.[58] Thus, the traditional elements of the "likeness" analysis under Art. III:4, such as (i) physical characteristics of the product, (ii) end uses of the product, (iii) consumers' tastes and habits, and (iv) tariff classification of the products, remain in principle relevant for determining "likeness" under Art. 2.1 of the TBT Agreement. Consequently, based on these factors and following the analysis of Art. III:4 above, it is possible that a panel/Appellate Body could find ENDS to be "like" cigarettes.

4. ADDITIONAL RELEVANT WTO PROVISIONS FOR ASSESSMENT OF ENDS BANS

4.1 Prohibition of Quantitative Restrictions (Art. XI of GATT 1994)

The GATT/TBT national treatment and most favored nation obligations are concerned with internal measures, but complete bans may also be designed as a border measure applicable to importation (either *de jure* or *de facto*). In this case, Art. XI of GATT 1994 ("General Elimination of Quantitative Restrictions") may be applicable. This provision requires that WTO Members do not apply "prohibitions or restrictions other than duties, taxes or other charges . . . on the importation of any product of the territory of any contracting party." Although it is highly unlikely that most ENDS bans are designed as border measures, this possibility can differ on a market by market basis. A complete ban could be seen as a quantitative restriction—that is, a quota of zero—and thus falls within the scope of Art. XI. The linkage between the applications of GATT 1994 Art. XI and Art. III should be analyzed—either in parallel or singularly to the exclusion of one another—on a case by case basis by examining the design of the relevant legislation.

4.2 General Exceptions (Art. XX(b) of GATT 1994)

This chapter examines whether ENDS and conventional cigarettes may be found to be a "like product" under WTO law, which is an important step in

---

[58] Appellate Body Report, *United States—Measures Affecting the Production and Sale of Clove Cigarettes* (n 49) para 120.

finding discrimination in the case of a complete ban on ENDS. It is important, however, to stress that a positive finding of discrimination along this line does not automatically result in a win for the party challenging the ban in the WTO. It is commonplace for a defendant in these type of cases (that is, the country that would have imposed an ENDS ban) to invoke a defense under Art. XX of GATT 1994 ("General Exceptions"). In the case of an ENDS ban, and in line with a certain division of opinions in the health community over the harmfulness of ENDS, the defendant is most likely to invoke the exception contained in subparagraph (b). It is difficult to predict how the WTO judiciary would rule on this matter, given that this exercise will be highly dependent on the available scientific evidence at the point in time when the case may be examined by a WTO panel.

However, in the event of a positive finding on discrimination, and provided the defendant's justification under Art. XX (b) is not supported by solid scientific evidence (in particular with regard to harm), such a measure may ultimately be found inconsistent with WTO law. This is particularly the case given the growing evidence that ENDS are less harmful than cigarettes (and provided that they do not produce other significant concerns from the public health point of view). Given that, a general ban may be considered as a "disguised restriction on international trade" as per the chapeau of Art. XX, which provides as follows:

> Subject to the requirement that such measures are not applied in a manner which would constitute a means of arbitrary or unjustifiable discrimination between countries where the same conditions prevail, or a disguised restriction on international trade, nothing in this Agreement shall be construed to prevent the adoption or enforcement by any contracting party of measures: [(b) necessary to protect human, animal or plant life or health].

Arguably, one would need to look here not only at the comparative health assessment (ENDS versus combustible tobacco), but also at the broader consequences of ENDS use. For example, it may be necessary to consider public health risks relating to the alleged gateway effect of ENDS (particularly for young users) and the problem of renormalization.[59] The pertinent decisions of the FCTC Conference of the Parties (despite their non-binding character) may be also relevant in this context, not so much as external normative materials (since they are of a nonbinding character) but as a source of scientific information.[60]

---

[59] For a discussion of both risks, see Chapters 2 and 3 in this volume.

[60] See for example Panel Report, *United States—Measures Affecting the Production and Sale of Clove Cigarettes* (n 51) para 7.414; and Panel Reports, *Australia—*

It is also worth noting that, unlike the exhaustive list of legitimate exceptions under Art. XX of GATT 1994, the scope of measures' regulatory purposes considered legitimate under the TBT Agreement is not very clear, as the list found in Art. 2.2 is open-ended. The drafters therefore assumed that the regulatory power of WTO Members which may fall under the TBT Agreements is potentially wider in health-related matters. This means that even if a health justification for the ban is not accepted under Art. XX, the WTO judiciary still may consider the purpose of the measure legitimate under Art. 2.2 of the TBT Agreement (provided of course that the measure is found to fall under this Agreement).[61]

4.3 Necessity Requirement (Art. 2.2 of the TBT Agreement)

Although the TBT Agreement recognizes that WTO Members should not be prevented from taking measures necessary for the protection of human life or health at the level they consider appropriate, if such measures are applied in a manner which constitutes a means of arbitrary or unjustifiable discrimination, this leeway is more restricted. The provision limits the degree of trade restrictiveness resulting from technical regulations to the extent necessary to fulfill legitimate objectives.[62] So even a non-discriminatory measure, which applies equally to domestic and imported products, could violate Art. 2.2 if it

---

Certain Measures Concerning Trademarks, Geographical Indications and Other Plain Packaging Requirements Applicable to Tobacco Products and Packaging (WT/DS435/R, WT/DS441/R, WT/DS458/R, and WT/DS467/R, not yet adopted) paras 7.412, 7.1309, 7.1660, 7.664–7.665 (both looking not only at the FCTC but also at its guidelines that were adopted in the form of COP decisions). See also L. Gruszczynski, M. Melillo, "The FCTC and Its Role in WTO Law: Some Remarks on the WTO Plain Packaging Report" (2018) 9(3) EJRR 564 and Chapter 4 in this volume.

[61] In the context of the TBT Agreement it will also be necessary to look at the third condition of Art. 2.1, which operates similarly to Art. XX of GATT 1994. In particular, the panel will need to examine whether the alleged detrimental impact "stems exclusively from a legitimate regulatory distinction rather than reflecting discrimination against the group of imported products": Appellate Body Report, *United States—Measures Affecting the Production and Sale of Clove Cigarettes* (n 49) para 182; see also Appellate Body Report, *United States—Certain Country of Origin Labelling (COOL) Requirements* (WT/DS384/AB/R, WT/DS386/AB/R, adopted June 29, 2012) para 271.

[62] Appellate Body Report, *United States—Measures Affecting the Production and Sale of Clove Cigarettes* (n 49). See also Panel Report, *European Communities—Trade Description of Sardines* (WT/DS231/R, adopted May 29, 2002) para 7.120.

lacks a sufficient scientific basis or does not constitute the least trade restrictive alternative. Art. 2.2 reads as follows:

> Members shall ensure that technical regulations are not prepared, adopted or applied with a view to or with the effect of creating unnecessary obstacles to international trade. For this purpose, technical regulations shall not be more trade restrictive than *necessary* to fulfil a legitimate objective, taking account of the risks non-fulfilment would create. Such legitimate objectives are, inter alia: national security requirements; the prevention of deceptive practices; *protection of human health or safety*, animal or plant life or health, or the environment. In assessing such risks, relevant elements of consideration are, inter alia: available *scientific* and technical information, related processing technology or intended end-uses of products. [emphasis added]

Once the objective that a WTO Member seeks to achieve through a technical regulation at issue is identified, a panel should next turn to the question of whether this particular objective is "legitimate" within the meaning of Art. 2.2. These assessments will act as a reference point for the further analysis of whether a challenged measure is "more trade-restrictive than necessary" to fulfill its legitimate objective.

4.4 The Approach to Scientific Evidence in the WTO Dispute Settlement System

Analysis of the relevant GATT 1994 and TBT case law reveals that the assessment of science and scientific evidence is an important element in all health-related trade disputes, irrespective of which agreement they are brought under. The TBT Agreement openly refers to science in the context of its necessity requirement. Although the GATT 1994 is silent on this issue, the WTO dispute settlement bodies frequently refer to scientific evidence in the context of various GATT provisions (most notably under Art. XX). Overall, science may be used: (i) to assess the degree of the contribution made by the measure to the legitimate objective at issue; (ii) to determine the nature of the risks at issue and the gravity of consequences that would arise from nonfulfillment of the objective(s) pursued by a Member through the measure; and (iii) to determine whether alternative measures exist that are less trade restrictive, but which make an equal contribution to the relevant legitimate objective(s).

Science helps to establish the existence of a specific risk, a causal link between a measure and the risk, and the availability and effectiveness of other regulatory options. The existence of risk arising from a certain product can be shown both qualitatively and quantitatively. Domestic measures (such as a complete ban on ENDS) may be based on either majority or minority scientific opinions so long as they come from qualified and respected sources.

Additionally, in the WTO there is no requirement of a minimum magnitude of risk (although the risk needs to be ascertainable) and the standard of review applied to scientific determinations at the domestic level remains relatively deferential.[63] The concept of the standard of review, which has its origins in common law, can be generally described in the WTO context as the level of scrutiny used by panels and the Appellate Body when assessing certain determinations of a legal, factual, or mixed nature made by WTO Members. The TBT Agreement also confirms the right of a panel to seek advice from experts—both in the form of an expert group or on an individual basis—and sets out a relatively detailed procedure for the operation of such a group (Annex 2). A panel can also rely on the expertise provided by specialized international organizations or other interstate cooperation platforms. All these issues may potentially be relevant in any dispute concerning a ban on ENDS.

5. CONCLUSIONS AND FURTHER RESEARCH

In determining the likeness of ENDS and cigarettes, the key is to ascertain whether the products are in a competitive relationship. When doing so, a panel/Appellate Body will look to whether the products are "commercially interchangeable, or if they offer alternative ways of satisfying the same consumer demand in the marketplace."[64] As discussed above, ENDS and cigarettes share the ability to deliver nicotine and both are capable of performing the same end use, which is to satisfy consumers' desire for nicotine and provide the experience of smoking. The two products also share some physical characteristics—although perhaps to a limited extent—such as a similarity in design (for some categories). The two products do not at present share the same customs classification, although the WCO seems to be moving toward classifying ENDS in the HS tobacco chapter. The most difficult determination will concern consumers' tastes and habits, with the limited existing evidence being in conflict. Studies do show that ENDS can be considered by some consumers as an alternative to satisfy their smoking habits, and thus the possibility that a panel/Appellate Body could regard ENDS and cigarettes as commercially interchangeable and offering an alternative way to satisfy the same consumer demands cannot be completely discounted. The use of ENDS is growing, whereas cigarette use is

---

[63] See for example L. Gruszczynski, "Science and the Settlement of Trade Disputes in the World Trade Organization Settlement of SPS Disputes in the WTO" in B. Mercurio, K.-J. Ni (eds), *Science and Technology in International Economic Law Balancing Competing Interests* (Routledge 2014) 23.

[64] Appellate Body Report, *United States—Transitional Safeguard Measures on Combed Cotton Yarn from Pakistan* (WT/DS/192/AB/R, adopted October 8, 2001) para 96.

declining—in many cases, users of ENDS are not and have not been cigarette smokers. Trends such as these indicate that while perhaps ENDS may not be seen to be in a competitive relationship with cigarettes today, there is a likelihood that such a competitive relationship will evolve and grow in the future.

A finding of likeness in a particular dispute will depend, however, on the quality of the evidence in each step, in particular as relating to the substitutability of the two categories of products. The data on the substitutability of ENDS and conventional cigarettes is crucial in building a solid discrimination argument. The reason for this is that in determining the "likeness" between two products—with a subsequent determination that one category is treated less favorably than another—there must be solid evidence of such substitution between the products. The CPED tests conducted in two economic studies show that the two categories of products are substitutes. However, such evidence may not be consistent across nations and this analysis would need to be conducted in the markets in question under the WTO dispute settlement system.

It should be once again stressed that the scope of this chapter is limited to the issue of likeness; it does not analyze "less favorable treatment" or possible exceptions (such as justification of a ban under GATT Art. XX regarding public health), or other justifications available in the context of the TBT Agreement. Thus, we do not draw conclusions on the question of any ENDS ban's consistency with the WTO, but rather offer preliminary and instructive guidance. Further discussion of these issues is reserved for future research as new evidence on the possible harmfulness or health benefits of ENDS emerges.

What is clear is that, when introducing a general ban on ENDS, regulators should seek to better inform themselves on the possible legal problems that may emerge under their international obligations. This would entail legal checks of preexisting obligations, including their adherence to obligations under international trade agreements. Caution should also be taken to ensure that an ENDS ban is supported by solid scientific evidence and that there is a lack of otherwise reasonably available alternatives which could deliver the stated public health objective through less trade restrictive measures.

While this chapter examines general ENDS bans under the WTO, similar analyses can be conducted with regard to bans on the registration and use of intellectual property linked to ENDS, such as the denial of patent registrations to inventors of ENDS; display bans, especially in countries which still do not apply display bans on cigarettes; and indoor vaping bans (which may be relevant for countries which still do not apply indoor smoking bans). Additionally, these arguments could be extended to possible bans on other categories of newly emerging products not discussed in this chapter. Useful research could also be conducted exploring the applicability of arguments deriving from other agreements, such as bilateral international investment agreements, bilateral and regional free trade agreements, and other international and regional treaties, including those on public health, human rights, and other related issues.[65]

[65] Some of those issues are discussed in this volume: see for example Chapter 4 (discussing ENDS under the FCTC) and Chapter 5 (analyzing state obligations when regulating ENDS under international human rights law).

7. Regulating e-cigarettes at the EU level

Anna Pudło and Lukasz Gruszczynski[1]

1. INTRODUCTION

The market for electronic cigarettes (e-cigarettes) was harmonized at the European Union (EU) level only recently, through Directive 2014/40 on tobacco and related products (the TPD or the Directive).[2] The applicable rules—provided by Art. 20—were added to the Directive at the final stage of the legislative process as an amendment by the European Parliament, with little prior assessment and very limited involvement from the national parliaments. The relatively detailed regulation was subsequently challenged in the Court of Justice of the European Union (the CJEU or the Court)[3] with respect to its compatibility with various EU legal principles. However, the Court did not find any violation. As a consequence, a new EU-wide regime for e-cigarettes entered into force, entirely changing the rules of the game for producers, importers, sellers, and individual consumers in this segment of the market. For some, the Directive establishes a golden regulatory standard for the treatment of e-cigarettes—one which can be replicated in the future in other jurisdictions; for others it represents an example of overprotective regulation that stifles innovation, and which may actually have a negative impact on public health protection.

---

[1] This chapter is partially based on L. Gruszczynski, "The EU regime for e-cigarettes: a rationale compromise or regulatory failure?" (2018) 4(2) J Health Inequal 62.

[2] Directive 2014/40 (EU) of the European Parliament and of the Council on the approximation of the laws, regulations and administrative provisions of the Member States concerning the manufacture, presentation and sale of tobacco and related products [2014] OJ L 127/1.

[3] Technically speaking the case was decided by Court of Justice (CoJ), which is a part of the CJEU. Following the existing convention in the literature, the chapter simply refers to the CJEU rather than to CoJ or the previously functioning General Court.

The objective of this chapter is twofold. First, it analyzes the legislative process that led to the adoption of the new EU regulatory framework for e-cigarettes, presenting at the same time the main features of this framework. Second, it assesses the extent of regulatory space available to the EU institutions in this policy area. The structure of the chapter reflects those two objectives. Accordingly, section 2 looks at the genesis of the current EU regulatory regime for e-cigarettes and attempts to identify the factors that have had an impact on its ultimate shape. This part also summarizes the main obligations of the TPD which are applicable to e-cigarettes. Against this background discussion, section 3 examines various legal benchmarks that establish the limits for EU institutions when regulating e-cigarettes. In this context, special attention is paid to the recent judgment of the CJEU in the *Pillbox 38 (UK) Ltd v Secretary of State for Health* dispute,[4] in which the relevant provisions of the Directive were extensively analyzed. The final section offers conclusions.

2. THE EU REGIME FOR E-CIGARETTES

2.1 The Genesis of the Directive and Its Legislative Process

The EU began to regulate the tobacco sector in the 1990s, by adopting directives which aimed at creating equal conditions between the Member States with regard to the advertising, sale, and manufacture of tobacco products, simultaneously ensuring a high level of health protection.[5] Not surprisingly, the provisions of all those directives were challenged in the CJEU. In *Federal Republic of Germany v European Parliament and Council of the European Union*, the Court annulled Directive 98/43, finding that the law had an incorrect legal basis and that it did not contribute to the elimination of distortions of competition in the tobacco market in terms of sponsorship and advertising.[6]

---

4 C-477/14 *Pillbox 38 (UK) Ltd v Secretary of State for Health* [2016] ECLI:EU:C:2016:324.

5 Directive 98/43/EC of the European Parliament and of the Council of 6 July 1998 on the approximation of the laws, regulations and administrative provisions of the Member States relating to the advertising and sponsorship of tobacco products [1998] OJ L 213/9; Directive 2001/37/EC of the European Parliament and of the Council of 5 June 2001 on the approximation of the laws, regulations and administrative provisions of the Member States concerning the manufacture, presentation and sale of tobacco products [2001] OJ L 194/26; Directive 2003/33/EC of the European Parliament and of the Council of 26 May 2003 on the approximation of the laws, regulations and administrative provisions of the Member States relating to the advertising and sponsorship of tobacco products [2003] OJ L 152/16.

6 C-376/98 *Federal Republic of Germany v European Parliament and Council of the European Union* [2000] ECLI:EU:C:2:544.

Consequently, the European Commission had to propose two completely new legal acts (Directive 2001/37 and Directive 2003/33), which were also challenged, but this time unsuccessfully.[7]

In 2009 the European Commission decided to revise Directive 2001/37 (at that time the main piece of EU legislation in the field), taking into consideration changes in the market (for example the expansion of novel smokeless tobacco products, the introduction of conventional cigarettes with new features, and the emergence of e-cigarettes), scientific progress (for example new evidence concerning the impact of packaging on consumers' behavior), and legal developments at the international level, in particular the conclusion in 2003 of the World Health Organization (WHO) Framework Convention on Tobacco Control (FCTC), to which the EU and most of its Member States became parties in 2005.[8] The whole process took more than five years and was characterized by intense lobbying by the tobacco industry as well as stark disagreement between the Member States, EU institutions, and the private sector over the appropriate methods for achieving a balance between harmonization of the internal market and the protection of public health.[9]

The legal status of e-cigarettes was particularly complex before the adoption of the Directive, with EU Member States taking different regulatory approaches to this new category of products. The majority considered e-cigarettes as medicinal products (for example Austria, Belgium, Denmark, Germany, and the Netherlands); some applied selectively specific restrictions taken from the traditional tobacco control repertoire, such as advertising controls or age limits (for example Malta or Poland); others banned those products entirely from their markets (for example Greece or Lithuania for so-called imitation products). There was also a group of countries that left these products unregulated, subjecting them to general consumer protection rules (for example Bulgaria, the Czech Republic, Ireland, and the United

---

[7] C-491/01 *The Queen v Secretary of State for Health, ex parte British American Tobacco (Investments) Ltd and Imperial Tobacco Ltd* [2002] ECLI:EU:C:2002:741.

[8] See the Commission Staff Working Document, Impact Assessment, accompanying the document "Proposal for a Directive of the European Parliament and of the Council on the approximation of the laws, regulations and administrative provisions of the Member States concerning the manufacture, presentation and sale of tobacco and related products" (December 19, 2012, SWD(2012) 452 final) section 2. For more detailed analysis of the legal status of e-cigarettes under the FCTC regime, see Chapter 4 in this volume.

[9] See generally S. Peeters et al, "The revision of the 2014 European Tobacco Products Directive: an analysis of the tobacco industry's attempts to break the health silo" (2016) 25 Tob Control 108; R. Bartollini et al, "Tobacco control in Europe: a policy review" (2016) 25 Eur Respir Rev 151.

Kingdom).[10] The Commission maintained, however, that the development of minimum safety standards for e-cigarettes under the General Products Safety Directive was not a feasible option, as it would fail to address existing health risks. According to the Commission, since nicotine is toxic and addictive it was impossible to set any safety standards for products releasing nicotine.[11] Consequently, the Commission believed that those products should have been subject to more demanding rules, and proposed to classify them (but, paradoxically, only those with a nicotine level above the 4 mg/ml threshold[12]) as medicinal products (original Art. 18 of the TPD).[13] As a result of this classification e-cigarettes would have been subject to the existing EU rules applicable to such products. In practice, such an approach would eliminate most of them from the market due to the financial costs and technical difficulties connected with an authorization process.

It is not clear why the Commission decided to choose the pharmaceutical model for the regulation of e-cigarettes. Arguably its decision was influenced by the fact that most of the Member States that regulated e-cigarettes at that time took this approach.[14] Consequently, the TPD would have simply reflected the dominant regulatory model within the EU, allowing for smoother harmonization and ensuring sufficient support in the course of the legislative process. The Commission also argued that e-cigarettes enjoyed an unjustified advantage, undermining any level playing field as compared to nicotine replacement therapy (NRT) products and unfairly affecting the interests of the pharmaceutical companies.[15] This conclusion was reached despite the fact that the EU e-cigarette industry generally tried to avoid making any cessation claims. Instead it was based on various market surveys, which showed that the cessation aspect was an important factor among e-cigarette users.[16] The pharmaceutical model was also supported by a number of non-governmental health organizations, which expressed their concerns about the health risks connected

---

[10] Commission Staff Working Document (n 8) 26.

[11] Ibid 53.

[12] Note that the position of the Commission was self-contradictory. The impossibility of setting safety standards for nicotine should prevent the Commission from establishing any threshold level.

[13] See the Proposal for a Directive of the European Parliament and of the Council on the approximation of the laws, regulations and administrative provisions of the Member States concerning the manufacture, presentation and sale of tobacco and related products (COM(2012)788 final).

[14] RAND Europe, *Assessing the Impacts of Revising the Tobacco Products Directive Study to Support a DG SANCO Impact Assessment* (2011) 124.

[15] Commission Staff Working Document (n 8) 26 and 28.

[16] Ibid 17, 27–8, and 83.

with the use of e-cigarettes.[17] In addition, it seems that the recommendation of the WHO Study Group on Tobacco Product Regulation,[18] which proposed regulating e-cigarettes as a combination of drugs and medical devices, played some role.[19] Overall, it is clear from the impact assessment prepared by the Commission that the harm reduction aspect of e-cigarettes initially remained largely unappreciated.[20]

The subsequent legislative process was full of unexpected shifts. There was an attempt to take an even more restrictive approach by applying the pharmaceutical model to all e-cigarettes regardless of their nicotine content.[21] It also seems that some pharmaceutical companies attempted to lobby the EU institutions for stringent regulation of e-cigarettes (preferably as medicinal products). In particular, GlaxoSmithKline tried to pressure the EU law-makers by warning that e-cigarettes can act as gateway products.[22] Eventually, however, the European Parliament proposed a *sui generis* regime under which e-cigarettes would be subject to some restrictions (for example, a notification requirement and limits on nicotine content) but much more lenient than those which are applied to medicinal products (for example, no authorization requirement).[23] Specific obligations also evolved over time (for example, the

---

17 Ibid 82.

18 WHO Study Group on Tobacco Product Regulation, *Report on the Scientific Basis of the Tobacco Product Regulation: Third Report of a WHO Study Group* (World Health Organ Tech Rep Ser 2009 (955)) 1–41.

19 Commission Staff Working Document (n 8) 81.

20 A harm reduction approach should be distinguished from the pharmaceutical model (the latter aims at full recovery). It can be defined as "a policy or programme directed towards decreasing adverse health, social and economic adverse consequences of drug use even though the user continues to use psychoactive drugs at the present time" (E. Single, "Defining harm reduction" (1995) 14 Drug Alcohol Rev 287, 289). In the context of the TPD proposal, the Commission, for example, noted that any other option would have less positive impact on public health because it would not able to address identified safety concerns (Commission Staff Working Document (n 8) 83).

21 D. Saitta, G.A. Ferro, R. Polosa, "Achieving appropriate regulations for electronic cigarettes" (2014) 5(2) Ther Adv Chronic Dis 50, 54. See also Council of the European Union, Proposal for a Directive of the European Parliament and of the Council on the approximation of the laws, regulations and administrative provisions of the Member States concerning the manufacture, presentation and sale of tobacco and related products (First reading, June 24, 2013, 2012/0366 (COD)).

22 A. Ralph, "E cigarettes can be gateway to tobacco, warns rival Glaxo" (*The Times*, February 17, 2014), https://bit.ly/2snDZzK accessed October 31, 2018.

23 Amendments adopted by the European Parliament on 8 October 2013 on the proposal for a directive of the European Parliament and of the Council on the approximation of the laws, regulations and administrative provisions of the Member States concerning the manufacture, presentation and sale of tobacco and related products (COM(2012)0788 – C7-0420/2012 – 2012/0366(COD)1, October 8, 2013.

maximum level of nicotine in e-liquids was decreased from 30 to 20 mg/ml, limits on the size of e-liquid containers and tanks were established, and a ban on flavors was introduced and subsequently withdrawn),[24] but the overall regulatory philosophy behind the new regime remained unchanged.[25] Again, it is not clear why the EU institutions shifted the proposed EU regulatory regime so sharply. The decision seems to have been influenced not only by a public campaign launched by the e-cigarette industry and groups of individual vapers, but also by opinions publicly expressed by many health specialists, who argued that e-cigarettes should primarily be seen as harm reduction devices rather than an alternative to NRT.[26] These groups were able to find allies in the European Parliament (for example members from the ALDE group), who fought against taking a strict regulatory approach to e-cigarettes. It must be kept in mind that the final formulation of Art. 20 of the TPD is in the end a political compromise between the opponents and proponents of the new technology, not necessarily representing the best available science in the field.[27] It does not embody any one regulatory philosophy (risk-based, harm reduction, or precautionary) but rather constitutes a mixture of different approaches.

2.2 The EU Regulatory Regime for E-cigarettes

The main objective of the TPD is to approximate the national laws of Member States concerning the manufacture, presentation, and sale of tobacco and related products, while on one hand maintaining a high level of health protection, and on the other implementing international obligations under the FCTC.[28] As far as e-cigarettes are concerned,[29] the TPD regulates such issues

---

[24] For different versions of the relevant provision of the TPD, see C. Bates, "Info post: EU legislative proposals for nicotine containing products (e-cigarettes)" (*The Counterfactual*, November 30, 2013) https://bit.ly/2OMRsKd accessed October 31, 2018.

[25] Position of the European Parliament adopted at the first reading on 26 February 2014 with a view to adopt a Directive of the European Parliament and of the Council 2014/. . . /EU on the approximation of the laws, regulations and administrative provisions of the Member States on the manufacture, presentation and sale of tobacco and related products and repealing Directive 2001/37/EC (EP-PE_TC1-COD (2012)0366) https://bit.ly/2ALVfDH accessed October 31, 2018.

[26] See for example the open letter "E-cigarettes are helping smokers" (*Financial Times*, December 2, 2013) https://on.ft.com/2OMUxKh accessed October 31, 2018.

[27] See for example "Scientific errors in the Tobacco Products Directive" (letter sent by scientists to the European Union, January 17, 2014) https://bit.ly/2Tn30HQ accessed October 31, 2018.

[28] Compare with Art. 1 in fine and recitals no 5, 6, 8, and 36 of the TPD.

[29] E-cigarettes are defined by the Directive as a "product that can be used for consumption of *nicotine-containing* vapour via a mouth piece, or any component of

as their safety and quality, labeling and consumer information, advertising and sponsorship activities, and notification and reporting obligations. The Directive does not apply to either those e-cigarettes that are classified as medicinal products (that is, marketed as cessation devices)[30] or electronic non-nicotine delivery systems. Member States are free to regulate this latter category as they deem appropriate.

As far as the safety and quality of e-cigarettes is concerned, the Directive establishes a maximum size of e-liquid containers (10 ml) and pods, tanks, and disposable e-cigarettes (2 ml), and sets the maximum level of nicotine in e-liquids (20 mg/ml). Both the containers and the e-cigarettes need to be child and tamperproof and protected against breakage and leakage. In addition, the TPD mandates the use of only high purity ingredients in the production of e-liquids (meaning that only trace levels of impurities which are technically unavoidable during the manufacturing process can be present in a product) and, except for nicotine, does not permit any substance that poses a health risk (the TPD does not however provide any additional guidance in this regard). E-cigarettes also need to deliver, under normal conditions of use, nicotine doses at consistent levels (Art. 20.3).

The labeling and information obligations call for inclusion of: (i) health warnings on unit packaging of e-cigarettes and e-liquids that cover 30–35 percent of the surface (albeit only in the form of a textual message, the content of which is determined by the TPD);[31] (ii) a list of ingredients, together with an indication of the nicotine content; (iii) a leaflet which provides instructions for use and storage, warnings for specific risk groups, and information on addictiveness and toxicity, as well as a second warning specifically directed to young people and non-smokers (Art. 20.4). As with traditional tobacco products, certain elements are prohibited from e-cigarettes' packaging, for example any suggestion that a product is less harmful than others or that it has health or lifestyle benefits (Art. 20.4 read in connection with Art. 13).

The TPD establishes a comprehensive ban on cross-border advertising, promotion, and sponsorship activities related to e-cigarettes. This ban covers

---

that product, including a cartridge, a tank and the device without cartridge or tank. Electronic cigarettes can be disposable or refillable by means of a refill container and a tank, or rechargeable with single use cartridges" (Art. 2(17) of the TPD) [emphasis added].

30 In such cases the provisions of Directive 2001/83/EC of the European Parliament and of the Council of 6 November 2001 on the Community code relating to medicinal products for human use [2001] OJ L 311/67 and Council Directive 93/42/EEC of 14 June 1993 concerning medical devices [1993] OJ L 169/1 are applicable.

31 The TPD envisages two messages: "This product contains nicotine which is a highly addictive substance. It is not recommended for use by non-smokers" and "This product contains nicotine which is a highly addictive substance."

commercial communications on the internet, radio, and television (Art. 20.5). Member States may also (but are not required to) restrict cross-border distance sales of e-cigarettes (Art. 20.6 read in connection with Art. 18).

The Directive introduces a notification (but not authorization) requirement for manufacturers and importers of e-cigarettes. For products that were on the market on May 20, 2016, the deadline expired on November 21, 2016. Notification must be given of new products introduced, or substantially altered, after that date six months before their planned placement on the market. The TPD describes in detail the information that has to be provided as a part of a notification. This particularly includes a list of the product's ingredients and its emissions, toxicological data regarding both the product's ingredients and its emissions, information on the nicotine dose and uptake, and a description of the production process (Art. 20.2).[32] Member States may ask for additional information if the data provided in a particular notification are considered to be incomplete. As of July 2018, more than 185,000 such notifications had been submitted, relating to both e-cigarettes and e-liquids.[33]

Manufacturers and importers of e-cigarettes are obliged to submit to the competent national authorities, on an annual basis, information on sales volume, preferences of various consumer groups—particularly young people and non-smokers (of course, if such information is available to them, they are not obliged to conduct any market surveys), and modes of sale (Art. 20.7). They also need to establish their own system for collecting data on suspected adverse effects arising from the use of e-cigarettes (Art. 20.9).

The Directive requires Member States to monitor market developments in the e-cigarette sector. In this context, they need to pay special attention to new evidence relating to the gateway effect hypothesis (Art. 20.7). The TPD also gives Member States the right to take appropriate provisional measures (for example a marketing ban) if a particular product on the market is believed to present a serious health risk. In such a case the Member State should inform other Members as well as the Commission about a measure and the reasons that stand behind it (Art. 22.11). If a product is prohibited by at least three Members, the Commission is entitled to extend the ban to the whole Union. The Commission also monitors the EU e-cigarette market and follows scientific developments in the field. On that basis the Commission is expected to prepare an implementation report in 2021, which will address "market

---

[32] See also Commission Implementing Decision (EU) 2015/2183 of 24 November 2015 establishing a common format for the notification of electronic cigarettes and refill containers, OJ L 309/15.

[33] Answer given by Mr Andriukaitis on behalf of the European Commission (August 8, 2018, Question reference: E-003629/2018) https://bit.ly/2De1jXA accessed October 31, 2018.

developments and the role of these products for the initiation of consumption by young people and non-smokers and their impact on cessation efforts as well as measures taken by Member States regarding flavors."[34]

It is important to stress that the TPD does not harmonize all regulatory issues relating to e-cigarettes, and certain aspects are decided at the national level. In particular, Member States are free to regulate the flavoring of e-liquids, smoke-free environments, domestic sales arrangements (for example sales via vending or other automated machines; internal distance sales), domestic advertising (for example billboards and presentations at points of sale), and age restrictions.[35] So far no Europeanwide rules on the taxation of e-cigarettes have been adopted and Member States may apply national taxes to e-cigarettes as they deem fit. Although the European Commission undertook some preliminary studies with the aim of revising Directive 2011/64/EU on the structure and rates of excise duties applied to manufactured tobacco,[36] it concluded that the information on the e-cigarette market and the health effects of e-cigarettes was limited and therefore it was not possible to recommend any specific tax treatment.[37] The Commission is planning to reassess this issue in 2019. In the meantime, some Member States have decided to introduce excise taxes on e-cigarettes (arguably motivated by fiscal rather than public health concerns),[38] while others have taken a wait and see approach.

The deadline for implementation of the Directive passed on May 20, 2016. Although there were some delays, in principle all EU Member States have successfully implemented the provisions of the TPD into their national laws. All Members have also introduced some additional restrictions relating to those areas that were left by the Directive to national regulators. These restrictions particularly relate to domestic advertising and sponsorship activities (in most cases taking an approach similar to tobacco products), use of e-cigarettes in public places, and age limitations for the purchase of e-cigarettes and e-liquids. Of course, there are some significant differences between the regulatory regimes adopted by individual Members (the most liberal approach has been taken by the United Kingdom). Probably the most important difference, from

---

[34] Ibid.

[35] See recitals nos 47 and 48 of the TPD.

[36] OJ L 176/24. Note that currently neither e-cigarettes nor novel tobacco products are covered by the Directive.

[37] European Commission, *Report from the Commission to the Council on Directive 2011/64/EU on the Structure and Rates of Excise Duty Applied to Manufactured Tobacco* (Brussels, 12.1.2018 COM(2018) 17 final) 3.

[38] This group particularly includes Italy, Portugal, Romania, Slovenia, Latvia, Hungary, Finland, Greece, and Croatia. Other countries are planning to introduce such taxes in the near future. For example, Poland will do so starting from June 30, 2020.

the point of view of establishment of the internal market,[39] relates to marketing restrictions for flavored e-liquids. Their use remains a controversial issue among public health specialists. Some studies suggest that restricting access to non-tobacco flavors (for example fruity flavors) may discourage smokers from attempting to switch to e-cigarettes.[40] Others, however, are more concerned with the possibility that a great variety of available flavors—particularly those with fruity tastes—increases e-cigarettes' appeal to children and adolescents. Consequently, their availability may contribute to the "renormalizing" process and lead new generations to nicotine addiction.[41]

Finland took the most restrictive approach in this regard, and simply banned all flavored e-liquids except for tobacco flavor. Hungary is planning to implement a similar restriction starting from 2020, while other Members may follow suit in the future—currently at least one (Estonia) is considering an analogous ban. They may be particularly encouraged by the more assertive approach to flavored e-liquids taken recently by the US Food & Drug Administration (FDA) (a planned ban on the sale of most flavored e-cigarettes in convenience stores and gas stations).[42]

Not surprisingly, various provisions of the TPD have been legally challenged, in three separate proceedings.[43] Interestingly, all these cases mainly center on alleged violations of the general principles of EU law rather than the choice of a relevant legal basis for the instrument, as was the case in previous disputes.[44] The regulatory model for the e-cigarette sector was only relevant

---

[39] Note that in practice such a ban may prevent the establishment of an internal market for e-liquids, as most of them come in flavors other than tobacco.

[40] C. Russell et al, "Changing patterns of first e-cigarette flavor used and current flavors used by 20,836 adult frequent e-cigarette users in the USA" (2018) 15 Harm Reduct J 33.

[41] T.W. Ferkol, "Electronic cigarette use in youths: a position statement of the Forum of International Respiratory Societies" (2018) 51 Eur Respir J 1800278. On the renormalizing hypothesis see Chapter 3 in this volume.

[42] L. McGinley, "FDA plans curbs on e-cigarette sales over concerns about surge in teen vaping" (*The Washington Post*, November 8, 2018) https://wapo.st/2Dfxl58 accessed November 8, 2018. Note that the FDA action is focused on sales of flavored products for youth. Consequently, menthol-flavored products would still be available in convenience stores and gas stations, and other flavors in specific age-verified settings. For a more detailed discussion of the US regulatory regime for e-cigarettes, see Chapter 10 in this volume.

[43] In addition to *Pillbox 38 (UK) Ltd v Secretary of State for Health* this includes two other cases: C-358/14 *Poland v Parliament and Council* [2016] ECLI:EU:C:2016:323 and C-547/14 *Philip Morris Brands SARL and Others v Secretary of State for Health* [2016] ECLI:EU:C:2016:325.

[44] It should however be mentioned that the choice of the legal basis for the TPD (with respect to the provisions that prohibit the placing on the market of tobacco prod-

in the *Pillbox 38 (UK) Ltd* case—a challenge that was dealt with by the CJEU in the course of a preliminary ruling proceeding initiated by the High Court of Justice of England and Wales, Queen's Bench Division (Administrative Court, United Kingdom). Pillbox, a British retail seller of e-cigarettes, argued in the original proceeding that Art. 20 of the TPD violated a number of general principles of EU law, in particular the principles of proportionality, legal certainty, subsidiarity, and equality, as well as Arts 16 and 17 of the Charter of Fundamental Rights of the European Union (EU Charter).[45] The subsequent section will review those claims in more detail.

3. ANALYSIS OF THE LEGALITY OF THE DIRECTIVE

3.1 Introduction

During the period in which work on the TPD was ongoing, the EU legal order changed significantly. First of all, the Treaty of Lisbon entered into force and introduced procedural novelties for enacting new EU legal acts under the ordinary legislative procedure. These novelties included in particular the obligation to provide a statement of reasons under Art. 296 of the Treaty on the Functioning of the European Union (TFEU),[46] together with the obligation—both for a draft law and the act itself—to comply with general principles of law, including the principles of subsidiarity and proportionality (Arts 5(1), 5(2), and 5(4) of the Treaty on European Union (TEU)[47] in connection with its Protocol No 2). In addition, a key role was envisaged for national parliaments in the process of enacting legislation (Protocol No 1). The above changes fit into the concept of "better law-making,"[48] aimed at ensuring the compliance of draft legislative acts with the principles of subsidiarity and proportionality. Second, the EU Charter entered into force during work on the TPD. The Charter protects the right to health (Art. 35) as well as the right to conduct a business and the right to property (Arts 16 and 17 respectively). It applies to the EU institutions as well as to the Member States (Art. 51).

---

ucts containing menthol as a characterizing flavor) was unsuccessfully challenged in *Poland v Parliament and Council*.

[45] Charter of Fundamental Rights of the European Union [2012] OJ C 326/391.

[46] Consolidated version of the Treaty on the functioning of the European Union [2012] OJ C 326/47.

[47] Consolidated version of the Treaty on European Union [2012] OJ C 326/43.

[48] Interinstitutional agreement on better law-making [2003] OJ C 321/1.

3.2 Art. 20 of the Directive and the Principle of Subsidiarity

3.2.1 The nature of the principle of subsidiarity

Pursuant to Art. 5(3) of the TEU, in areas that do not fall within the scope of the exclusive competence of the EU, the Union takes action only if and to the extent that the objectives of the intended action cannot be sufficiently achieved by its Member States, either at the central, regional, or local level, and if, due to the scale or effects of the proposed action, the objective can be better achieved at the EU level. The aim of the subsidiarity principle is to rationally restrain the Union when it exercises the shared competences entrusted to it.[49] In other words, the principle answers the question of who should take a particular action.[50]

The principle of subsidiarity has two dimensions: substantive and procedural.[51] The first requires a finding that: (i) an objective of a proposed action cannot be sufficiently realized at the national level (for example because of inadequate means available to Member States); and (ii) such an objective can be better achieved at the EU level due to the scale or effects of required actions. The procedural dimension of the principle of subsidiarity calls for evaluation of the procedural duties imposed on the EU institutions (particularly on the European Commission) with regard to the required consultations for a planned action and its proper justification in terms of subsidiarity.[52] In this context, Art. 5 of Protocol No 2 sets out the guidelines for draft EU legislative acts with respect to their compliance with the principle of subsidiarity (in both the substantive and procedural sense). These guidelines call for, *inter alia*, a detailed statement of the reasons why the draft act is in compliance with the principles of subsidiarity and proportionality. Such a statement should include data on the financial effects of the draft act and, in the case of a directive, its implications for the rules to be put in place by Member States. It also needs to

---

[49] See C. Mik, "Raport i wytyczne do celów kontroli poszanowania zasady pomocniczości" [Report and guidelines for controlling the observance of the subsidiarity principle] in Biuro Analiz Sejmowych (ed), *Parlamenty narodowe wobec zasady pomocniczości w świetle prawa i praktyki Unii Europejskiej* [National parliaments and the principle of subsidiarity in the light of law and practice of the European Union] (Wydawnictwo Sejmowe 2015) 29.

[50] See the *Report from the Commission on Subsidiarity and Proportionality* (18th report on Better Lawmaking covering the year 2010, June 10, 2011, COM(2011) 344 final) 1–2.

[51] For further details see K. Granat, "Subsidiarity as a principle of EU governance" in R. Schütze (ed), *Globalisation and Governance: International Problems, European Solutions* (Oxford University Press 2018).

[52] F. Fabbrini, "The principle of subsidiarity" in R. Schütze, T. Tridimas (eds), *Oxford Principles of European Union Law* (Oxford University Press 2018) 228.

substantiate its claim that the objective can be better achieved at Union level with qualitative and, if possible, quantitative indicators.

The control over compliance with the principle of subsidiarity as such has a twofold nature. First of all, it is a political control exercised by national parliaments, in accordance with the procedures established in Protocol No 2, which may lead to the legislative process being blocked (the so-called orange card[53]). Second, there is a judicial control exercised by the CJEU. In this context, it should be noted that the applicable judicial control standards are not established very precisely, which is undoubtedly the result of the Court's previous restraint in specifying their content.[54] For example, in *Pillbox 38 (UK) Ltd*, neither the Court nor its Advocate General carried out any in-depth analysis of the compatibility of e-cigarette rules with the principle of subsidiarity (although they both looked at the substantive and procedural dimensions of the principle). Since the procedural dimension is more important for the purpose of this chapter, only this aspect will be analyzed in the subsequent subsection.[55]

3.2.2 The procedural dimension of the principle of subsidiarity

As far as the TPD is concerned, the draft of the directive was sent by the European Commission to the national parliaments on January 3, 2013,[56] and they had six weeks to express their reasoned opinions. The draft directive, being the subject of examination by the national parliaments, did not contain the current version of Art. 20 but instead Art. 18, which treated e-cigarettes

---

[53] The orange card refers to a situation when half of the national parliaments raise an objection to a draft legislation.

[54] See A. Biondi, "Subsidiarity in the courtroom" in A. Biondi, P. Eeckhout, S. Ripley (eds), *EU Law after Lisbon* (Oxford University Press 2012) 220.

[55] As far as the substantive aspect is concerned, the CJEU only confirmed that there had been significant differences between Member States as regards the rules applicable to e-cigarettes and to refill containers (C-477/14 *Pillbox 38 (UK) Ltd v The Secretary of State for Health* (n 4) paras 150–1), which required an EU action in order to improve the functioning of the internal market. See also the Opinion of Advocate General Kokott delivered on December 23, 2015 in case C-477/14 *Pillbox 38 (UK) Ltd v The Secretary of State for Health* [2015] ECLI:EU:C:2015:854 paras 162–70 (rightly noting in para 168 that "[i]n view of the fundamental differences between the Member States' rules on e-cigarettes, the flourishing cross-border trade in that field, the novelty of the products in question and the rapid development of the sector, the Union legislature cannot be accused of having committed a manifest error of assessment if it takes the view that there is a problem that has a cross-border dimension with respect to e-cigarettes, which cannot be resolved by measures taken by the Member States alone, but requires action to be taken at Union level").

[56] See http://ipex.eu/IPEXL-WEB/dossier/document/COM20120788.do accessed October 31, 2018.

as medical products, so the parliaments were not in fact able to evaluate the regulation that is currently in force.

As part of the examination (of the whole Directive, not only Art. 18), seven parliaments, representing 11 votes, submitted reasoned opinions relating to the violation of the principle of subsidiarity,[57] a number which was not enough to launch the "yellow card"[58] procedure from Art. 7(2) of Protocol No 2 or the suspensive veto procedure (orange card), which would result in suspension of the legislative procedure and the need to reanalyze the draft. In addition, eight national parliaments sent opinions in the framework of political dialogue; these opinions contained statements that the proposal was incompatible with the principle of subsidiarity.[59] Two chambers sent opinions in which they claimed that the proposal was not in line with the principle of subsidiarity,[60] but these were submitted after the deadline and therefore could not be taken into account when calculating whether the threshold was reached. Consequently, the threshold of 19 votes to launch the yellow card procedure, as required by Art. 7(2) of Protocol No 2, was not achieved, and thus according to Art. 7(1) of Protocol No 2 the European Commission was not obliged to take those opinions into account.

In response to the statement of reasons, the European Commission specified that the submitted draft directive complied with the subsidiarity principle, as it did not impose restrictions on the placing on the market of low risk products. As regards delegated acts (another issue that was contested by the national parliaments), the Commission explained that in order to ensure the operation of the Directive, its exercise of the power to adopt acts in accordance with Art. 290 of the TFEU was considered necessary.[61] The Commission also noted that the draft largely pursues the same objectives as the directive then in force, the

---

57 Czech Republic: Poslanecká sněmovna (1 vote), Denmark: Folketing (2 votes), Greece: Vouli ton Ellinon (2 votes), Italy: Senato della Repubblica (1 vote), Portugal: Assembleia da República (2 votes), Romania: Camera Deputaților (1 vote) and Sweden: Riksdag (2 votes).

58 Yellow card refers to a situation when at least a third but not yet half or more of all national parliaments raise an objection.

59 Austria: Bundesrat, Czech Republic: Sénat, Germany: Bundesrat, France: Assemblée nationale, Poland: Senat, Romania: Senat, Slovakia: Národná Rada, Hungary: Országgyűlés.

60 Bulgaria: Narodno Sabranie and Italy: Camera dei Deputati.

61 See for example Commission's reply to Czech Senate (Brussels, 23.7.2013 C(2013) 4563 final) http://ipex.eu/IPEXL-WEB/scrutiny/COD20120366/czsen.do; Commission's reply to National Council of the Slovak Republic (Brussels, July 25, 2013 C(2013) 4562 final) http://ipex.eu/IPEXL-WEB/scrutiny/COD20120366/skrad.do; Commission's reply to Bulgarian National Assembly (Brussels, July 18, 2013 C(2013) 4564 final) http://ipex.eu/IPEXL-WEB/scrutiny/COD20120366/bgnar.do, all accessed October 31, 2018.

legality of which (in terms of its legal basis) was already confirmed by the CJEU.

The Advocate General, in her opinion in *Pillbox 38 (UK) Ltd*, pointed out that none of the reasoned opinions of the national parliaments contained properly supported arguments regarding e-cigarettes.[62] The Court itself did not address this aspect of the procedural dimension of the principle of subsidiarity because, as it rightly held, examination of the procedural safeguards of the principle provided for by Protocol No 2 was not raised in the question for the preliminary ruling.[63]

The Advocate General also noted that the statement of reasons for a legal act had to be appropriate to the measure at issue and contain a clear explanation of the reasoning followed by the EU institution when adopting such a measure.[64] Such a statement of reasons, however, does not need to include all relevant legal or factual circumstances,[65] while the subsequent review is not limited to the explanatory memorandum that accompanies the draft. Overall, the Advocate General found sufficient reasons in the various legal materials to allow for the conclusion that the principle of subsidiarity had not been violated.[66] The Court, on its part, did not address this issue at all.

3.2.3 Assessment of Art. 20's compliance with the principle of subsidiarity

As has been noted, observance of the principle of subsidiarity requires the fulfillment of two types of elements: procedural and substantive. When considering the compliance of a given act with the principle of subsidiarity in its procedural sense, one should particularly answer two questions: Did the drafter formulate the statement of reasons from the perspective of the principle of subsidiarity? Is the statement of reasons precise enough that it respects the criteria of the principle of subsidiarity?[67] The answers to those questions will also affect the extent to which other obligations arising under the procedural dimension of the principle of subsidiarity are met.

---

[62] See the Opinion of Advocate General Kokott in case C-477/14 *Pillbox 38 (UK) Ltd v The Secretary of State for Health* (n 55) para 161.

[63] C-477/14 *Pillbox 38 (UK) Ltd v The Secretary of State for Health* (n 4) para 147.

[64] Opinion of Advocate General Kokott in case C-477/14 *Pillbox 38 (UK) Ltd v The Secretary of State for Health* (n 55) para 172.

[65] Ibid para 176.

[66] Ibid para 179.

[67] See P. Kiver, *The Early Warning System for the Principle of Subsidiarity: Constitutional Theory and Empirical Reality* (Routledge 2012) 98. This approach is confirmed by the practice of the Committee of the Regions and the Conference of Parliamentary Committees for Union Affairs of Parliaments of the European Union (COSAC).

Art. 20 of the TPD was introduced as an amendment of the European Parliament in February 2014, and therefore was not the subject of the statement of reasons and the impact assessment that accompanied the draft directive presented by the European Commission in December 2012; thus it was not examined by the national parliaments. One of the conditions of the assessment of compliance with the principle of subsidiarity is that the EU proposal should be submitted to national parliaments in a form that allows for such assessment (among others, of the justification for the project).[68] This does not exclude the possibility that a preliminary draft legal act may be and normally is subject to changes in the further stages of legislative work.[69] This was also the case for the regulations concerning e-cigarettes. Indeed, if the EU legislative bodies would need to limit themselves only to adopting provisions which had been subject to an impact assessment of effects made by the Commission, their scope of powers would be limited and the law-making procedure would become meaningless.[70] But in the case of the regulations contained in Art. 20 of the Directive, one needs to recognize the Article's independent nature and its special character due to the nature of the regulated products,[71] which in fact leads to the conclusion that we are dealing with what is a new legislative proposal. This raises the question whether the lack of assessment of the new regulation by national parliaments could result in its annulment because of its failure to comply with the procedural dimension of the principle of subsidiarity.

It seems that such a defect could indeed constitute a basis for challenging the act in the CJEU, because its key aspect was not subject to political and legal assessment under the early warning procedure. Unfortunately, this aspect was not raised by Pillbox, so the Court did not investigate the procedural element.

Considering that the function of the principle of subsidiarity is to contribute to improvement of the quality and consistency of legislation at the EU level,[72] the fact that the TPD provisions on e-cigarettes were not scrutinized by national parliaments can hardly be seen as meeting the criterion of smart regulation,[73] which constitutes a part of the concept of better law-making. The

---

68 Ibid 100–1.

69 See the Opinion of Advocate General Kokott delivered on March 19, 2015 in case C-398/13 P *Inuit Tapiriit Kanatami and Others v European Commission and Others* [2015] ECLI:EU:C:2015:190 para 30.

70 Ibid.

71 Ibid para 15.

72 See for example European Parliament resolution of May 7, 2009 on the development of the relations between the European Parliament and national parliaments under the Treaty of Lisbon (20018/2120(INI)) OJ C 212E/13 para 11.

73 See Communication from the Commission to the European Parliament, the Council, the European Economic and Social Committee and the Committee of the Regions, Smart Regulation in the European Union (COM/2010/0543 final) and F.-X.

examination by national parliaments of a draft legislative act's compliance with the principle of subsidiarity is designed to give the Commission and other EU institutions the opportunity to record political moods, and consequently to take concrete actions in the form of making a proposal more specific, or withdrawing it if it is met with strong resistance. Taking into consideration that most of the Member States had very different regulatory models for e-cigarettes from the one introduced by the Directive, it is possible that had the proposed Directive been properly scrutinized, a sufficient number of objections would have been lodged.

3.3 Art. 20 of the Directive and the Principle of Proportionality

According to the settled case law of the CJEU, the principle of proportionality is one of the general principles of EU law.[74] This principle has underlain the EU decision-making process since the European Council meeting in Edinburgh in 1992. In addition, the Treaty of Lisbon, through its Protocol No 2, introduced the possibility for national parliaments to express their opinions on the compliance of a draft legislative act with the principle of proportionality.

The principle requires that measures adopted by the EU do not exceed the limits of what is appropriate and necessary in order to achieve a particular objective set out in the Treaties.[75] At the same time, the EU institutions are granted a broad margin of discretion in all the areas which entail political, economic, and social choices that require complex assessment. In such cases, an adopted measure can be struck down by the CJEU as being illegal only if it is manifestly inappropriate, having regard to the objective which the competent institution is seeking to pursue.[76] In practice, when examining compliance with

---

Priollaud, D. Siritzky, *Le Traité de Lisbonne. Texte et commentaire article par article des nouvaux traités européens (TUE-TFUE)* (La documentation française 2008) 430.

[74] See for example the judgments in C-331/88 *The Queen v Ministry of Agriculture, Fisheries and Food, ex parte FEDESA and Others* [1990] ECLI:EU:C:1990:391 para 13; C-157/96 *The Queen v Ministry of Agriculture, Fisheries and Food and Commissioners of Customs & Excise, ex parte National Farmers' Union and Others* [1998] ECLI:EU:C:1998:191 para 60.

[75] C-265/87 *Hermann Schräder HS Kraftfutter GmbH & Co. KG v Hauptzollamt Gronau* [1989] ECLI:EU:C:1989:303 para 21; C-379/08 *Raffinerie Mediterranee (ERG) SpA, Polimeri Europa SpA and Syndial SpA v Ministero dello Sviluppo economico and Others* [2010] ECLI:EU:C:2010:127 para 86; C-491/01 *The Queen v Secretary of State for Health, ex parte British American Tobacco (Investments) Ltd and Imperial Tobacco Ltd* (n 7) para 122; C-62/14 *Peter Gauweiler and Others v Deutscher Bundestag* [2015] ECLI:EU:C:2015:400 paras 67 and 91.

[76] See for example C-491/01 *The Queen v Secretary of State for Health, ex parte British American Tobacco (Investments) Ltd and Imperial Tobacco Ltd* (n 7) para 123;

the principle of proportionality the Court conducts the so-called proportionality test, which verifies whether the measure in question is adequate to achieve the proposed objective, whether it is necessary, and finally whether there are other, less intrusive measures to achieve the same objective (proportionality *stricto sensu*).

In the *Pillbox 38 (UK) Ltd* case the applicant made a number of allegations regarding Art. 20 of the TPD's violation of the principle of proportionality. In particular, the company made its claims with regard to the overall legitimacy of the regulatory scheme for e-cigarettes and its specific elements, such as the advanced notification requirement, maximum size of e-liquid containers and threshold for nicotine level, obligation to attach an information leaflet, ban on advertising and sponsorship, restrictions on cross-border distance sales of e-cigarettes, and reporting obligations. Due to space constraints, it is not possible to discuss all those claims in detail here.[77] The subsequent analysis therefore concentrates only on the general, and probably the most important, challenge, which related to the overall legitimacy of the EU regime applicable to e-cigarettes.

Pillbox argued that e-cigarettes should not have been subject to any special rules as they were less harmful than tobacco (or even beneficial for public health). The Court disagreed and ruled, as has already been noted above, that at the time of designing the provisions of the TPD, the laws of the Member States with regard to the e-cigarette sector differed to great extent, thereby creating obstacles to the free movement of goods.[78] The CJEU also noted—with reference to the WHO report on e-cigarettes prepared for the FCTC—the existence of genuine scientific disagreement as to the health risks connected with the consumption of e-cigarettes, both at the level of individual users as well as at the macro level of the entire population.[79] In this context the CJEU particularly mentioned the addictive, toxic, and carcinogenic properties of nicotine, the potential normalization and gateway effects, as well as the issue of the effectiveness of e-cigarettes as a cessation device. In addition, the Court also referred to the precautionary principle, according to which if it is

> impossible to determine with certainty the existence or extent of the alleged risk because of the insufficiency, inconclusiveness or imprecision of the results of studies conducted, but the likelihood of real harm to public health persists should

---

C-62/14 *Peter Gauweiler and Others v Deutscher Bundestag* (n 75) paras 74, 81, and 91.

77 Note, however, that the considerations addressed here are also relevant for specific elements of the EU regulatory regime for e-cigarettes questioned by Pillbox.

78 C-477/14 *Pillbox 38 (UK) Ltd v The Secretary of State for Health* (n 4) para 58.

79 Ibid para 51.

the risk materialize, the precautionary principle justifies the adoption of restrictive measures.[80]

Last but not least, the Court recalled one of the decisions of the Conference of the Parties (COP) to the FCTC, which recommended the consideration of specific restrictions for e-cigarettes (for example with regard to advertising and sponsorship) and monitoring of their use.[81] In this context, the CJEU explained that the Union legislature, by adopting the relevant TPD provisions, intended to meet the EU's obligations under the FCTC.[82]

It is hard to disagree with the CJEU as to its ultimate conclusion on the validity of Art. 20 of the Directive insofar as it establishes a specific regime applicable to e-cigarettes. It is true that Member States have adopted very diverse regulatory solutions for e-cigarettes, ranging from the laissez-faire approach to total sales bans. Considering the dynamic development of the e-cigarette market (including the growing cross-border sales), those different national rules would indeed restrict the flow of the goods within the internal market. It is equally true that, at least at the time of adoption of the TPD, there was a considerable level of scientific uncertainty (which some claim still persists[83]) as to the health risks and potential benefits connected with the use of e-cigarettes. If one recognizes that the Court has traditionally expressed judicial restraint in all cases involving complex scientific questions (particularly when a dispute concerned an EU act rather than an act taken at the national level by an individual Member State) and has granted regulators a considerable margin of discretion—extended even further by the presence of the precautionary principle[84]—then the outcome of the Court's analysis is hardly surprising. The role of the CJEU is not to assess whether the approach taken by the EU institutions is correct,[85] or even the optimal one, but rather to determine whether it meets a certain (in fact rather low) level of rationality,

---

80 Ibid para 55. For extensive discussion of this aspect of the case see Chapter 8.

81 For additional analysis of the FCTC COP recommendations see Chapter 4 in this volume.

82 C-477/14 *Pillbox 38 (UK) Ltd v The Secretary of State for Health* (n 4) paras 59 and 61.

83 For analysis of scientific evidence relevant for e-cigarettes see Chapters 2 and 3 in this volume.

84 See further P. Dąbrowska-Kłosińska, "Risk, precaution and scientific complexity before the Court of Justice of the European Union" in L. Gruszczynski, W. Werner (eds), *Deference in International Courts and Tribunals: Standard of Review and Margin of Appreciation* (Oxford University Press 2014).

85 For example, it was persuasively argued that the limitation on the strength of e-liquids and size of their containers have a weak scientific basis (see "Scientific errors in the Tobacco Products Directive" (n 27)).

that is, whether it *manifestly* exceeds the limits of what is necessary in order to achieve the stated objective. It should be noted that a similar approach has been taken by many other national and international courts and reflects a recognition on the part of judicial bodies of their limited epistemic competences in scientific matters.[86]

Having said this, one may however question the strength of the final argument advanced by the Court. The FCTC does not apply to e-cigarettes as they cannot be classified as tobacco products. Even though the FCTC COP, having a broad mandate, has adopted a decision on e-cigarettes, due to its non-binding character this document cannot create any international obligations.[87] This non-binding nature is actually reflected in the decision itself, which simply invites the FCTC Parties to *consider* taking measures that would meet specific enumerated objectives. Consequently, insofar as e-cigarettes are concerned, one cannot claim that the EU regulators intended to comply with certain obligations under the FCTC, because no such obligations exist.

3.4 Art. 20 of the Directive and the Principle of Equal Treatment

The principle of equal treatment requires that comparable situations cannot be treated differently, and different situations should not be treated in the same way unless such treatment is objectively justified.[88]

Pillbox claimed that Art. 20 of the TPD infringed the principle of equal treatment because it provides less favorable treatment to e-cigarette manufacturers and retailers as compared to conventional cigarette manufacturers and retailers, despite the fact that e-cigarettes are less harmful than tobacco products. In this context, Pillbox pointed out several specific obligations of the TPD (which partially overlapped with those raised in the context of the proportionality analysis): the advance notification requirement, reporting duties, requirement of childproof packaging, restrictions on nicotine content and size

---

86 See for example L. Gruszczynski, V. Vadi, "Standards of review in international investment law and arbitration: multilevel governance and the commonweal" (2013) 16(3) JIEL 613.

87 In particular, Art. 23.5 of the FCTC cannot be regarded as explicitly granting the power to an FCTC COP to adopt binding substantive rules. It merely states that the FCTC COP can take decisions necessary to promote the effective implementation of the Convention. For additional discussion, see L. Gruszczynski, "Tobacco and international trade: recent activities of the FCTC Conference of the Parties" (2015) 49(4) J World Trade 670–5.

88 See in particular C-579/13 *P and S v Commissie Sociale Zekerheid Breda and College van Burgemeester en Wethouders van de gemeente Amstelveen* [2015] ECLI: EU:C:2015:369 para 41.

of refill containers and cartridges, and restrictions imposed on commercial communications (the advertising ban).

The Court, rightly in our opinion, held that e-cigarettes are sufficiently different from tobacco products and therefore cannot be compared with them.[89] Although both categories of products are partially in a competitive relationship and are covered by the same measure (that is, the TPD), there are also a number of objective differences between them. This particularly includes the physical characteristics of the two products; their different patterns of consumption (combustion versus vaporization); their risk profile (clearly established risks versus uncertain risks); and consumers' familiarity with both categories of products.[90] Since e-cigarettes and combustible tobacco products are not similar, the EU legislator was free to establish a separate legal system with its own requirements for the e-cigarette market.

However, irrespective of whether e-cigarettes and traditional tobacco products could be regarded as similar, it should be noted that if such comparison takes into account all—rather than just individual—elements of the relevant regulatory regimes, the treatment of e-cigarettes is not necessarily less favorable.[91] Note, for example, that the labeling requirements for tobacco products are far more demanding and include the obligation to include a combined (textual–pictorial) health warning of much larger size (65 percent on both sides of the package versus 30–35 percent of the front of the package), with a different mode of formulation reflecting the different risk profiles (appealing to smokers' emotions versus neutral information).[92] Similarly, the TPD introduces a ban on flavors in tobacco products, but leaves this issue unregulated for e-cigarettes, and it also extensively standardizes the packaging of tobacco products but contains only limited requirements with respect to e-cigarettes. Some other instances of discrimination identified by Pillbox seem to be questionable as well. For example, restrictions on commercial communications with respect to e-cigarettes mirror those applicable to tobacco products. The TPD also sets maximum emission levels of nicotine and other chemical sub-

---

89 For a discussion on the likeness/similarity of e-cigarettes and traditional tobacco products (and possible discrimination claims) under the law of the World Trade Organization, see Chapter 6 in this volume.

90 C-477/14 *Pillbox 38 (UK) Ltd v The Secretary of State for Health* (n 4) paras 37–41.

91 See also the Opinion of Advocate General Kokott in case C-477/14 *Pillbox 38 (UK) Ltd v The Secretary of State for Health* (n 55) para 41.

92 Compare for example "This product contains nicotine which is a highly addictive substance" (e-cigarettes) with "Smoking can kill your unborn child" (traditional tobacco products).

stances for cigarettes (1 mg of nicotine per cigarette), which may be regarded as roughly equivalent to the maximum nicotine level requirement for e-liquids.

Last but not least, one has to bear in mind that the principle of non-discrimination is not absolute. Different treatment of comparable situations is possible if there is an objective justification for doing so. In this context, it seems that the requirement of childproof packaging can be easily justified (particularly if the EU legislator is granted a broad margin of discretion) as it addresses a specific risk of poisoning that is present in the context of e-liquids.[93] As far as notification and reporting requirements are concerned, it should be recalled that e-cigarettes are relatively novel products on the market and there are significant gaps in our knowledge about them as compared to traditional tobacco products, for example concerning their long-term safety as well as the existence of gateway and renormalization effects. The collection of additional data therefore appears to be a rational approach that will allow better control of potential risks in the future.

3.5 Art. 20 of the Directive and the EU Fundamental Freedoms

Art. 16 of the EU Charter stipulates that "[t]he freedom to conduct a business in accordance with Community law and national laws and practices is recognized." Art. 16 has the nature of a non-specific rule.[94] It is limited to declaring the freedom to conduct a business without defining its content. The scope of this principle is subject to clarification via both national and EU legal acts. The principle of Art. 16 should be seen, in the process of the adoption and interpretation of secondary law, as a postulate that calls for restraint on the part of the EU legislator when intervening on the market, as well as a justification for those interventions that are aimed at opening access to the market, increasing the scope of choice for consumers, and expanding business opportunities for other entities.[95] As indicated in the doctrine, the freedom deriving from Art. 16 of the EU Charter should not be equated with the freedoms of the internal market.[96] The freedom in question is a fundamental right aimed at protecting

---

[93] See for example A. Kamboj et al, "Pediatric exposure to e-cigarettes, nicotine, and tobacco products in the United States" (2016) 137(6) Pediatrics e20160041.

[94] See D. Miąsik, "Art. 16 Karty Praw Podstawowych" [Art. 16 of the Charter of Fundamental Rights] in A. Wróbel (ed), *Karta Praw Podstawowych Unii Europejskiej. Komentarz* [Charter of Fundamental Rights of the European Union. Commentary] (CH Beck 2013) 614.

[95] See Opinion of Advocate General Ruiz-Jarabo Colomer delivered on May 14, 2009 in case C-192/08 *TeliaSonera Finland Oyj* [2009] ECLI:EU:C:2009:309 para 88.

[96] See A. Szafrański, *Przedsiębiorca publiczny wobec wolności gospodarczej* [A public entrepreneur and economic freedom] (CH Beck 2008) 25 and 57.

individuals. On the other hand, the rights deriving from the freedoms of the internal market do not have as an objective the protection of individuals, but rather the achievement of the objectives of the EU.[97]

Art. 20 of the TPD undoubtedly interferes with the freedom to conduct a business. This is particularly true when it comes to the advertising ban (an element of the regime specifically identified by Pillbox), which prevents economic operators from promoting their products. However, according to well-established case law the freedom to conduct a business is not an absolute right; it may be subject to various interferences by public authorities, which have the right to impose restrictions on its exercise to protect the general interest.[98] At the same time, any limitation on the exercise of rights and freedoms protected under the EU Charter must be provided for by law and may not violate the essence of those rights and freedoms. In addition, such limitations need to comply with the principle of proportionality, meaning that they must be necessary and genuinely meet the objectives of the general interest recognized by the Union, or arise from the need to protect the rights and freedoms of others (Art. 52(1) of the EU Charter).

The CJEU was very brief in addressing this claim. It simply stated that the relevant provision was included in a directive (a legal act), did not affect the essence of the right (economic operators could still produce and sell their products), and complied (for the reasons discussed above) with the requirements set out by the principle of proportionality.[99] More interesting in this regard is the opinion of the Advocate General, who explicitly stated that the assessment of proportionality of the advertising ban under Art. 16 of the EU Charter had to be considered from the point of view of economic interests as well as the protected good (in this case public health).[100] At the same time, the Advocate General pointed out that public health is particularly high in the EU hierarchy of values,[101] and arguably always takes precedence over the right to conduct a business (as well as other rights provided by the EU Charter).

The Court took a similar position with regard to the right to property under Art. 17 of the EU Charter, the scope of which also covers intellectual prop-

---

[97] See M. Szydło, *Krajowe prawo spółek a swoboda przedsiębiorczości* [National company law and freedom of establishment] (LexisNexis 2007) 140–1.

[98] See for example C-283 *Sky Österreich GmbH v Österreichischer Rundfunk* [2013] ECLI:EU:C:2013:28 para 46; C-544/10 *Deutsches Weintor eG v Land Rheinland-Pfalz* [2012] ECLI:EU:C:2012:526 para 54.

[99] C-477/14 *Pillbox 38 (UK) Ltd v The Secretary of State for Health* (n 4) paras 161–2.

[100] Opinion of Advocate General Kokott in case C-477/14 *Pillbox 38 (UK) Ltd v The Secretary of State for Health* (n 55) para 190.

[101] Ibid.

erty rights.[102] According to the CJEU, although the advertising ban limited Pillbox's opportunities to use its trademark, it did not affect the essence of the right to property as it was still possible for the company to use such trademark in other circumstances (for example on a product). For the same reasons indicated above, the interference did not exceed the limits of what was appropriate and necessary to achieve the objectives of the TPD.[103] One may also recall here an additional observation made by the Advocate General, although it was not repeated by the Court. Note that pursuant to existing case law, the protection of property rights does not cover business interests or expectations. An economic entity, such as Pillbox, cannot rely on a right acquired, or even legitimate expectations regarding the maintenance of an existing situation, that may change as a result of changes in the law. According to the Advocate General, Pillbox's claim was essentially about its future earnings prospects, as the advertising ban was conceptualized as an element of the new regulatory regime, which impairs the future opportunities for marketing e-cigarettes in the internal market.[104]

The conclusions reached by the Court, although accompanied only by a brief analysis, do not seem to raise any significant legal controversies.

4. CONCLUSIONS

The judgment of the Court in the *Pillbox 38 (UK) Ltd* case confirmed that the EU legislature has the power to harmonize rules relating to e-cigarettes. Interestingly, this assessment was mostly limited to the compliance of the relevant provisions of the TPD with general principles of EU law, rather than the appropriate legal basis. In this context, the Court confirmed that general principles, that is, the principle of subsidiarity or proportionality, have not only political value, but above all legal value. The only serious concern which arises in the context of the TPD provisions for e-cigarettes relates to the procedural aspect of the subsidiarity principle. This non-compliance (if it did exist) does not however affect the substantive legitimacy of the mechanisms introduced by the Directive.

---

[102] Art. 17 specifically provides "[e]veryone has the right to own, use, dispose of and bequeath his or her lawfully acquired possessions. No one may be deprived of his or her possessions, except in the public interest and in the cases and under the conditions provided for by law, subject to fair compensation being paid in good time for their loss. The use of property may be regulated by law in so far as is necessary for the general interest."

[103] C-477/14 *Pillbox 38 (UK) Ltd v The Secretary of State for Health* (n 4) para 164.

[104] Opinion of Advocate General Kokott in case C-477/14 *Pillbox 38 (UK) Ltd v The Secretary of State for Health* (n 55) para 198.

Overall, the TPD, with its *sui generis* legal regime for e-cigarettes, can be seen as a realistic (albeit not perfect) compromise between the proponents and opponents of the new technology. It recognizes the harm reduction potential of the products (for example by establishing less strict standards than those which are applied to combustible tobacco products), but also acknowledges the existing uncertainties resulting from gaps in knowledge and contradictory scientific views (for example on the long-term consequences of e-cigarette use, or the gateway potential of the products), as well as the systemic problems that the technology may create (the renormalization effect).[105] At the same time, it also creates mechanisms, such as the notification and reporting requirements, that will facilitate its revision as our knowledge about e-cigarettes develops. Finally, the TPD leaves a certain regulatory space to the EU Member States, allowing them to reflect on particular national risk preferences and providing room for regulatory experimentation. Consequently, as an overall approach (but not necessarily with respect to its specific elements), it may act as an inspiration for other countries, at least until more complete data on e-cigarettes and related public health risks and benefits becomes available.

---

105 See A. McNeill et al, *E-Cigarettes: An Evidence Update* (A Report Commissioned by Public Health England, Public Health England 2015). For a less optimistic view, see European Public Health Association, "Facts and fiction on e-cigs" (undated) https://eupha.org/repository/advocacy/EUPHA_facts_and_fiction_on_e-cigs.pdf accessed October 31, 2018.

8. Vaping and the precautionary principle in EU law

Giancarlo A. Ferro and Costanza Nicolosi[1]

1. INTRODUCTION

Despite years of research, we still lack scientific certainty as to the extent of human health risks (or their actual existence) resulting from use of electronic nicotine delivery systems (ENDS or e-cigarettes). Scientists as well as anti-tobacco activists seem to be genuinely divided on this issue. For example, some researchers claim e-cigarettes should be regarded as a solution to the tobacco epidemic, while others believe that they simply constitute yet another variation of a well-known deadly product.[2] In a similar vein, some anti-tobacco organizations advocate for a more liberal approach that recognizes the harm reduction potential of e-cigarettes,[3] while others call for strict regulations, arguing that the many uncertainties surrounding ENDS use demand aggressive regulatory action to ensure a high level of human health protection in the face of "potential risks."[4] This latter position seems to be dominant in the current regulatory practice. The underlying assumption in many jurisdictions is that vaping is potentially just as harmful as regular smoking. Therefore, a general regulatory trend is to apply the—often taken for granted—precautionary principle in order to extend the restrictions already applied to tobacco products to e-cigarettes as well, or even to prohibit ENDS altogether. In the EU, the

[1] G.A. Ferro wrote sections 3, 4 and 6 of the chapter while C. Nicolosi wrote sections 1, 2 and 5.

[2] For a discussion on the differences among public health experts, see Chapter 2 in this volume.

[3] See for example Action on Smoking and Health, "Briefing: Electronic Cigarettes" (February 2016) https://bit.ly/2PpDqPO accessed October 31, 2018.

[4] See for example Southeast Asia Tobacco Control Alliance, "Statement on Singapore's ban on emerging tobacco products like e-cigarettes" (January 31, 2018) https://seatca.org/?p=12027 accessed October 31, 2018.

elements of such a trend were recently evidenced by the passage of Directive 2014/40 on tobacco and related products (the TPD or the Directive).[5]

Generally speaking, the precautionary principle is invoked in order to justify preemptive measures whenever the potentially harmful effects from a phenomenon, product, or process cannot be scientifically determined with certainty. Precautionary measures ought to be non-discriminatory and proportional to the level of protection sought by a regulator. In some jurisdictions, the application of the principle may also result in the alteration of the traditional allocation of the burden of proving the "potential" risk (or lack of it) associated with a specific product. As a consequence, the burden of proof may fall not on regulators, but rather on producers, manufacturers, or importers. However, establishing a product's safety with *absolute certainty* is often exceedingly difficult (or even impossible) and may, in many cases, take years (or even decades) to determine. This is arguably the case for ENDS.

Following a brief assessment of the precautionary principle, both in international and in EU law, this chapter investigates its application to vaping and attempts to identify certain distortions caused by precautionary regulations. The chapter argues that the precautionary principle, as it currently stands, is too vague, and that its application sacrifices legal certainty and industrial innovation in the name of rather undefined concerns about public safety. The chapter also submits, in the context of the TPD, that the precautionary principle has been used not for its original purpose of balancing public health concerns with market principles, but rather to further harmonize the EU internal market. While this is unquestionably an important objective, it is certainly not best served by the application of the principle meant for rather different aims.

Thus the chapter proceeds as follows. Section 2 traces the origins of the precautionary principle and summarizes its evolution as a legal principle of international law. Section 3 discusses the normative content of the principle in EU law. Against this background, section 4 moves on to the TPD and analyzes how the precautionary principle was used in the context of the EU's approach to vaping. Section 5 provides a critical assessment of the stance taken by the European institutions, particularly the Court of Justice of the European Union (CJEU or the Court),[6] and section 6 offers conclusions.

---

5 Directive 2014/40 (EU) of the European Parliament and of the Council on the approximation of the laws, regulations and administrative provisions of the Member States concerning the manufacture, presentation and sale of tobacco and related products [2014] OJ L 127/1.

6 For the terminological clarifications see fn 3 in Chapter 7 of this volume.

2. THE PRECAUTIONARY PRINCIPLE IN INTERNATIONAL LAW

Defining the precautionary principle is not an easy task. Indeed, it has been said that there exist at least 20 different definitions of the principle—many of which are incompatible with each other.[7] The precautionary principle is originally rooted in sociology and philosophy,[8] where it stood as an ethical rule regulating human behavior in the so-called risk society, and only relatively recently has it come to assume a central role as a legal concept.

The distinguishing feature underlying the precautionary principle is the impossibility to meaningfully assess the risks deriving from (un)identified sources. Hence, it does not concern so much the *actual risks*, but rather the *potential risks* that cannot (yet) be fully established because of scientific uncertainty. From this perspective, it is necessary to distinguish the precautionary principle from the prevention principle, which allows interventions aimed at preventing the occurrence of certainly existing and already proven risks. In other words, the precautionary principle is aimed not at *actual risks* (which are covered by the prevention principle) but at potential ones, that is, risks about which there are scientific uncertainties. Indeed, if prevention takes place to avoid the occurrence of a certain risk, precaution aims at regulating a still uncertain risk whose occurrence cannot be excluded, but nevertheless cannot be proven with certainty. Prevention needs sufficient data to identify a certain or probable risk, whereas precaution kicks in when such information is missing and it is therefore impossible to determine relevant probabilities. This also means that the precautionary principle requires early intervention, so as to prevent the transformation of a potential risk into a real one. Generally such an intervention is justified only in order to avoid potentially grave and irreversible damage (but that depends on the version of the principle). Precautionary measures also need to be based on at least plausible scientific hypotheses. The precautionary principle therefore stands for the approach that scientific uncertainty should not prevent the application of preventive and cost effective measures in cases of potentially serious or irreversible harmful effects—

[7] See generally C.R. Sunstein, *The Laws of Fear: Beyond the Precautionary Principle* (Cambridge University Press 2005).

[8] This meaning dates back to the classical works of Hans Jonas, *Das Prinzip Verantwortung. Versuch einer Ethik für die technologische Zivilisation* (Suhrkamp Verlag 1979) and *Technik, Medizin und Ethik. Zur Praxis des Prinzips Verantwortung* (Suhrkamp Verlag 1985). See also U. Beck, *Risk Society: Towards a New Modernity* (Sage Publications 1992). For further references to the precautionary principle in philosophy, see particularly L. Marini, L. Palazzani (eds), *Il principio di precauzione tra filosofia, biodiritto e biopolitica* (Studium 2008).

effects which can be identified mainly by scientific progress and technological developments.[9] The precautionary principle is activated as a way to assess (to the extent possible) and manage potential risks in cases of uncertainty as to the existence and scope of negative effects of specific activities or products.

The precautionary principle as a legal concept appeared for the first time in German environmental law, where it was aimed at providing a rationale for regulation in cases of an unclear causal relationship between the source of the harm and the potential damage.[10] There is no agreement as to when the principle made its first appearance in international law, even though its origins can probably be traced back to the 1980s, when several charters and conventions made reference to some elements of precaution.[11] Finally, the 1992 Rio Declaration provided the first relatively precise articulation of the precautionary principle, stating that "where there are threats of serious or irreversible damage, lack of full scientific certainty shall not be used as a reason for postponing cost-effective measures to prevent environmental degradation."[12] This definition has quickly become the most accepted and most commonly referred to formulation of the principle, nowadays widely (even if not

---

9 More precisely, the precautionary principle applies in any case where activities might cause risks for human health and—in more general terms—for the enjoyment of rights, but such risks are only potential, as there is not yet definitive evidence as to their existence and scope. In such cases, public authorities can allow the activities only after collecting data which might reasonably exclude the potential for grave dangers, therefore complying with the principles of proportionality, non-discrimination, and coherency. There is also a disclosure obligation imposed on the public authorities toward those who are exposed to such risks. Such understanding of the precautionary principle has been shaped by the case law of the European Court of Human Rights (ECtHR). See in particular *Guerra et al v Italy* (1998) App. No 14967/89; *Tatar v Romania* (2009) App. No 67021/01; *McGinley v United Kingdom* (1998) App. No 21825/93; *Roche v United Kingdom* (2005) App. No 32555/96. Compare also with D. Xenos, "Asserting the Right to Life (Article 2, ECHR) in the Context of Industry" (2007) 3 Ger Law J 231.

10 See L. Gruszczynski, *Regulating Health and Environmental Risks under WTO Law: A Critical Analysis of the SPS Agreement* (Oxford University Press 2010) 158 (quoting S. Boehmer-Christiansen, "The Precautionary Principle in Germany—Enabling Government" in T. O'Riordan, J. Cameron (eds), *Interpreting the Precautionary Principle* (Earthscan 1994)).

11 See for example the 1982 World Charter for Nature (requiring special precautions to be taken in order to prevent discharge of radioactive or toxic wastes) and the 1989 Montreal Protocol on Substances that Deplete the Ozone Layer (determined to protect the ozone layer by taking precautionary measures to equitably control total global emissions).

12 Rio Declaration on Environments and Development, June 14, 1992, UN A/Conf 151/5/Rev 1 (1992), reprinted in 31 ILM 876 (1992) principle 15.

uniformly[13]) applied in different countries as well as at the international level, including in areas other than environmental law (for instance the protection of human life and health).[14] More recently, this formulation was reaffirmed by several eminent scholars and ecological non-governmental organizations in the "Wingspread Statement," which states that "when an activity raises threats of harm to human health or the environment, precautionary measures should be taken even if some cause-and-effect relationships are not fully established scientifically."[15]

However, given the mutable formulations of the precautionary principle in different international instruments, it comes as no surprise that no uniform definition or application of the principle has been achieved in international law. At a certain general level, one may say that "the essence of the precautionary principle is that positive action . . . may be required before the existence of a risk has been scientifically established."[16] However, when it comes to details, any overall consensus disappears.[17]

3. THE PRECAUTIONARY PRINCIPLE IN EU LAW AND PRACTICE

The precautionary principle has gradually taken on a central role in EU law even though, as we will see in more detail below, it still remains vague in its definition. Given the heterogeneity of definitions in international law and the vagueness of the concept in EU law, it is difficult to analyze the principle's different meanings in the two legal systems. Nevertheless, such an attempt

---

13 For instance, differences exist with respect to the thresholds of scientific uncertainty for the principle's application, the requirement (or lack thereof) to carry out a cost–benefit analysis, the proportionality test, and allocation of the burden of proof. See generally Gruszczynski (n 10) 160–1.

14 See for example the Cartagena Protocol on Biosafety (touching upon the protection of human health as a part of its objective of safeguarding biodiversity); the Stockholm Convention on Persistent Organic Pollutants (asking for a precautionary approach with regard to the protection of human life and health).

15 Wingspread Statement on the Precautionary Principle, January 25, 1998, reprinted in C. Raffensperger, J. Ticker (eds), *Protecting Public Health and the Environment: Implementing the Precautionary Principle* (Island Press 1999); compare also with Regulation (EC) No 178/2002 of the European Parliament and of the Council of January 28, 2002 laying down the general principles and requirements of food law, establishing the European Food Safety Authority and laying down procedures in matters of food safety [2002] OJ L 031.

16 J. Bohanes, "Risk Regulation in WTO Law: A Procedure-Based Approach to the Precautionary Principle" (2002) 40 Columbia J Trans Law 331.

17 Gruszczynski (n 10) 160.

is meaningful to our discussion, as it provides a useful focus on some of the principle's peculiarities.

First, it seems there are different thresholds for the application of the principle in international and EU law. Indeed, the Rio Declaration seems to imply that only *serious or irreversible threats* can trigger the application of the principle. On the other hand, EU law provides for a much lower threshold, having recourse to the precautionary principle simply in cases of *potential* risks.[18] Second, prior to invoking the precautionary principle, EU law requires a scientific (and as complete as possible) risk analysis in order to identify and assess uncertainties.[19] International law adopts a more permissible approach in this regard, referring only to "the lack of full scientific certainty" (Rio Declaration) or to a situation in which "some cause and effect relationships are not fully established scientifically" (Wingspread Statement). The most important difference between the precautionary principle in international law and in EU law is probably that in the latter the principle is formulated as a mere signpost for risk managers, meaning that it simply gives a justification for regulatory action, without compelling risk managers to act in the first place.[20] On the other hand, in international law the principle is usually formulated as an imperative, requiring action in cases of uncertainty (if there is a threat of serious or irreversible damage).

Similarly to the case in international law, the precautionary principle made its first appearance in EU law in the area of environmental protection. Still today the connection in EU law between the principle and the environment remains very strong. Indeed, Art. 191 of the Treaty on the Functioning of the European Union (TFEU) (ex-Art. 174 of the Treaty establishing the European Community), which introduces the principle, provides that:

---

[18] Communication from the Commission on the Precautionary Principle, February 2, 2000, COM/2000/0001 final, 17. Note, however, that other instruments of international law also provide for lower thresholds. See for instance the Biosafety Protocol, which only speaks about a "potential adverse effect" without qualifying its seriousness and probably presuming the irreversible character of threats connected with genetically modified organisms, or the Convention on Biological Diversity, which refer to "threats of significant reduction or loss."

[19] Communication from the Commission on the Precautionary Principle (n 18) 13–14.

[20] Ibid 15–16 (stating that "the Commission or any other Community institution has broad discretionary powers, notably as regards the nature and scope of the measures it adopts" and "responding does not necessarily mean that measures always have to be adopted. In this case, the decision to do nothing may be a response in its own right").

2. Union policy on the environment shall aim at *a high level of protection* . . . based *on the precautionary principle and on the principles that preventive action* should be taken . . .
3. In preparing its policy on the environment, the Union shall take account of: *available scientific and technical data* . . . *the potential benefits and costs of action or lack of action* . . . [emphasis added].

However, the entire European regulatory process—also in areas other than environmental law—is greatly inspired by the realization of a *high level of protection*, especially in risk-related fields (for example food, work, commercial products, and so on). Indeed, in practice the precautionary principle has found application far beyond environmental protection and become a normative principle for the protection of public health. EU case law has consistently upheld this "expansion in scope."[21] In *Artegodan GmbH*,[22] the Court of First Instance explicitly defined the precautionary principle as a general principle of EU law:

> [A]lthough the precautionary principle is mentioned in the Treaty only in connection with environmental policy, it is broader in scope. It is intended to be applied in order to ensure a high level of protection of health, consumer safety and the environment in all the Community's spheres of activity.[23]

In the subsequent paragraph, the Court also explained:

> [T]he precautionary principle can be defined as *a general principle of Community law* requiring the competent authorities to take appropriate measures to prevent specific potential risks to public health, safety and the environment, by giving precedence to the requirements related to the protection of those interests over economic interests. Since the Community institutions are responsible, in all their spheres of activity, for the protection of public health, safety and the environment, the precautionary principle can be regarded as an autonomous principle stemming from the abovementioned Treaty provisions. [emphasis added][24]

---

21 This was the case up until the 1980s, as evidenced by Case C-104/75 *De Peijper, Managing Director of Centrafarm BV* [1976] ECLI:EU:C:1976:67; Case C-97/83 *Criminal proceedings against CMC Melkunie BV* [1984] ECLI:EU:C:1984:212. See also J. Scott, "The Precautionary Principle before the European Courts" in R. Macrory (ed), *Principles of European Environmental Law* (Europa Law Publishing 2004); V. Heyvaert, "Facing the Consequences of the Precautionary Principle in European Community Law" (2006) 31 EL Rev 185.

22 Joined Cases T-74/00, T-76/00, T-83/00, T-84/00, T-85/00, T-132/00, T-137/00, and T-141/00 *Artegodan and Others v Commission* [2002] ECLI:EU:T:2002:283.

23 Ibid para 183.

24 Ibid para 184.

The case law that followed has confirmed this understanding.[25]

This "expansion in scope" is also reflected in EU secondary law, as evidenced by the previously cited European Commission's Communication on the Precautionary Principle, currently the main document produced by the European institution regarding the principle.[26] A thorough analysis of the Communication is beyond the scope of this contribution, and for our discussion it is enough to say that in EU law, as depicted by the Communication, the precautionary principle provides a methodology for organizing the decision-making process in all cases of scientific uncertainty. Indeed, the principle is the instrument balancing free market principles with protection of the primary legal values and corresponding rights—such as health and safety—of European citizens.

According to the Communication, invoking the precautionary principle requires: (a) identification of the potentially negative effects; (b) evaluation of the available scientific data; and (c) consideration of scientific uncertainty. Consequently, a decision as to whether to apply preventive measures *per* the precautionary principle needs to be based on a scientific evaluation and risk assessment of the potential consequences of action, as well as of non-action, that is as comprehensive as possible. The elaboration process leading to the adoption of the preventive measures also needs to be transparent and inclusive. Finally, any measure adopted on the basis of the precautionary principle must—at the very least—comply with five other principles:

(1) proportionality between the measures adopted and the level of protection that is sought;[27]
(2) non-discriminatory application;
(3) coherence between the measures to be adopted and actions taken in similar circumstances;
(4) assessment of the costs of actions (and non-actions);

---

[25] See for example Case T-392/02 *Solvay Pharmaceuticals BV v Council of the European Union* [2003] ECLI:EU:T:2003:277; Joined Cases C-154/04 and C-155/04 *The Queen, ex parte: Alliance for Natural Health Stores and Health Food Manufacturers Ltd v Secretary of State for Health and National Assembly for Wales* [2005] ECLI:EU:C:2005:449. See also J. Scott (n 21); K. Garnett, D.J. Parsons, "Case Review of the Application of the Precautionary Principle in European Union Law and Case Law" (2017) 3 Risk Analysis 502.

[26] For an excellent analysis of this point, see N. McNelis, "EU Communication on the Precautionary Principle" (2000) 3 J Intl Econ L 545.

[27] Proportionality has two distinctive dimensions. First, it calls for a certain coherence between the means used and ends pursued. Second, a measure has to be the least onerous alternative available to regulators to achieve a specific objective (without, however, a need to compromise it).

(5) provision for re-evaluation of the measures taken in light of ongoing scientific developments.

The broadening scope of the precautionary principle in all fields affecting public health and its vague conceptualization may have serious consequences as it can forestall and undermine technical innovation. Indeed, resolving the "balancing dilemma" in the context of a principle, which escapes a conclusive definition, provides a very shaky foundation for its application. As the appropriate amount of precaution derives from balancing several different interests, identification of the level of protection for precautionary purposes cannot avoid being influenced by consideration of *ad hoc* circumstances and—possibly—a high degree of political discretion, given the exceedingly discretionary nature of choosing the level of (scientifically unprovable) risk that society can or cannot tolerate. Moreover, in deciding cases involving the precautionary principle, judges must proceed on a case-by-case basis, thereby undermining the legal certainty and providing fertile ground for judicial activism.

It is also important to note that the legal evaluation of preemptive measures based on the precautionary principle shifts the general rules on the burden of proof, thereby further undermining product innovation. Indeed, with some notable exceptions,[28] EU law does not require a system of preventive authorization before products' entry into the market. Therefore, any harmful effect will have to be shown either by regulators or by end consumers or their associations after the product's entry into the market. Conversely, in cases involving the precautionary principle, the burden of proving a product's *safety* is shifted on producers, manufacturers, or importers, and in addition is evaluated on a case-by-case basis. Therefore, the reasonableness of judicial decisions will depend on the reliability—and accurate assessment—of the available (yet inconclusive) scientific evidence. Consequently, application of the precautionary principle will ultimately depend very little on legal arguments and more on both the intended level of protection (mainly a political choice) and the evaluation of the available scientific data. It is therefore fair to conclude that application of the precautionary principle is an issue more of a *political* rather than *legal* nature, aimed at developing an ever more *harmonized* common market (as purposed by Art. 114(3) of the TFEU) based on a high degree of protection.

---

[28] Concerning products such as medicines, fungicides, and food additives.

The Commission has acknowledged the political nature of the precautionary principle, stating that:

> [D]ecision-makers are constantly faced with the dilemma of balancing the freedom and rights of individuals, industry and organisations with the need to reduce the risk of adverse effects to the environment, human, animal or plant health. Therefore, finding the correct balance so that the proportionate, non-discriminatory, transparent and coherent actions can be taken, requires a structured decision-making process with detailed scientific and other objective information.[29]

The EU case law has further affirmed the political nature of the initial decision on the appropriate degree of protection sought by regulators. In *Pfizer Animal Health*,[30] the Court of First Instance—explicitly referring to the Communication on the Precautionary Principle—found that:

> [I]n the assessment of risk, it is for the Community institutions to determine the level of risk—that is the critical probability threshold for adverse effects on human health and for the seriousness of those possible effects—which in their judgment is no longer acceptable for society and above which it is necessary, in the interests of protecting human health, to take preventive measures in spite of any existing scientific uncertainty.[31]

4. REGULATING ENDS: THE TPD AND THE CJEU CASE LAW

In considering specifically the regulation of ENDS, one cannot but refer to the TPD. The Directive seems to be inspired by the same considerations that led to the introduction and application of the precautionary principle in EU law. In particular, in its introduction the TPD stresses the need to set up precise rules in order to facilitate the smooth functioning of the internal market, based on a *high level of protection of human health*, above all for youth.[32] It also refers to the 2003 WHO Framework Convention on Tobacco Control (FCTC),[33] which however does not itself contain any explicit vaping regulations, but only a generic provision requiring signatories to "take measures to prevent the initi-

---

29 Communication from the Commission on the Precautionary Principle (n 18) 7.

30 Case T-13/99 *Pfizer Animal Health SA v Council of the European Union* [2002] ECLI:EU:T:2002:209.

31 Ibid para 151.

32 See recitals 36, 43, and 47 of the TPD; see also Arts 1 and 20.7 of the Directive.

33 WHO Framework Convention on Tobacco Control, opened for signature June 16, 2003 (entered into force February 27, 2005) 2302 UNTS 166.

ation . . . of tobacco products in any form."[34] This reference is understandable as the TPD regulates not only e-cigarettes but above all traditional tobacco products, which are at the center of the FCTC's interest. However, the reference to the FCTC may also show that the EU institutions believe that vaping (particularly when it comes to products containing nicotine) might represent a gateway or "rite of passage" toward consumption of traditional cigarettes,[35] and produce a "normalization effect" (that is, increase social acceptance of smoking as a result of the growing popularity of e-cigarettes). Supposing this assumption to be true, several precautions should be taken in the manufacturing and sale of e-cigarettes and related products. Such a reading of the TPD is reinforced by the approach taken by the Court in the *Pillbox 38 (UK) Ltd v The Secretary of State for Health* dispute (discussed in detail below).[36] In particular, the judgment includes a number of references to the FCTC, notwithstanding the fact that it only deals with those parts of the Directive that regulate e-cigarettes. Moreover, both the CJEU and the Advocate General explicitly referred in their analysis to the gateway and normalization risks.[37]

Art. 20 of the TPD subjects ENDS to a regulatory regime inspired by traditional tobacco control policies, but sufficiently distinctive to consider e-cigarettes a *sui generis* product category. In particular, the Directive distinguishes ENDS from traditional tobacco products and defines them as "a product that can be used for consumption of nicotine-containing vapour via a mouth piece, or any component of that product, including a cartridge, a tank or a device without cartridge or tank."[38] As explained in detail in Chapter 7 of this volume, the TPD requires that all e-liquids offered on the market meet certain requirements relating to their composition (for example, there is a maximum level of nicotine)[39] and size (for example, containers cannot be larger than 10 ml). Both e-liquids and ENDS can be sold only in unit packets containing specific information (some of it directly on the packaging, some in the form of an attached leaflet), such as mandatory health warnings (although such warnings are less strict than in case of traditional tobacco products),

---

[34] Ibid Art. 4.2(b). For a detailed discussion of other FCTC provisions that may be relevant for regulation of ENDS, see Chapter 4 in this volume.

[35] See also Art. 20.7 of the TPD, which requires Member States to monitor market developments concerning ENDS, in particular with respect to evidence relating to ENDS as a potential gateway product.

[36] Case C-477/14 *Pillbox 38 (UK) Ltd v Secretary of State for Health* [2016] ECLI: EU:C:2016:324.

[37] Ibid para 53. See also Opinion of Advocate General Kokott delivered on December 23, 2015 in Case C-477/14 *Pillbox 38 (UK) Ltd v Secretary of State for Health* [2015] ECLI:EU:C:2015:854 para 62.

[38] Art. 2(16) of the TPD.

[39] See for example ibid Art. 20.3.

instructions on products' use and storage, and information on their addictiveness and toxicity.[40] The TPD also envisages a comprehensive ban on advertising and promotional activities concerning ENDS, which however only applies to the transnational (that is, European) level and online activities.[41]

A separate set of requirements relates to notification and reporting duties. Manufacturers and importers of ENDS are required to notify relevant Member States of any new product prior to its commercialization (this obligation is also activated whenever a particular product is substantially altered).[42] Such a notification needs to include a number of specific items of information, such as toxicological data regarding the product's ingredients and emissions. In addition, manufacturers and importers are required to transmit to the competent national authorities each year relevant data on sales volumes and the preferences of various consumer groups, including young people (of course, if they possess such data).[43] The Directive also provides for an emergency mechanism that allows Member States to restrict, on a temporary basis, the marketing of specific products.[44]

Although the TPD is a comprehensive piece of legislation, it does not cover all relevant matters. In particular, Member States are free to regulate issues such as smoke-free environments, domestic advertising, age limits for the purchase of e-cigarettes and related products, nicotine-free e-cigarettes, and e-liquid flavorings. In addition, the TPD does not cover so-called medical e-cigarettes (that is, ENDS meant for therapeutic and medical purposes), which are covered either by Directive 2001/83/EC or Directive 93/42/EEC.

The legality of the TPD has been contested in several different proceedings.[45] For the purpose of this chapter, the most important one is the challenge brought by Pillbox 38 (UK) Ltd (Pillbox), a British reseller of ENDS and related accessories. The High Court of Justice of England and Wales, Queen's Bench Division—where the proceeding was initiated—decided to refer a number of preliminary questions relating to the interpretation of EU law to the CJEU, which delivered its judgment on May 4, 2016. Due to the limited scope of this chapter, we will only focus here on the Court's findings relating to the compatibility of Art. 20 of the TPD with the principle of proportionality and the role that precaution played in this context.

---

[40] Ibid Art. 20.4(a) and (b).

[41] Ibid Art. 20(5).

[42] See ibid Art. 20.2 for a comprehensive list of the information to be produced.

[43] Ibid Art. 20.7–20.9.

[44] Ibid Art. 20(11).

[45] Besides Pillbox 38 (UK) Ltd, this group included cases C-358/14 *Poland v Parliament and Council* [2016] ECLI:EU:C:2016:323 and C-547/14 *Philip Morris Brands SARL and Others v Secretary of State for Health* [2016] ECLI:EU:C:2016:325.

Pillbox argued that Art. 20 of the TPD is invalid because it infringed a number of the EU law principles, such as the principles of proportionality, legal certainty, non-discrimination, free competition, and subsidiarity, as well as Arts 16 and 17 of the Charter of Fundamental Rights of the European Union (Charter).[46] In this context, Pillbox specifically submitted that, given that e-cigarettes might have a beneficial effect on public health, they ought not to be subject to any regulation, or at least not a regulation as restrictive as the one applicable to tobacco products. Pillbox also pointed to the lack of a required impact assessment before the adoption of the TPD (note that Art. 20 was added at a later stage of the legislative process, and hence was not covered by the initial assessment conducted by the Commission[47]) and the vague nature of the formulation of certain provisions relevant for ENDS in the Directive.[48]

The CJEU disagreed. According to the Court, given that e-cigarettes, unlike tobacco products, are relatively new products, the harmful effects on human health of which have yet to be understood,[49] EU law-makers had reasonably set up a different—and, according to the Court, actually less restrictive—legal regime for vaping products. In the context of the proportionality analysis, the Court stated that, given European law-makers' discretionary power in regulating industries (such as the e-cigarette industry) which require complex assessments of political, economic, and social interests, only measures that are manifestly inappropriate to achieve the regulatory objectives pursued by the EU institutions can be invalidated.[50] In the case at issue, the Court found no such manifest non-compliance. Even though the Court acknowledged that the question of the harmfulness (or lack thereof) of vaping is very controversial,[51] it ultimately agreed with EU law-makers on the existence of potential risks resulting from vaping. The Court clarified that, given the lack of scientific certainty surrounding e-cigarettes, European law-makers had to take account of the precautionary principle, as it allows for the adoption of restrictive measures in cases where, despite a lack of scientific certainty, there is a probability of actual harm for human health.[52] Consequently, the creation of a specific

---

[46] Those aspects of the CJEU judgment are extensively analyzed in Chapter 7 of this volume.

[47] For more details, see Chapter 7 in this volume.

[48] Case C-477/14 *Pillbox 38 (UK) Ltd v Secretary of State for Health* (n 36) paras 34 and 47.

[49] Ibid para 56.

[50] Ibid para 49.

[51] The Court referred for instance to a WHO document of 2014, "Electronic nicotine inhalators," which, while acknowledging the lack of any conclusive scientific evidence, states that electronic nicotine inhalators find themselves "somewhere on a floating point between aid and threat in the fight against smoking": ibid para 50.

[52] Ibid para 55.

regime for this type of product was justified (despite their possible potential as a harm reduction device).[53] Technically speaking, the precautionary principle was used by the Court to extend the margin of discretion available to the EU decision-makers, as it made it easier to conclude that a measure does not manifestly infringe the limits of regulatory intervention. The principle was also referred to by the Court when examining the notification requirements for all new and substantially altered products, as well as when analyzing restrictions on commercial communications and sponsorship for ENDS. In this context, the CJEU again confirmed that the principle eased the threshold for establishing the appropriateness of the measure under the proportionality analysis.[54]

The analysis of the Court therefore suggests that the existence of uncertainty, combined with the presence of some—real or potential—health risks (although their seriousness was not addressed in the judgment at all),[55] requires the EU institutions to take account of the precautionary principle (but not necessarily to apply it). Based on this premise, the Court confirmed that the Commission enjoys a very broad discretion as to the choice of measures aimed at addressing those risks or uncertainties.

At the same time, however, the conclusion that the measure at issue was supported by the precautionary principle might have been influenced by the political nature of the principle. Indeed, the Court highlighted that, given the expansion of the market of vaping products (as evidenced by point 43 of the TPD's recitals), national requirements might, without any harmonization in this sense, hamper the free circulation of goods.[56] Therefore, the case at issue reveals the need to regulate the industry *not only* to protect public health, *but also* to increase economic harmonization within the EU. No consideration was given as to whether—in the case of ENDS—recourse to the precautionary principle was the best way to achieve such harmonization.

5. VAPING AND THE PRECAUTIONARY PRINCIPLE IN EU LAW: A CRITICAL ASSESSMENT

The evaluation of the EU regulatory regime for e-cigarettes leads to both positive and negative conclusions. The TPD is a welcome example of European

---

53 Ibid para 60.

54 Ibid paras 71, 111, and 116.

55 The CJEU particularly mentioned the inhalation of nicotine and toxicants in aerosol, nicotine exposure by means other than inhalation (irrespective of the fact that these risks can actually be much lower as compared to combustible tobacco products), and the gateway and normalization effects: ibid paras 52–3.

56 Ibid paras 61, 84, and 97.

law-makers' attention to a new sector where it is necessary to establish a balance between market rules and other objectives (such as a high level of protection of public health) identified by EU primary law (that is, Arts 9, 114(3), and 168(1) of the TFEU, and Art. 35 second sentence of the Charter). Such a balance stems from a precise political choice, which as such is neither good nor evil per se. The precautionary principle aims at achieving a "dual responsibility" effect. On one hand, it suggests that consumers are responsible for a "cautionary" use of a product whose possible harmfulness has not yet been established, while on the other it compels the relevant industry to work toward reaching high standards of safety for human health.

However, the TPD's "original sin" was to borrow too excessively from the regulatory standards for traditional tobacco products, thus bypassing the opportunity to set up a truly innovative regulatory regime which could take into account the peculiarities of vaping products. Indeed, even if we do not yet have conclusive evidence as to the harmfulness of e-cigarettes, the general sentiment in the scientific community is that the lack of combustion makes ENDS less dangerous than traditional cigarettes (at least at the level of an individual user).[57] This is even truer for nicotine-free e-cigarettes (which, however, are not covered by the TPD). Given the relative novelty of ENDS and their arguably safer nature, one may reasonably posit that some restrictions provided by the TPD might end up working as a barrier to innovation. For instance, contrary to the Court's opinion in *Pillbox 38 (UK) Ltd* (distinguishing between *notification* and *authorization*[58]), the requirement for a six-month notification period before the introduction of a new product might turn out to be unduly burdensome. Rather than immediately introducing new products on the market that could better serve actual and potential consumers (many of them being ex- or current smokers), companies will need to wait for a rather extended period of time to introduce them. According to the Court, this obligation seeks to give the competent national authorities sufficient time to examine all of the relevant data and thus enable them to carry out their surveillance and control tasks.[59] However, considering that about 185,000 notifications had already been submitted as of August 2018,[60] it is unlikely that any thorough consid-

57 For the detailed discussion of scientific evidence concerning ENDS see Chapter 3 in this volume.

58 Case C-477/14 *Pillbox 38 (UK) Ltd v Secretary of State for Health* (n 36) paras 70–5.

59 Ibid para 73.

60 See the answer given by Mr Andriukaitis on behalf of the European Commission in the course of Parliamentary questions on August 8, 2018, question reference E-003629/20 http://europarl.europa.eu/doceo/document//E-8-2018-003629-ASW_EN .html accessed October 31, 2018.

eration was given to them in order to assess the existence of any potential risks. Consequently, from a precautionary point of view the six-month waiting period before launching a product onto the market seems to make little sense, while unduly stifling innovation.

The TPD regulatory regime also runs against the precautionary principle's original intent, which was to always "leave the window open" to scientific progress. In this sense, preventive measures based on the precautionary principle ought to be *temporary* and *revocable*. In other words, application of the precautionary principle should not be considered an end in itself. It ought always to be the beginning of further collaboration and cooperation among all the stakeholders involved (policy-makers, consumers, and producers), with an aim to address the relevant issue(s).[61] While Art. 28(1) of the TPD[62]—as well as various statements by the European Commission—shows an intention to review new evidence and consider possible changes to the TPD in 2021,[63] this appears to be a very long period of time just for beginning to think about the appropriateness of the precautionary regulation applicable to ENDS—all the more so if one takes into account that it took five years to pass the original directive. It would not be surprising to see an equally long delay in making any future revisions of the TPD. This slow pace of reaction seems to frustrate the original intent behind the application of the precautionary principle, depriving it of the flexibility and adaptability that originally made it appear so fitting to cases of scientific *uncertainty*.

Therefore, despite its noble intent, the TPD *de facto* leaves little (if any) room for future "softening" of the regulation of electronic cigarettes and vaping e-liquids. On the contrary, the precautionary principle can—and already has—become the legitimizing reasoning for the adoption of more and more restrictive e-cigarette regulations by EU Member States[64]—above all, relating to tax matters and restrictions on e-liquid flavoring[65]—thereby impos-

[61] For a very interesting analysis of this point, see A.M. Bush, J.W. Holsinger, Jr, L.D. Prybil, "Employing the Precautionary Principle to Evaluate the Use of E-Cigarettes" (2016) 4:5 Front Public Health 1.

[62] Art. 28(1) provides that "[n]o later than five years from 20 May 2016, and whenever necessary thereafter, the Commission shall submit to the European Parliament, the Council, the European Economic and Social Committee and the Committee of the Regions a report on the application of this Directive."

[63] See the answer given by Mr Andriukaitis on behalf of the European Commission (n 60).

[64] For more detailed discussion of implementation strategies in different EU Member States, see Chapter 7 in this volume.

[65] Italy provides an example relative to the taxation of e-liquids. The Italian legal system indeed imposes the very same tax regime on both e-liquids and traditional tobacco products. Initially, the law-makers had imposed the same level of taxation for

ing an unreasonable leveling,[66] whereas the principle's application should instead allow room to differentiate the level of regulation for products whose likeliness of harm has yet to be conclusively proven.

A critical reading of the Directive suggests that it uses the precautionary principle for purposes different than the original ones. Indeed, in the context of ENDS regulation the principle is no longer a tool to balance economic and public interests, but rather has become an instrument to legitimize the application of the same (or similar) restrictions in force for traditional tobacco products—whose harmfulness is today established beyond doubt—to vaping products, whose actual harmfulness has yet to be conclusively proven or accepted by the medical community, while much evidence indicates that their risk profile is much lower. Rather than being based on the *precautionary* principle, such a restrictive attitude toward ENDS seems more inspired by the *principle of prevention*, which is more appropriate for regulating traditional tobacco products (or other products or activities having clearly identified risks). In this regard, TDP's recital No 43 is very telling, as it provides that:

> Disparities between national laws and practices on advertising and sponsorship concerning electronic cigarettes *present an obstacle to the free movement of goods and the freedom to provide services and create an appreciable risk of distortion of competition.* Without further action at Union level, those *disparities are likely to increase over the coming years*, also *taking into account the growing market for electronic cigarettes and refill containers. Therefore, it is necessary to approximate the national provisions on advertising and sponsorship of those products having cross-border effects*, taking as a base a high level of protection of human health. Electronic cigarettes can develop into a gateway to nicotine addiction and ultimately traditional tobacco consumption, as they mimic and normalize the action of

---

both tobacco products and e-cigarettes, but the Italian Constitutional Court, in decision no 83 of 2015, declared illegitimate the imposition of the same level of taxation in light of the lack of scientific evidence on the risks deriving from vaping (on this issue, see G.A. Ferro, "Note minime sulla regolamentazione della sigaretta elettronica. Aspettando la pronuncia della Corte costituzionale" (*Ambientediritto.it*, July 8, 2014) https://bit.ly/2P3PEBw (accessed October 31, 2018). Following the Italian Constitutional Court's decision, the law-makers modified the taxation but imposed the very same fiscal treatment for e-liquids with and without nicotine. The Constitutional Court delivered a second decision (no 240) in 2017, surprisingly finding the initial decision to have the same level of taxation for both types of products to be reasonable. The Court declared that, notwithstanding the belief that traditional smoking is more harmful than vaping, the taxation regime cannot be considered illegitimate in light of the TPD, which acknowledges that electronic cigarettes can become gateway products toward nicotine addiction and consumption of traditional tobacco products.

[66] Despite the level of nicotine (if any) contained in the liquids, as shown by the Italian case in n 65.

> smoking. For this reason, it is appropriate to adopt a restrictive approach to advertising electronic cigarettes and refill containers. [emphasis added]

This passage is very revealing for our discussion, as it shows that the TPD takes for granted certain scientific assumptions about the potential harmfulness of vaping, notwithstanding the existence of studies to the contrary (for example, those showing that electronic cigarettes help overcome addiction to traditional smoking[67]), and reflects the more cautious approach of the CJEU, which has highlighted existing uncertainties and the need for EU legislators to rely on the precautionary principle. Most telling is that the Directive builds its whole rationale for its restrictiveness on considerations about the need to protect and foster the internal market.[68] Therefore, the true rationale for restricting vaping advertisement might be less a lack of scientific certainty—as the precautionary principle would require—and more the need to further harmonize the common market.

What is even more troublesome is that medical science might show (or already has?) that the very premise of the TPD is wrong and that vaping, rather than being a gateway to traditional smoking, can instead serve as an aid to *quit* traditional smoking (perhaps through progressively diminished dosages of nicotine). If that were the case, the TPD would actually disfavor consumption of a useful tool for the promotion of public health policies. Indeed, the assessment of the potential risk—which should be the main basis for applying the precautionary principle—seems to be skewed by its reliance on the scientific evidence as to the risks resulting from consumption of traditional smoking products, rather than evidence as to the potential benefits of using ENDS.[69]

---

[67] A growing body of scientific studies on e-cigarettes and liquids shows that smokers may quit when introduced to e-cigarettes and that the overall level of risk is much lower than that of cigarette smoking, with no chemicals raising serious health concerns in the e-liquids. See for instance a recent study by K. Farsalinos, V. Tomaselli, R. Polosa, "Frequency of Use and Smoking Status of U.S. Adolescent E-Cigarette Users in 2015" (2018) 54(6) Am J Prev Med 814. For further evidence on this point, see D. Saitta, G.A. Ferro, R. Polosa, "Achieving Appropriate Regulations for Electronic Cigarettes" (2014) 5(2) Ther Adv Chronic Dis 50 (highlighting that from a public health perspective, regulatory authorities have expressed concern about e-cigarette use by youngsters or by non-smokers, with e-cigarettes becoming a gateway to smoking or becoming a new form of addiction. However, such concerns are unsubstantiated by existing data; in fact the use of e-cigarettes may serve as a gateway "out" of smoking). See also Chapters 2 and 3 in this volume.

[68] One reason for such an approach may be the limited EU competence with respect to regulation of public health. For more details, see Chapter 7 in this volume.

[69] See Sunstein (n 7) 112, linking recourse to the precautionary principle with precise political choices, whereby overstating potential dangers and calling for *precaution* can in fact better build a political consensus and favor lobbies.

There does not seem to be any room left for the production of an unbiased assessment of medical studies regarding, instead, the usefulness of vaping products as a cessation aid for traditional smokers.

Arguably, the Court in *Pillbox 38 (UK) Ltd* should not have passed over the opportunity to take into account such considerations while evaluating the proportionality of the precautionary measures set up by the EU legislator. On its face, as well as in light of the existing judicial practice, the Court's position seems to be understandable given the EU institutions' broad discretion to make complex assessments, set policies, and choose the most appropriate instruments to pursue them. These turn out to be political issues, on which the EU judicial bodies can only exercise a limited review, aimed at verifying the lack of manifest error, misuse of powers, or manifest abuse of institutional discretion.[70] Therefore, the Court cannot substitute its own assessment of complex (technical or scientific) facts for the institutions. However, it can—and should—review the plausibility of evidence on which the institutions based their assessments,[71] in order to verify whether the evidence substantiates the conclusions—that is, whether the evidence "contains all the information which must be taken into account in order to assess a complex situation," and whether the evidence is "factually accurate, reliable and consistent."[72] Moreover, the (formally limited) scope of judicial review not only does not preclude, but in fact requires, a *de facto* substantive evaluation of the plausibility of the evidence, a kind of substantive evaluation that we believe did not take place in *Pillbox 38 (UK) Ltd.*[73]

---

[70] See for example Case T-257/07 *French Republic v European Commission* [2011] ECLI:EU:T:2011:444 para 265.

[71] The CJEU explained that in the EU legal order "those guarantees include, in particular for the competent institution, the obligations to examine carefully and impartially all the relevant elements of the individual case and to give an adequate statement of the reasons for its decision." Case C-405/07 *Kingdom of the Netherlands v Commission of the European Communities* [2008] ECLI:EU:C:2008:613 paras 56–7; see also Case C-192/01 *Commission of the European Communities v Kingdom of Denmark* [2003] ECLI:EU:C:2003:492 para 56. What is more, the risk assessment process belongs to these guarantees, as it has been specified in judgments that "a scientific risk assessment carried out as thoroughly as possible . . . is an important procedural guarantee whose purpose is to ensure the scientific objectivity of the measures adopted and preclude any arbitrary measures." Case C-236/01 *Monsanto Agricoltura Italia SpA and Others v Presidenza del Consiglio dei Ministri and Others* [2003] ECLI:EU:C:2003:431 para 107.

[72] Case C-405/07 *Kingdom of the Netherlands v Commission of the European Communities* (n 70) para 55. See also Case C-41/02 *Commission of the European Communities v Kingdom of the Netherlands* [2004] ECLI:EU:C:2004:762 para 59.

[73] See generally P. Dąbrowska-Kłosińska, "Risk, Precaution and Scientific Complexity before the Court of Justice of the European Union" in L. Gruszczynski, W.

6. CONCLUSIONS

As societies develop and scientific processes become more complex, law-makers have to assign ever increasing importance to human health and well-being. Therefore, the scope of products and activities that *might* prove harmful to health necessarily becomes more and more inclusive, which will likely call for an ever more widespread reliance on application of the precautionary principle. However, despite its popularity, its ever broadening scope, and its far reaching application, the precautionary principle itself remains a very difficult concept to define in legal terms, and its formulation remains vague. Its vagueness, coupled with the aforementioned ever increasing recourse to the principle cannot but create controversy about the very nature and appropriateness of the precautionary principle itself.

The current regulation of ENDS provides a good example of all the contradictions inherent in the application of the precautionary principle in EU law. By adopting the TPD, the EU has for the most part extended to ENDS products the restrictions already in place for traditional tobacco products, even though it seems highly likely that the latter are much less safe than ENDS. The reason for such a strict approach might be that the precautionary principle has (perhaps unconsciously) transformed itself from a tool aiming at balancing market and public interests to an instrument to further harmonize the EU internal market (that is, to the common denominator suitable either for the European institutions or the most important Member States).

Indeed, as we have tried to show in this chapter, in the context of the EU's regulation of ENDS, application of the precautionary principle seems to have been inspired (for the most part) by considerations originally alien to its scope. However important it is, harmonization of the single market is not the purpose of the precautionary principle and therefore, we believe, should not further distort its already vague meaning or create confusion as to the (arguably equally important) objectives the principle is actually meant to protect (human health and the environment, against uncertainties and potential and unknown risks).

Moreover, in the case of the EU's regulation of ENDS, the very triggering of the precautionary principle appears to be based on a shaky legal foundation. While many countries indeed claim that the precautionary principle compels them to restrict the consumption of ENDS product, as we have shown in this chapter, this does not appear to be the case. Even if the precautionary principle does provide a legal basis for regulating potentially risky products, in no way

---

Werner (eds), *Deference in International Courts and Tribunals: Standard of Review and Margin of Appreciation* (Oxford University Press 2014).

does it compel the taking of any regulatory action—this essentially remains a political decision to be taken by balancing paramount objectives (such as health and environmental protection) with the advancement of innovation and freedom of economic enterprise, with the latter being not only a requirement for social and industrial development, but also a fundamental right enshrined in many European and other western liberal constitutions. Such confusion between political choices and legal requirements is not conducive to a well-functioning EU, whose legitimacy is—in light of the much discussed democratic deficit—becoming more and more controversial.

PART III

National law perspectives

9. E-cigarette regulation in Taiwan and China

Chuan-Feng Wu, Ching-Fu Lin and Mao-Wei Lo

1. INTRODUCTION

As scientific evidence solidly demonstrates that smoking cigarettes and using other tobacco products over time can cause death from various cancers and pulmonary and cardiac diseases, and that such risks are higher for those exposed to secondhand tobacco smoke, the World Health Organization (WHO) Framework Convention on Tobacco Control (FCTC) was adopted as an evidence-based platform to assist countries in developing regulatory strategies for tobacco control and to reaffirm the right of all people to the highest standard of health. However, the growing use of electronic cigarettes (e-cigarettes)—battery-powered devices which turn a flavored liquid solution normally containing nicotine into an aerosol mist that enables users to inhale and imitate the act of conventional smoking[1]—may undermine tobacco control efforts and can ultimately increase smoking prevalence.[2] In particular, the WHO has asserted that e-cigarettes might undermine existing tobacco control efforts,[3] set back decades of public education on the health hazards of tobacco use, contribute to lasting nicotine addiction,[4] and actually promote smoking.[5]

---

1 D.S. Kenkel, "Healthy Innovation: Vaping, Smoking, and Public Policy" (2016) 2 J Policy Analysis & Mgmt 473.

2 T. Clarke, "E-Cig Use Soared, Cigarette Use Fell among U.S. Youth in 2014: CDC" (*Reuters*, April 16, 2015) https://reut.rs/2Qr3klW accessed October 31, 2018.

3 WHO, "Electronic Nicotine Delivery Systems, Including Electronic Cigarettes: Report by the Convention Secretariat" (June 18, 2012) para 33 https://bit.ly/2Rk9HJn accessed October 31, 2018.

4 Ibid para 34.

5 Ibid para 35.

Studies also show a trend of increasing e-cigarette use among teenagers,[6] as well as increasing advertising expenditures.[7]

In Taiwan, although the conventional cigarette smoking rate has dropped sharply in the past two decades,[8] the rate of e-cigarette use has increased in recent years.[9] In 2015 the rate of e-cigarette use in adults above the age of 18 was 0.9 percent (about 180,000 people);[10] it was higher for younger people aged 15–24 years and current or former smokers.[11] Among Taiwan's teenagers, the rate of e-cigarette use has doubled in the past two years.[12] In a survey of junior high and senior high school students in 2016, 3.7 percent and 4.9 percent, respectively, had used e-cigarettes, an increase of 185 percent for junior high students (from 2.0 percent) and 233 percent (from 2.10 percent) for high school students as compared to 2014.[13] Among these two groups, 52 percent were dual users of conventional and e-cigarettes.[14] Evidence shows that e-cigarette use, especially among the younger Taiwanese population, has become a serious public health concern and preventive measures need to be implemented.

Furthermore, while there is neither sufficient nor specific scientific evidence demonstrating that e-cigarettes can effectively help people quit smok-

---

6 See for example S. Schneider, K. Diehl, "Vaping as a Catalyst for Smoking? An Initial Model on the Initiation of Electronic Cigarette Use and the Transition to Tobacco Smoking among Adolescents" (2016) 18 Nicotine Tob Res 647; V.H. Murthy, "E-Cigarette Use among Youth and Young Adults: A Major Public Health Concern" (2017) 171(3) Jama Pediatr 209.

7 See for example A.E. Kim, K.Y. Arnold, O. Makarenko, "E-Cigarette Advertising Expenditures in the U.S., 2011–2012" (2015) 46(4) Am J Prev Med 409.

8 The current smoking rate in Taiwan has declined from 32.5 percent in 1995 to 15.3 percent in 2016. HPA (Taiwan), *2017 Taiwan Tobacco Control Annual Report* (2018) 99.

9 For example, an increase was observed in e-cigarette use from 1.0 percent in 2014 to 2.1 percent in 2016, with an increase in dual use (using both electronic and traditional cigarettes) from 0.9 percent to 1.9 percent. P.-C. Chen et al, "Dual Use of E-Cigarettes and Traditional Cigarettes among Adolescents in Taiwan, 2014–2016" (2018) Nicotine Tob Res https://doi.org/10.1093/ntr/nty003; see also R. Salmonsen, "Estimated 52,000 Taiwan Teens Hooked on E-Cigs" (*Taiwan News*, April 14, 2018) http://taiwannews.com.tw/en/news/3395773 both accessed October 31, 2018.

10 HPA (Taiwan), *2016 Taiwan Tobacco Control Annual Report* (2017) 110.

11 H.-C. Chang et al, "Elucidating Challenges that Electronic Cigarettes Pose to Tobacco Control in Asia: A Population-Based National Survey in Taiwan" (2017) 7 BMJ Open 1.

12 HPA (Taiwan), *2016 Taiwan Tobacco Control Annual Report* (n 10) 110.

13 Ibid.

14 Chen et al (n 9).

ing,[15]some studies suggest that e-cigarettes may become a gateway to the use of regular cigarettes,[16] without significantly reducing harm to health (e-cigarettes still contain chemicals, including fine particulate matter, metals, and nicotine, that can harm health and cause addiction),[17] the tobacco industry consistently uses "harm reduction"[18] as a strategy to persuade governments, including those in Taiwan (where e-cigarettes are currently illegal products) and China (where their regulation is unclear), to open the market to e-cigarettes and/or to loosen their strict e-cigarette regulations.[19] Additionally, since the relationship between e-cigarettes and the objective of conventional tobacco control laws—to reduce the harm caused by tobacco consumption—has not been fully explored, the tobacco industry has seen this as an opportunity to attack evidence-based tobacco control measures.[20]

In light of this tension, this chapter carefully examines the obstacles to effective e-cigarette regulations in Taiwan. It also explores similar regulatory obstacles in Chinese law, but with less thoroughness due to the limited scope and focus of this chapter. Section 2 reviews existing regulatory hurdles in Taiwan from the angle of conventional tobacco control measures as well as legal

---

[15] For example, the US Committee on the Review of the Health Effects of Electronic Nicotine Delivery Systems has argued that "the potential health risks and benefits of e-cigarettes requires an understanding of the risks of e-cigarettes relative to both cigarette smoke as well as never using any tobacco" and identified a great need for more research and evidence regarding every aspect of the public health risks/benefits of e-cigarettes (for example, only limited evidence was available about whether e-cigarettes can be effective aids to promote smoking cessation, and no evidence was available about whether or not e-cigarette use is associated with clinical cardiovascular outcomes). K. Stratton et al (eds), *Public Health Consequences of E-Cigarettes* (National Academy Press 2017) 1–8, S-9, SA-1, and SA-3.

[16] See L.O. Gostin, A.Y. Glasner, "E-Cigarettes, Vaping, and Youth" (2014) 312 Jama 1.

[17] See generally J.L. Pearson et al, "E-Cigarette Awareness, Use, and Harm Perceptions in US Adults" (2013) 102(9) Am J Public Health 1758.

[18] For example, the tobacco industry has argued that, compared to the fact that regular cigarettes have been scientifically proven to pose serious risks to humans, e-cigarettes, marketed as a device that transforms liquid nicotine into a vapor, seem therapeutically capable of helping people quit smoking and thus should be promoted as harm reduction devices. Some studies also support this claim, although substantial and conclusive evidence is still lacking. See for example Stratton et al (n 15); K.O. Fagerstrom, K. Bridgman, "Tobacco Harm Reduction: The Need for New Products that Can Compete with Cigarettes" (2014) 39(3) Addict Behav 507. See also the discussions in Chapters 2 and 3 of this book.

[19] See for example E.A. Feldman, C. Yue, "E-Cigarette Regulation in China: The Road Ahead" (2016) 11 U Penn Asian L Rev 409.

[20] S. Sing Churk, "E-Cigarette Regulation and Harm Reduction: The Case of Hong Kong" (2016) 71 Food Drug Law J 634.

definitions and characterizations. Section 3 evaluates potential approaches to effective e-cigarette regulation, covering regulations related to Electronic Nicotine Delivery System (ENDS) and Electronic Non-Nicotine Delivery System (ENNDS). The legal and regulatory contexts and challenges in relation to e-cigarettes in China are briefly discussed in section 4. Section 5 concludes with recommendations and suggested topics for further investigation.

2. OBSTACLES TO REGULATING E-CIGARETTES IN TAIWAN

While the contents and delivery mechanism of e-cigarettes are different from those involved in conventional tobacco smoking, they arguably result in a similar user effect and experience. In this sense, it has been difficult for both the FCTC and its Parties to decide whether current tobacco control regulations—such as increased taxes on tobacco products, strictly restricting the use of tobacco in public spaces, and banning tobacco advertising and promotion—can be applied directly to e-cigarettes. For example, recent FCTC Conference of Parties (COP) decisions show that even though the Parties reached a certain degree of consensus over the gradual inclusion of e-cigarette controls under the FCTC framework, the FCTC has not yet agreed upon a set of comprehensive guidelines for e-cigarettes, due to the lack of conclusive scientific evidence on their health effects.[21] Similar challenges are also reflected in Taiwan's tobacco control legislation, resulting in discrepancies among policy-makers, tobacco control advocates, and e-cigarette manufacturers as to the scope and regulatory rigor of e-cigarette control.

2.1 Tobacco Control Regulation in Taiwan

Inspired by the FCTC and the general background of global tobacco control, Taiwan amended its Tobacco Hazards Prevention Act (THPA) in 2009 after ten years of its enforcement.[22] That amendment adopted most of FCTC's tobacco control strategies, such as protecting the public from secondhand smoke, increasing the size of health warnings (including graphic warnings) on tobacco packaging, banning written content or pictures that could lure people into smoking or that downplay tobacco's hazardous effects, limiting point of sale tobacco product displays, banning pregnant women from smoking, banning

---

[21] For a detailed analysis of the applicability of FCTC standards to ENDS and the disagreement between State Parties, see Chapter 4 in this volume.

[22] Bureau of Health Promotion, *Taiwan Tobacco Control Annual Report 2010* (2010) 5 http://tobacco.bhp.doh.gov.tw/Upload/FTB/UpFiles/2010en.pdf accessed October 31, 2018.

tobacco product sales to teenagers, and increasing the tobacco tax (via a health and welfare surcharge).[23] Based upon the THPA regulatory framework, which contains two types of tobacco control measures—demand reduction and supply reduction—Taiwan has developed a comprehensive tobacco control mechanism. Additionally, through the government's effective implementation of the THPA and anti-smoking groups' efforts to control tobacco advertising and health effect labeling, the Taiwanese public has increasingly been making healthy lifestyle choices, both in terms of quitting smoking and not taking it up in the first place. For instance, the general population's smoking rate dropped from 21.9 percent in 2008 to 17.1 percent in 2015 (for males from 38.6 percent to 29.9 percent; for females from 4.8 percent to 4.2 percent).

In 2017, the Taiwanese government continued to push for strengthened tobacco control measures by proposing and seeking approval of an amendment to the THPA, including requiring cigarette producers to increase the size of health warning graphics from 35 percent to 85 percent of the size of a cigarette package, banning flavored cigarettes, extending the list of smoke-free public places (for example, outside schools; inside bars and nightclubs), and requiring the government to provide legal and medical assistance to people (for example store clerks and restaurant owners) who have sustained injuries or damage after attempting to dissuade people from smoking or refusing to sell cigarettes to underage people.

2.2 The First Challenge: The Legal Definition of Tobacco Products

Despite efforts to strengthen tobacco control regulations, Taiwan's current legal tobacco control regime does not directly address e-cigarettes, thus creating a high degree of uncertainty when the 2009 THPA is applied to e-cigarettes.

The courts, politicians, government officials, scholars, tobacco interests, and health advocates have argued over whether it is justifiable to fold e-cigarettes directly into the existing 2009 THPA regulations on combustible cigarettes, or whether they constitute their own unique category. The first challenge faced by the government is whether e-cigarettes are tobacco products subject to tobacco control, and fall under Ministry of Health and Welfare authority. The answer seems to be negative. According to THPA Art. 2(I), "tobacco products" subject to tobacco control measures "refer to cigarettes, cut tobacco, cigars and other products entirely or partly made of the tobacco leaf or its substitute as a raw material, which are manufactured to be used for smoking,

[23] C.-F. Wu, "Tobacco Control in Taiwan" in A.D. Mitchell, T. Voon (eds), *The Global Tobacco Epidemic and the Law* (Edward Elgar Publishing 2014) 279.

chewing, sucking, snuffing or other methods of consuming."[24] Despite such a broad definition, e-cigarettes are basically excluded from the scope of the THPA since they are not "entirely or partly made of the leaf tobacco as a raw material."[25] More specifically, according to the THPA text, tobacco products are those "made of" rather than "made from" the tobacco leaf; nicotine which is extracted from the tobacco leaf therefore cannot be legally defined as a "tobacco product" because it is "made from" the tobacco leaf.[26] E-cigarettes with nicotine-containing liquids thus cannot be legally classified as tobacco products.[27]

Therefore, since the THPA's definition of tobacco products is limited to products "made of" tobacco leaves,[28] a literal interpretation of the THPA disqualifies e-cigarettes from being considered tobacco products and the THPA cannot fully address the health concerns related to increased adolescent use of e-cigarettes. E-cigarettes in Taiwan thus remain beyond the reach of the THPA and related tobacco control measures, unless tobacco products can be redefined or more loosely interpreted in the THPA text.

To resolve this regulatory problem, some scholars have proposed extending the definition of tobacco products in the THPA to include e-cigarettes by focusing on "substitutes" for leaf tobacco rather than on "leaf tobacco" per se. They have argued that since Art. 2(I) of the THPA defines tobacco products as products "made of the leaf tobacco or its substitute as raw material," the raw material of the tobacco products need not be leaf tobacco and can be a replacement or substitute for leaf tobacco insofar as the product is manufactured to be used for smoking or to produce an experience similar to the inhalation of smoke from an ignited tobacco product. In other words, the material used in the liquid solution for e-cigarettes, including not only nicotine extracted from tobacco leaves but also other non-nicotine substances, could be regarded as a "substitute" for leaf tobacco. This would mean that both ENDS and ENNDS products could fall within the definition of tobacco products under Art. 2(I) of

---

24 To clarify the interpretation of official legal documents, the term "tobacco" is defined in THPA Art. 2(I) in the original Taiwanese context as "菸品：指全部或部分以菸草或其代用品作為原料，製成可供吸用、嚼用、含用、聞用或以其他方式使用之紙菸、菸絲、雪茄及其他菸品."

25 Letter of Interpretation No 0980700249 (Guo Jian Jiao Zi No. 0980700249) issued by Bureau of Health Promotion, Department of Health Bureau of Health Promotion, Department of Health (國健教字第0980700249號函).

26 Ibid.

27 Compare also with the discussion of this term in the context of the FCTC (see Chapter 4 in this volume).

28 T.-Y. Lin, "The Status of FCTC in the Interpretation of Compensable Indirect Expropriation and the Right to Adopt 'Stricter' Tobacco Control Measures under BITs" (2014) 9 Asian J WTO Int Health L Policy 123.

the THPA. However, the government has not adopted this expansive approach to THPA Art. 2(I).

From our perspective, the expansive interpretation of Art. 2(I) of the THPA might be too vague and too broad.[29] For example, by adopting such an interpretation, the sandalwood powder or the incense sticks which are burned in traditional religious ceremonies in Taiwan would legally qualify as tobacco products and would be banned from use in public places in accordance to Art. 15 of the THPA.[30] The pharmaceutical products approved by the Taiwan Food, Drug and Cosmetic Administration (TFDA) for smoking cessation (such as nicotine patches) would also be categorized as tobacco products and inappropriately subject to tobacco control measures. We are however not against a broad definition of tobacco products within which e-cigarettes would then fall; we merely argue that an expansive interpretation which contains no exemptions might cause concerns about overreach.

Another regulatory issue related to the legal definition of tobacco products in the THPA is that, even if the broadest interpretation (that is, e-cigarettes contain nicotine liquid derived from tobacco and thus can be legally regarded as tobacco products) is adopted, e-cigarettes that do not contain nicotine cannot be categorized as tobacco products and are beyond the current tobacco control regulations. Therefore, unless the definition of tobacco products in the THPA is amended, the THPA's inflexible legal definition of tobacco products would prevent the government from extending the scope of current tobacco control measures to non-nicotine infused e-cigarettes, which might have the effect of promoting the sale or consumption of nicotine-infused e-cigarettes or conventional tobacco products as well, and thus impair tobacco control efforts.[31]

3. THE REGULATORY APPROACH TOWARD E-CIGARETTES IN TAIWAN: A DETOUR

Due to the unstated legal status of e-cigarettes in the THPA, the Taiwanese government cannot regulate e-cigarettes through the THPA directly, because

---

29 For example, when analyzing the spread of electronic smoking device regulation in California, Katherine Florey also argued that the definition of e-cigarettes, which applies unequivocally to all electronic smoking devices whether or not they are used to deliver tobacco or nicotine, might be too broad. K. Florey, A. Doan, "A Successful Experiment: California's Local Laboratories of Regulatory Innovation" (2018) 66 UCLA L Rev Discourse 80.

30 In alignment with the FCTC, Taiwan's THPA Art. 15(I) extends the number of smoke-free places in communities, schools, military bases, and workplaces.

31 Asian Center for WTO & International Health Law and Policy (ACWH), "ACWH Comments on FCTC COP 7" (2017) 12 Asian J WTO Int Health L Policy 205.

e-cigarettes cannot be legally categorized as tobacco products. Therefore, before amending the legal definition of tobacco products, the government has adopted a two-tiered regulatory approach based upon the Pharmaceutical Affairs Act (PAA) and THPA Art. 14 (which prohibits the manufacturing, import, or sale of objects in the form of tobacco products) to regulate ENDS and ENNDS. The PAA is applied to e-cigarettes based on their nicotine content and THPA Art. 14 is applied based upon their shape/appearance (which frequently mimics the look of conventional cigarettes). However, the regulations are not applicable to e-cigarettes that contain no nicotine, claim no therapeutic properties, and/or do not resemble cigarettes.[32] The following sections explain how the current regulations concerning ENDS and ENNDS have formed in Taiwan, and outline possible legal challenges.

3.1 ENDS Regulations

First, according to the legal interpretations issued by the Health Promotion Administration (HPA) and the TFDA,[33] both authorities classify e-cigarettes that use a liquid solution with nicotine (that is, ENDS) as pharmaceutical products that fall within the scope of the PAA. The reason for this is that some e-cigarette manufacturers claim that their products can help smokers cease smoking. On the other hand, for e-cigarette manufacturers that make no health claims about their products (which are used merely as an alternative to smoked tobacco), nicotine contained in e-cigarettes is still regarded as a drug as defined in the PAA and e-cigarette carriers, if sold separately from the cartridge/e-liquid, are regarded as medical devices.

According to Arts 6(I)(3) and 13(I) of the PAA, the term “drug” refers to substances that “are sufficient to affect the human body or organ structure and physiological functions of human beings,” and the term “medical devices” refers to “any instruments, machines, apparatuses, materials, software, reagent for in vitro use, and other similar or related articles that . . . may affect the body structure or functions of human beings.”[34] Because nicotine is also an

---

32 Chang et al (n 11).

33 See Letter of Interpretation No 1000701214 (Guo Jian Jiao Zi No 1000701214) issued by the HPA on September 14, 2011 (國健教字第1000701214號函) and Letter of Interpretation No 1000086333 (Xiao Zi No 1000701214) issued by the TFDA on February 10, 2012 (消字第1000086333號函).

34 PAA Art. 13(I) states: “[t]he term ‘medical device,’ as used in this Act, shall refer to any instruments, machines, apparatus, materials, software, reagent for in vitro use, and other similar or related articles, which are used in diagnosing, curing, alleviating, or directly preventing human diseases, regulating fertility, or which may affect the body structure or functions of human beings, and do not achieve its primary intended function by pharmacological, immunological or metabolic means in or on the human body.”

ingredient of tobacco cessation adjuvant drugs (for example nicotine patches), the HPA argued that nicotine used in e-cigarettes qualifies as a drug under the PAA and that ENDS products are listed under drug management and need to be evaluated by the TFDA for safety and efficacy before they can be commercially marketed.[35] Since nicotine is regarded as a drug under the PAA, smoking devices, including components of e-cigarettes such as the nicotine cartridge and atomizers, are thus regarded as "medical devices" and are subject to the same strict premarketing approval process and standards.

The rationale underlying this regulatory approach is based on the precautionary principle: regulators must be authorized and required to withhold approval of a product that *could* pose human health risks.[36] Since the precise health risks and effects of nicotine-infused e-cigarettes (including both the probable facilitation of nicotine addiction and the delivery of other harmful substances)[37] are different from those of conventional cigarettes,[38] and because definitive scientific studies on their health effects—particularly in terms of prolonged use of e-cigarettes[39]—and their possible influence on the implementation and continuity of tobacco control measures have not yet been confirmed,[40] it is thus appropriate and justified to apply the precautionary principle when regulating these new products,[41]

---

35 HPA (Taiwan), *2016 Taiwan Tobacco Control Annual Report* (n 10) 108.

36 E. Soule, "The Precautionary Principle and the Regulation of U.S. Food and Drug Safety" (2004) 29(3) J Med Philos 333.

37 Stratton et al (n 15). R.P. Jensen et al, "Hidden Formaldehyde in E-Cigarette Aerosols" (2015) 374 N Eng J Med 392.

38 See for example J. Ralof, "Health Risks of E-Cigarette Emerge" (*Science News*, June 3, 2014) http://sciencenews.org/article/health-risks-e-cigarettes-emerge accessed October 31, 2018.

39 C. Dinakar, G.T. O'Connor, "The Health Effects of Electronic Cigarettes" (2016) 375 N Eng J Med 1372; see also Stratton et al (n 15).

40 Sing Churk (n 20).

41 The precautionary principle has frequently been mentioned in the field of environmental risks and corresponding regulations to manage uncertain risks. For example, the Rio Declaration on Environment and Development issued in 1992 by the United Nations Conference on Environment and Development defined the principle as follows: "Where there are threats of serious and irreversible damage, lack of full scientific certainty shall not be used as a reason for postponing cost-effective measures to prevent environmental degradation." The principle is also used in bioethics, initially to evaluate the regulation of new technologies which might cause irreparable harm to human health. G.E. Marchant, R.A. Lindor, "Prudent Precaution in Clinical Trials of Nanomedicines" (2012) 40 J Law Med Ethics 831; L.M. Kopelman et al, "What is the Role of the Precautionary Principle in the Philosophy of Medicine and Bioethics?" (2004) 29(3) J Med Philos 255. See also Chapter 8 in this book for a discussion on the precautionary principle in the context of EU law.

and to adopt stricter regulatory measures.[42] From the perspective of the precautionary principle, the uncertainty about the potential public health risks of ENDS requires strict regulatory management to avoid such risks,[43] and thus it would be unreasonable to authorize the marketing of e-cigarettes without a more complete understanding of their health risks, in particular their long-term effects.

Therefore, taking extensive precautionary measures to prevent the public from the potential health risks posed by ENDS by regulating them as pharmaceutical products is a justified policy option. This is because the PAA is stricter than the THPA in terms of marketing (for example, premarketing approval is required) and manufacturing practices, including the qualifications of pharmaceutical manufacturers, drug component review, drug safety monitoring, factory establishment standards, guides to good manufacturing practices, improvements in safety or therapeutic effect concerns within a limited period of time, and the prohibition of manufacturing after major hazards are discovered. In other words, in the absence of sufficient scientific evidence that guarantees the safety of nicotine-based e-cigarette products, adopting the pharmaceutical regulation framework can help the Taiwanese government to keep these products off the market, or strictly limit their availability, until their relative safety is established.

To date, to the best of our knowledge no e-cigarette company has sought TFDA approval, partly because the PAA premarketing review process requires time consuming and expensive data collection with no guarantee of product approval. This fact alone makes ENDS illegal in Taiwan, at least theoretically.[44] The HPA and the TFDA have both publicly stated that all ENDS on the Taiwanese market appear to be unapproved and are "counterfeit drug-device combinations" (that is, the products are manufactured without prior approval per PAA Art. 20(I)(1)) or "prohibited/banned drug-device combinations" (that is, products imported without prior approval per PAA Art. 22(I)(2)). Therefore, they fall within the TFDA's broad regulatory authority over pharmaceutical products. Both regulatory authorities have asserted that the manufacture,

---

42 See for example C.-C. Chen, *The Application and Boundary of Precautionary Principle in Risk Regulation—Regulating Electronic Cigarettes as an Example* (Master's Thesis in Chinese, National Taiwan University 2016) 104–26; Some US government officials, such as the Director of the Center of Disease Control (CDC) Thomas Frieden, also took a similar position. See for example S. Tavernise, "A Hot Debate Over E-Cigarettes as a Path to Tobacco, or From It" (*New York Times*, February 22, 2014) https://nyti.ms/1hpCCmK accessed October 31, 2018.

43 E.A. Feldman, "Layers of Law: The Case of E-Cigarettes" (2014)10 FIU L Rev 111.

44 T. Schmid, "Asia's E-Cig Regulations: Confusion & Uncertainty" (*Tobacco Asia*, May 26, 2016) https://bit.ly/2Oqoy6I accessed October 31, 2018.

importation, and/or sale of ENDS in Taiwan is thus illegal and prohibited, as they are unapproved drugs/devices. Under PAA Art. 82, anyone or any company who manufactures or imports ENDS is subject to punishment for violating the PAA (for manufacturing or importing counterfeit or prohibited drugs) and can face a prison sentence of up to ten years and/or a fine up to NT $100 million (~US $3.36 million). Anyone knowingly trading in or circulating ENDS can face up to seven years' imprisonment and/or a fine of up to NT $50 million (~US $1.68 million) in accordance with PAA Art. 83. Furthermore, PAA Arts 77 and 79 state that the TFDA is also authorized to confine or seize ENDS, and/or to incinerate or destroy these products if necessary.

3.2 Challenges to Current ENDS Regulations

It is worth noting that the possession and use of unapproved ENDS is legal, because there is no law against users of counterfeit or prohibited drugs set out in the PAA. This regulatory loophole may erode the nation's current smoke-free policy and undermine the effort to regulate ENDS. For example, Art. 15(I) of the THPA bans smoking in most public places so as to provide protection for the general public from exposure to tobacco smoke. With regard to ENDS, potential harm to others might occur from exposure to secondhand vapor or from "renormalizing" smoking-like behavior (that is, eroding the negative public opinion of cigarette smoking),[45] thus it is necessary to include ENDS in the ban on smoking in public places. However, because ENDS are not regarded as tobacco products under the THPA, its smoke-free provisions do not cover these products. The PAA cannot help resolve this problem either, because it was designed to ensure the safety and efficacy of drugs/devices and to prevent their misuse rather than to protect nonconsenting individuals in public places from being exposed to secondhand vapor. Users of counterfeit drugs/devices (unapproved ENDS) are treated as victims who need to be protected rather than punished. In other words, neither the THPA nor the PAA provide legal grounds for the Taiwanese government to ban individuals from using ENDS in public places, even if the TFDA has not approved those products. Therefore, under the pharmaceutical regulatory framework, vapers may be able to secure a legal route to use ENDS and get a nicotine fix in public places despite smoking bans.[46]

---

45 C. Bullen, "Regulatory Policy and Practical Issues Arising from A Disruptive Innovation: A Public Health Perspective on E-Cigarettes" (2016) 11 Asian J WTO Int Health L Policy 1, 11.

46 J. Paradise, "No Sisyphean Task: How the FDA Can Regulate Electronic Cigarettes" (2013) 13 Yale J Health Policy Law Ethics 326.

Additionally, the PAA's "personal use" exemption could also lead to more e-cigarette control challenges. According to PAA Art. 22(I)(2),[47] the importation of pharmaceutical products (for example ENDS) without TFDA approval is not illegal if those products are for personal use. In Taiwan's pharmaceutical regulatory framework, this exemption is necessary because it can alleviate individual hardships caused by a general ban on the importation of unapproved therapies and protect the right to health. However, it is questionable whether the personal use exemption can be applied directly to ENDS. First, even though the retail sale of ENDS in Taiwan is currently illegal, by applying the personal use exemption it is generally legal (on a case-by-case basis) for consumers to purchase or import small quantities of ENDS for their personal use from other countries. The exemption would thus enable vapers to import ENDS for personal use despite the fact that nicotine-containing liquid is strictly regulated by the TFDA and illegal to manufacture or sell in Taiwan. Second, the exemption would also make the implementation of the ban on ENDS use in public places more difficult, because inasmuch as it is legal to carry ENDS products into Taiwan for personal use even without TFDA's premarketing approval for such products, it would be illogical to forbid individuals' "medical use" of these "legitimate drugs/devices" in public places.

These challenges, which arise from regulating ENDS as pharmaceuticals, show that the Taiwanese framework for pharmaceutical regulation does not wholly address all e-cigarette control issues. When developing ENDS control strategies, it is important to recognize the differences in the nature of pharmaceutical and tobacco control regulations. The pharmaceutical regulations are basically a front end/ex ante regulatory framework that focuses on marketing authorization, safety, efficacy review, and import and border control, while the tobacco control regulations are a back end/post ante regulatory framework that focuses on advertising (bans), on bans on smoking in public places and on cigarette sales to minors, on requiring graphic health warnings, and on cigarette taxes. Since both regulations serve different policy purposes, adopting a regulatory model for pharmaceutical products that addresses only the safety and efficacy issues of ENDS while ignoring certain essential elements of tobacco control measures can run counter to the policy purpose of protecting public health from health risks potentially caused by e-cigarettes.

For example, as discussed earlier, because the PAA focuses mainly on regulating the safety and efficacy of drugs and drug delivery devices, it

[47] Art. 22(I)(2) specifically provides: "The term 'prohibited drugs' as used in this Act shall refer to any of the following: . . . The drugs that are imported without prior approval, except drugs that are carried into this country for personal use by passengers or service personnel on board of the means of transportation."

contains no smoking restrictions on the places where ENDS can be used. In other words, it is not illegal to use ENDS in public places where it is illegal to smoke cigarettes. But it is problematic, because using these products looks like smoking, and this may undermine anti-smoking norms.[48] Another example regards e-cigarette adverting. Even though PAA Art. 66(I) stipulates that advertisements for drugs must be reviewed and approved in advance (that is, manufacturers and/or suppliers, under the law, must submit texts, drawings, or images to the TFDA for approval prior to the publication or broadcast of advertisements), it is still a looser regulation than the THPA's, in which advertising, promotion, and sponsorship are banned, not only with respect to tobacco manufacturers/importers, but also by advertising and media outlets. Additionally, the PAA's advertisement regulation for ENDS is different from the WHO's proposal, which states:

> Given that the same promotional elements that make ENDS attractive to adult smokers could also make them attractive to children and non-smokers . . . an outright ban on ENDS advertising, promotion and sponsorship is preferable to the implementation of voluntary codes on ENDS marketing, given the overwhelming evidence that similar codes for tobacco and alcohol products have failed to protect young people from such advertising.[49]

The final point is that from the socio-cultural perspective, the word "drug" generally leaves a far better impression than the word "cigarette." Therefore, as the existing scientific evidence on the risks of e-cigarettes and the influence that e-cigarettes have on human health is still far from definitive, applying the PAA directly to regulate ENDS without careful consideration may deliver a false message to the public that ENDS offer a certain therapeutic effect, which can hamper efforts to curb tobacco use. In legal parlance, this false message can undermine the denormalization of tobacco use. Some might argue that ENDS cannot safely and effectively promote a legitimate therapeutic purpose unless they go through a formal approval process and qualify as drugs

---

48 K. Voigt, "Smoking Norms and the Regulation of E-Cigarettes" (2015) 105(10) Am J Public Health 1967. The WHO's report also confirmed that "since the reasonable expectation of bystanders is not a diminished risk in comparison to exposure to second-hand smoke but no risk increase from any product in the air they breathe, ENDS users should be legally requested not to use ENDS indoors, especially where smoking is banned, until exhaled vapour is proven to be not harmful to bystanders and reasonable evidence exists that smoke-free policy enforcement is not undermined." See WHO, *Electronic Nicotine Delivery System* (FCTC/COP/6/10 REV.1, September 1, 2014) para 41 http://apps.who.int/gb/fctc/PDF/cop6/FCTC_COP6_10Rev1-en.pdf accessed October 31, 2018.

49 Ibid para 42 and 43.

or medical products.[50] But the problem is that it is not easy for the public to assess whether or not ENDS are approved for therapeutic purposes. The confusion about the nature of ENDS (are they tobacco products or pharmaceuticals?) could lead to a reversal of smoking denormalization and the use of such products in smoke-free areas rather than promotion of cessation. A number of youth who would never have smoked cigarettes might start using such products.[51]

However, we are not proposing here that the pharmaceutical regulatory framework is inappropriate for e-cigarette regulation. It is important to introduce the pharmaceutical regulatory framework into e-cigarette regulation because the former, compared to tobacco control regulations, is stricter in terms of premarketing approval requirements and in assessing and managing uncertain health risks. Additionally, by applying the pharmaceutical model, e-cigarettes could be subject to a higher level of obligations. Here, we merely propose as follows:

(1) Neither the regulatory model for pharmaceuticals nor the regulatory model for tobacco use is adequate on its own to regulate e-cigarettes. In fact, the pharmaceutical regulation model's strengths are the tobacco control model's weaknesses, and vice versa. Therefore, to regulate emerging products like e-cigarettes, a new model is needed—one that combines the pharmaceutical regulatory framework and tobacco control measures.

(2) To avoid misleading information about the nature of e-cigarettes, the new products should not be directly treated and marketed as pharmaceuticals with therapeutic purposes in the PAA unless solid and conclusive scientific evidence is carefully reviewed and accepted by the TFDA on a case-by-case basis. Instead of treating e-cigarettes as pharmaceuticals, the government should treat them as special tobacco (nicotine delivery) products with uncertain health risks. Also, the government should amend the THPA to incorporate the pharmaceutical regulatory model (especially the premarketing approval process) into current tobacco control measures in order to develop a more comprehensive e-cigarette regulatory regime. It would be similar to the US's e-cigarette regulatory framework. In accordance to the US Tobacco Control Act, any new or significantly changed e-cigarette (or other tobacco product) cannot be legally sold in the market unless its manufacturer or importer submits a Premarket Tobacco Application and obtains new product permission

---

50 E.N. Lindblom, "Effectively Regulating E-Cigarettes and Their Advertising and the First Amendment" (2015) 70 Food Drug Law J 55.

51 S. Kalkhoran, "Modeling the Health Effects of Expanding E-Cigarette Sales in the United States and United Kingdom" (2015) 175(10) Jama Intern Med 1671.

from the Food and Drug Administration, ensuring that it would be "appropriate for the protection of the public health" to allow the product to be marketed and sold.[52]

3.3 ENNDS Regulations

Even though ENDS fall under the PAA regulation in Taiwan and currently no ENDS product may be legally manufactured, imported (except for personal medical use), or sold in Taiwan, ENNDS remain largely unregulated. On the one hand, because ENNDS are not made of leaf tobacco and do not fit the legal definition of tobacco products, they are not covered by the THPA regulations (similarly to ENDS). On the other, because ENNDS contain no nicotine or other drugs which are subject to the PAA regulation, they cannot be categorized as pharmaceutical products either. The lack of clear and explicit regulations with regard to ENNDS thus might create tobacco control loopholes and leave the consumer vulnerable to unknown health risks. For example, sellers could actively market these non-nicotine e-cigarettes and devices, which come in a variety of fruit, confectionery, and other flavors that appeal to children and teenagers, as a way of encouraging future tobacco use.[53] In addition, the marketing of ENNDS could provide cover for the marketing of illicit unapproved ENDS,[54] since authorities cannot easily tell the difference between ENDS and ENNDS simply by their appearance; lab testing would be necessary for this.

To close the regulatory gap, THPA Art. 14[55]—like FCTC Art. 16.1(c), which bans the sale of goods not containing tobacco designed to resemble tobacco products—seems like an effective textual hook for the regulation of ENNDS that closely resemble conventional tobacco products. In other words, if the shape of ENNDS products resembles that of actual tobacco products (for example cigarettes), they will fall within the scope of Art. 14 of the THPA and thus their manufacture, import, and sale can be banned in Taiwan.[56] Violations

---

52 21 U.S.C. § 387j. E.N. Lindblom, "Should FDA Try to Move Smokers to E-Cigarettes and Other Less-Harmful Tobacco Products and, If So, How?" (2018) 73 Food Drug Law J 276. See also Chapter 10 in this volume.

53 Lindblom, "Effectively Regulating E-Cigarettes and Their Advertising and the First Amendment" (n 50) 92.

54 Ibid.

55 Art. 14 THPA, "No person shall manufacture, import or sell candies, snacks, toys or any other objects in form of tobacco products."

56 Scholars also proposed that, in order to avoid the need to decide on the nature of e-cigarettes and to make finegrained regulatory decisions, the government can ban all e-cigarettes, as the Singapore government did, by simply prohibiting the import, distribution, sale, or offer for sale of any article that is designed to resemble a tobacco

can result in fines ranging from NT $10,000 to NT $50,000 (~US $336–$1,682), and the products are subject to mandatory recall within a limited period of time (THPA Art. 30).

Additionally, THPA Art. 14 can also be applied to ENDS because, in addition to the PAA regulation that prohibits ENDS without prior TFDA premarketing approval, it covers those products that are designed to resemble tobacco products.

3.4 Challenges to Current ENNDS Regulations

Despite the fact that the manufacture, import, and sale of ENNDS—e-cigarette-like products designed to physically resemble actual cigarettes (for example by using a LED light that resembles a lit cigarette)—is prohibited, there is no regulation regarding the use of these products. It is also important to extend the ban on smoking in public places to the use of ENNDS because, as noted earlier regarding ENDS, allowing their use in public places could complicate the enforcement of smoke-free laws. Additionally, their public use could undermine the public's compliance with and recognition of smoke-free laws. It is perhaps for this reason that several smoke-free laws now also prohibit the use of e-cigarettes,[57] and advocacy organizations recommend that the use of e-cigarettes, regardless of whether they contain nicotine (that is, ENDS) or do not (ENNDS), should be prohibited in public.[58] This regulatory loophole needs to be closed.

Another difficult regulatory issue is that e-cigarettes come in a variety of shapes in addition to the conventional cigarette type. Because THPA Art. 14 bans only the manufacture, import, and sale of objects "in form of" tobacco products, it has been easy for e-cigarette manufacturers to bypass the regulations by simply creatively redesigning their e-cigarettes.[59] Some e-cigarettes (allowing people to inhale nicotine or non-nicotine vapor) do not resemble cigarettes, pipes, or cigars, but pens, lipstick, perfume bottles, USB drives, or

---

product, including vaporizers such as e-cigarettes, e-pipes, e-cigars and the like. See Art. 16 of the Tobacco (Control of Advertisements and Sale) Act, Singapore. See also Feldman (n 43) 121; M.A. Rahman et al, "Electronic Cigarettes: Patterns of Use, Health Effects, Use in Smoking Cessation and Regulatory Issues" (2014) 12 Tobacco Induced Diseases 1; M. Johnson, "Regulatory Response to E-Cigarettes" (2017) 45 Ga J Int Comp Law 645.

[57] See for example N.J. Stat. Ann. 26:3D-57 (2010).

[58] M. Freiberg, "Options for State and Local Governments to Regulate Non-Cigarette Tobacco Products" (2012) 21 Annals Health Law 407.

[59] D. Palacios Rubio, "Taiwan Braced for Legal U-Turn on Nicotine vs Non-Nicotine" (*ECigIntelligence*, December 20, 2016) https://ecigintelligence.com/taiwan-brace-for-legal-u-turn-on-nicotine-v-non-nicotine/ accessed October 31, 2018.

even small tools. In other words, because the current laws for e-cigarettes are based upon their nicotine content and shape, ENNDS that do not resemble the shape of conventional cigarettes and cigars fall outside of the PAA and THPA Art. 14. By designing their ENNDS to look dissimilar from conventional tobacco products, e-cigarette manufacturers can carefully remove their products from the PAA's and HPA's jurisdictions and legally sell their products in the market. This regulatory loophole could then potentially undermine the tobacco control measures because, as noted earlier, ENNDS may appeal to children and younger non-smokers and could motivate their use and subsequent experimentation with actual tobacco products.[60]

To resolve this problem, the HPA has broadly interpreted THPA Art. 14 and asserted that any object used to imitate the feel of smoking tobacco in order to attract users, regardless of whether it resembles or is designed to resemble the shape of a tobacco product, is subject to THPA Art. 14.[61] In other words, manufacturing or selling ENNDS which resemble USB drives and look dissimilar from conventional cigarettes is prohibited because, according to the HPA, such products allow users to imitate the act of conventional smoking.[62] The HPA defended its position by arguing that even if the shape of e-cigarettes is different from conventional products, e-cigarettes producing a vapor can still mimic the effects of actual tobacco-based cigarettes, and the inhaling and exhaling of e-cigarette aerosol can also produce some of the same sensory experiences as smoking a cigarette. This is similar to the WHO's argument that e-cigarettes' resemblance to conventional tobacco products, coupled with the fact that "exhaled vapor looks like tobacco smoke," would likely hamper the enforcement of tobacco control measures such as smoke-free policies.[63] THPA Art. 14 was therefore interpreted broadly to include all vaping devices in the ban, regardless of whether or not such products are in the shape of and/or made to appear like cigarettes.

However, the HPA's expanded interpretation of THPA Art. 14 has been criticized and challenged by the e-cigarette industry. Opponents have argued that the legal text in THPA Art. 14 focuses on the physical appearance and properties of the objects for sale, that is, being physically "in the form of" regular cigarettes. Therefore, non-tobacco products designed to physically resemble

---

60 WHO, *Electronic Nicotine Delivery Systems and Electronic Non-Nicotine Delivery Systems (ENDS/ENNDS)* (FCTC/COP/7/11) para 23 https://bit.ly/2IuisNd accessed October 31, 2018.

61 Letter of Interpretation No 1040701069 (Guo Jian Jiao Zi No 1000701214), issued by the HPA on August 13, 2014 (國健教字第1000701214號函).

62 Letter of Interpretation No 1039906918 (Guo Jian Jiao Zi No 1039906918), issued by the HPA on November 1, 2014 (國健教字第1039906918號函).

63 WHO, *Electronic Nicotine Delivery System* (n 48) para 8 and 9.

tobacco products (for example cigarettes or e-cigarettes), subject to THPA Art. 14, should also be banned from manufacturing, import, or sales within Taiwan. However, when the THPA's ban was expanded to include objects that can be smoked or may be used to mimic the act of smoking (for example, by vaping) regardless of their physical appearance, it was argued that the ban was unjustified because it went beyond the legislators' intent.

This issue has been reviewed by several administrative courts in Taiwan, but without reaching any consensus. Some administrative courts agreed with the HPA's expansive interpretation when determining the resemblance between e-cigarettes and conventional tobacco products. They argued that the physical appearance of an e-cigarette is only one criterion, and the intended purpose of the product and how it is actually used are also relevant. For example, in 2016 the Kaohsiung High Administrative Court, in Judgment No 45 (Jian-Shang-Zi No 45), stated that ENNDS designed to imitate conventional smoking are subject to the ban set out by THPA Art. 14, "even if the length, width, shape, weight, texture and material, and flavor and odor are not exactly the same as the conventional tobacco products."[64]

However, some administrative courts disagreed with the HPA and found that because the ban would seriously restrict citizens' property rights, the interpretation of THPA Art. 14 should be restricted in order to properly regulate the authority's power and to protect individuals' rights. Therefore, ENNDS are subject to the ban set out in THPA Art. 14 when, and only when, their physical design resembles tobacco products, whether the resemblance is in the product itself and/or its packaging. For example, the Kaohsiung High Administrative Court Judgment No 497 (Su-Zi No 497) did not support the HPA's confiscation of component parts of ENNDS based upon THPA Art. 14.[65] The Court ruled in favor of the ENNDS retailer because, according to the Court, separate components of e-cigarettes are not "in the form of" tobacco products and thus are not subject to Art. 14. In other words, according to the Court the HPA has jurisdiction over e-cigarettes only because the finished product, not the separate components, can be considered "in the form of" conventional tobacco products. In 2017 the Kaohsiung High Administrative Court, in Judgment No 21 (Jian-Shang-Zi, No 21), held that the HPA's expansive interpretation of THPA Art. 14 violates "the principle of legal reservation" (*Gesetzesvorbehalt*),[66] according to which restrictions or regulations

---

64 2016 Kaohsiung High Administrative Court Judgment No 45 (2016 Jian-Shang-Zi No 45) (高雄高等行政法院105年度簡上字第45號).

65 2016 Kaohsiung High Administrative Court Judgment No 497 (2016 Su-Zi No 497) (高雄高等行政法院105年訴字第497號).

66 2017 Kaohsiung High Administrative Court Judgment No 21 (2017 Jian-Shang-Zi No 21) (高雄高等行政法院106年簡上字第21號).

of people's freedoms and rights can occur only if a formal law is passed by a legislative body.[67] Furthermore, the Court argued that if the HPA wants to regulate e-cigarettes that do not physically resemble tobacco products, rather than adopting an extensive interpretation, the authority should persuade the legislators to amend the relevant law.

4. THE (LACK OF) REGULATION IN CHINA

Across the Taiwan Strait, in China, a rather different regulatory environment exists. With the largest production capacity of tobacco and highest per capita tobacco use worldwide, China does not have a rigorous legal framework for tobacco control in general, and no regulatory steps have been taken to address the emerging issues surrounding e-cigarettes. China accounts for 38 percent of global cigarette production and sales.[68] Currently, China has more than 300 million smokers (among whom 100 million smokers are younger than 30 years of age),[69] as well as 740 million non-smokers exposed to secondhand tobacco smoke.[70] About 1.4 million (16.5 percent) of all deaths in China in 2010 were linked directly or indirectly to tobacco use.[71] As for e-cigarettes, China—the country in which the e-cigarette was invented—has emerged not only as a huge market for domestic consumption but also as the largest global e-cigarette manufacturer, producing more than 90 percent of the world's e-cigarettes.[72] Given the country's key position in the global tobacco/e-cigarette supply chain

---

67 In the case being considered in Judgment 21, the ENNDS manufacturer's property rights were restricted because ENNDS could be confiscated by the HPA.

68 See J. Jin, "Why FCTC Policies Have Not Been Implemented in China Domestic Dynamics and Tobacco Governance" (2014) 39(3) J Health Politics Policy Law 633 (citing Euromonitor, Cigarettes-China 2010).

69 B.-Q. Liu et al, "Emerging Tobacco Hazards in China: 1. Retrospective Proportional Mortality Study of One Million Deaths" (1998) 317 BMJ 1411.

70 G. Yang et al, "The Road to Effective Tobacco Control in China" (2015) 385 Lancet 1019; see also Chinese Center of Disease Control and Prevention, *Global Adults Tobacco Survey (GATS): China 2010 Country Report* https://bit.ly/2OoKajU accessed October 31, 2018.

71 G. Yang et al, "Rapid Health Transition in China, 1990–2010: Findings from the Global Burden of Disease Study 2010" (2013) 381 Lancet 1987.

72 In addition, the vast majority of the world's e-cigarettes are manufactured in Shenzhen Provence, China. See Feldman, Yue (n 19) 410; see also G. Lidian (高工锂电) [Engineering Institute of the Lithium Battery Industry], "Dianzi Yan Shichang San Niannei Guimo Jiang Da 96 Yi Yuan (电子烟市场三年内规模将达96亿元) [The Electronic Cigarette Market is Expected to Reach 9.6 Billion Yuan in Three Years]" (December 3, 2013) http://gg-lb.com/asdisp2-65b095fb-11448-.html accessed October 31, 2018.

and the sheer size of its market, there is certainly an urgent need for tobacco control legislation in general, and e-cigarette regulation in particular.

However, regulatory rigor in relation to domestic tobacco control has been comparatively weak in China. Due to a myriad of economic, social, and political factors (for example positive social image of tobacco use, tobacco industry interference in tobacco control efforts, government economic-oriented policy, and inefficient interministerial coordination), little tobacco control effort has been made by governmental agencies in China since its ratification of the WHO FCTC in 2005.[73] One major reason for China's tobacco regulatory lacuna is the state-owned tobacco industry's influence in national, provincial, and local tobacco policy-making. China's State Tobacco Monopoly Administration (STMA) is in charge of supervising and regulating the entire tobacco supply chain in China, and the China National Tobacco Corporation (CNTC), a wholly state-owned enterprise, runs the nation's tobacco business management with the full support of the STMA. As pointed out by prominent Chinese scholars, "[t]he STMA and CNTC are effectively the same organization, representing the complete absence of separation between the government and the tobacco industry."[74] The STMA and CNTC are composed of multiple levels and types of organizations, including 33 provincial level companies, 17 industrial enterprises, 446 city level companies, 2,283 county level branches, and many other training, research, and planning offices with a total of 50,000+ employees.[75] The STMA/CNTC contributed more than one trillion RMB (~US $156 billion) to China's national tax revenue in 2016,[76] hence representing a powerful interest group with solid government connections in the tobacco control realm. In fact, the State Council established the FCTC Implementation Inter-Ministerial Coordination Lead Group in 2007, which includes powerful member organizations, including the Ministry of Industry and Information Technology (the group's head agency), the former National Health and Family Planning Commission (now the National Health Commission), the Chinese Ministry of Foreign Affairs, the Ministry of Finance, the General Administration of Customs, the State Administration for Industry and Commerce, the General Administration of Quality Supervision,

---

73 United Nations Treaty Collection, WHO Framework Convention on Tobacco Control (May 21, 2003) 2302 UNTS 166 https://bit.ly/2nxt0k1 accessed October 31, 2018.

74 Yang et al (n 70) 1020.

75 See China Tobacco, "Zhongguo Yancao Gaikuang (中国烟草概况) [An Overview of China Tobacco]" http://tobacco.gov.cn/html/10/1004.html accessed October 31, 2018.

76 Ibid.

Inspection and Quarantine, and the STMA.[77] The head agency of the FCTC Implementation Inter-Ministerial Coordination (the Lead Group) was shifted to the newly rebranded National Health Commission in April 2018 following a government reorganization.[78] Nevertheless, the fact that the STMA continues to occupy a seat in this eight-member lead group responsible for the implementation of the WHO FCTC and for setting national tobacco control policies (in particular those regarding labeling, packaging, and content regulation)[79] may constitute a violation of Art. 5.3 of the FCTC.

Against this backdrop of weak tobacco control in China (that is, no dedicated tobacco control law, a highly valued tobacco industry, greater social acceptance of tobacco use, and so on), it comes as no surprise that the production, distribution, sale, and use of e-cigarettes in China is primarily unregulated.[80] Government health and public welfare agencies have been reluctant to take action toward tighter regulatory control over e-cigarettes ever since they first entered the market in 2006.[81] Occasionally some government officials have expressed opinions on whether and how e-cigarettes could be regulated. For instance, officials from the Maternal Child and Community Health Division hinted that, given that the main ingredient of e-cigarettes is nicotine, they should be regulated under the Dangerous Chemicals Regulations administered by the State Council.[82] This view was echoed by the STMA/CNTC due to its legal implication: the preemption of tobacco or e-cigarette

---

77 State Council of People's Republic of China, "Guowuyua Guanyu Tongyi Chengli Yancao Kongzhi Kuangjia Gongyue Luyue Gongzuobu ji Xietiao Lingdao Xiaozu de Pifu (国务院关于同意成立烟草控制框架公约履约工作部际协调领导小组的批复) [Reply by the State Council on the Agreement to Establish the FCTC Implementation Inter-Ministerial Coordination Leading Group]" (State Council Letter No 41, 2007) http://gov.cn/zwgk/2007-04/30/content_603299.htm accessed October 31, 2018.

78 State Council of People's Republic of China, "Guowuyuan Jigou Gaige Fangan (国务院机构改革方案) [State Council Organizational Reform Program]" (June 2, 2018) https://bit.ly/2NWysxs accessed October 31, 2018.

79 In fact, STMA published a research report on countermeasures and strategies to weaken the WHO FCTC due to its potential impact on the tobacco industry the same year (2005) that China ratified the treaty. Yang et al (n 70) 1022.

80 D. Yan, "Dianzi Yan: Silue Zai Wuzhu Zhi Di (电子烟：肆虐在无主之地) [E-cigarettes: Rampaging in No-Man's-Land]" (*Southern Weekend*, March 24, 2015).

81 See Feldman, Yue (n 19) 416–20.

82 Ibid 417 (citing National Health and Family Planning Commission/Ministry of Health, "2006 Nian Zhongguo Xiyan Yu Jiankang Baogao Fabuhui Neirong Shilu—Kongyan Yu Fang'ai Fangzhi (卫生部《2006 年中国"吸烟与健康" 报告》发布会内容实录—控烟与防癌防治) [Press Conference Record of the "Smoking and Health" Report in 2006 by the Ministry of Health—Tobacco Control and Prevention of Lung Cancer]" (May 29, 2006).

regulation in the future.[83] In addition, officials from the Chinese Food and Drug Administration (CFDA) have stated that e-cigarettes are not approved as either a medical device or pharmaceutical product (that is, to help smokers quit).[84] Other agencies may also be responsible for certain aspects of the regulation of e-cigarettes, such as advertising and marketing, labeling, product safety, and toxicological content limits, yet such agencies have remained silent and evasive. Overall, the production, distribution, and sale of e-cigarettes is subject to the background requirements of product quality law and tort liability law, in the absence of legal documents that define and characterize e-cigarettes as tobacco products, medical devices, or pharmaceutical products.[85]

The STMA/CNTC entered the e-cigarette market with a nicotine-based e-cigarette in 2014,[86] which has complicated and exacerbated existing public health challenges to tobacco control in China. As mentioned above, the STMA/CNTC enjoy premium access to the government's tobacco policy-making process and can mobilize tremendous economic and political capital to domestically promote the production, distribution, sale, and use of e-cigarettes. In addition, China's dominance as the world's largest producer of e-cigarettes suggests that its lack of a regulatory framework could have serious global implications.[87] In the most recent Party's Implementation Report submitted to the FCTC, China did not answer the question as to whether it had "adopted and implemented any policy or regulation" for specific tobacco products, including ENDS and ENNDS, but only indicated that "China participates in the TobLabNet and is planning to submit a report of smokeless tobacco and electronic nicotine delivery systems as discussed in COP 7."[88] Yet it is unclear whether, when, and how China plans to regulate e-cigarettes. Given that China produces more than 90 percent of the world's e-cigarettes, a set of basic rules and standards for product safety, nicotine limits, and health control is urgently needed.[89] One sign of movement toward this was the city government of Shenzhen's stipulation of certain technical requirements for the production

---

[83] Ibid.

[84] Ibid 418.

[85] Ibid 418–20.

[86] See M. O'Neill, "How China is Lighting Up the E-Cigarette Market" (*EJ Insight*, August 11, 2014) http://ejinsight.com/20140811-china-e-cigarette/ accessed October 31, 2018.

[87] See Feldman, Yue (n 19) 419.

[88] Department of Consumer Goods Industry, Ministry of Industry and Information Technology, *China's Implementation Report of the WHO Framework Convention on Tobacco Control* (2016) 33 and 64.

[89] See D. Barboza, "China's E-Cigarette Boom Lacks Oversight for Safety" (*New York Times*, December 12, 2014) https://nyti.ms/2RjbGOr accessed October 31, 2018; D. Ding, "Guowai Dianziyan Guanzhi Gaikuang yi ji dui Woguo de Qishi" (国外电子

of e-cigarettes in 2015. At the national tobacco work conference in 2018, an STMA representative said that it planned to create some national standards for e-cigarettes.[90] Nevertheless, beyond mere technical standards, much more needs to be immediately done in various other areas that fall within the jurisdictions of national and local agencies, including the State Administration for Market Regulation, State Standardization Administration, and CFDA. In the near future, regulatory agencies in China also need to define and characterize e-cigarettes as either conventional or special tobacco products, medical devices, pharmaceutical products, or products with hybrid characteristics (as Taiwan did), and to design compatible regulations addressing the different public health risks posed by e-cigarettes. Lastly, more generally, the STMA/CNTC should cease to be involved in the tobacco control policy-making process due to their interests in selling such products. Regulations targeted at conventional cigarettes and other tobacco products, together with e-cigarettes, should be created where necessary and reinforced at both the national and local levels.

5. THE ROAD AHEAD

As discussed earlier, even though e-cigarettes arose in a legal vacuum in Taiwan, the Taiwanese government has responded prudently to the regulatory challenges which e-cigarettes pose to tobacco control. However, comprehensive legislative action remains necessary to address the potential health risks of e-cigarettes—both with and without nicotine—and the vague regulatory options must be clarified. The bans on e-cigarettes (both ENDS and ENNDS) in Taiwan are currently implemented through administrative orders issued by the Ministry of Health and Welfare and are not yet codified in laws, leaving legal wiggle room for manufacturers, sellers, and users. Additionally, because of the complex nature and potentially negative effects of e-cigarettes, these administrative orders follow either the THPA and/or the PAA, thus fragmenting the current e-cigarette regulatory framework.

Therefore, in 2017 the Taiwanese government proposed to amend the THPA to incorporate e-cigarettes and comprehensively ban the manufacture, import,

---

烟管制概况及其对我国的启示) [Overview of E-Cigarette Regulation Situation and Some Suggestions] (2017) 23(4) Acta Tabacaria Sinica 128.

[90] C. Ling, "Quanmian Quanche Dang de Shijiuda Jingshen Nuli Kaichuang Yancao Xingye Wenzhong Xianghao Xinjumian" (全面贯彻党的十九大精神 努力开创烟草行业稳中向好新局面) [Fully implementing the principles set forth at the 19th CPC National Congress and Pursuing the stable and positive progress for the tobacco industry] (*China Tobacco*, June 2, 2018) http://tobacco.gov.cn/history_filesystem/2018ycgzh/ldjh1.html accessed October 31, 2018.

sale, and use of both ENDS and ENNDS, including e-cigarette accessories such as liquid cartridges.[91] However, if an e-cigarette manufacturer can obtain TFDA approval for marketing and sale as pharmaceutical or medical devices, such products can be marketed and sold for "therapeutic" purposes. In other words, Taiwanese authorities seem to agree upon a two track system whereby e-cigarettes marketed to treat or prevent diseases (including nicotine addiction) are subject to pharmaceutical regulations (the PAA), while those that do not make therapeutic claims are banned in accordance with the THPA.

Additionally, even if e-cigarettes are marketed as pharmaceutical products with TFDA approval, the advertisement or use of such products remains subject to tobacco control regulations. In accordance with the new THPA amendment recently proposed by the HPA, the use of e-cigarettes is to be banned in public places where smoking is banned in accordance with THPA Arts 15–19. Other tobacco measures, such as bans on advertising, promotion, and sponsorship, and on sale to minors and pregnant women, will also apply to e-cigarettes. Under the proposed amendment, the manufacture and import of e-cigarettes would be punishable with a fine of NT $50,000–250,000 (~US $1,680–8,397), while the sale of e-cigarettes and their use in non-smoking areas would be punishable with a fine of NT $10,000–50,000 (~US $336–1,680).

The adoption of an integrated rather than a simple two track regulatory model for emerging products such as e-cigarettes considers their dual nature as pharmaceuticals and tobacco: for e-cigarettes with therapeutic claims, the HPA has proposed to first adopt a premarket approval approach similar to the pharmaceutical regulatory framework under the PAA in relation to the manufacture and import of such products. In addition, existing THPA regulations on conventional tobacco products (for example bans on smoking in public spaces, as well as on advertisement, promotion, sponsorship, and sale to minors and pregnant women) will also apply when such e-cigarettes enter into the market. For e-cigarettes without therapeutic claims, the HPA has proposed to impose a comprehensive ban on such products.

On one hand, e-cigarettes and conventional tobacco products are similar in terms of their method of use and effects; on the other, e-cigarettes may contain addictive content (for example nicotine) but may also come with therapeutic claims. Therefore, an integrated regulatory model that is not only directed against e-cigarettes' features but also integrates the merits of the models regulating tobacco and pharmaceuticals should be able to thoroughly regulate

---

91 D. DeAeth, "Taiwan Moves towards a Total Ban on 'Vaping'" (*Taiwan News*, December 27, 2017) http://taiwannews.com.tw/en/news/3329032 accessed October 31, 2018.

e-cigarettes and protect the public's health until the scientific evidence on their health effects is definitive.

A recent survey showed that 91 percent of citizens support reinforced regulation of e-cigarettes, while 73 percent support the strictest version (which imposes import and manufacture bans on e-cigarettes) and 63 percent support the idea that the ENDS should be listed as a prescription medication.[92] Additionally, anti-smoking civil society organizations in Taiwan enjoy great influence over public opinion and policy-makers. Such organizations' strong media advocacy regarding strict e-cigarette regulation may underpin the government's position of imposing a ban on e-cigarettes.[93] Therefore, while e-cigarette manufacturers have proposed the regulation of e-cigarettes as conventional tobacco products in Taiwan (or at least adoption of the US model of allowing the manufacture and sale of these products with a premarket approval mechanism),[94] in the recently proposed THPA amendment the government has refused to legalize e-cigarettes.

Some studies have shown that e-cigarettes may potentially be useful as a harm reduction tool and may ease the health burden on both individuals and the general population in terms of tobacco control (for example, helping current smokers to quit smoking expeditiously).[95] However, the scientific evidence regarding the safety of e-cigarettes and their efficacy in harm reduction and treatment of tobacco dependence is far from conclusive. In response to the scientific uncertainty, the integrated regulatory model embraced by the current THPA amendment proposal is not a comprehensive ban of e-cigarettes, hinting at the possibility that a modified/reduced risk tobacco product claim may be submitted and approved by the TFDA in the future.

Another important factor that influences the HPA's attitude toward e-cigarette regulations is a lack of resources. In Taiwan, the HPA, unlike the TFDA, does not have sufficient expertise, personnel, or financial resources to conduct a thorough cost–benefit analysis and carry out empirical studies to authoritatively determine whether e-cigarettes are less harmful than conventional tobacco or are effective in reducing conventional cigarette consumption and/or achieving cessation. As a result, the HPA appears to be incapable of adopting and implementing the US model of premarket approval and licensing

---

[92] HPA (Taiwan), *2017 Taiwan Tobacco Control Annual Report* (n 8) 126.

[93] See for example L. I-chia, "Foundation Warns over E-Cigarettes" (*Taipei Times*, May 2, 2016) http://taipeitimes.com/News/taiwan/archives/2016/05/02/2003645325 accessed October 31, 2018.

[94] D. Lawrence, "Taiwan Considers 100% Ban on Vaping" (*Vaporizer Wire*, February 6, 2018) https://vaporizerwire.com/taiwan-considers-ban-on-vaping accessed October 31, 2018.

[95] Stratton et al (n 15).

schemes and may be incentivized to leave the hard question (that is, whether e-cigarettes are harm reduction products and can be approved for sale) to the TFDA under the pharmaceutical regulatory framework.

However, the ENDS/ENNDS industry (partially controlled by Big Tobacco) may persist in objecting to such a regulatory structure, or may lobby for more lenient alternatives. Tobacco corporations have continued to position themselves to take a seat at the table when discussing what can be done with the "harm reducing" e-cigarettes,[96] arguing that the products are a healthier alternative to conventional tobacco.[97] Additionally, by making contributions, lobbying, and establishing third party front groups (such as e-cigarette user groups), the tobacco corporations have been trying to change public opinion toward e-cigarette regulation and to defeat the HPA's proposed THPA amendment.

As far as China is concerned, the absence of a regulatory framework and laws dedicated to tobacco control in general, and e-cigarettes in particular, has posed serious challenges to public health. An adverse spillover effect has taken place, which is worth noting given China's dominance as the largest producer of e-cigarettes in the world. While there have been signs that a few governmental agencies might start technical standard setting work in relation to the production of e-cigarettes, much of the discussion has been focused on the economics of e-cigarettes (that is, how e-cigarette profits support China's economy). It remains unclear whether, when, and how China will lay out regulations to address the legal challenges posed by e-cigarettes. Overall, the STMA/CNTC's role in the nation's tobacco control policy should be curbed, given the related interests in profits from the cigarette industry. Instead, a fundamental regulatory framework for conventional tobacco products should be established and supported by both central and local governments. Given that China produces most of the global e-cigarette supply, a set of basic rules and standards for product safety, nicotine limits, and health control is necessary. This will require more research and dedication of resources by the central and local governments. And it will require a sincere desire to put the health and welfare of the public before profits. Lastly, China needs to mobilize interministerial efforts to define and characterize e-cigarettes as either conventional tobacco products, special tobacco products, medical devices, pharmaceutical

---

[96] D. Sweanor, R.C. Grunberger, "The Basis of a Comprehensive Regulatory Policy for Reduced Harm Tobacco Products" (2008) 11 J Health Care Law Policy 83.

[97] J. Bickford, "New Vape Ban Proposed for Taiwan" (*VapingDaily Blog*, February 24, 2018) https://vapingdaily.com/blog/new-vape-ban-proposed-taiwan/; see also Y.-Y. Wang, "E-Cigarettes: A New Rising Industry" (in Chinese) (*Liberty Times*, January 27, 2018) http://talk.ltn.com.tw/article/paper/1172213, both accessed October 31, 2018.

products, or products with hybrid characteristics, and to stipulate compatible regulations to address the public health challenges they pose.

This chapter has focused primarily on the regulation of e-cigarettes in Taiwan (reviewing existing regulatory hurdles in Taiwan and evaluating potential approaches to effective regulation of e-cigarettes), while also offering a general account of the current regulatory landscape in China so as to situate our analysis in the greater regional context. Given the legal and policy recommendations discussed above, this chapter will hopefully pave the way for future research in similar historical, cultural, and legal settings.

10. Regulation of e-cigarettes in US law

Patricia I. Kovacevic

1. INTRODUCTION

The United States (US) product legislative framework for electronic nicotine delivery systems (ENDS or e-cigarettes) is unusual in its severity and lack of nuance. This chapter argues that at present the framework is substantially inadequate (as well as internally inconsistent) with respect to the protection of public health because it does not differentiate between ENDS and traditional cigarettes, does not acknowledge the risk differential between tobacco products and ENDS, and places a much higher—and economically unsustainable—regulatory burden on the fledgling ENDS industry than on the conventional cigarette industry.

The US ENDS products market is characterized by diversity. According to the Food & Drug Administration's (FDA) establishment registration list, there are more than 2,500 US-based ENDS products manufacturers; to date, non-US manufacturers do not have an obligation to register with the FDA.[1] One banking analyst estimated the total volume of the ENDS market in 2018 at US $5.5 billion, of which the convenience store channel—the only channel tracked by Nielsen—accounts for a total of US $1.433 billion.[2] There is no reliable market share data for the other channels. In the Nielsen-tracked convenience channel, rechargeable refills (which include e-liquids and cartridges) dominate, with 76 percent of the market, while the disposable market has shrunk to 7 percent. Kits (device plus liquids packaged together, or only devices) account for the remainder. Subsidiaries of four large tobacco manufacturers (Altria, British American Tobacco, Imperial Brands, and Japan Tobacco International) manufacture and sell ENDS products on the US market. The vast majority of US ENDS manufacturers are, however, small and medium enterprises, privately

---

1 See FDA, "Database: Establishment Registration & Tobacco Product Listing" https://bit.ly/2q6izpW accessed October 31, 2018.

2 See Wells Fargo Securities, "Our Evening with blu" (March 28, 2018) https://bit.ly/2y7iQwh accessed October 31, 2018.

held and not controlled by the tobacco industry. Chinese manufacturers export to the US, but their total number and identity is difficult to establish because of a lack of accurate data and tracking.

In order to understand why the ENDS regulatory environment is particularly hostile for harm reduction and innovation in the US, it is essential to characterize the US legal framework, primarily driven at the federal level by the 2009 Family Smoking Prevention and Tobacco Control Act (TCA),[3] which gives the FDA—a US government agency—primary jurisdiction over tobacco products, with concurrent jurisdiction by another US agency, the Federal Trade Commission (FTC). Less limitative, but evolving, is product legislation at the state level.

This chapter analyzes selected court challenges that have been initiated against the FDA and ENDS regulation promulgated under the TCA, and looks at the different trade associations' engagement in initiatives that arguably seek to reach an optimal regulatory balance between the precautionary principle favored by regulators and the harm reduction approach, which could entail encouragement of reduced risk ENDS alternatives. It proceeds as follows. Section 2 provides a short description of the TCA. Against this background, section 3 discusses the FDA's authority over ENDS products, and the challenges this brings for the industry. Section 4 briefly discusses industry litigation initiatives currently on appeal, challenging the FDA's regulation of ENDS products. Section 5 provides conclusions on the adequacy of the current US ENDS regulatory regime to promote tobacco harm reduction.

2. THE FAMILY SMOKING PREVENTION AND TOBACCO CONTROL ACT

The FDA is a mammoth US government agency with authority over one trillion dollars' worth of products per year introduced into interstate commerce in the US,[4] including the following: all food except for meat, poultry, and some egg products; drugs; biological products (including blood, vaccines, and tissues for transplantation); medical devices; animal drugs and feed; cosmetics; medical and consumer products that emit radiation; and tobacco products. The FDA's current authority derives from the Federal Food, Drug and Cosmetic Act of 1938 (FD&C Act),[5] which has subsequently been amended several times.

---

3 Family Smoking Prevention and Tobacco Control Act, Pub. L. No 111-31, 123 Stat. 1776 (June 22, 2009).

4 See FDA, "Laws Enforced by FDA" https://bit.ly/2NgVji5 accessed October 31, 2018.

5 Federal Food, Drug and Cosmetic Act, Pub. L. No 75-717, 52 Stat. 1040 (1937 and as subsequently amended). The history of the FDA can be traced back to the nine-

Until 2009, tobacco was prominently left outside the FDA's authority. In the 1990s FDA attempted to regulate cigarettes and smokeless tobacco products as drugs under the FD&C Act.[6] The FDA issued proposed rules and allowed for comments, and when the rules were finalized one of the US tobacco companies affected by the FDA rules, Brown & Williamson, filed suit in federal district court to enjoin the rules on the grounds that they exceeded the FDA's statutory authority. The case made its way to the US Supreme Court, which found for the plaintiff, Brown & Williamson, in 2000.[7]

The FDA's current tobacco products authority was granted by Congress through the TCA, signed into law by President Obama on June 22, 2009, following decades of patchwork legislation of tobacco products and a voluntary agreement between the tobacco industry and 46 US States—the Master Settlement Agreement, or MSA—which was not superseded but rather complemented by the TCA. A new Center for Tobacco Products (CTP) was thus established within the FDA, with authority to regulate the manufacture, distribution, and marketing of tobacco products.

A "tobacco product" is defined by the TCA as follows:

a. Definition of Tobacco Products. Section 201 of the Federal Food, Drug, and Cosmetic Act (21 U.S.C. 321) is amended by adding at the end the following:
    1. The term "tobacco product" means any product made or derived from tobacco that is intended for human consumption, including any component, part, or accessory of a tobacco product (except for raw materials other than tobacco used in manufacturing a component, part, or accessory of a tobacco product).
    2. The term "tobacco product" does not mean an article that is a drug under subsection (g)(1), a device under subsection (h), or a combination product described in section 503(g).
    3. The products described in paragraph (2) shall be subject to chapter V of this Act.

---

teenth century and the US Department of Agriculture's Division of Chemistry (later rebranded to the USDA Bureau of Chemistry). In the 1920s, the bureau was reorganized into the Food, Drug and Insecticide organization. The FDA received its current name in 1930. For details see FDA, "FDA's Origin & Functions" https://bit.ly/2yaHRGW accessed October 31, 2018.

6 See W.B. Schultz, "The FDA's Decision to Regulate Tobacco Products" (1997) 18 Pace L Rev 27 https://digitalcommons.pace.edu/plr/vol18/iss1/2/ accessed October 31, 2018.

7 *Brown & Williamson Tobacco Corp. v. FDA*, 153 F.3d 155, 167 (4th Cir. 1998) (concluding that the FDA has no authority to regulate tobacco under the Federal Food, Drug, and Cosmetic Act), affd. *FDA v. Brown & Williamson Tobacco Corp.*, 120 S. Ct. 1291 (2000).

4. A tobacco product shall not be marketed in combination with any other article or product regulated under this Act (including a drug, biologic, food, cosmetic, medical device, or a dietary supplement).[8]

Upon the passage of the TCA, four types of tobacco products were specifically regulated under it: cigarettes, cigarette tobacco, smokeless tobacco, and roll-your-own tobacco. Added to these were "any other tobacco products that the Secretary by regulations deems to be subject to this chapter."[9] Congress thus allowed the FDA to bring additional tobacco-derived nicotine products under the TCA authority by deeming them "tobacco products" at a later date through notice and comment rulemaking.

The most impactful provision of the TCA is the requirement for premarket review by the FDA of any change to a grandfathered tobacco product (which creates a new tobacco product) and prior to the introduction of any new tobacco product on the US market. A "new tobacco product" is defined as:

a. any tobacco product (including those products in test markets) that was not commercially marketed in the United States as of February 15, 2007; or
b. any modification (including a change in design, any component, any part, or any constituent, including a smoke constituent, or in the content, delivery or form of nicotine, or any other additive or ingredient) of a tobacco product where the modified product was commercially marketed in the United States after February 15, 2007.[10]

No new tobacco product may be introduced on the US market unless the manufacturer first obtains a premarketing authorization from the FDA under one of the three premarket authorization pathways provided for in the TCA, namely: (i) substantial equivalence; (ii) exemption from substantial equivalence (also termed minor modification); or (iii) a premarket tobacco product authorization (PMTA) (specific pathways are discussed below). It is worth adding that the US approach is unique in this respect, as no other country requires an actual authorization of a tobacco product based on a comprehensive dossier review. Most other tobacco regulatory schemes require a notification and a waiting period, as is the case, for example, under the Tobacco Products Directive.[11] Some jurisdictions, however, classify nicotine-containing products, including

---

8 Family Smoking Prevention and Tobacco Control Act para 101(a).

9 Ibid para 901(b).

10 Ibid para 910(a).

11 Directive 2014/40/EU of the European Parliament and of the Council of 3 April 2014 on the approximation of the laws, regulations and administrative provisions of the Member States concerning the manufacture, presentation and sale of tobacco and related products and repealing Directive 2001/37/EC. For additional details see Chapters 7 and 8 in this volume.

e-cigarettes, as medicinal (that is, as cessation devices) and require their premarket authorization.[12]

Another novel requirement is the prohibition against any comparative harm or comparative product construction/ingredients claim unless such claim receives an authorization by the FDA under the Modified Risk Tobacco Product (MRTP) application scheme. This provision was primarily meant to disallow the "lights" and "low tar" descriptions on cigarette packaging, but when applied to ENDS it eventually resulted in a blanket prohibition against even truthful and measurable statements such as "this product does not contain leaf tobacco," or "does not emit cigarette smoke." It would eventually be challenged by several plaintiffs, as will be discussed below.

Products that were on the market on February 15, 2007 are "grandfathered in" and therefore do not require any premarket authorization from the FDA to be sold.[13] A class of products that was on the market with changes made between February 15, 2007 and March 22, 2011 could continue to be sold provided that the manufacturers filed a product dossier with the FDA, termed a "substantial equivalence report" (SE Report), by March 22, 2011. Those products are commonly referred to as "provisionals" and the FDA refers to that group of SE Reports as "provisional SE Reports," to distinguish them from SE Reports filed for products not on the market before March 22, 2011, and which cannot be introduced into interstate commerce before FDA premarket authorization is obtained.

The SE premarket authorization pathway is relatively straightforward if the manufacturer can demonstrate that the characteristics of the product it seeks to introduce (the "new" product) are almost identical to the characteristics of a grandfathered predicate product that was on the market on February 15, 2007. The costs of preparing an SE application, while not negligible, primarily consist of internal staff, product testing, and outside consultant costs.

In reviewing an SE application, the FDA will seek to determine whether the new product's side by side differences versus the grandfathered predicate product chosen by the manufacturer for comparison raise "different questions of public health."[14] Based on the FDA's SE actions and industry engagement to date, the FDA will only approve very similar—almost identical—products under the SE pathway after a comprehensive and lengthy review of the product information, including a review of product features, chemistry, and other

---

[12] Such a system was introduced, for example, in Jamaica, the Philippines, and Taiwan (with respect to the latter see a detailed discussion in Chapter 9 of this volume). So far, no entity has overcome this regulatory hurdle.

[13] Family Smoking Prevention and Tobacco Control Act para 910(a)(1).

[14] Ibid para 910(a)(3).

data, generally consistent with requirements outlined in an FDA guidance.[15] However, the FDA has not issued a set of pass/fail criteria for SE evaluations, and manufacturers are not given sufficient feedback on the SE applications to estimate the likelihood of a favorable decision. In addition, the FDA decision-making process appears to be subjective because of, *inter alia*, a lack of pass–fail criteria and owing to inconsistent reviews of past SE applications, as demonstrated by the Summary of the Applications published by the FDA following the issuance of various SE marketing orders.[16] Traditionally, courts do not second guess the FDA's scientific determinations in a product application. It is therefore possible that legal challenges to findings of non-substantial equivalence (NSE), such as the recently filed lawsuit by the US Smokeless Tobacco Company LLC (an Altria Group, Inc. subsidiary) challenging an NSE finding ordering product withdrawal for its Copenhagen Bold Wintergreen Flavor Packs brand products,[17] will be rejected.

Inasmuch as the cigarette and smokeless tobacco industry can largely continue to sell most of the products that were on the market in 2011 without major impediment and can line-extend products following the relatively affordable SE premarket authorization pathway, they have not suffered great impediments following the passage of the TCA, as reflected by robust company earnings in spite of declining sales volume.[18] It can be said that the TCA did not make a dent in the conventional tobacco industry. In contrast, as will be seen below, the SE pathway is not available to ENDS products. According to the FDA's own estimate in the preamble to the Deeming Rule, the same TCA, when applied to ENDS products—which present a much lower comparative risk of disease than combustible cigarettes—is likely to decimate the number of industry participants (manufacturers) and products available for sale within a few years, although it will not dampen demand.[19] Compliance with the rule does not allow for innovation after the cutoff date of August 8, 2016, and any

---

[15] Guidance for Industry and Food and Drug Administration Staff, "Section 905(j) Reports: Demonstrating Substantial Equivalence for Tobacco Products" https://bit.ly/2OvRlXj accessed October 31, 2018.

[16] FDA, "Marketing Orders for SE" https://bit.ly/2OvZSd2 accessed October 31, 2018.

[17] *US Smokeless Tobacco Company LLC v. FDA et al*, United States District Court for the District of Columbia, Case 1:18-cv-00251.

[18] See J. Maloney, S. Chaudhuri, "Against All Odds, the U.S. Tobacco Industry is Rolling in Money" (*The Wall Street Journal*, April 23, 2018) https://on.wsj.com/2q4h8pY accessed October 31, 2018.

[19] FDA, "Deeming Tobacco Products to Be Subject to the Federal Food, Drug, and Cosmetic Act, as Amended by the Family Smoking Prevention and Tobacco Control Act; Regulations on the Sale and Distribution of Tobacco Products and Required Warning Statements for Tobacco Products. Final Rule" (2016) 81 Fed Regist 79. The

innovation would be in violation of the law.[20] The rule thus places a much higher regulatory burden on a relatively less risky set of products. That is primarily because, as will be discussed in more detail below, the only premarket pathway available to ENDS either to remain on the market or to make any product improvements is the PMTA pathway.

Thus, the most onerous—and still largely unexplored and unclear—premarket pathway under the TCA is the PMTA, which must be used by a manufacturer which wishes to introduce a new product that cannot be compared with (predicated upon) a similarly designed February 15, 2007 grandfathered product. Under the PMTA pathway, the manufacturer must demonstrate with compelling scientific evidence that the introduction of the new product is "appropriate for the protection of public health," taking into consideration, *inter alia*, "the risks and benefits to the population as a whole, including users and non-users of the tobacco product."[21] To date, only one set of eight variations of the same snus product received marketing orders under the PMTA pathway in November 2015,[22] while the same manufacturer applicant was denied the MRTP applications for the same snus products in 2016.[23] However, snus products by the same manufacturer which were very similar to the snus products subject to the successful PMTA application had already been sold on the US market for several years. The PMTA application in question could have been an SE application were it not for the lack of an available 2007 predicate. Therefore, in connection with the respective snus PMTAs, the FDA was really only called upon to evaluate small changes made to commercially available products with a long track record of sales and other available consumer data, and did not have to evaluate an entirely novel product.

To date there have been relatively few attempts to file PMTAs, and it seems that none have been filed by the ENDS industry—and all but eight of those which were filed were swiftly rejected by the FDA (or, in FDA parlance, received "refuse to accept" or "refuse to file" letters), most likely for being vastly insufficient. From time to time the FDA updates its dashboard Summary

---

FDA itself has conservatively estimated that more than 87 percent of the industry would not be able to comply, and additional consolidation would occur.

[20] Note that despite the existence of the rule, new products (albeit not necessarily innovative) have been introduced on the market.

[21] Family Smoking Prevention and Tobacco Control Act para 910(c)(4).

[22] FDA, "FDA Issues First Product Marketing Orders through Premarket Tobacco Application Pathway" (November 10, 2015) https://bit.ly/2xVcwsA accessed October 31, 2018.

[23] FDA, "FDA Takes Action on Applications Seeking to Market Modified Risk Tobacco Products" (December 14, 2016) https://bit.ly/2ybys1X accessed October 31, 2018.

of Premarket Tobacco Applications Final Actions.[24] At present only a couple of PMTAs are under active review by the FDA, most notably a PMTA for the Philip Morris International (PMI) IQOS device,[25] with PMI also separately seeking an MRTP claim authorization from the FDA. IQOS is not covered by the Deeming Rule (see below), since the Marlboro HeatSticks it uses fall under the definition of conventional cigarettes under the TCA.[26]

We can therefore conclude that to date the FDA has never authorized the sale of a completely new (and never before sold) product under the PMTA pathway, and may not have formulated a firm set of criteria defining the novel "appropriate for the protection of public health" standard. This conclusion is important for the US ENDS industry, for, as we shall see below, all ENDS are now required to follow the largely unexplored, costly, and time consuming PMTA pathway to be reviewed by a relatively novice FDA, with no clear set of pass–fail criteria either having been developed or communicated to the industry to date. This seems to promise a very opaque and subjective review.[27]

3. BRINGING ENDS UNDER FDA JURISDICTION

In April 2009 the FDA, using its 1990s tobacco regulatory strategy, attempted to ban the sale of e-cigarettes by denying their importation to a couple of US companies. The FDA stated that the products were unapproved drug device combination products intended to treat nicotine withdrawal symptoms. One importer sought an injunction, and another party joined the lawsuit.[28] As the TCA became law in June 2009 it was relatively easy for a federal appellate court in 2011 to find that the FDA could not regulate the respective electronic cigarettes as drug devices, because the TCA gave the FDA authority to regu-

---

24 FDA, "Premarket Tobacco Applications" https://bit.ly/2O6BHCE accessed October 31, 2018.

25 Philip Morris International, "Philip Morris International (PMI) Files Premarket Tobacco Product Application for its Electronically Heated Tobacco Product (EHTP) with the US Food and Drug Administration (FDA)" (*Business Wire*, March 31, 2017) https://bit.ly/2Oxz77W accessed October 31, 2018.

26 Family Smoking Prevention and Tobacco Control Act para 900(3).

27 It should be noted however that compliance with the deadline was extended to 2022 (for more details see the subsequent discussion in this text), possibly giving the FDA some additional time to elaborate more precise criteria. Having said this, it also needs to be stressed that the existing draft PMTA guidance still remains unclear, while the time necessary to develop rules through the notice and comment rulemaking procedure may not allow for sufficient time to prepare necessary studies. For example, if the rules are to be adopted in 2021, it is already too late, given that the required studies take substantially longer to complete.

28 *Smoking Everywhere, Inc. v. U.S. Food and Drug Admin.*, No 09-771 (D.D.C. January 14, 2010).

late them as tobacco products if the products did not make therapeutic claims (for example *Sottera v. FDA*).[29] The plaintiffs may have believed at the time that tobacco products regulation was more desirable and less onerous than drug approval requirements. The *Sottera* litigation delayed FDA regulation by a few years and enabled the creation of an ENDS market in the US, which grew exponentially between 2009 and about 2015. While *Sottera* had the desired outcome at the time it was issued, its effects are merely palliative care for a deeper problem. The FDA's subsequent deeming regulation failed to distinguish harm reduction-promoting products such as ENDS from conventional cigarettes.

Between 2009 and 2014, the FDA was well aware of the proliferation of ENDS products and other nicotine-containing consumer products, such as hookahs and gels, on the US market. The FDA's website at the time sought to deter consumers from even trying these products, expressing cautious adverse warnings and directing those who wanted to quit smoking to FDA-approved smoking cessation drugs instead. The FDA's actions and statements were impactful even outside of the US borders. Several foreign governments, such as Brazil's,[30] acted to ban ENDS pursuant to a 2009 FDA report on e-cigarettes (since then deleted from the FDA website),[31] raising concerns about ENDS in connection with decisions to make them illegal in their respective jurisdictions.[32] Most of these bans are still in place. The precautionary principle featured prominently in many FDA statements and research between 2009 and 2014,[33] laying the foundation for the issuance of a proposed rule which was to bring ENDS, tobacco cigars, and "other products" under the authority of the TCA.

---

29 *Sottera, Inc. v. U.S. Food and Drug Admin.,* 627 F.3d 891 (D.C. Cir. 2011).

30 See for example V. Queiroz Galvao, "Cigarros eletrônicos contêm agente cancerígeno, diz FDA" (*Folha de Sao Paulo*, July 23, 2009) https://bit.ly/2zP1w1h accessed October 31, 2018. It should be noted that those decisions were also influenced by other factors, such as pressure from local non-governmental organizations. At the same time, it seems the Conference of the Parties to the Framework Convention on Tobacco Control did not play any role at that time and ENDS were not yet on its agenda (for detailed discussion see Chapter 4 in this book).

31 See S. Reinberg, "E-Cigarettes Pose a Health Hazard, FDA Warns" (*ABC News*, July 22, 2009) https://abcn.ws/2NZgDOd accessed October 31, 2018.

32 See "E-Cigarette Bans Growing // Sellers Seek Liability Insurance" (*PRLOG*, September 2, 2009) https://bit.ly/2IzcScd accessed October 31, 2018.

33 See for example FDA, "FDA Warns of Health Risks Posed by E-Cigarettes" https://bit.ly/2ICbYM2 accessed October 31, 2018. For a detailed discussion of the precautionary principle and its application to ENDS in the context of European law, see Chapter 8 of this book.

Thus, the proposed rule, deeming ENDS as well as some other tobacco products, was issued in April 2014.[34] As required by the Administrative Procedure Act (APA),[35] a docket was established, and a total of 119,031 comments were received from all interested parties—manufacturers; importers; retailers; public health advocates, including academics and non-governmental organizations; and consumers.[36] The FDA did not appear to give much weight to industry and consumer comments, and in May 2016 it issued a final rule (the Deeming Rule) in a form substantially similar to the 2014 proposed rule.[37]

According to the FDA's own summary of the Deeming Rule:

> The final rule, published on 10 May 2016 [and with certain provisions effective as of 8 August 2016] extends the FDA's "tobacco product" authority to all other categories of tobacco products meeting the statutory definition of "tobacco product" in the FD&C Act, except accessories of such products. The final rule, among other things, also:
>
> - prohibits the sale of "covered tobacco products" to individuals under the age of 18;
> - prohibits vending machine sales of covered tobacco products (except in facilities that prohibit individuals under the age of 18 years from entering at any time);
> - requires the display of health warnings on covered tobacco products, cigarette tobacco, and roll-your-own tobacco (RYO tobacco) packages and advertisements;
> - requires the submission and approval of cigar warning plans for packaging and advertisements; and
> - results in the prohibition of free sample distribution of newly regulated tobacco products.[38]

The Deeming Rule contains some so-called automatic provisions, meaning that ENDS, among other newly deemed products, must comply with all provisions regarding "tobacco products" in the TCA and FDA regulations issued to date. These provisions require, where applicable, manufacturers, importers, and retailers of ENDS to take certain actions, including:

---

34 FDA, "Deeming Tobacco Products to Be Subject to the Federal Food, Drug, and Cosmetic Act" (n 19).

35 See Administrative Procedure Act, para 553, Pub. L. No 79-404, 60 Stat. 237 (1946) (codified as amended in scattered sections of 5 U.S.C.).

36 See FDA, "Deeming Tobacco Products to Be Subject to the Federal Food, Drug, and Cosmetic Act" (n 19).

37 Ibid.

38 FDA, "Summary of the Deeming Final Rule" https://bit.ly/2IAYm3J accessed October 31, 2018.

- ensure that ENDS are not adulterated or misbranded;[39]
- provide the FDA with ingredient listings for all ENDS by a certain date (eventually extended to May 8, 2018 for all except small scale manufacturers,[40] which had a compliance date of November 8, 2018);[41]
- register manufacturing establishments and provide the FDA with product listings (deadline eventually extended to October 12, 2017);[42]
- allow the FDA to exercise its inspection authority over ENDS manufacturers, importers and retailers;
- submit certain types of health information about the ENDS products created between June 22, 2009 and December 31, 2009 (a timeframe when most ENDS products on the market as of the effective date of the Deeming Rule, that is, August 8, 2016, were not in fact being manufactured);[43]
- not introduce into interstate commerce modified risk tobacco products (including ENDS), meaning products that make a modified (that is reduced) risk or modified (that is reduced) exposure claim, without an FDA MRTP order;[44]
- obtain premarket authorization for newly deemed products that meet the definition of a "new tobacco product"[45] via one of the pathways specified in the TCA (SE, minor modification, or PMTA, while *de facto* only the PMTA is available to ENDS products because there are no eligible and substantially similar ENDS predicate products that were on the market on February 15, 2007). Initially, the Deeming Rule required all ENDS manufacturers to submit PMTAs by August 8, 2018 as a prerequisite to continue to sell their respective products, pending PMTA review by the FDA, and for no longer than a year thereafter should the PMTA review not finish by August 8, 2019. However, following the victory of the Republican presidential candidate in the 2016 US presidential elections, on July 28, 2017 a newly appointed FDA Commissioner issued a statement extending the compliance deadline to August 8, 2022.[46]

---

39 Family Smoking Prevention and Tobacco Control Act para 902 and 903.

40 For the purposes of the FDA and the compliance policy for ENDS, a "small-scale tobacco product manufacturer" is a manufacturer of any regulated tobacco product that employs 150 or fewer full-time equivalent employees and has annual total revenues of US $5 million or less. See FDA, "Summary of the Deeming Final Rule" (n 38).

41 FDA, "Listing of Ingredients in Tobacco Products (Revised)—Guidance for Industry" https://bit.ly/2zPCAqf accessed October 31, 2018.

42 FDA, "Registration and Product Listing for Owners and Operators of Domestic Tobacco Product Establishments (Revised)—Guidance for Industry" https://bit.ly/2wgyQ0X accessed October 31, 2018.

43 FDA, "Health Document Submission Requirements for Tobacco Products (Revised)—Guidance for the Industry" https://bit.ly/2xXjSM5 accessed October 31, 2018.

44 Family Smoking Prevention and Tobacco Control Act para 911.

45 Ibid para 910(a).

46 FDA, "FDA Announces Comprehensive Regulatory Plan to Shift Trajectory of Tobacco-Related Disease, Death" (July 28, 2017) https://bit.ly/2w6oeNF accessed October 31, 2018.

- report harmful and potentially harmful constituents[47]—a one-off requirement, with a deadline theoretically established for May 8, 2019 but clearly requiring additional FDA rulemaking, or at least additional guidance, before ENDS manufacturers may proceed with testing. Realistically, this requirement will not be due before 2021.

The Deeming Rule imposes additional restrictions specific to "covered tobacco products,"[48] according to which ENDS must comply with the following:

- An immediate requirement for a federal minimum age of purchase (18) and verification of age via photographic identification, also applicable to online sales (note that some US states and localities have a minimum age of purchase of 19 or 21).
- Prohibition of vending machine sales, unless the vending machine is located in a facility where the retailer ensures that individuals under 18 years of age are prohibited from entering at any time, and such age prohibition also limits the age of the store clerk to be over 18.
- Health warnings for product packages and advertisements:
  - All "covered tobacco products" manufactured by August 8, 2018 must bear the following warning regarding the addictiveness of nicotine: "WARNING: This product contains nicotine. Nicotine is an addictive chemical." The warning must cover 30 percent of the two principal display panels of the product packaging. The FDA offers a self-certification option for manufacturers who certify that their product, although derived from tobacco, does not contain nicotine (and who have data to support that assertion). Such a product will be required to bear the statement "This product is derived from tobacco." Note that conventional cigarette products at present are not required to carry 30 percent front and back warnings and an FDA attempt to impose graphic health warnings was struck down by a federal court.[49] Consequently, cigarette products must display one of four health warning

---

[47] FDA, "'Harmful and Potentially Harmful Constituents' in Tobacco Products as used in Section 904(e) of the Federal Food, Drug and Cosmetic Act (Revised)" https://bit.ly/2xVwenJ accessed October 31, 2018.

[48] The FDA defines "covered tobacco product" as any tobacco product deemed to be subject to TCA under para 1100.2 of TCA, but excludes any component or part that is not made or derived from tobacco; thus vaping devices and device spare parts and accessories would be exempted from such additional provisions, as these are not made or derived from tobacco.

[49] The TCA requires the FDA to include new warning labels on cigarette packages and in cigarette advertisements. On June 22, 2011, the FDA published a final rule requiring the use of color graphics depicting the negative health consequences of smoking to accompany the nine new textual warning statements. However, the final rule was challenged in a court by several tobacco companies, and on August 24, 2012 the United States Court of Appeals for the District of Columbia Circuit vacated the rule on First Amendment grounds and remanded the matter to the agency. On December 5, 2012, the Court denied the government's petition for a panel rehearing and rehearing en banc. *R.J. Reynolds Tobacco Co., et al, v. Food & Drug Administration, et al*, 696 F.3d

statements under the federal Cigarette Labeling and Advertising Act (15 U.S.C. paras 1331–1340) in a less conspicuous manner on the side of each cigarette pack.

- Tobacco products with packages too small to bear the warning and for which there is no carton or other outer container or wrapper that is large enough to carry the warning must carry the warning on a tag firmly and permanently affixed to the package.

An immediate effect of the Deeming Rule was a complete halt to innovation, as manufacturers and importers were not allowed to introduce any "new tobacco products" after August 8, 2016. This disallows any change, however small and inconsequential, to any product that was on the market on August 8, 2016. Initially most manufacturers complied, but it became apparent that the FDA was not going to be able to enforce the rule against a market of more than 1,500,000 distinct ENDS stock-keeping units (SKUs) (according to a November 2017 count, since deleted, from the FDA's own Registration and Product Listing section of its website). Thus new ENDS products seem to appear and then disappear from the US market, marketed mostly online but also through a network of vape shops that themselves appear and disappear, sometimes seemingly overnight. Such is the market fragmentation and fluctuation that only a handful of brands and companies in the e-liquid, disposable, and cartridge space have demonstrated resilience and gained consumer loyalty (JUUL, blu, Vuse, MarkTen, Halo, Space Jam), generally when supported by consistent distribution through convenience channels, while the vast majority of the rest veer between instant popularity and oblivion within a span of a couple of years, and some of the early well-known manufacturers (Johnson Creek, NJOY) either disappeared or had to be rescued from bankruptcy.[50]

Another impact, subsequently mitigated by deadline extensions, was a general panic among the ENDS industry regarding the expenditure and research inevitably accompanying the putting together of viable PMTAs. Costs of the research, drafting, and testing that manufacturers will incur, based on the FDA ENDS PMTA guidance,[51] range from conservative estimates of US $2 million per SKU to more realistic estimates of US $7–10 million, due

---

1205 (D.C. Cir. 2012). In 2013, the government decided not to seek further review of the Court's ruling.

[50] See R. Romeli, "E-Cigarette Juice Maker Johnson Creek Enterprises Abruptly Shuts Down" (*Milwaukee Journal Sentinel*, October 10, 2017) https://bit.ly/2O2YPSb; L. Fickenscher, "E-Cigarette Maker Files for Bankruptcy" (*New York Post*, September 19, 2017) https://nyp.st/2yamENq both accessed October 31, 2018.

[51] FDA, "Premarket Tobacco Product Applications for Electronic Nicotine Delivery Systems (ENDS), Guidance for Industry, Draft Guidance" https://bit.ly/2ODXTmK accessed October 31, 2018.

primarily to the cost of clinical and pharmacokinetic studies,[52] but also to the stability studies and in vitro/in vivo studies required in the Guidance. This is particularly the case where there are no synergies within the product portfolio, meaning that the individual SKUs are very different and testing cannot address multiple product characteristics.

Active and engaged oversight by the FDA—meaning a thorough exploration by the FDA of the properties and possible risks posed by individual ENDS, inspection of manufacturing facilities, and product recalls—has not yet begun. The FDA does not even have a complete picture of all ENDS products circulating on the US market because its own guidance on registration and product listing specifically exempts importers of foreign-made products as well as foreign manufacturers from product listing requirements, though ingredient reporting is required for everyone. Given the millions of ENDS SKUs on the US market, most of which are manufactured in China, how will the FDA know who should have filed ingredient reports but did not, when not all products are on record with the FDA through product listing submissions?

Furthermore, the sheer volume of information on ENDS ingredients—due May 8 and November 8, 2018 for large and small sized manufacturers, respectively—will likely take years to review, if a review is even planned by the FDA. A review is unlikely, judging by the complete absence of any ingredients inquiry regarding conventional cigarette products, for which ingredients filings were due December 22, 2009. Cigarette products are presumed to contain questionable ingredients in their composition, yet the FDA has never investigated, or ordered a recall of, any cigarette product based on the lack of safety of ingredients alone. It is therefore not expected that the FDA will approach ENDS manufacturers to discuss any potentially unsafe ingredients in ENDS based on ingredients reporting alone.

However, the TCA provides the FDA with a very powerful tool that could implement safeguards in the area of questionable ENDS ingredients—the authority to issue product standards under Section 907 of the TCA.[53] To establish a tobacco product standard, the FDA must find that the standard is appropriate for the protection of the public health, taking into consideration scientific evidence concerning the risks and benefits to the population as a whole, including users and non-users of tobacco products; the increased or decreased likelihood that existing users of tobacco products will stop using such products; and the increased or decreased likelihood that those who do not

---

[52] For a US government estimate of respiratory studies costs in general, see US Department of Health and Human Services, "Examination of Clinical Trial Costs and Barriers for Drug Development" https://bit.ly/29RQ1th accessed October 31, 2018.

[53] Family Smoking Prevention and Tobacco Control Act para 907.

use tobacco products will start using such products. Thus, under section 907 the FDA may issue product standards concerning the construction, components, ingredients, additives, constituents, and properties of tobacco products, including ENDS, and it may impose, *inter alia*, a cap, range, or ban on certain substances (with the exception of nicotine).

The FDA exercised its product standard authority for the first time through the issuance of a proposed rule on Tobacco Product Standard for N-Nitrosonornicotine Levels in Finished Smokeless Tobacco Products, on January 23, 2017.[54] With respect to ENDS products, the FDA expressed its interest in limiting flavor availability in an earlier draft of the Deeming Rule that was sent to the Office of Management and Budget for review in 2017, but was dropped in the final version of the Deeming Rule.[55] The preamble of the Deeming Rule raises certain issues regarding the potential benefits and detriments of ENDS flavors (other than tobacco and menthol) to tobacco harm reduction. Following the promulgation of the Deeming Rule, there was sustained pressure on the FDA from various advocacy groups and members of the legislative branch to address the perceived appeal to children of certain flavored ENDS products. Consequently, the FDA took two important steps to appease those stakeholders expressing concerns regarding the potential appeal of ENDS to youth.

First, on March 21, 2018 the FDA issued an Advance Notice of Proposed Rulemaking on the Regulation of Flavors in Tobacco Products,[56] a nonmandatory first step toward the issuance of a proposed, and then possibly a final, rule on flavors in tobacco products, including ENDS. The issuance of an Advance Notice does not necessarily mean that the FDA will move into actual rulemaking; it is rather an exploration of issues surrounding flavors in tobacco products in the form of a list of questions to the various stakeholders.

Second, on May 1, 2018 the FDA enlisted the help of the FTC, which has concurrent jurisdiction over ENDS products as consumer products, to issue 13 joint warning letters to several e-liquid manufacturers,[57] alleging that "those companies misleadingly labelled or advertised nicotine-containing e-liquids as kid friendly food products such as juice boxes, candies, and cookies." The warning letters requested the recipients to undertake certain actions within

---

[54] Tobacco Product Standard for N-Nitrosonornicotine Level in Finished Smokeless Tobacco Products, Proposed Rule, 82 FR 8004.

[55] See FDA, "Deeming Draft RIA as Submitted to Office of Management and Budget" https://bit.ly/2zPMLLE accessed October 31, 2018.

[56] Regulation of Flavors in Tobacco Products, Advance Notice of Proposed Rulemaking, 83 FR 12294.

[57] See FDA, "E-Liquids Misleadingly Labeled or Advertised as Food Products" https://bit.ly/2jJ30kP accessed October 2, 2018.

15 working days from the date of receipt. Namely, with regard to the FD&C Act violation described in the respective warning letter, the manufacturer was required to submit a written response to the warning letter describing the corrective actions taken, including the dates on which the manufacturer discontinued the violative labeling, advertising, sale, and/or distribution of the respective ENDS products and the manufacturer's plan for maintaining compliance with the FD&C Act. If the manufacturer *did not* believe that the respective ENDS products were in violation of the FD&C Act, the manufacturer was urged to include the relevant reasoning and any supporting information for the FDA's consideration in the response to the warning letter. Additional enforcement action on similarly advertised products is expected.

Following extensive media reports and a proliferation of online ads and videos depicting the increasing popularity among school-age children of a vaping device manufactured in China for JUUL Labs, Inc. (JUUL), on April 24, 2018 the FDA also sent a document request letter to the company. The FDA requested that JUUL:

> submit documents relating to marketing practices and research on marketing, effects of product design, public health impact, and adverse experiences and complaints related to JUUL products. This request applies to research relating to all such tobacco products and their components or parts, including those products for research, investigational use, developmental studies, test marketing, and/or commercial marketing.
>
> The FDA is requesting these documents based on a growing concern about the popularity of JUUL products among youth. JUUL product use appears to be common in middle and high schools based on widespread media reporting describing a rapid growth of use among youth in general and on school property, numerous complaints that have been received by CTP, small research studies that have raised concerns, and social media evidence of youth use.[58]

The documents were due on June 19, 2018. Subsequently, on September 12, 2018, the FDA issued separate letters to five vaping products manufacturers, including JUUL, asking the companies to submit plans to reverse youth use trends.[59]

While age verification enforcement at the retail level is routinely performed by FDA agents and contracted state agents with respect to all tobacco products,

---

[58] See FDA, "Letter to Juul Labs, Inc." (April 24, 2018) https://bit.ly/2Kvyi9Q accessed October 31, 2018.

[59] FDA, "FDA Takes New Steps to Address Epidemic of Youth E-Cigarette Use, Including a Historic Action against more than 1,300 Retailers and 5 Major Manufacturers for Their Roles Perpetuating Youth Access" (September 12, 2018) http://fda.gov/NewsEvents/Newsroom/PressAnnouncements/ucm620184.htm accessed October 31, 2018.

the joint FDA/FTC warning letters and the document request sent to JUUL are unprecedented since the passage of the TCA and may indicate that the FDA might presently be deploying more efforts to scrutinize ENDS products than conventional cigarette products.

Ultimately, the FDA will rely on the PMTA process and on the 2,022 mandatory ENDS PMTA submissions to determine which ENDS products will remain on the market. At present the FDA repeats that the health impact of ENDS cannot be reliably determined based on the data currently available, and places the onus on manufacturers to demonstrate the eventual impact of ENDS on the population as a whole through the PMTA process.

In contrast, grandfathered conventional cigarette products need not demonstrate *anything* in order to remain on the market, and cigarette manufacturers may extend their product offering through the relatively accessible SE process. Thus, the population health standards envisaged by the TCA do not seem to be put into practice by the FDA,[60] whose Deeming Rule effectively discriminates against ENDS products in the post-2016 and especially the post-2022 marketplace, disallowing robust competition against conventional cigarettes protected by the grandfather clause.

4. THE INDUSTRY FIGHTS BACK—THE *NICOPURE* LITIGATION AND OTHER INITIATIVES

The Deeming Rule was challenged by a US-based ENDS manufacture, Nicopure Labs, LLC (Nicopure), as to its legality under the APA. The challenge stated that the FDA violated the APA (which, among other things, prohibits federal agencies from acting in an "arbitrary and capricious" manner) in connection with the Deeming Rule rulemaking process, and that the TCA, as applied to ENDS through the Deeming Rule, violated First Amendment free speech protections.

As to the APA claim, Nicopure argued that the FDA exceeded its statutory authority by defining "tobacco products" to include products that are neither made or derived from tobacco nor intended for human consumption (such as vaping devices).[61] Nicopure also claimed that, in drafting the Deeming Rule, the FDA "arbitrarily" ignored the benefits of e-cigarettes as compared to smoking. The plaintiff also contended that the grandfather date of February 15, 2007 was arbitrary and capricious, and thus ENDS manufacturers could not

---

60 Family Smoking Prevention and Tobacco Control Act para 3(9).

61 Although most nicotine in e-liquids comes from tobacco, technically speaking the devices as such are not "made or derived from" tobacco.

avail themselves of two of the premarket pathways available under the TCA. Furthermore, Nicopure argued that the FDA cost–benefit analysis conducted in connection with the Deeming Rule, while mandatory, was flawed, in that the FDA discounted the costs and in fact stated it could not fully quantify the costs or benefits.

With respect to the First Amendment claims, the plaintiff stated that the Deeming Rule's implementation of the TCA MRTP provision prohibits ENDS manufacturers from making truthful and non-misleading statements related to their products, and that such prohibition violates the US Constitution. Nicopure also questioned the Deeming Rule's prohibition against free sample distribution (which the FDA interpreted to mean a prohibition against even offering a consumer a free puff from a vaping product), which, according to Nicopure, represented a violation of protected speech.

At a later date, a coalition of several trade associations filed suit in the same court.[62] The two law suits were consolidated shortly thereafter.[63] Various parties filed *amici curiae* briefs in support of both Nicopure and other plaintiffs as well as the FDA.[64] Meanwhile several other law suits were filed in 2016,[65] but none proceeded very fast.

On July 21, 2017 Judge Jackson disagreed with the plaintiffs' arguments and found in favor of the FDA on all counts.[66] In its decision, the court largely deferred to the FDA as follows: (1) non-nicotine containing products, such

---

[62] *Right to Be Smoke-Free, American E-Liquid Manufacturing Standards Assoc., American Vaping Assoc., Electronic Vaping Coalition of America, Georgia Smoke Free Assoc., Kentucky Vaping Retailers Assoc., Inc., Louisiana Vaping Assoc. Maryland Vape Professionals, LLC, New Jersey Vapor Retailers Coalition, Ohio Vapor Trade Association and Tennessee Smoke Free Assoc. vs. Food & Drug Administration* 1:16-cv-01210 (D.D.C. June 20, 2016).

[63] See M. Rowland, "Federal Judge Consolidates Historic Lawsuits: Nicopure Labs vs. FDA E-Cig Regulations" (*Vapes*, July 18, 2016) https://bit.ly/2b8eivP accessed October 31, 2018.

[64] See J. Harlay, "SFATA Submits Amicus Curiae Brief in Lawsuit against FDA, Others Follow" (*VapingPost*, August 12, 2016) https://bit.ly/2P6oZju. See also J. McDonald, "Deeming News: FDA Responds to the Vaping Legal Challenge" (*Vaping360*, August 22, 2016) https://bit.ly/2zPr7XB both accessed October 31, 2018.

[65] *Lost Art Liquids, LLC v. U.S. Food & Drug Administration* 2:16-cv-3468 (C.D. Cal. May 19, 2016); *Icaza et al v. Food & Drug Administration et al*, 1:16-cv-21967 (S.D. Fla. June 1, 2016); *Larry W. Faircloth v. U.S. Food & Drug Administration* 2:16-cv-5267 (S.D.W.V. June 10, 2016) (partially dismissed in October 2017), and *Cyclops Vapor 2, Tiger Vapor and Karma S. v U.S. Food & Drug Administration* 2:16-cv-556 (M.D. Ala. July 8, 2016).

[66] For a comprehensive overview of the decision, see S.L. Ehrlich, J.W. Woodlee, "Nicopure Labs, LLC v. Food and Drug Administration et al" (*Food and Drug Law Institute*) http://fdli.org/2018/07/nicopure-labs-llc-v-food-and-drug-administration-et-al/ accessed October 31, 2018.

as devices sold without liquids and zero-nicotine and zero-tobacco liquids, were found to fall under the definition of tobacco products; (2) the FDA's decision to subject ENDS to its tobacco product authority was not arbitrary and capricious and not in violation of the APA, with the judge commenting that the plaintiffs' concerns were mainly policy arguments that should have been directed to Congress; (3) the FDA was not required to undertake a cost–benefit analysis when it implemented the statutory deeming provision, and even if had to do so, the FDA's cost–benefit analysis was adequate and was not "a clear error of judgment"; (4) the FDA did not violate the Regulatory Flexibility Act because FDA completed a Regulatory Impact Analysis that "contains a discussion of all of the required topics"; and (5) the rule does not violate the plaintiffs' substantive due process rights under the US Constitution, because Congress articulated a number of rational reasons for the premarket review requirement in the purposes section of the TCA. With respect to the plaintiffs' argument that two provisions of the Deeming Rule violated their right to free speech under the First Amendment to the US Constitution,[67] the court found that samples were conduct, not speech, and therefore not protected under the First Amendment; and also stated that the sampling ban directly and materially advances and serves the government interest and is not more extensive than necessary to do so, and that the preapproval requirement "does not ban truthful statements about health benefits or reduced risks; it simply requires that they be substantiated."[68]

A week later, Commissioner Gottlieb announced a "comprehensive nicotine policy,"[69] which promised an earnest exploration of very low admissible nicotine limits in cigarettes but also extended certain compliance deadlines, most notably the 2018 ENDS PMTA deadline, to 2022. By 2022 a new political administration may be in power, and it may not be the same as the present one. This could mean a new Commissioner will have to deal with the incoming PMTA reports and may set new priorities.

Support for, and understanding of, the vaping industry is to a certain extent split along party lines,[70] with the Democrats advocating for ever stricter oversight of the industry and some even for flavor and advertising bans (with the notable exception of Representative Sanford Bishop from Georgia), and

---

[67] The ban on free samples and the preapproval requirement for modified risk claims.

[68] *Nicopure Labs, LLC v. FDA,* 266 F. Supp. 3d at 421 (D.D.C. 2017).

[69] See FDA, "FDA Announces Comprehensive Regulatory Plan to Shift Trajectory of Tobacco-Related Disease, Death" (n 46).

[70] See for example D. Caruana, "Senate Democrats Propose a Bill that Would Raise E-Cig Taxes" (*VapingPost*, October 24, 2017) https://bit.ly/2QqtYf0 accessed October 31, 2018.

the Republicans taking a more moderate view on vaping products, probably reflecting their overall attitude toward business and regulation.

During 2016 and 2017 the most important legislative initiative at federal level regarding vaping was the so-called Cole–Bishop Amendment (Cole–Bishop), a bipartisan amendment sponsored by Rep. Tom Cole (R-OK) and Rep. Sanford Bishop (D-GA) to the 2017 fiscal year Agricultural Appropriations bill, which the House Appropriations Committee voted for inclusion on April 19, 2016, just days before the Deeming Rule was published. Cole–Bishop strove, among other things, to amend the February 15, 2007 grandfather date for ENDS to coincide with the effective date of the Deeming Rule, that is, August 8, 2016. After sustained deadlock in Congress with respect to the budget bill, the Cole–Bishop rider was not included in the final "omnibus" budget bill passed on March 21, 2018.[71]

Days after Gottlieb's announcement, the parties to the *Nicopure* litigation announced an appeal to the Court of Appeals of the District of Columbia. Shortly after the *Nicopure* appeal was filed, in September 2017 several public health-oriented non-governmental organizations—the American Association of Pediatrics, American Cancer Society, Cancer Action Network, American Heart Association, American Lung Association, Campaign for Tobacco-Free Kids, and Truth Initiative—filed a motion to intervene as defendants, contending that the FDA, under the new leadership, was not going to vigorously defend the *Nicopure* appeal. The Intervenors cited the FDA's agreement to delay and eventually stay the *Cyclops Vapor 2, LLC v. FDA* litigation, as well as the announcement of the July 2017 Deeming Rule deadline extensions, as evidence that the FDA was likely to take a passive stance in the *Nicopure* appeal. In fact, the FDA proved to be anything but passive in the *Nicopure* litigation. The FDA's answer to the motion to intervene, filed on September 28, 2017, was brief: "The government takes no position on the intervention motion and defers to the judgment of the Court, but we note that the movants may present their arguments as amici."[72]

In November 2017 the judges assigned to hear the motion to intervene declined to rule and ordered "that the motion for leave to intervene be referred to the merits panel to which this case is assigned." The Court also directed the parties to brief the intervention issue again "rather than incorporate . . . arguments by reference" to briefs already filed both in support of and against the Intervenors' motion.

---

[71] See J. Castle, "Cole–Bishop Removed from 2018 Omnibus Bill" (*Vape News*, March21,2018)https://vapenews.com/vape-news/cole-bishop-removed-2018-omnibus-bill/ accessed October 31, 2018.

[72] Document on file with the author.

Shortly after the plaintiffs filed their appellate brief, which dedicated several pages to arguments against the Intervenors' motion to intervene, in March 2018 the Intervenors withdrew their motion in the *Nicopure* case, only to promptly file their own litigation against the FDA, contending that the FDA violated the APA and the Constitution by granting ENDS manufacturers (and others) extensions of the Deeming Rule deadlines via Commissioner Gottlieb's July 28, 2018 announcement.[73] In an even more interesting twist, though procedurally precluded from discussing evidence not found in the Deeming Rule's administrative record, the FDA's response to the *Nicopure* appellate brief, filed on May 3, 2018, contained abundant references to recent FDA actions, including the joint FDA/FTC warning letters that had been issued a mere two days before the FDA's deadline to file their answer. The FDA's answer read in places as a vigorous, yet unsubstantiated, indictment of the vaping industry, whereas the core of the FDA's legal arguments could be summarized as "Judge Jackson was right to rule in FDA's favor."

Oral arguments in the *Nicopure* appeal were held on September 11, 2018. A decision is expected in 2019. Should Nicopure Labs et al prevail, the Deeming Rule's application might be limited to the extent that its revision by the FDA becomes practically inevitable. Moreover, if the First Amendment MRTP claim is successful, ENDS companies—as well as other manufacturers of regulated tobacco products—will be able to make claims pertinent to the absence of any substance in the respective products, as well as comparative safety claims. However, FTC's broad, concurrent jurisdiction over tobacco products, including ENDS, provides the necessary safeguards that any advertising claim made by tobacco products manufacturers, including ENDS manufacturers or retailers, must be truthful and substantiated as per the FTC Act.[74]

Appeals to the Supreme Court of the United States are not a matter of right. A party seeking to appeal the future *Nicopure* decision of the United States Court of Appeals for the District of Columbia may only file a petition for a writ of certiorari.[75] In the US Supreme Court four Justices must agree to review the case in order for the Court to grant certiorari. In recent years the

---

73 *American Academy of Pediatrics, et al v. FDA, et al*, No 8:18-cv-00883 (D. Md.).

74 15 U.S.C. para 45.

75 As explained in the official webpage of the US courts: "Parties who are not satisfied with the decision of a lower court must petition the US Supreme Court to hear their case. The primary means to petition the court for review is to ask it to grant a *writ of certiorari*. This is a request that the Supreme Court order a lower court to send up the record of the case for review. The Court usually is not under any obligation to hear these cases, and it usually only does so if the case could have national significance, might harmonize conflicting decisions in the federal Circuit courts, and/or could have precedential value" https://bit.ly/1VPZ8YX accessed October 31, 2018.

Court has heard fewer and fewer cases. If the FDA prevails in the currently pending appeal, it is possible that the plaintiffs/appellants might seek certiorari and the 2018 US Supreme Court composition suggests that at least the First Amendment arguments could be of interest to more than four of its Justices. If certiorari is denied and the rule remains in place as written, the future of the industry will depend, among other factors, on the FDA's appetite to exercise enforcement discretion in connection with ENDS regulation, and on Congress's willingness to change the TCA to make it more favorable to vaping products. If the plaintiffs prevail in the currently pending appeal, the FDA will likely revisit its Deeming Rule through notice and comment rulemaking rather than deferring to a potential grant of certiorari by the Supreme Court.

It is also possible that other cases filed in other jurisdictions may be heard before a grant of certiorari by the Supreme Court (if such would actually be the case). It is not impossible for a different district or circuit court to reach a different conclusion on the same set of facts. In fact, it has happened in the past that litigation against the FDA has been resolved in diametrically opposed ways by two different circuit courts, which is termed a "circuit split." In that case, the Supreme Court might well be more inclined to hear an appeal, but this is still discretionary, not a matter of right.[76] One can only speculate on what the practical consequences would be for the industry and the FDA, in a precedent-based legal system, if one federal district court were to find, for instance, that the MRTP speech restriction violates the First Amendment, while another has already issued an opposite ruling.

5. CONCLUSIONS REGARDING THE ADEQUACY OF THE CURRENT US ENDS REGULATORY REGIME TO PROMOTE TOBACCO HARM REDUCTION

Due to the timing of ENDS' entry to the US market (after February 15, 2007) and due to certain ENDS-specific requirements in the Deeming Rule, the US regulatory framework for ENDS, while overlapping in theory with that for conventional cigarettes, places ENDS at a competitive disadvantage versus conventional cigarettes in three areas: (1) innovation—ENDS can only line-extend through the much more costly and as yet unexplored PMTA pre-market pathway, while cigarettes can line-extend through the less onerous SE pathway; (2) sustainability past 2022—ENDS products must file PMTAs by 2022, and according to the FDA's own estimates it is likely to take most ENDS

[76] Rules of the Supreme Court of the United States of America (2017) 10(a) https://bit.ly/2NE6ouV accessed October 31, 2018.

products off the market at that point,[77] whereas cigarette manufacturers do not have to do anything additional to continue selling past 2022; (3) ENDS is at a severe disadvantage with respect to the resources required to manage the regulatory filings for a more diverse product portfolio. Since each SKU is treated as a separate product, for which all kinds of regulatory filings are needed, the typical ENDS manufacturer will have thousands or even tens of thousands of SKUs to manage through regulatory processes, or else most of these SKUs must be discontinued;[78] meanwhile, the largest tobacco company would only have at most a few hundred cigarette SKUs (and vastly more resources).

To add to the complexity, due to recent state developments in cannabis legislation (still banned at the federal level and in most states), ENDS must also compete with vaporized cannabis products for the same consumer profile, and federal authorities such as the FDA and the Drug Enforcement Agency (DEA) do not appear to be very active in curbing the use of cannabis products or the advertising of the medicinal properties of cannabis and kratom—which is not allowed under the FD&C Act for unapproved drugs. The bigger tobacco harm reduction picture requires a thorough exploration of the interplay between the regulatory regimes for ENDS, cigarettes, and other inhaled, non-tobacco-based "recreational" products, as well as the impact of selective action by federal enforcement agencies such as the FDA and DEA among various types of inhaled recreational products.

US regulation, coupled with spotty enforcement and unfair competition on the marketplace from illicit ENDS and other types of recreational products, does not at present create a transparent and consistent tobacco harm reduction environment. Despite regulatory smoking reduction tools deployed by the government in the past—such as smoking bans, hiking tax rates, and limiting the cigarette manufacturers' ability to introduce new products through the 2009 TCA—their effects on smoking rates (although effective in the past when those measures were first deployed) appear to have slowed since the mid-1990s.[79] This situation can be attributed in part to states' inappropriate use

---

[77] FDA, "Deeming Tobacco Products to Be Subject to the Federal Food, Drug, and Cosmetic Act" (n 19) 79 and 97 (assuming only 2,500 PMTAs for vaping products).

[78] Some deadlines have already passed, and ENDS manufacturers did file ingredients reports for a large number of products. Most small manufacturers rely on a large number of products to realize a profit. Shrinking their portfolio (by refining their product offerings to a much smaller set) will also mean shrinking their profits proportionally.

[79] Centers for Disease Control and Prevention, "Trends in Current Cigarette Smoking Among High School Students and Adults, United States, 1965–2014" https://bit.ly/2AefA2X accessed October 31, 2018.

of Master Settlement Agreement funds.[80] Arguably, the only modest incremental reduction in cigarette consumption can still be attributed to those residual mechanisms at present, and it is not clear how much is attributable to traditional tobacco control measures and how much to switching to non-combustible products after 2009. Furthermore, some authors find underfunding of cessation programs to be both a reality and an issue.[81] This means that the most impactful harm reduction tool for reducing smoking rates in the marketplace may in the future be switching to less harmful nicotine consumption alternatives, such as ENDS. This encouraging trend was documented in, *inter alia*, government surveys quoted in a 2017 University of California study.[82] However, US government actions and statements toward ENDS are contradictory and clearly do not recognize, stimulate, or reward the likely positive impact on individual (if not public) health of ENDS substitution, documented in various surveys over the past few years, extrapolated from the decline in cigarette volumes and distinct improvements in the health of cohorts of individual smokers, who submitted tens of thousands of comments to the various FDA ENDS-related dockets (the latter of which is dismissed as "merely anecdotal evidence" by the FDA CTP leadership).

In conclusion, absent the FDA's willingness to enforce the TCA in a differentiated manner, and one that is supportive of ENDS's harm reduction value proposition, Congress is the only US body that may, and should, revisit the TCA to account for the beneficial position of ENDS on the nicotine risk continuum, while imposing safeguards regarding product design and responsible communication to various audiences. At present, there does not appear to be sufficient political will to engage in the overhaul of nicotine regulation in the US which is desired by both consumers and industry advocacy groups. However, I am hopeful that long-term ENDS population studies and the

---

80 See American Heart Association & American Stroke Association, "FACTS: Reducing the Burden of Tobacco Establishing Sustainable Funding for Tobacco Prevention and Cessation Programs" https://bit.ly/2AnuiWZ; L. Stroud, "Using the Tobacco Settlement to Pay for Public Employee Pensions, while Doubling Down against Safer Tobacco Products" (*The American Spectator*, July 10, 2018) https://spectator.org/tobacco-funds-are-filling-government-coffers-not-helping-people-quit/ both accessed October 31, 2018.

81 See D. Mapes, "US Public Health Funding Steadily Falling, New Study Shows" (*Fred Hutch*, November 12, 2015) https://bit.ly/2nDbs5c; see also The National Academies of Sciences, Engineering, and Medicine, "Smoking Cessation Programs" http://sites.nationalacademies.org/tobacco/smokingcessation/tobacco_051286 both accessed October 31, 2018.

82 See S.-H. Zhu, "E-Cigarette Use and Associated Changes in Population Smoking Cessation: Evidence from US Current Population Surveys" (2017) 358 BMJ j3262. See also the detailed review of the scientific evidence in Chapter 3 of this book.

unquestionable reduction in smoking due to ENDS will persuade legislators that ENDS may hold the promise—and comparatively little danger when compared to smoking combustible cigarettes—to effect meaningful improvements in public health.

11. One does not simply sell e-cigarettes in Australia: an overview of Australian e-cigarette regulations

Coral Gartner and Marilyn Bromberg

1. INTRODUCTION

Australia is globally recognized as a leader in tobacco control because it has implemented innovative tobacco control strategies which have contributed to a substantial decline in smoking prevalence over the past 50 years. Adult smoking prevalence declined from 35 percent in 1980 to 14.2 percent in 2016. However, smoking prevalence did not significantly change between 2013 (14.7 percent) and 2016 (14.2 percent), prompting concerns that the rate of decline in smoking seen over the past 15 years may be slowing. Moreover, the socio-economic disparity in smoking prevalence may be increasing in Australia because smoking has declined faster among more advantaged groups than among those most socially disadvantaged.[1] These trends have increased discussions of tobacco harm reduction strategies, and particularly whether Australian smokers should have access to nicotine-containing e-cigarettes.

Australia embraced tobacco harm reduction in the form of "low tar" cigarettes in the 1960s. This strategy was promoted by the Anti-Cancer Council of Victoria (now Cancer Council Victoria), which campaigned to reduce cigarette tar yields in 1966.[2] After referral from the federal health minister, the National Health and Medical Research Council (NHMRC), the government funding body for health research, recommended that information on tar content be included on cigarette packs along with a health warning. This policy was voluntarily implemented in 1982 and mandated in 1994. The tobacco indus-

---

1 Australian Institute of Health and Welfare, *Tobacco indicators: measuring mid-point progress—reporting under the National Tobacco Strategy 2012–2018* (Drug statistics series no 30. PHE 210, Canberra: AIHW 2016).

2 W. King et al, "The Australian tar derby: the origins and fate of a low tar harm reduction programme" (2003) 12 Tob Control iii61.

try resisted the low tar program until filter ventilation was introduced in the 1970s, a modification that facilitated compensatory smoking while producing very low tar yields according to FTC/ISO tests. The Australian government removed quantitative smoke yield information from cigarette packs in 2006 after concluding that the information was misleading to consumers because the FTC/ISO test results did not accurately reflect human exposure.

After it became clear that filter ventilation did not reduce harm, the Australian public health community abandoned harm reduction approaches for tobacco. It focused instead on deterring smoking uptake and encouraging smokers to quit. The experience of "low tar" cigarettes came to be seen as a failed experiment in tobacco harm reduction that resulted in increased population harm. Experiences such as this have developed a deep mistrust of the tobacco industry and of tobacco harm reduction. Australian regulation of e-cigarettes has developed against this historical background.

The remainder of this chapter discusses Australian policy and laws regarding nicotine and e-cigarettes, including enforcement activities, government inquiries into e-cigarette regulation, and attempts to liberalize the recreational nicotine market. It concludes by discussing whether the current policy is consistent with the precautionary principle.

2. AUSTRALIAN TOBACCO POLICY

Australian tobacco control policy-making is guided by a National Tobacco Strategy (NTS), which is a substrategy of the National Drug Strategy (NDS). E-cigarettes emerged during the period covered by the 2004–9 NTS,[3] which anticipated the development of new non-medicinal nicotine products, referred to in the Strategy as "tobacco substitutes," "other nicotine products," and "alternative nicotine delivery systems." Replacing cigarettes with less harmful nicotine delivery systems, such as e-cigarettes, is consistent with objective 4 of the 2004–9 NTS ("where feasible, to reduce harm associated with continuing use of, and dependence on, tobacco and nicotine"). Fourteen outcome indicators were specified to show the success of the Strategy, including "a reduction in the exposure of remaining users of tobacco (or tobacco substitutes) to dangerous smoke constituents." A footnote to this indicator states: "Exposure to tobacco might be reduced by replacing some or all tobacco products with medicinal nicotine or other nicotine products." The 2004–9 NTS contains discussion of the possibility of achieving harm reduction through tobacco product regulation, including a section on alternative nicotine delivery systems, which

[3] Ministerial Council on Drug Strategy, *National Tobacco Strategy 2004–2009* (Commonwealth of Australia 2004).

recommended regulations be developed for these products as unregulated products could reduce quitting, or act as a gateway to smoking. The Strategy acknowledged that there was no policy "in place in Australia to guide therapeutic goods and food regulators about how best to regulate such products, and we have no mechanism at all for regulating some classes of products" and that the "absence of measures that reduce harm from continuing smoking results in greatest harm among socially disadvantaged smokers." In terms of addressing this issue, as signatories to the Strategy, all Australian jurisdictions aimed to "develop a regulatory system for tobacco and tobacco replacement products that, if it is feasible, allows us to reduce the overall harm associated with dependence on tobacco and nicotine." There is evidence that the Ministerial Council on Drug Strategy took some early steps toward developing a policy on regulation of all tobacco and nicotine products as it "commissioned the Department of Human Services, Victoria to undertake a project to investigate regulatory options for the control of tobacco and other nicotine products in Australia." However, the outcome of this project is unknown and at the time of writing, in 2018 (14 years after the commencement of the Strategy), Australia still does not have a coherent regulatory system for the full spectrum of nicotine and tobacco products to achieve the harm reduction policy intention stated in the 2004–9 NTS.

In 2007, a federal election saw a change in government from the Coalition of Liberal and National parties, which had been in power since 1996, to a Labor government. The new government commenced an agenda of substantial policy reform. Health Minister Nicola Roxon established the National Preventative Health Taskforce (NPHT) in April 2008, which was chaired by Professor Rob Moodie and Professor Mike Daube (as deputy chair).[4] The NPHT was tasked with developing a National Preventative Health Strategy with an initial focus on obesity, tobacco, and excessive consumption of alcohol. Working groups prepared topic-specific technical reports.

The NPHT held a series of policy consultations (by invitation only) between October 2008 and February 2009. The tobacco technical report, released in July 2009,[5] discussed alternative nicotine delivery systems including e-cigarettes. It stated that Australian laws only allowed them to be marketed as therapeutic goods. The report acknowledged differing views, but emphasized

---

[4] National Preventative Health Taskforce, "Australia: the healthiest country by 2020" (Discussion paper, Australian Government Preventative Health Taskforce 2008) vii.

[5] Tobacco Working Group, *Australia: the healthiest country by 2020 Technical Report 2. Tobacco control in Australia: making smoking history. Including addendum for October 2008 to June 2009* (Australian Government Preventative Health Taskforce 2009).

the potential risks of e-cigarettes attracting young non-smokers and then acting "as a gateway to cigarettes," and maintaining nicotine addiction among "adults who might otherwise have given up tobacco completely" who might also then "return to cigarettes, which are always likely to be a superior delivery device." Potential benefits were briefly acknowledged, but in the context of needing to restrict use to long-term smokers who can't quit, which was presented as a "conundrum." The strategy recommended establishing or nominating a body with "power to regulate the design, contents and maximum emissions for all tobacco products (and any alternative nicotine delivery devices that may be allowed onto the market)." This recommendation appears as Action 5.4 in the National Preventative Health Strategy which was published in June 2009.[6] It is notable that some members of the NPHT and the Tobacco Working Group, including the chairs of both,[7] signed a 2014 letter to the Director General of WHO urging greater restrictions on e-cigarettes, which cited the Australian ban on nicotine cartridges as a country showing "evidence of success."[8]

The next NTS covered the period 2012–18. The introduction states that like its parent strategy, the 2010–15 NDS, the 2012–18 NTS is based on "the three pillars of demand reduction, supply reduction and harm reduction."[9] However, the focus of tobacco policies in the strategy is overwhelmingly on demand reduction strategies, via high tobacco excise rates, mandatory plain packaging with large graphic health warnings, anti-smoking media campaigns, and public smoking bans. Although reduction of harm "associated with continuing use of tobacco and nicotine products" is a stated objective of the 2012–18 NTS, the only action listed related to cigarette substitutes is to "[c]onsider further regulation of the contents, product disclosure and supply of tobacco products and alternative nicotine delivery systems."[10] The Strategy states that "the sale of nicotine in cartridges is prohibited as a Schedule 7 poison under the Standard for Uniform Scheduling of Medicines and Poisons."[11] It also notes a "need to better understand the potential risks and/

---

6 National Preventative Health Taskforce, *Australia: the healthiest country by 2020—national preventative health strategy. The roadmap for action* (Australian Government Preventative Health Taskforce 2009).

7 Professors Rob Moodie (Chair, NPHT), Mike Daube (Chair, Tobacco Working Group), Simon Chapman, and Melanie Wakefield.

8 S.A. Glantz, "129 public health and medical authorities from 31 countries write WHO DG Chan urging evidence-based approach to ecigs" (*UCSF Center for Tobacco Control Research and Education*, June 15, 2014) https://tobacco.ucsf.edu/129-public-health-and-medical-authorities-31-countries-write-who-dg-chan-urging-evidence-based-approach-ecigs#_edn1 accessed October 31, 2018.

9 Australian Government Department of Health Intergovernmental Committee on Drugs, *National tobacco strategy 2012–2018* (Commonwealth of Australia 2012) 7.

10 Ibid 30.

11 Ibid 31.

or benefits of these products, determine whether there is a need to increase restrictions on their availability and use, and identify the most appropriate policy approach for Australia."

The most recent NDS (2017–26) states that "[s]trategies to prevent and minimize alcohol, tobacco and other drug problems should be balanced across the three pillars."[12] The NDS includes many harm reduction strategies for alcohol and other drugs, such as mandatory plasticware in high risk venues to stop glassings and clean needle and syringe programs to reduce transmission of bloodborne infections. However, the NDS does not include any non-abstinence strategies to reduce harms to tobacco smokers and it does not mention e-cigarettes. Therefore, despite nominal support for tobacco harm reduction, in practice the NDS does not include any harm reduction strategies for tobacco smokers and does not support smokers switching to e-cigarettes.

The Australian government has commissioned two assessments of the regulation of e-cigarettes. The first of these was a regulatory impact assessment of e-cigarettes and smokeless tobacco products in 2012. The process was not open to public submissions. The NTS states that this assessment was "due to report in early 2013" but no results were publicly released. A subsequent assessment of "[o]ptions to minimize the risks associated with the marketing and use of electronic nicotine delivery systems [ENDS] in Australia" was commissioned in late 2014. This included a closed consultation on policy options in 2016 by invitation only. The contract was awarded to a consortium of the University of Sydney and Cancer Council New South Wales,[13] which included individuals who were strong public advocates for tight restrictions on e-cigarettes, including during the period in which the consultancy was in progress. The background discussion paper was leaked via a blog which questioned the impartiality of the process.[14] The final report has not been publicly released.

In January 2018, the Department of Health published a statement of "Principles that Underpin the Current Policy and Regulatory Approach to Electronic Cigarettes (E-Cigarettes) in Australia,"[15] which defended current

---

[12] Australian Government Department of Health, *National drug strategy 2017–2026* (September 18, 2017) https://campaigns.health.gov.au/drughelp/resources/publications/report/national-drug-strategy-2017-2026 accessed October 31, 2018.

[13] Dr Becky Freeman, Mr James Kite, Professor Nicholas Buckley, Dr Blythe O'Hara, Professor Simon Chapman, Mr Scott Walsberger, Professor Bill Bellew, and Professor Adrian Bauman.

[14] T. Barnes, "Guest post: Terry Barnes—regulating e-cigarettes: read all about it!" (*Catallaxy Files*, May 29, 2016) http://catallaxyfiles.com/2016/05/29/regulating-e-cigarettes-read-all-about-it/ accessed October 31, 2018.

[15] Australian Government Department of Health, *Principles that underpin the current policy and regulatory approach to electronic cigarettes (e-cigarettes) in Australia* (January 11, 2018) https://bit.ly/2GIWTqp accessed October 31, 2018.

e-cigarette policies. The statement also acknowledged that there was public confusion concerning "the legality of e-cigarettes and/or nicotine, especially in terms of the regulations that apply to their importation, marketing (including sale) and use," and highlighted the government's important role in clarifying legal obligations relating to these products. However, the clarification provided—that "[t]he commercial supply of nicotine for use in e-cigarettes is prohibited under all State and Territory poisons legislation"—was an oversimplification of Australian laws and did not address non-commercial supply; possession and use of nicotine; supply of nicotine-free e-cigarettes; or prescribing, supplying, or using nicotine in an e-cigarette for therapeutic purposes.

3. REGULATION OF E-CIGARETTES IN AUSTRALIA

Australian laws covering e-cigarettes are complex. Drugs and poisons laws apply to nicotine, tobacco control laws apply to e-cigarettes and their use (irrespective of whether they contain nicotine or not), and therapeutic goods laws apply to products which make therapeutic claims or are for therapeutic use. Regulations vary between jurisdictions. As a rule, Australian federal law prevails over the laws of the states and territories if there are inconsistencies. In the following subsections we first describe the laws that apply to nicotine with respect to use in an e-cigarette (subsection 3.1), and then the laws that apply to e-cigarettes, regardless of whether they contain nicotine or not (subsection 3.2). It should be noted that, despite the overlap between those two regimes, they operate independently.

3.1 Regulation of Nicotine

Nicotine-containing products are classified according to the Standard for the Uniform Scheduling of Medicines and Poisons (also known as the Poisons Standard).[16] The ten schedules (nine of which are in use) provide a classification system for medicines and poisons according to the level of access deemed appropriate for consumers given the substances that they contain. The Poisons Standard includes recommended requirements related to scheduled substances such as packaging and labeling, and restrictions on sale, possession, and use.[17]

---

[16] Unless otherwise stated, this chapter references the March 2018 version of the Poisons Standard.

[17] Australian Government, Department of Health, Therapeutic Goods Administration, *Scheduling handbook: guidance for amending the Poisons Standard version 1.0* (January 2018) http://tga.gov.au/publication/scheduling-handbook-guidance-amending-poisons-standard accessed October 31, 2018.

Scheduling of substances occurs at the federal level, but the provisions of the Poisons Standard are implemented through state and territory legislation.[18] The purpose of this arrangement is to achieve uniformity in how medicines and poisons are regulated across the country while retaining state and territory responsibility for regulation and enforcement. All states and territories have adopted the Poisons Standard by reference. While there are differences in drugs and poisons laws between each jurisdiction, they all achieve much the same outcomes with respect to nicotine, albeit with minor variations. It is theoretically possible for an individual state or territory to depart from the Poisons Standard Schedules, but this is unlikely to occur because it is inconsistent with Recommendation 4 of the Galbally Review,[19] which was endorsed by the Council of Australian Governments.[20]

Nicotine is listed in multiple Schedules of the Poisons Standard. Which Schedule applies to a particular nicotine product depends on the type of preparation that it is in and its intended use. Nicotine in e-liquids is in Schedule 7 (labeled "Dangerous Poison") when for non-therapeutic use or in Schedule 4 (labeled "Prescription Medicine Only") when for therapeutic use. Schedule 7 products containing nicotine are also included in Appendix J, which applies further controls on non-therapeutic nicotine products. All nicotine-containing products are automatically Schedule 7 poisons unless one of the following exemptions applies: (i) when a product is included in Schedule 6; (ii) when it is in a preparation for human therapeutic use; or (iii) when it is in tobacco prepared and packed for smoking.

In all jurisdictions it is an offense to sell or supply nicotine when it is a Schedule 7 poison unless authorized, such as by a license or permit.[21] In all jurisdictions it is also either illegal to possess (QLD, ACT, VIC, TAS, WA,

---

[18] Australian Government Department of Health Therapeutic Goods Administration, *AHMAC—Scheduling policy framework for medicines and chemicals version 1.0* (January 2018) http://tga.gov.au/publication/ahmac-scheduling-policy-framework-medicines-and-chemicals accessed October 31, 2018.

[19] R. Galbally, *National competition review of drugs, poisons and controlled substances legislation: final report* (Australian Government, Department of Health, Therapeutic Goods Administration 2000) http://tga.gov.au/sites/default/files/review-galbally-050628-parta.pdf accessed October 31, 2018, Part A. Commonwealth of Australia. Recommendation 4: Adoption by jurisdictions of the SUSDP Schedules.

[20] Australian Government Department of Health Therapeutic Goods Administration, *Inquiry into the use and marketing of electronic cigarettes and personal vaporisers in Australia submission 297—supplementary submission 1* (September 8, 2017) https://bit.ly/2P11hVY accessed October 31, 2018.

[21] Australian Government Department of Health Therapeutic Goods Administration, *Australian state & territory regulatory controls on Schedule 7 poisons: scheduling medicines & poisons* (November 2017) http://tga.gov.au/sites/default/files/state-and-territory-schedule-7.pdf accessed October 31, 2018.

NT) or illegal to use (QLD, NSW, SA, WA, NT)[22] nicotine for vaping when it is a Schedule 7 poison unless the possession or use is authorized.[23] In NSW and SA, a person does not commit an offense for possession of nicotine when it is a Schedule 7 poison. A factsheet bearing the emblems of the South Australian Health Department, the Heart Foundation, and Cancer Council SA states that "possession of e-cigarettes (containing nicotine or otherwise) is not illegal."[24]

Nicotine "in preparations containing 3 percent or less of nicotine when labelled and packed for the treatment of animals"[25] is in Schedule 6. These preparations may be sold by general retailers. Tobacco prepared and packed for smoking is not listed under any other Schedule, hence is unscheduled.

The remaining exemption from Schedule 7 for nicotine products is for preparations intended for human therapeutic use.[26] The Schedule 4 entry for nicotine covers "preparations for human therapeutic use except for use as an aid in withdrawal from tobacco smoking in preparations for oromucosal or transdermal use." This means that oromucosal and transdermal nicotine replacement therapies (for example nicotine patches, nicotine gum, and so on) are unscheduled and may be sold by general retailers, while all other therapeutic nicotine products, including "nicotine when used in e-cigarettes," are "in Schedule 4 (Prescription Medicine Only)."

The classification of nicotine used in e-cigarettes as Schedule 4 when used therapeutically was introduced in 2011 when the Schedule 2 entry for nicotine

---

[22] QLD: Queensland; ACT: Australian Capital Territory; VIC: Victoria; TAS: Tasmania; WA: Western Australia; NT: Northern Territory; NSW: New South Wales; SA: South Australia.

[23] Medicines, Poisons and Therapeutic Goods Act 2008 (ACT), ss 20, 26, 36; Medicines Poisons and Therapeutic Goods Act 2012 (NT), ss 36, 42–4; Medicines and Poisons Act 2014 (WA), ss 16, 25, 26; Controlled Substances Act 1984 (SA), ss 13–16, 23–7; Controlled Substances (Poisons) Regulations 2011 (SA), rr 9–13, 30, 47; Health (Drug and Poisons) Regulation 1996 (Qld), Appendix 9 (Dictionary: regulated poison, S2–S9); Appendix 7, rr 5, 7, 271; Drugs, Poisons and Controlled Substances Act 1981 (Vic), ss 4, 12, 13, 18a, 20, 23, 26–7, 46; Drugs, Poisons and Controlled Substances Regulations 2017 (Vic), rr 5, 148, 149; Poisons and Therapeutic Goods Act 1966 (NSW), ss 4, 8, 9, 11; Poisons and Therapeutic Goods Regulations 2008 (NSW), rr 3, 11, 12, 20; Part 8; Poisons and Therapeutic Goods (Poisons List) Proclamation 2016 (NSW).

[24] Cancer Council SA, "E-cigarette fact sheet: information for smokers" (December 2013) http://cancersa.org.au/assets/E-cigarette%20brochure%20December%202013%202015%20branding.pdf accessed October 31, 2018.

[25] Poisons Standard March 2018 (Cth).

[26] The definition of therapeutic use in the Cmwlth Therapeutic Goods Act 1989 includes: "use in or in connection with . . . preventing, diagnosing, curing or alleviating a disease, ailment, defect or injury in persons; or influencing, inhibiting or modifying a physiological process in persons."

"for use as an aid in withdrawal from tobacco smoking in preparations for inhalation" was deleted. In making the 2011 decision, the scheduling committee "noted that the current Schedule 2 entry for nicotine for inhalation was intended to capture oromucosal inhalators and not nicotine vaporizer products (for example e-cigarettes). Members clarified that e-cigarettes should be captured by Schedule 4 when for human therapeutic use or by Schedule 7 if for non-therapeutic use."[27] Prior to this scheduling change, e-cigarettes containing nicotine for therapeutic use were considered to be a Schedule 2 medicine,[28] which does not require a prescription to obtain or use. In this context, it should be noted that in all states and territories, it is an offense to possess, sell, or supply Schedule 4 medicines without being an authorized person (such as a pharmacist or medical practitioner) or having been prescribed or supplied the medicine by an authorized person.[29]

In general, therapeutic goods must be approved by the Therapeutic Goods Administration (TGA)[30] and listed on the Australian Register of Therapeutic Goods (ARTG) before they can be supplied within Australia. The TGA confirmed during the 2017 Parliamentary Inquiry into the Use and Marketing of Electronic Cigarettes and Personal Vaporisers in Australia that no e-cigarettes had been approved as a therapeutic good, so none were listed on the ARTG. The TGA also confirmed that Australians can legally access nicotine-containing e-cigarettes for therapeutic use via a number of exemptions that allow

---

27 National Drugs and Poisons Scheduling Committee, Therapeutic Goods Administration, *Record of reasons for decisions: September 2011* (2011) http://tga.gov.au/ndpsc-records-reasons accessed October 31, 2018.

28 National Drugs and Poisons Scheduling Committee, Therapeutic Goods Administration, *Record of reasons for decisions: June 2008* (2008) http://tga.gov.au/ndpsc-records-reasons accessed October 31, 2018.

29 Medicines, Poisons and Therapeutic Goods Act 2008 (ACT), ss 20, 26, 36; Medicines Poisons and Therapeutic Goods Act 2012 (NT), ss 39–41; Medicines and Poisons Act 2014 (WA), ss 14, 25; Controlled Substances Act 1984 (SA), ss 13–15, 18; 23–7; Controlled Substances (Poisons) Regulations 2011 (SA), rr 6, 47; Health (Drug and Poisons) Regulation 1996 (Qld), rr 5, 7, Appendix 9 (Dictionary: restricted drug, S2–S9); most of chapter 3, in particular r 146, Division 3 and 4; Part 4, in particular rr 204–5; Drugs, Poisons and Controlled Substances Act 1981 (Vic), ss 4, 12, 13, 20, 23, 26–7, 36B, 46; Drugs, Poisons and Controlled Substances Regulations 2017 (Vic), ss 7–8, Part 3, Part 5, Part 6 [Division 1 (rr 47, 50, 53–8), Division 2 (rr 59–62; 67–70)], 105; Poisons and Therapeutic Goods Act 1966 (NSW), ss 4, 9, 10–12, 16–18, 31, 36A; Poisons and Therapeutic Goods Regulations 2008 (NSW), r 23; Part 3, Part 8. Poisons and Therapeutic Goods (Poisons List) Proclamation 2016 (NSW).

30 The definition of therapeutic goods in the Cmwlth Therapeutic Goods Act 1989 includes: "goods that are represented in any way to be, or that are, whether because of the way in which the goods are presented or for any other reason, likely to be taken to be for therapeutic use."

access to unapproved therapeutic goods.[31] These include extemporaneously compounded medicines, the TGA Special Access Scheme, the Authorised Prescriber Scheme, and the Personal Importation Scheme. Australians may import up to a three-month supply (total of 15-month supply in a 12-month period) of nicotine as an unapproved therapeutic good for their own or an immediate family member's treatment. However, consumers must have a prescription for the nicotine before importing because under state and territory law a prescription is required to obtain, possess, and use Schedule 4 medicines.

There has been inconsistent interpretation of the Poisons Standard regarding nicotine in e-cigarettes. Some State Health Departments have advised the public that access to nicotine, even for therapeutic use as a cessation aid, is not permitted. For example, a Queensland Health factsheet states:

> There are no legal ways to import e-cigarettes containing nicotine into Queensland. Some websites suggest that e-cigarettes can be imported into Queensland under the TGA's personal importation scheme for the purpose of quitting smoking. This is misleading and deceptive. This is because these products once imported, are classified as a poison, not a therapeutic good.[32]

However, Queensland Health have since amended their interpretation to be consistent with the TGA's advice, acknowledging that nicotine in e-cigarettes is a Schedule 4 medicine when prescribed for therapeutic use.[33] Other jurisdictions (for example Tasmania) have also amended their public advice to include the possibility of personally importing nicotine for therapeutic use with a prescription.[34]

---

31 Australian Government Department of Health Therapeutic Goods Administration, *Inquiry into the use and marketing of electronic cigarettes and personal vaporisers in Australia submission 297—supplementary submission 1* (September 8, 2017) https://bit.ly/2P11hVY accessed October 31, 2018.

32 Queensland Government, Tobacco and Alcohol Branch, Preventive Health Directorate, *Electronic cigarettes—the facts* (September 2011) https://bit.ly/2zIiVZ1 accessed October 31, 2018.

33 H. Spelitis, "Vapers targeted in Queensland health crackdown" (*The Queensland Time*, July 10, 2018) https://bit.ly/2KUf2Xx accessed October 31, 2018.

34 Tasmanian Government, Department of Health and Human Services, *Electronic Cigarettes Fact Sheet* https://bit.ly/2P88nYw accessed October 31, 2018.

3.2 Regulation of E-cigarettes Not Containing Nicotine

In 2008, the National Drugs and Poisons Scheduling Committee considered whether e-cigarettes were therapeutic goods. The committee speculated:

> given that electronic cigarettes claim to aid the user in replacing "real" cigarettes by imitating the taste, smell, feel and action of smoking (as well as delivering nicotine via inhalation), it could be suggested that these devices could be seen to be therapeutic goods, even without the nicotine cartridge. Further claims made on various Australian websites and claims made in documents lodged with the Australian patent application also add weight to these devices being considered therapeutic goods whether they include the nicotine cartridge or not.[35]

However, so far the TGA has not regulated e-cigarette devices that do not contain nicotine as therapeutic goods unless the sellers of those products make explicit claims that they will assist smoking cessation.[36] Consequently, the Australian Competition and Consumer Commission (ACCC) is the federal regulator for nicotine-free e-cigarettes that are not marketed as therapeutic goods. Nicotine-free e-cigarette vendors must comply with general consumer protection and safety laws. In addition to federal consumer law, state and territory tobacco control laws may also apply to the sale and use of such e-cigarettes.

3.3 Restrictions on Sale and Public Use of E-cigarettes

Queensland was the first Australian jurisdiction to implement legislation that restricted the sale and use of e-cigarettes. These laws do not specify whether the e-cigarette product contains nicotine or not and they apply in addition to drugs and poisons laws which control the sale, possession, and use of nicotine. The Tobacco and Other Smoking Products Act 1998 (QLD) and the Tobacco and Other Smoking Products Regulation 2010 (QLD) were amended in 2014 to apply the same restrictions that apply to tobacco and other smoking products to e-cigarettes and related products. These include bans on advertising, retail displays, and sales to persons aged under 18, and on vaping in non-smoking areas. Other jurisdictions have since implemented laws related to sale and use of e-cigarettes. In 2015, New South Wales prohibited the sale of e-cigarettes to people under the age of 18 years and applied similar restrictions to e-cigarettes

---

35 National Drugs and Poisons Schedule Committee, *Record of reasons*, 54th Meeting, October 14–15, 2008 http://tga.gov.au/sites/default/files/ndpsc-record-54.pdf accessed October 31, 2018, 134.

36 Delegates' final decisions and reasons for decisions (March 23, 2017) 78.

as to tobacco products in terms of retail display and advertising.[37] Using an e-cigarette in a car carrying children was also banned. In 2018, New South Wales also banned the use of e-cigarettes in smoke-free areas, but allowed specialist vape shops to apply for an exemption to allow use on the premises.[38] In 2016, the Australian Capital Territory also applied restrictions to e-cigarettes similar to those already in existence for cigarettes, including prohibiting sales to people aged under 18 years and use in smoke-free areas and placing restrictions on advertising, retail displays, and other marketing practices.[39] The laws were introduced following a public consultation conducted in late 2014, which received 242 submissions.[40] The Tasmanian government conducted a public consultation on proposed new regulations for e-cigarettes in 2015 which received 56 submissions.[41] The laws implemented in late 2017 applied the same restrictions on supply and use of e-cigarettes as apply to cigarettes, including prohibitions on supply to people aged under 18 (including parental supply) and on possession and use by people aged under 18. In 2017, Victoria applied similar restrictions. Provision of free samples and use within retail shops were also prohibited. A factsheet on the laws advised that a TGA-approved e-cigarette may be excluded from these restrictions if prescribed in the relevant regulations.[42]

4. ENFORCEMENT OF LAWS REGARDING E-CIGARETTES

The enforcement activities in Australia related to e-cigarettes fall under four different categories. They are: (1) sale of e-cigarettes without nicotine; (2) prosecutions by the ACCC for misleading representations about e-cigarettes; (3) prosecutions for possessing nicotine for use in e-cigarettes and selling it; and (4) seizing imported nicotine intended for use in e-cigarettes.

---

[37] NSW Government Department of Health, *Are electronic cigarettes legal in NSW* http://health.nsw.gov.au/tobacco/Factsheets/e-cigs-are-they-legal.pdf accessed October 31, 2018.

[38] Smoke-Free Environment Amendment Bill 2018 (NSW).

[39] ACT Government Department of Health, *Electronic cigarettes* https://bit.ly/2IsgLQn accessed October 31, 2018.

[40] ACT Government Department of Health, *Electronic cigarettes—community consultation* https://bit.ly/2zHU0VS accessed October 31, 2018.

[41] TAS Government Department of Health and Human Services, *Submissions received for the e-cigarette public consultation* https://bit.ly/2y4otv5 accessed October 31, 2018.

[42] Victoria State Government, *Health and human services, e-cigarette reforms: factsheet for the community* (May 2017) https://health.vic.gov.au/about/publications/factsheets/e-cigarette-reforms-factsheet accessed October 31, 2018.

4.1 The Sale of E-cigarettes without Nicotine: The *Van Heerden* Case

Vincent Van Heerden ran a business called "Heavenly Vapours" that sold refillable e-cigarettes (that is, devices) and nicotine-free liquids.[43] He was charged with selling products that were not a tobacco product but were designed to resemble a tobacco product, thereby breaching section 106(a) of the Tobacco Products Control Act 2006 (WA).[44] This provision pre-dates e-cigarettes and was originally intended to capture toys and novelty items that might promote smoking to children. In the first instance, Van Heerden was acquitted. The Magistrate did not believe that Van Heerden's e-cigarettes "resemble a cigarette or cigar."[45] This decision was appealed to the Supreme Court of Western Australia. Two of the grounds of appeal were successful, resulting in Van Heerden being convicted and fined AU $1,750;[46] the maximum was AU $10,000. The primary judge held that a "description of the appearance of someone using an electronic cigarette could be taken into account as evidence of the appearance of one of the items during use."[47] This decision was unsuccessfully appealed to the Western Australian Supreme Court of Appeal.

This decision clarified that selling e-cigarettes without nicotine, including devices that do not physically resemble cigarettes, is illegal in Western Australia. The sale of any e-cigarette device that is approved as a therapeutic good by the TGA would also likely be illegal in that state. This ruling would also be a persuasive decision for the courts of any other Australian state with similarly worded legislation, which previously included Queensland, New South Wales, and South Australia; however, the Tobacco and Other Smoking Products Act 1998 (QLD) was amended in 2014 to exclude e-cigarettes from Section 26ZS (Supply of objects resembling tobacco products). The New South Wales government has stated in a factsheet that e-cigarettes "fall outside the definition of products resembling tobacco products under section 21 of the *Public Health (Tobacco) Act 2008* (NSW)."[48] The Tobacco Products Regulation (E-Cigarette Regulation) Amendment Bill 2017 (SA) excludes

---

[43] *Van Heerden v Hawkins* [2016] WASCA 42, para 21.

[44] Ibid para 2.

[45] Ibid para 38.

[46] *Hawkins v Van Heerden* [No 2] [2014] WASC 226, para 41.

[47] *Van Heerden v Hawkins* (n 43) para 59.

[48] New South Wales Government, Health, *Are electronic cigarettes legal in NSW?* http://health.nsw.gov.au/tobacco/Factsheets/e-cigs-are-they-legal.pdf accessed October 31, 2018.

e-cigarettes from this provision in South Australia.[49] Section 15O of the Tobacco Act 1987 (VIC) allows for the Minister to implement a ban order "in respect of a specified product or a specified class of products," including a product that "is not a tobacco product but resembles a tobacco product." In 2017, this section was amended to allow ban orders on products that are not e-cigarette products but that resemble an e-cigarette product and that have "packaging that appeals to children or young people."[50] Hence, these jurisdictions show no intention of banning non-nicotine e-cigarette sales as occurred in Western Australia.

4.2 Misleading Representations Concerning E-cigarettes

In 2017, Justice Gilmour handed down three separate, highly similar judgments in the Federal Court of Australia concerning representations made about e-cigarettes: *Australian Competition and Consumer Commission v Social-Lites Pty Ltd*;[51] *Australian Competition and Consumer Commission v Burden*;[52] and *Australian Competition and Consumer Commission v The Joystick Company Pty Ltd*.[53] In each instance the ACCC prosecuted an e-cigarette company and its director or CEO for breaching the Australian Consumer Law (ACL) by making representations that were misleading or deceptive or that were made in a way that was likely to mislead or deceive.[54] They made these representations on the companies' websites and, in the case of Social-Lites, also on social media.[55] Justice Gilmour stated that none of the respondent companies had scientific evidence to substantiate their representations.[56] The ACCC tested the

---

49 Tobacco Products Regulation (E-Cigarette Regulation) Amendment Bill 2017 (South Australia).

50 s15O of *Tobacco Act 1987* No 81 of 1987 incorporating amendments as at August 1, 2017.

51 [2017] FCA 398.

52 [2017] FCA 399.

53 [2017] FCA 397. For further commentary on the *Joystick* case in particular, see R. Pillay, "Mere puffery" (2017) 33 Competition and Consumer Law News 56.

54 The Australian Consumer Law is the second schedule in the Competition and Consumer Act (No 2) 2010 (Cth); Social-Lites breached ss 18, 29(1)(a), 33 of the ACL; Elusion breached ss 18, 29(1)(a), 33 ACL para 2.

55 *Australian Competition and Consumer Commission v Social-Lites Pty Ltd* (n 51) para 4.

56 Ibid para 67; *Australian Competition and Consumer Commission v The Joystick Company Pty Ltd* (n 53) paras 51, 64; *Australian Competition and Consumer Commission v Burden* (n 52) paras 59, 72.

e-cigarettes from the three companies and found that they contained carcinogens and toxic chemicals.[57]

Each party admitted liability and none of the matters proceeded to trial. The parties also agreed on the pecuniary penalty that they should pay. These amounts were as follows: Social-Lites to pay AU $50,000 and its CEO to pay AU $10,000;[58] Elusion to pay AU $40,000, and its director to pay AU $15,000;[59] Joystick to pay AU $50,000 and its director to pay AU $10,000.[60] The penalties were at the lower end of the range of possible pecuniary penalties for this conduct.[61] Each party also agreed to an injunction that they would not sell or promote e-cigarettes for three years.[62] It is significant that all the parties in the cases mentioned admitted liability without the need for a trial. Elusion and Social-Lites were self-represented, which may have been relevant to this decision. Elusion Australia Limited was liquidated on March 17, 2017;[63] Joystick Company Pty Ltd was voluntarily deregistered on April 21, 2017.[64]

Following the court action, the ACCC sent letters to 30 Australian e-cigarette companies and instructed them to apply the ACL to the information that they provide on their websites.[65]

---

57 Australian Competition and Consumer Commission, *Cigarette Companies to Pay Penalties* (May 8, 2017) http://accc.gov.au/media-release/e-cigarette-companies-to-pay-penalties accessed October 31, 2018.

58 *Australian Competition and Consumer Commission v Burden* (n 52) para 64.

59 Ibid para 99.

60 *Australian Competition and Consumer Commission v The Joystick Company Pty Ltd* (n 53) para 3.

61 In *Social-Lites*, J Gilmour relevantly stated that s 224(3) of the ACL had the maximum penalties for this conduct as AU $1.1 million for a body corporate and AU $22,000 for a natural person.

62 *Australian Competition and Consumer Commission v The Joystick Company Pty Ltd* (n 53) paras iv, v, 7; *Australian Competition and Consumer Commission v Social-Lites Pty Ltd* (n 51) paras iii, 29, 32; *Australian Competition and Consumer Commission v Burden* paras (n 52) 28, 34.

63 New Zealand Government, Te Tare Tariwhenua Internal Affairs, *Elusion Australia Limited (in Liquidation)* (March 23, 2017) https://gazette.govt.nz/notice/id/2017-al1377 accessed October 31, 2018.

64 ASIC, "Published notices: notice of proposed deregistration—voluntary" (April 21, 2017) https://bit.ly/2QkjuOA accessed October 31, 2018.

65 Australian Competition and Consumer Competition, *E-cigarette companies to pay penalties* (May 8, 2017) http://accc.gov.au/media-release/e-cigarette-companies-to-pay-penalties accessed October 31, 2018.

4.3 Prosecution for Possessing, Selling, and Advertising Nicotine

The potential maximum penalties for breaching drugs and poisons regulations related to nicotine products can be severe, and they vary across the country. At the higher end of the potential penalties are the Australian Capital Territory, the Northern Territory, and Western Australia. In the Australian Capital Territory, if a person supplies nicotine when they are not authorized to, they can face a maximum sentence of a fine of AU $75,000 and imprisonment for five years or both.[66] If they possess nicotine when they are not authorized to, they can face a fine of AU $30,000 or imprisonment for two years or both.[67] In the Northern Territory, if a person supplies nicotine to another person when they are not permitted to, they can face a maximum sentence of a fine of AU $30,800 or imprisonment for two years;[68] if they possess nicotine when they are not permitted to, they can face a fine of AU $15,400 or imprisonment for 12 months.[69] In Western Australia, the maximum fine for unauthorized possession is fixed at AU $45,000.[70] One example of a state which has lower penalties for offending in this area is South Australia. There, possessing or supplying nicotine without authority can attract a maximum fine of AU $10,000.[71]

Very few prosecutions related to nicotine have been reported in the media. In Queensland, a man advertised and sold liquid nicotine at a university campus. He was charged with possessing and advertising for sale a regulated poison (nicotine). He entered a plea of guilty and received a fine of AU $2,500 and a spent conviction.[72] Also in Queensland, a police officer found two bottles of nicotine e-liquid (50 ml and 40 ml) at the house of Benjamin Vittle. He pleaded guilty in the Bundaberg Magistrates Court to charges that he must not dispense, manufacture, obtain, possess, prescribe, sell, or use a regulated poison unless under an approval and received a spent conviction. Vittle had informed police that when he bought the liquid he did not know this was illegal. He stated that he wanted to use the product to start an online business selling e-cigarettes. He also stated that on learning it was illegal, he tried unsuccessfully to return the

66 Medicines, Poisons and Therapeutic Goods Act 2008 (ACT) s 26.
67 Ibid s 3.
68 Medicines, Poisons and Therapeutic Goods Act 2012 (NT) s 40.
69 Ibid s 3.
70 Medicines and Poisons Act 2014 (WA) s 115.
71 Controlled Substances Act 1984 (SA) s 22 and s 15 respectively.
72 Queensland Government, Queensland Health, "News: e-cigarettes ruling" (*Queensland Health*, July 10, 2014) http://health.qld.gov.au/cairns_hinterland/html/e-cigarette accessed October 31, 2018.

liquid to the vendor, who refused a refund. He then attempted to surrender it to a pharmacy, which declined to accept it.[73]

4.4 Seizures of E-cigarettes and Nicotine

There are reports that imported nicotine for use in e-cigarettes has been seized on arrival in Queensland and Western Australia.[74] The New South Wales Ministry of Health undertook sampling of e-cigarette products offered for sale in that state, reporting in 2013 that 70 percent of the samples contained "high levels of nicotine."[75] The inspectors seized e-cigarette products containing nicotine from 18 stores, but there were no prosecutions.[76] The New South Wales Health Minister, Jillian Skinner, stated that the government was "modernising the poisons legislation to make it easier to prosecute, where necessary."[77] Further sampling and testing undertaken between 2015 and 2018 found that 63 percent of e-liquids labeled as nicotine-free contained nicotine and 40 percent of the 227 retailers sampled illegally sold e-cigarette products containing nicotine.[78]

[73] R. Irby, "Liquid nicotine 'poison' lands man in court" (*NewsMail*, September 6, 2017) http://news-mail.com.au/news/liquid-nicotine-an-honest-mistake/3220549/ accessed October 31, 2018.

[74] "Imported cigarettes can be fatal" (*Hervey Bay Observer*, May 18, 2011) 8; House of Representatives Standing Committee on Health, Aged Care and Sport, *Report on the Inquiry into the Use and Marketing of Electronic Cigarettes and Personal Vaporisers in Australia* (2018) 139 para 17; see for example *AussieVapers.com* (May 2017) https://bit.ly/2NdyADe; *AussieVapers.com* (May 2017) https://bit.ly/2Ncri2U both accessed October 31, 2018.

[75] NSW Government Department of Health, "NSW health alert—warning on e-liquids" (October 23, 2013) http://health.nsw.gov.au/news/Pages/20131023_00.aspx accessed October 31, 2018.

[76] N. Hasham, "Health officials admit failure to prosecute potentially lethal e-cigarettes" (*The Sydney Morning Herald*, May 14, 2015) https://bit.ly/2P1K4LZ accessed October 31, 2018.

[77] Ibid.

[78] F. Duxfield, "NSW Health Department finds not all e-juices are as nicotine free as they claim" (*Australian Broadcasting Corporation*, June 12, 2018) http://abc.net.au/news/2018-06-12/not-all-e-juices-are-as-nicotine-free-as-they-claim/9857540 accessed October 31, 2018.

5. OFFICIAL INQUIRIES AND ATTEMPTS TO LIBERALIZE THE REGULATION OF NICOTINE-CONTAINING E-CIGARETTES

5.1 TGA Applications

In 2008, the National Drugs and Poisons Scheduling Committee received a submission to amend the Schedule 7 entry for nicotine to add the exemption: "(d) in electronic cigarettes prepared and packed as an alternative to traditional smoking," essentially extending the exemption for smoked tobacco to e-cigarettes. The submission argued that the product (EGAR electronic cigarette with cartridges containing 0, 11, 14, and 18 mg nicotine) was not a therapeutic good and "claimed that the product does not achieve its principal intended action by chemical means on the body of a human." In arguing this, "it claimed that the device does not produce any changes to the pharmacology or neurotransmitters of the human body," which is inconsistent with scientific evidence.[79] The record of reasons for the decision not to amend the Poisons Standard cited "[s]everal submissions critical of the devices" and included the key concern that "e-cigarettes actually widen the appeal of nicotine," highlighting "the fast delivery of nicotine. And while the devices claim to be free of tobacco carcinogens, there are other chemicals involved besides pure nicotine, such as acetaldehyde." The committee also considered a proposal by the Victorian jurisdictional member to amend the Schedule 4 entry for nicotine to cover all non-tobacco internal human use, including non-therapeutic use, so that access to nicotine-containing e-cigarettes would be restricted in a nationally consistent manner to prescription only access.[80] This proposal was in response to the retailing of nicotine-containing e-cigarettes in Victoria, which could not be prevented under Victorian laws. At the time, only wholesale supply of Schedule 7 poisons required a license in Victoria and Victoria had not adopted Appendix J of the SUSMP. It was argued that Schedule 7 was inappropriate for a recreational consumer product intended for internal use as

[79] US Department of Health and Human Services, *The health consequences of smoking: nicotine addiction: a report of the Surgeon General* (US Government Printing Office 1988): "Nicotine is a powerful pharmacologic agent that acts in a variety of ways at different sites in the body. After reaching the blood stream, nicotine enters the brain, interacts with specific receptors in brain tissue, and initiates metabolic and electrical activity in the brain. In addition, nicotine causes skeletal muscle relaxation and has cardiovascular and endocrine (that is hormonal) effects."

[80] National Drugs and Poisons Scheduling Committee, Therapeutic Goods Administration, *Record of reasons for decisions: June 2008* (2008) http://tga.gov.au/ndpsc-records-reasons accessed October 31, 2018.

"most of the substances included in Schedule 7 are agricultural products and industrial chemicals which have certain controls on use."[81] The committee did not amend the Poisons Standard and recommended instead that Victoria amend its legislation to prevent unlicensed retail supply of Schedule 7 poisons. The resulting Victorian amendment also prohibited the issuing of a license for the supply of Schedule 7 poisons for human non-therapeutic use.

In 2017, the New Nicotine Alliance, a nonprofit consumer organization, submitted an application to the TGA to "exempt nicotine from Schedule 7 at concentrations of 3.6 percent or less of nicotine for self-administration with an electronic nicotine delivery system (personal vaporizer or electronic cigarette) for the purpose of tobacco harm reduction."[82] The proposed amendment would require such nicotine preparations to be packaged in a child resistant container with a maximum nicotine content of 900 mg and labeled with nicotine concentrations, other ingredients, and the statements "Keep out of reach of children" and "Not to be sold to a person under the age of 18 years." There were 54 public submissions in support of the application, from consumers (35), business owners and manufacturers (6), peak bodies (2), advocacy groups (3), medical professionals (7), and a consultant. Seventeen submissions—from academia (one), government health departments (seven), non-government organizations (four), and peak bodies (five)—opposed the application. The joint Advisory Committee on Chemicals Scheduling and Advisory Committee on Medicines Scheduling recommended retaining the existing scheduling of nicotine. Twenty-one public submissions were received in response to the Delegate's interim decision not to amend the Schedule 7 entry for nicotine, with 5 supporting and 16 opposing the decision. The Delegate's final decision confirmed the interim decision. Among the reasons cited for the decision was the statement that "[c]urrent government policy supports the cessation of smoking rather than harm reduction."

5.2 Inquiry into Personal Choice and Community Impacts

In 2015, the Australian Senate referred an inquiry "into measures introduced to restrict personal choice 'for the individual's own good'" to the Senate Economics References Committee. The inquiry's terms of reference included the economic and social impact of legislation, policies, or Commonwealth guidelines, in reference to the sale and use of tobacco, tobacco products, nico-

---

[81] Ibid.

[82] Australian Government Department of Health Therapeutic Goods Administration, *Final decisions and reasons for decisions by delegates of the Secretary to the Department of Health* (March 23, 2017) http://tga.gov.au/sites/default/files/scheduling-delegates-final-decisions-23-march-2017.pdf accessed October 31, 2018.

tine products, and e-cigarettes, including any impact on the health, enjoyment, and finances of users and non-users. The inquiry lapsed with the dissolution of the Senate on May 9, 2016 ahead of a federal election on July 2, 2016. However, an interim report was released on May 6, 2016, which focused on e-cigarettes. The committee provided in-principle support for making nicotine-containing e-cigarettes available as a prescription only therapeutic good once approved by the TGA; that is, it endorsed the status quo. One committee member, Senator David Leyonhjelm, provided dissenting comments that argued for exempting nicotine-containing e-cigarettes from Schedule 7 of the Poisons Standard "as a matter of urgency, so that vapers have access to the nicotine e-liquids that enable them to quit without fear of prosecution or having to go to a doctor."[83]

5.3 Senate Select Committee on Red Tape

In October 2016, the Senate established a Select Committee "to inquire into [the] effect of restrictions and prohibitions on business (red tape) on the economy and community," which included tobacco retailing. The inquiry, which was chaired by Senator David Leyonhjelm, received 19 submissions and 11 form letters. A number of submissions addressed the inability to market nicotine-containing e-cigarettes and heated tobacco products in Australia. The committee's interim report recommended "that Commonwealth, State and Territory governments develop and implement an appropriate framework for alternative nicotine delivery systems." Senator Murray Watt issued a dissenting report on behalf of Labor senators strongly opposing the report recommendations and stating that "Labor will continue to follow the advice of independent experts on this issue—including the recent advice of the Therapeutic Goods Administration and National Health and Medical Research Council on e-cigarettes."[84]

5.4 Senate Inquiry into the Vaporised Nicotine Products Bill 2017

In June 2017, the Senate referred the Vaporised Nicotine Products Bill 2017, which was sponsored by Senators David Leyonhjelm and Malcolm Roberts, to the Senate Community Affairs Legislation Committee for inquiry and report.

---

[83] Australian Senate, Economics References Committee, *Personal choice and community impacts. Interim report: the sale and use of tobacco, tobacco products, nicotine products and e-cigarettes (term of reference a)* (May 2016) https://bit.ly/23D4N8u accessed October 31, 2018.

[84] The Senate Select Committee on Red Tape, *Effect of red tape on tobacco retail. Interim report* (June 2017) http://aph.gov.au/Parliamentary_Business/Committees/Senate/Red_Tape/Tobacco/Interim_Report accessed October 31, 2018.

If passed, this private members' bill would amend various federal legislation to exempt e-cigarettes from: smoking bans within airports (Airports Act 1996); bans on advertising of tobacco products (Tobacco Advertising Prohibition Act 1992); and regulation by the TGA as a therapeutic good (Therapeutic Goods Act 1989). With regard to the latter, the amendment would ensure that the Poisons Standard would treat "nicotine in electronic nicotine delivery systems in concentrations no greater than 20 mg/mL" and "nicotine in tobacco prepared and packed for heating" in the same way as it treats nicotine in tobacco prepared and packed for smoking. The inquiry received 67 submissions and 2,023 form letters supporting the Bill. The committee recommended that the bill not be passed "until further scientific evaluation of the efficacy and safety of e-cigarettes and related products has been undertaken." Senator David Leyonhjelm issued a dissenting report recommending that the Bill be passed.[85]

5.5 Parliamentary Inquiry into the Use and Marketing of Electronic Cigarettes and Personal Vaporisers in Australia

Following referral from the Minister for Health and Sport, Greg Hunt, the Standing Committee on Health, Aged Care and Sport conducted an inquiry into the use and marketing of e-cigarettes and personal vaporizers in Australia. The terms of reference included their use for smoking cessation, health impacts, international approaches to regulation, the appropriate regulatory framework for Australia, and any other related matter. The inquiry was conducted over ten months, during which it received 352 submissions and three different form letters submitted by 2, 7, and 1,695 individuals. Six hearings were held and committee members visited New Zealand to interview relevant stakeholders, including members of parliament, public servants, a government advisory group, peak health organizations, and university academics, about current regulatory reforms concerning nicotine-containing e-cigarettes. The committee's majority report recommended that: the National Health and Medical Research Council fund an independent and comprehensive evidence review on the health impacts of e-cigarettes; an international meeting of health experts from similar economic jurisdictions be convened to discuss different policy and legislative approaches; the TGA retain responsibility for nicotine-containing e-cigarettes; a national approach to the regulation of non-nicotine e-cigarettes be adopted; and a regulatory process be established for assessing and regulating e-cigarette ingredients. The committee report included two dissenting reports from three committee members. One was coauthored by the committee Chair, MP Trent Zimmerman, and MP Tim Wilson, and recommended: exempting nicotine in

---

85 Vaporised Nicotine Products Bill 2017 (Cth).

e-cigarettes from Schedule 7 of the Poisons Standard; legislating to permit the sale, purchase, and possession of e-cigarettes with restrictions similar to those adopted in the European Union, including prohibiting sale to minors; marketing and advertising restrictions; child resistant packaging; a limit on nicotine strength; safety features to reduce battery explosions; ingredient listing and health warnings; establishment of a notification system for e-cigarette products; and a regulatory process for assessing and regulating e-cigarette ingredients. The second dissenting report, authored by MP Andrew Laming, consisted of two sentences: "Life is short and shorter for smokers. Just legalize vaping."[86]

5.6 Political Responses to Heated Tobacco and E-cigarette Products

A number of Australian politicians have made public statements concerning their position on tobacco harm reduction products. These statements have ranged from strong support for liberalization to strong opposition. There have also been differences in interpretation of the law.

In 2005, the then Parliamentary Secretary for Health, Christopher Pyne, allowed the marketing of a heated tobacco product (Philip Morris' Heatbar) in Australia, stating: "The Government welcomes scientific exploration into the production of a product that might minimize the harmful effects of tobacco smoke."[87] In 2017, Assistant Health Minister David Gillespie stated, in response to a question regarding whether the exemption from Schedule 7 of the Poisons Standard for smoked tobacco would apply to Philip Morris' IQOS product (a heated tobacco product similar to Heatbar): "The department is of the view that these exemptions would not likely apply to heat-not-burn products as the nicotine in them would not be in the form of tobacco prepared and packed for smoking."[88] Hence, the legal status of heated tobacco products in Australia is unclear.

---

[86] House of Representatives Standing Committee on Health, Aged Care and Sport, *Report on the Inquiry into the Use and Marketing of Electronic Cigarettes and Personal Vaporisers in Australia* (March 2018) https://bit.ly/2GTRtK0 accessed October 31, 2018.

[87] M. Metherell, "Smoking to get a little less deadly" (*Sydney Morning Herald*, March 24, 2005) http://smh.com.au/news/National/Smoking-to-get-a-little-less-deadly/2005/03/23/1111525226018.html# accessed October 31, 2018.

[88] T. Wright, "Philip Morris's 'smoke-free' cigarette seems unlikely to ignite in Australia" (*Sydney Morning Herald*, February 16, 2017) http://smh.com.au/politics/federal/philip-morriss-smokefree-cigarette-seems-unlikely-to-ignite-in-australia-20170215-gudjx5.html accessed October 31, 2018.

In 2009, then Federal Health Minister Nicola Roxon described e-cigarettes as an "insidious, manipulative attempt to hook people on smoking."[89] Another former federal health minister, Sussan Ley, also opposed liberalization of nicotine-containing e-cigarettes, stating: "If it worked and helped people give up cigarettes I'd be delighted, but unfortunately there's no evidence it helps people give up smoking."[90] In 2017, in response to a question from a journalist about the then current Parliamentary Inquiry into e-cigarettes, the Federal Health Minister, Greg Hunt, stated:

> [H]aving met with the head of the Therapeutic Goods Administration today, so one of Australia's most senior medical officials, his point to me, and this is my clear view, is there is no strong evidence at all that this is a pathway of people quitting. There is clear evidence that it's likely to lead to the uptake of . . . cigarette smoking. It creates the habit.[91]

He also emphatically ruled out any change to current laws, stating: "It's not going to be happening on my watch."[92] The public statements made by the Health Minister while the inquiry was ongoing were interpreted as appearing to undermine the inquiry.[93] When queried as to why he had started the inquiry, Minister Hunt stated:

> [T]he parliamentary process is a good way of dealing with and exposing those claims, but frankly it's Big Tobacco which is arguing the case for these e-cigarettes and they're only doing it because it's in their interests. I have a very strong clear categorical view that this is not something that should occur in Australia.[94]

Following the recommendation of the House of Representatives Standing Committee on Health, Aged Care and Sport to maintain current restrictions on nicotine-containing e-cigarettes, Senator David Leyonhjelm announced that he and "a critical number of crossbenchers in the Senate" would block all future government health bills unless the Health Minister reversed his

---

[89] S. Cauchi, "Close, but no cigarette" (*Sydney Morning Herald*, March 8, 2009) http://smh.com.au/national/close-but-no-cigarette-20090307-8rz7.html accessed October 31, 2018.

[90] A. Bunn, "Building up steam on bid to legalise nicotine vaping" (*The Border Mail*, February 2, 2018).

[91] S. McPhee, "Getting private health insurance, and cigarette company quits smoking" (*Triple J Radio*, October 16, 2017) http://abc.net.au/triplej/programs/hack/hack/9055592 accessed October 31, 2018.

[92] Ibid.

[93] A. Creighton, "Health experts lash ban on e-cigs" (*The Australian*, October 23, 2017).

[94] Ibid.

position on e-cigarettes.[95] A number of conservative and libertarian federal politicians have publicly supported liberalization of the regulations governing nicotine-containing e-cigarettes, including MP Tim Wilson,[96] MP Trent Zimmerman, MP Andrew Laming,[97] Senator James Paterson,[98] Senator Eric Abetz,[99] Senator Linda Reynolds,[100] Senator James McGrath,[101] Senator Cory Bernandi,[102] Senator Pauline Hanson,[103] Senator Malcolm Roberts, and Senator Derryn Hinch.[104] While in opposition in 2018, the Western Australian Liberal Party voted 76 to 56 in support of a motion to "adopt a policy to legalize the sale of nicotine in vaping and welcome the associated technology as a method to help Western Australians quit smoking."[105] It was also reported in September 2018 that "an overwhelming majority of [federal] Liberal parliamentarians now support legalizing vaping [nicotine]."[106] The Health Minister, Greg Hunt, agreed to commission independent research on the issue as a compromise to changing current regulations.

---

95 D. Lyonhjelm, "Media release: more smokers will die on Hunt's watch" (*Medium*, March 28, 2018) https://medium.com/leyonhjelm/more-smokers-will-die-on-hunts-watch-8ed5cf594413 accessed October 31, 2018.

96 B. Fordham, "Federal MP backs Ben on the fight to scrap strict vaping rules" (*2 GB Radio*, May 23, 2018) http://2gb.com/federal-mp-backs-ben-on-the-fight-to-scrap-strict-vaping-rules/ accessed October 31, 2018.

97 Commonwealth of Australia, *Parliamentary Debates* (House of Representatives, March 30, 2017) 3860 (Andrew Laming, MP).

98 Commonwealth of Australia, *Parliamentary Debates* (Senate, September 14, 2016) 829 (Senator James Paterson).

99 E. Abetz, "Media release: UNSW report underscores need for vaping" (April 6, 2018) https://abetz.com.au/news/unsw-report-underscores-need-for-vaping accessed October 31, 2018.

100 Commonwealth of Australia, *Parliamentary Debates* (Senate, September 14, 2016) 834 (Senator Linda Reynolds).

101 Commonwealth of Australia, *Parliamentary Debates* (Senate, September 16, 2015) 6972 (Senator James McGrath).

102 Commonwealth of Australia, *Parliamentary Debates* (Senate, March 28, 2017) 2462 (Senator Cory Bernardi).

103 P. Hanson (*Twitter*, May 9, 2017, 2:35 AM) https://bit.ly/2xPWmjX accessed October 31, 2018.

104 D. Hinch (*Sky News Australia*, April 12, 2018, 5:11 AM) https://bit.ly/2zHYeww accessed October 31, 2018.

105 B. Fordham, "Highlights" (*2 GB Radio*, August 13, 2018) www.2gb.com/podcast/august-13th-highlights/ accessed October 31, 2018.

106 S. Powell, "Hunt bows to MP pressure to reverse vaping ban" (*The Australian*, September 20, 2018).

5.7 Public Health and Medical Organization Policies on E-cigarette Regulation

A number of Australian health and medical organizations have released position statements or made submissions to government inquiries about e-cigarette regulation. Some organizations support banning the sale of non-therapeutic e-cigarette products with or without nicotine (for example Cancer Council Australia and the National Heart Foundation,[107] the Thoracic Society of Australia and New Zealand and the Lung Foundation Australia,[108] and Australian Council on Smoking or Health[109]). A number of organizations, mostly based in Western Australia, also endorsed the Australian Council on Smoking or Health statement calling for a complete ban on all e-cigarettes that have not been approved as a therapeutic good.[110]

Some organizations have stated that e-cigarettes should be regulated in the same way as tobacco products (for example the Australian Medical Association,[111] the Australian Dental Association,[112] and the Royal Australasian

---

[107] Cancer Council Australia, *Position statement electronic cigarettes* https://wiki.cancer.org.au/policy/Position_statement_-_Electronic_cigarettes accessed October 31, 2018.

[108] Thoracic Society of Australia and New Zealand and Lung Foundation Australia, *Submission to inquiry into the use and marketing of electronic cigarettes and personal vaporisers in Australia* http://thoracic.org.au/documents/item/1051 accessed October 31, 2018.

[109] M. Swanson, K. Faulkner on behalf of ACOSH, *Inquiry into the use and marketing of electronic cigarettes and personal vaporisers in Australia submission 285* (July 10, 2017).

[110] Royal Australasian College of Surgeons, Australian and New Zealand College of Anaesthetists, Australian Nursing Federation, Lung Foundation Australia, Thoracic Society of Australia & New Zealand, Australian and New Zealand Society of Respiratory Science, Royal College of Pathologists of Australasia (WA Branch), Cancer Council WA, Public Health Advocacy Institute of WA, Environmental Health Australia (WA), Western Australian Council of State School (WACOSS), University of Western Australia (Department of Paediatrics), The University of Notre Dame Australia (Broome Branch), Westcare Inc., Mental Illness Fellowship of Western Australia, Puntukurnu Aboriginal Medical Service.

[111] Australian Medical Association, *Tobacco smoking and e-cigarettes: the AMA position* (December 16, 2015) https://ama.com.au/position-statement/tobacco-smoking-and-e-cigarettes-2015 accessed October 31, 2018.

[112] H. Sachs, President of Australian Dental Association, *Inquiry into the use and marketing of electronic cigarettes and personal vaporisers in Australia* http://ada.org.au/News-Media/News-and-Release/Submissions/Use-and-Marketing-of-E-Cigarettes-and-Personal-Vap/20170706-E-cigarettes accessed October 31, 2018.

College of Surgeons[113]). Such a policy is consistent with liberalizing the nicotine market (for example exempting nicotine e-cigarettes from Schedule 7 of the Poisons Standard, as is applied to tobacco intended for smoking); however, it is unclear whether these organizations support applying the same exemption to e-cigarettes that applies to tobacco. The Public Health Association of Australia has specifically called for a ban on e-cigarette advertising and promotion, enacting "strict emission and control measures," prohibiting "unproven health claims about e-cigarettes," and applying the same smoke-free laws to e-cigarettes.[114] The Royal Australasian College of Physicians has called for a "nationally defined and coordinated approach" to e-cigarette regulation,[115] and set out specific recommendations including: prohibiting supply to minors; restrictions on promotion of e-cigarettes; including e-cigarettes in smoke-free environments legislation; regulating as a therapeutic good if claims about therapeutic benefit (or claims about toxicity) are made; applying a lower excise tax relative to cigarettes; and applying manufacturing quality and safety standards (Good Manufacturing Practice) and packaging and labeling requirements (childproof packaging; plain packaging; health warnings and disclosure of ingredients).

A small number of Australian health and medical organizations have publicly supported reforming current e-cigarette regulations to provide Australian smokers with greater access to nicotine-containing e-cigarettes. Generally these have been health and medical organizations with a focus on priority populations that have high smoking prevalence, such as people living with mental illness (The Royal Australian & New Zealand College of Psychiatrists[116]), substance use disorders (Drug and Alcohol Nurses of Australasia[117]), and HIV

---

113 Royal Australasian College of Surgeons, *Inquiry into the use and marketing of electronic cigarettes and personal vaporisers in Australia* (July 7, 2017) http://surgeons.org/media/college-advocacy/inquiry-into-the-use-and-marketing-of-electronic-cigarettes-and-personal-vaporisers-in-australia/ accessed October 31, 2018.

114 Public Health Association of Australia, *Statement by the Public Health Associations of Australia on electronic cigarettes* http://phaa.net.au/documents/item/704 accessed October 31, 2018.

115 Royal Australasian College of Physicians, *Policy on electronic cigarettes* (May 2018) http://racp.edu.au/docs/default-source/advocacy-library/policy-on-electronic-cigarettes.pdf accessed October 31, 2018.

116 The Royal Australian and New Zealand College of Psychiatrists, *RANZCP submission on the use of e-cigarettes and personal vaporizers in Australia* (July 20, 2017) https://bit.ly/2ysiWPl accessed October 31, 2018.

117 Drug and Alcohol Nurses of Australasia, *Position statement #3: electronic cigarettes for tobacco harm reduction* (September 2017) http://danaonline.org/wp-content/uploads/2017/09/DANA-Position-Statement-on-E-Cigarettes-2017.pdf accessed October 31, 2018.

(Australasian Society for HIV Medicine and the Sexual Health Society of Queensland).

6. IS CURRENT AUSTRALIAN POLICY ON E-CIGARETTES CONSISTENT WITH A PRECAUTIONARY APPROACH?

In justifying the current ban on non-therapeutic nicotine products, Australian governments and non-government organizations have described the current policy as a "precautionary approach."[118] The precautionary approach, also known as the precautionary principle, originated in the environmental protection field.[119] However, it is arguable whether the current policy is consistent with a precautionary approach for a number of reasons. First, nicotine-containing e-cigarettes are a lower risk delivery system for a substance (nicotine) that is already legally (and widely) available in a much more harmful delivery system (tobacco cigarettes). The ban perversely favors a more harmful over a less harmful nicotine product for the same intended purpose (non-therapeutic use), whereas a precautionary approach should "encourage the replacement of dangerous substances and activities with less dangerous substances or technologies where suitable alternatives are available."[120]

Second, there are many precautionary measures other than a complete ban that could be adopted to minimize the potential public health risks of non-therapeutic nicotine-containing e-cigarettes. Examples include limits on nicotine strength, child resistant packaging, accurate labeling, age restrictions on purchase, and licensing of retailers. Policies that encourage smokers to switch to lower risk products, such as lower taxation compared to smoked tobacco, could also achieve better public health outcomes. A precautionary approach does not require, nor does it justify, a complete ban; this is a disproportionate policy response. The following quotes from the decision of Preston CJ of the New South Wales Land and Environment Court,[121] which is seen

---

118 Australian Government Department of Health, *Principles that underpin the current policy and regulatory approach to electronic cigarettes (e-cigarettes) in Australia* (January 11, 2018) https://bit.ly/2GIWTqp; Australian Government Cancer Australia, *Statement on e-cigarettes in Australia* (February 2018) https://bit.ly/2GJmwHn both accessed October 31, 2018.

119 J. Peel, "Precaution—a matter of principle, approach or process?" (2004) 5(2) MJIL 483.

120 M. Martuzzi, J. Tickner, *The precautionary principle: protecting public health, the environment and the future of our children* (World Health Organization 2004) 5.

121 *Telstra Corporation Limited v Hornsby Shire Council* [2006] NSWLEC 133, Land and Environment Court of New South Wales http://caselaw.nsw.gov.au/decision/549f8a6b3004262463ad5606 accessed October 31, 2018, paras 123–83.

as the "leading Australian reference point" on the precautionary principle,[122] provide guidance on the appropriate application of the precautionary principle/approach in Australia:

> "The precautionary principle should not be used to try to avoid all risks."
> "A zero-risk precautionary standard is inappropriate."
> "Measures based on the precautionary principle must not be disproportionate to the desired level of protection and must not aim at zero risk, something which rarely exists."
> "The precautionary principle embraces the concept of proportionality."
> "The selection of the appropriate precautionary measures must involve examining both sides of the ledger: the costs associated with the project, process or product (which tends to increase the degree of precaution) as well as the benefits of the project, process or product (which tends to decrease the degree of precaution commensurate with realizing the benefit)."
> "The precautionary principle, where triggered, does not necessarily prohibit the carrying out of a development plan, programme or project until full scientific certainty is attained."

Accordingly, a precautionary approach is consistent with adopting risk-proportionate regulatory measures. Considering the most appropriate regulation for nicotine-containing e-cigarettes in the context of existing similar products (smoked tobacco) would be a more coherent policy and consistent with the approach adopted for other chemical regulation. For example, the National Industrial Chemicals Notification and Assessment Scheme is currently being reformed to "make regulatory effort more proportionate to risk" and "promote safer innovation by encouraging the introduction of lower risk chemicals."[123] It is also the approach currently being adopted by the New Zealand government.[124]

---

[122] Australian Government Department of the Environment, Water, Heritage and the Arts, *The Australian Environment Act—report of the independent review of the Environment Protection and Biodiversity Conservation Act 1999 final report* (Commonwealth of Australia, October 2009).

[123] Australian Government Department of Health National Industrial Chemicals Notification and Assessment Scheme, *Implementing reforms to the National Industrial Chemicals Notification and Assessment Scheme (NICNAS): consultation paper 5* (Commonwealth of Australia, June 2017).

[124] Ministry of Health, Manatū Hauora, "Vaping, smokeless, including heated tobacco" (Update June 6, 2018) http://health.govt.nz/our-work/preventative-health-wellness/tobacco-control/vaping-smokeless-including-heated-tobacco accessed October 31, 2018.

7. CONCLUSIONS

There are conflicting statements concerning the place of harm reduction in Australian tobacco control policy. The 2004–9 NTS supported tobacco harm reduction as a strategy and included the aim of developing a regulatory system for tobacco and tobacco replacement products that would reduce the harm from nicotine dependence. The 2017–26 NDS and the 2012–18 NTS state that harm reduction is one of the three pillars that underpin these strategies. The 2012–18 NTS also includes as an objective to "reduce harm associated with continuing use of tobacco and nicotine products." However, in denying an application to allow Australian smokers access to nicotine for the purpose of harm reduction, the delegates of the Secretary to the Department of Health asserted that current government policy does not support harm reduction regarding smoking.[125]

The Australian laws concerning e-cigarettes are complex and have been inconsistently interpreted by different jurisdictions and government ministers. The type of enforcement action related to e-cigarettes has varied by jurisdiction. Currently, nicotine-free e-cigarettes can be legally possessed and used throughout Australia wherever smoking is permitted. Some jurisdictions have not implemented any bans on public use, while others have applied the same restrictions as apply to smoking. One jurisdiction (Western Australia) has banned the sale of e-cigarettes, regardless of whether they contain nicotine or not. Others have imposed restrictions on sales similar to those imposed on tobacco products.

Nicotine for non-therapeutic use is a Schedule 7 poison and requires state or territory approval to sell, obtain, or use. Potential penalties can be severe, including the possibility of jail terms. Nicotine for therapeutic use in e-cigarettes, such as to alleviate tobacco withdrawal symptoms, is a Schedule 4 medicine. As there are no nicotine-containing e-cigarettes approved as therapeutic goods in Australia, the only legal access for this purpose is via legal pathways for accessing unapproved therapeutic goods and requires a medical prescription. It is unknown how many Australian medical practitioners are willing to prescribe nicotine for vaping as a smoking cessation aid.

There have been a number of (so far) unsuccessful attempts to liberalize the Australian nicotine e-cigarette market. Liberalization has been strongly opposed by a number of influential public health and medical organizations, state and territory government health departments, the Federal Health Department,

---

[125] Australian Government Department of Health Therapeutic Goods Administration, *Final decisions and reasons for decisions by delegates of the Secretary to the Department of Health 23 March 2017* (March 23, 2017) 91 http://tga.gov.au/sites/default/files/scheduling-delegates-final-decisions-23-march-2017.pdf accessed October 31, 2018.

public health academics, and Australian health ministers, although some Australian health organizations, academics, and politicians have supported widening access to nicotine-containing e-cigarettes for Australian adults. The hostility to tobacco harm reduction is likely to have been influenced by the previous Australian experience with low tar cigarettes and an enduring distrust of and animosity toward the tobacco industry. However, there are practical and ethical issues associated with the current policy which penalizes smokers for switching to a lower risk nicotine product. A more coherent and ethical policy approach would be to allow the legal sale of non-therapeutic nicotine-containing e-cigarette products to adults, with regulations imposed to minimize potential risks.

Index